Penguin Education

Consumer Behaviour

Edited by A. S. C. Ehrenberg
and F. G. Pyatt

Penguin Modern Management Readings

General Editor
D. S. Pugh

Consumer Behaviour

Selected Readings

Edited by A. S. C. Ehrenberg and F. G. Pyatt

Penguin Books

Penguin Books Ltd, Harmondsworth,
Middlesex, England
Penguin Books Inc., 7110 Ambassador Road,
Baltimore, Md 21207, U.S.A.
Penguin Books Australia Ltd,
Ringwood, Victoria, Australia

First published 1971
Reprinted 1972
This selection copyright © Aske Publications and F. G. Pyatt, 1971
Introduction and notes copyright © Aske Publications and
F. G. Pyatt, 1971

Made and printed in Great Britain by
Richard Clay (The Chaucer Press) Ltd,
Bungay, Suffolk
Set in Monotype Times

Contents

Introduction 7

Part One Buyer Behaviour for Non-Durables 11

Part Two Consumer Attitudes 109

Part Three Durable Goods 179

Introduction

This book is concerned with understanding the private consumer's behaviour in acquiring goods or services for consumption. It consists of a selection from the wide range of writings that have appeared on this subject in the last twenty years and is intended for the student of consumer behaviour – whether he is in a practical marketing or management function, taking a course in social science, business studies, or economics, or is more generally concerned with the development of our society.

The area of consumer behaviour is important. Total expenditure accounts for some 80 per cent of the national income, and has remained roughly the same over many years. It follows that a corresponding fraction of our standard of living is directly geared to consumer behaviour. More specifically, the success or failure of a particular product sold to the consumer market, and hence the well-being of the people who produce it, depends directly on how consumers react to the product. Will they buy it or not? Will they go on buying it? And what products should be produced anyway?

For the individual consumer, the greater part of his expenditure, and a large part of his leisure time, revolves around the consumption of goods and services, including not only food and household products but also communication media, travel, housing, insurance, medical care, education, etc.

A fundamental precept of Western society is consumer sovereignty. Narrowly defined, this means the right of an individual, or group of individuals such as a household, to spend their money as they like. More broadly, it carries with it the connotation that the structure of society – especially what goods and services are produced and in what quantities – will be determined by consumers' wants to the extent that these are expressed in a willingness to spend money. It has been said that every shilling spent is a vote for a particular kind of society. But these are not the only kinds of votes cast, and consumer sovereignty must be limited if it is to exist at all. The limitations of sovereignty are an important aspect of consumer behaviour, in fashioning the kind of society that we seek to live in.

The study of consumer behaviour from this point of view is a part of sociology, economics and politics. However, the significance of consumer behaviour in *management*, which is the accent of this series of readings, derives from the consumer's role in *marketing*. Marketing concerns the interchange of goods or services between producer and consumer. Consumer behaviour is therefore part of the environment in which the producer operates and in which management has to make its decisions and implement them.

Our basic orientation in selecting readings for this particular book has been with the consumer himself, and not with the executive marketing function as such. We have been concerned less with papers discussing how to influence the consumer as with ones which describe how his behaviour in the market varies in response to the products and brands, the distribution channels and pricing policies, the packaging and promotion to which he is exposed. This has narrowed the range of topics that needed to be covered.

Our selection has been determined by the material's relevance to understanding consumer behaviour rather than with its intrinsic ease or difficulty. Some of the papers involve quite technical discussions, including mathematics beyond secondary school level. For the student there ought to be no difficulty, since it should by now be axiomatic that he has a basic foundation in mathematics. To our contemporaries who lack this we cannot apologize, but note that such technicalities are a part of the study of consumer behaviour today. And even mathematicians find other people's mathematics difficult, at least to begin with. Technicalities cannot be omitted altogether, but few people master them fully (or need to master them) at a first or second reading.

Some readers may at the other extreme find certain of the readings here relatively light-weight. They will find meatier work in many of the references to the individual papers and in the further readings listed at the end of this volume. Our endeavour in the main text has been to include papers which are typical of the recent development of the subject. The heterogeneity of the papers derives from the wide variety of literature from which the present sample has been selected – almost all of this literature is post-war, and reflects a rapid development in sophistication if not in understanding.

In general, this volume contains a rather personal selection of papers. Our individual tastes entered significantly into the choice from amongst the vast literature open to consideration. The basic conclusion on the present stage of knowledge is, however, inescapably that we know very little. At one level, economists know enough to be able to predict with some accuracy how expenditure on broad classes of commodities will change over time with shifts in income and price levels. At the other extreme, certain regularities have been uncovered in the purchasing of numerous different branded goods and in the extent to which consumers are loyal to particular items. Both these achievements are exemplified in papers which follow, but neither is well-founded in theoretical concepts. The traditional economic theory of a utility-maximizing consumer yields theorems on the relationship between rates of consumption, prices and incomes for an individual, but these do not hold for a group. The observed regularities in purchasing of brands are as yet largely unexplained, beyond a demonstration that they are consistent with certain probability models. More generally, very little indeed is known – in an empirically-validated form – about how consumers *change* their behaviour.

The book is in four main parts. The first two parts concern non-durable consumer goods and centre on people's buying behaviour and on their motivation respectively. The focus of interest tends to be the brand: brand-share, brand-loyalty and market segmentation are what matter to particular firms and hence to their marketing executives. The selected papers concern empirical information and its examination, rather than presenting well-constructed theories of consumer behaviour – as other writings do – without, however, giving any indication of their factual validity.

Part Three of the book turns to consumer durables, where much of the published work concerns forecasting the total demand for particular durable goods or – largely as a specific means to this end – understanding the order with which individual consumers tend to acquire different kinds of durables.

The last part of the book provides a survey of some of the more modern forms of economic analysis in this area: this – the economic study of the relationship between demand, supply, and price – is where the systematic examination of consumer behaviour largely began.

The editors are grateful to Mrs Jacqueline Hoque for her extensive help in the preparation of this book.

Part One Buyer Behaviour for Non-Durables

The last twenty-five years have seen an explosive growth in the measurement of individual consumers' buying behaviour, primarily by means of sample surveys using questionnaires and diary-panel techniques. A great many measurements have been collected and efficiently, if usually rather superficially, classified and tabulated. Interest in proceeding beyond this 'natural history' stage towards some deeper understanding of buyer behaviour is growing.

The first paper indicates that consumer behaviour is an area where regular patterns can be uncovered by simple and traditional scientific endeavour. The second paper by George Brown, for many years market research director at Fords and now Director of the U.S. Bureau of the Census, is a classic, though dating only from the early fifties: in it Brown began to put the notion of 'brand-loyalty' on a quantitative empirical basis.

In the third paper, Ronald Frank from the Wharton School summarizes a series of studies from the mid-sixties showing that there are at best very *weak* relationships between characteristic features of consumers' buying behaviour and their socio-economic status. In Reading 4, Yankelovitch, heading one of the companies now in the Leasco Group, discusses market segmentation in more general terms – the way in which even mass-produced products may most appeal to some particular sub-group or segment of the consuming public. Really distinct market segmentation, however, seems to be relatively rare for most branded consumer-products. The positive reflection of this and of Frank's low correlations with socio-economic variables seem to be manifested in the existence of patterns or laws of consumer behaviour which generalize across different brands and product-fields.

'Buyer behaviour' extends beyond the acquisition of household goods and the like to the consumption of services like mass-media. Mass-media are of interest primarily as vehicles of information and entertainment which themselves need to be successfully 'marketed', and also, where relevant, as possible carriers of advertisements for the promotion of other goods or services. In Reading 5, Agostini of the Elvinger Agency in Paris established one of the earliest patterns in the build-up of the 'unduplicated' audience of different print-media, i.e. in the extent to which *different* people are reached by different newspapers or magazines.

Related findings for television viewing, and some practical applications to programming problems, are briefly summarized in section 3 of the final paper in this Part, a review of a wider range of studies of buyer behaviour for frequently-bought products and services. Included are some early relationships between buying or usage and the attitudinal responses which people have towards the items in question. The area of consumer attitudes and motivations is covered more fully in Part Two.

1 A. S. C. Ehrenberg

Regularities of Behaviour

A. S. C. Ehrenberg, 'Laws in marketing: a tail-piece',[1]
Applied Statistics, vol. 15, 1966, pp. 257–67.

One of the commonest beliefs about marketing is that it is much more complex and variable than natural science. Physics and chemistry deal with simple, well-behaved and highly regular phenomena. Their study easily yields the absolute and invariant laws of science with which we are all so familiar. In contrast, marketing is thought to be far more complex to study. There are more factors at work. It involves intangibles, human beings, and so on. Nothing is constant. Everything varies. There may never be any stable scientific laws in marketing.

Such comments on the difficulties, the complexities and the instability of marketing processes are only too familiar, both in public and in private. One or two specific references may suffice. One is to the eight or nine talks by Churchman, Kuhn, Kuehn, Green, Starr, Littauer and others given here at the Market Research Council in the 1961–2 season, edited since by Dr Peter Langhoff (1965) and published under the title *Models, Measurement and Marketing*. The special complexities and instabilities of marketing problems are emphasized, together with the probabilistic rhetoric with which we are nowadays supposed to grapple with such problems.

The popular view of marketing complexity was also summarized by Professor Charles K. Ramond, as quoted by Buzzell (1963) in the *Harvard Business Review*: 'Variables affecting human behaviour interact to such an extent that the familiar "other things-being-equal" assumption can lead to mistaken conclusions. Further, physical scientists have generally been able to represent real systems by relatively simple models which can

1. A lunch-time talk given to the Market Research Council at the Yale Club, New York, 15 April 1966.

readily be manipulated. But such simple models have not been found adequate to describe human behaviour. And finally, while relationships among physical phenomena are characteristically *stable* over extended time-periods, marketing is thought to be highly *dynamic*. Thus, relationships which seem to describe a system at one time may not hold at some future time.'

Personally, I have found nothing in all this talk of special complexities and of new methods which resembles either the known facts of marketing or any successful scientific work that I have come across, whether it was work for establishing generalized knowledge in the first place or work for then applying such knowledge to practical problems. But I do not here want to criticize the detailed past, except by broadly attempting to demonstrate that there is nothing special about studying marketing (or social science topics generally): ordinary and simple law-like relationships can and do exist, and they can be established by old-fashioned and simple methods of data-handling, such as discovering that variable y varies with variable x under such-and-such a range of empirical conditions, or that so-and-so is a constant.

Laws can be of two broad kinds. There are the scientific generalizations which are derived from empirical data, and which for convenience are usually put in a quantitative form. And there are the generalized twaddle kind of laws which are based on insight and armchair experience. Both kinds of law have their uses.

The fundamental law of science

Taking first the twaddle type of law, Ramond (1965) gave us several in a recent editorial in the *Journal of Advertising Research*. For example:

Smith's law: 'If it's worth doing at all, it's worth doing twice.'
McAllister's law: 'If you talk long enough, you will say something intelligent', with its frightful corollary:
Corollary: 'If you talk long enough, you will say something stupid.'

A further armchair or twaddle law to enunciate now is the fundamental law of science, as follows:

The fundamental law of science: 'In general, nothing changes.'
Corollary: 'A lot of factors *might* affect what one observes, but in practice they don't seem to.'

This law has the double advantage of greatly simplifying one's problems and of being true to the facts. If one studies the things which are regular, one will find regularities. Science is as simple as that. All one has to do is to pick on some regular things to study.

This law obviously applies also to marketing. Take any product or brand. Lots of things may vary. But its sales will – *in general* – be pretty much the same as last year. So will the brand's market share and its advertising appropriation and its distribution channels and consumer attitudes and the segmentation of its market. So will the problems of producing the product and of marketing it profitably. Take any sequence of successive market research reports, and all the figures will also be the same from one report to the next: any figure which looks different and therefore interesting is usually wrong – a coding or computing error.

There may be a lot of 'intangible' factors in the situation as well, but they only remain intangible because of the fundamental law's corollary, i.e. because they do not seem to have affected the situation anyway. Thus some of the advertising may have changed, and also the price and the package, and the weather is different too. But sales are pretty much the same as they were and so these variable factors just did not matter.

The remarkable thing about the fundamental law that in science nothing changes is that it holds not only for 'complex' subjects like marketing where our knowledge is as yet very simple, but also in 'simple' fields like physics and chemistry where so much is already known that it all becomes highly complex.

Open a textbook on physics to learn about factor X and it is very complicated: factor X is known to vary approximately with so-and-so and so-and-so in such-and-such a manner, as long as variables A and B are controlled and C is negligible, and given that this and that adjustment has been made and all the standard corrections for so-and-so are applied. Outside this limited range of conditions nothing general and systematic is known about

15

factor X at all. Mr L's long series of pre-war results on factor X have been contradicted by 375 experiments carried out under diverse conditions by Professors P, Q, R and S since. Dr Z has thoughtfully suggested that differences in the conditions of observation might have been relevant, but his actual results go in the wrong direction and are internally inconsistent, as well as being discrepant with some French and German findings in 1864 and 1897–8 respectively.

In contrast, open a textbook on economics, on management, on marketing, and it is all very simple: there is nothing there. There is not even any empirical evidence of all these *discrepancies* which are always said to exist, of all this alleged change and variance! When people state that something in marketing is not or cannot be constant, what they really mean is that they have hardly observed or measured it at all, and almost certainly not more than once!

Yet irrespective of the state of development of one's subject-matter – whether it is physics or marketing – by studying the things which *are* regular, we come up with regularities: factor X is systematically related to so-and-so under such-and-such conditions, and last year's brand-leader is still brand-leader.

Empirical generalization

One very real difficulty does arise in establishing scientific laws, i.e. laws with a full empirical content. It is that people tend to overrate the status of any such law, especially in the natural sciences. Thus they will think of the older and simpler type of physical law either as an almost self-evident universal statement or as deriving its validity from some background of 'theory', instead of its being simply a description of empirical regularities which have been laboriously isolated under a limited range of specified conditions of observation, and which are equally known *not* to occur under certain other conditions of observation.

Take for example Boyle's law in physics. This is that the pressure P of a body of gas goes up as its volume V goes down, and vice versa, i.e. that $P \doteq k/V$, where k is some constant. This approximate relationship has been found to hold for different gases, for different amounts of gas, for different containers, different kinds of apparatus and different experimenters. It is what has been found to hold when the pressure goes up and when the pressure goes down, and when the pressure has gone up fast and when it has done so slowly, and so on. Equally, however, it has been found that pressure does *not* vary as k/V when the temperature changes, when there is a chemical reaction, when there is a leak in the apparatus, when there is physical absorption or condensation of the gas, or when we tried to prove the law at school.

Boyle's own empirical results relating pressure directly to volume were only obtained in defending his earlier and more general 'Doctrine touching on the Spring and Weight of Air'. Indeed, his results relate only to air as such, which he studied in one type of apparatus (of at least two sizes because the smaller one broke), and he spent much time explaining away his (small) discrepancies. But the relationship $P \doteqdot k/V$ became established as a general 'law' only a good deal later, because Boyle's initial work had then been followed by vast and laborious amounts of extremely repetitive and tiresome empirical data collection and analysis: the behaviour of this kind of gas and that kind of gas had been examined, under almost unbearably innumerable different conditions. To repeat: large amounts of gas and small amounts of gas have been studied. And one kind of container and another kind of container. Pressure going up and pressure going down. Pressure going up fast and pressure going down slowly. And so on and so on. If the law is also known to hold to a close approximation at different times and for different places, this is only because of all the massive and direct empirical observation that something like it has in fact held here and there, in the morning and at night, this year and last year, and so on.

All the cases where the law does *not* hold involve still further work, still further empirical observation and analysis. Thus it is very much a part of really establishing Boyle's law to have shown empirically that $P \doteqdot k/V$ does *not* hold when the temperature changes, or when there is a leak in the apparatus, or when there is a chemical reaction or physical condensation – and it has of course also been empirically established that these failures occur for this kind of gas and for that kind, for large amounts of gas and for small ones, and so on.

The apparent *simplicity* of many scientific laws is only a reflec-

17

tion of all the work which has been done empirically to rule out the complicating conditions where the simple result does *not* hold (changing temperature, leaks, etc). The *power* of a law depends on the extent to which theoretical analysis has shown it to inter-relate with other empirical laws and with general background knowledge. But the *validity* of a scientific law depends only on its range of empirical generalization, i.e. on the different conditions for which it is known to hold or not to hold, as shown by direct observation and analysis.

The law of methodology

The same approach of course applies to laws in marketing. All that is necessary is to isolate simple regularities in marketing processes by observing and analysing the extent to which they do or do not occur under all the different conditions of observation which are at all relevant – different products, different brands, different countries and different times, and varying marketing conditions generally. Instead of the common doubts of the 'will it hold over extended time-periods?' or 'won't so-and-so matter?' kind, we need only observe and analyse whether or not it does.

To establish generalized laws, we therefore have the basic law of scientific methodology:

The basic law of methodology: 'If in doubt, find out.'
Corollary: 'If you don't, you won't.'

Some illustration of empirical marketing laws derived by this old-fashioned approach may be relevant. Three examples are given. Two are taken from papers published last month, the third is from some more recent work. The examples concern general laws from three fields: media, consumer attitudes, and purchasing behaviour. They illustrate that although the marketing laws which we can establish at this stage are of course much simpler than the complex laws which are now current in the natural sciences, there is no difference in kind. The complexity of the present-day laws in physics is due to the very much larger amount of work which has already gone into studying the subject-matter there: the physicist already knows so much more, but does not always have the mathematics to describe it very simply and concisely.

Duplication of viewing

The first example of a simple empirical marketing law concerns some recent results on the viewing patterns of television audiences, as relating for instance to work for JICTAR, and CEIR Inc., and ARB. I hasten to add that the example does not concern itself with the popular OR kinds of 'media model' which are meant to optimize something. Instead, it is an example of establishing what actually happens, by way of 'duplicated' viewing of any TV channel or station at any two specific times on any two different days of any week. For instance, given that 30 per cent of the population view on Monday night at 8 p.m., and that on Tuesday night at 9 p.m. the 'rating' is 20 per cent, what is the duplicated audience at these two times, i.e. how many per cent of the population view the station *both* on Monday night at 8 and on Tuesday at 9?

The traditional view of 'everything in marketing is complex and variable' is of course readily countered by simply looking at some actual duplication data. Examination of any table of the duplicated audiences for two days of the week makes the existence of a regular pattern almost immediately obvious. Thus for some recent data collected by the American Research Bureau, this pattern could be summarized as follows:

1. The higher the rating at one time, the higher the duplicated audience with any other point in time.

2. The tendency for people who view at one time also to view at another time is positive, i.e. there is positive correlation.

3. This correlation can virtually all be accounted for by a single constant. Thus the duplicated audience r_{ts} at times t and s with ratings r_t and r_s is given by the simple law

$$r_{ts} \doteq kr_t r_s,$$

where k is a constant.

4. The law $r_{ts} = kr_t r_s$ holds for the data in question with deviations averaging at a rating point or so. (The larger deviations which occur within these small average limits are not only rare

19

but tend themselves to be highly regular, i.e. susceptible to further law-like description.)

The audience data analysed here refer to the viewing of station WRBC on Mondays and Tuesdays in November last year in Birmingham, Alabama. It may seem absurd to describe some apparent regularities in Alabama last November as a 'law'. Will such a result also hold for other pairs of days, and at other points in time, for other stations or in other places, and under other conditions generally? 'If in doubt, find out.' All that has to be done is to observe and analyse some comparable data for other points in space and time, and other conditions generally.

Table 1 Empirical Conditions under which $r_{ts} = kr_t r_s \pm 1$ is Known to Hold

(r_{ts} is the duplicated audience at two times s and t on two different days of the week with ratings r_s and r_t.)

Any two programmes	1959
Any two days of the week	1965
Any two ratings levels from 0 to about 50	1966
Any two times of day from 2 p.m. to 11.15 p.m.	
	Summer
Adults	Winter
HWs	
Sets on	London, ITV
	Great Britain, ITV
Continuous meter panels	Alabama, WRBC
Continuous diary panels	
1-week diary surveys	Two-channel
1-week recall surveys	Poly-channel[1]

1. The phrase 'poly-channel' has been devised by Mr N. L. Webb to distinguish multi-channel viewing situations with three or more operating channels from the two-channel situation which has been traditional in Great Britain until recently.

Other analyses have therefore also been carried out. They cover so far some sets-switched-on and housewife-viewing data measured by Television Audience Measurement in the London region in January 1966, and the earlier 1959 Granada Viewership Surveys of the adult population of Great Britain. Space and time, including seasons, are therefore beginning to be covered. And also different 'kinds of gas', i.e. the viewing behaviour of individual people and of TV sets, and different measurement techniques – ARB's weekly household diaries, Tam's continuous minute-by-minute meter and quarter-hour diary panels, and Granada's individual seven-day aided recall interviews. Even the few hundred cases analysed so far therefore begin to cover quite a wide range of empirical conditions, as set out in Table 1. And the same simple law – that $r_{ts} = kr_t\, r_s \pm 1$ – continues to emerge.

The relation between I and U

The second illustration of a simple law concerns an attitudinal variable, namely people's expressed intentions-to-buy any stated brand. In work for J. Walter Thompson, no evidence has been found that this variable measures what it says it measures, e.g. in the sense of predicting changes in people's buying behaviour (Bird and Ehrenberg, 1966).

There is of course nothing unusual or wrong about that, as long as one knows. After all, in physics and in everyday life one does not look at the length of a column of mercury in a glass tube just to see how long a column of mercury in a glass tube is, but as a measure of something quite different – temperature or pressure, or whatever it is that empirical validation has told us the length of this particular type of mercury column is correlated with.

In thus empirically investigating the percentage I of people who express an intention-to-buy the brand in question, it was found that this variable tends to be systematically and closely related to the current usership level of the brand. Thus I is directly proportional to the square root of the percentage U of informants who currently use the brand, i.e.

$$I = k\sqrt{U},$$

within a mean deviation of about three percentage points for the discrepancies $I - k\sqrt{U}$ on the 0 to 100 per cent scale of intentions-to-buy. This simple relationship between I and U, which has already been briefly quoted by Ramond (1965), is known to hold under a wide range of empirical conditions (Table 2). Thus, $I \doteq k\sqrt{U}$ holds for large brands and small brands in each

21

product-field, and for brands with stationary and with fluctuating usage levels. It holds, with different values of the single parameter k, for some thirty different product-fields investigated by JWT so far, and for various different measuring techniques. It holds at different points in time stretching back over five years or more, and in Great Britain and in the U.S.

Table 2 Empirical Conditions under which $I = k \sqrt{U} \pm 3$ is Known to Hold
(I is the % of informants expressing an intention-to-buy a brand which is used by U%)

Intentions-to-buy levels ranging from 0% to almost 100%

The 4 to 10 leading brands in each product-field
Brands with stationary usage level
Brands with increasing usage level
Brands with decreasing usage level

Great Britain
USA

Demographic sub-groups – young, old, etc.
From 1960 to 1966
Summer/winter
Usage measures varying from 'ever use' to 'used in last 7 days'

Several intentions-to-buy measures

Different product-fields, including beer, biscuits, breakfast cereals, chocolate assortments, chocolate bars, corned beef, cough syrups, frozen foods, indigestion remedies, margarine, meat extracts, milk drinks, shampoos, tinned soups, toilet papers, toilet soap, voluntary grocery chains, washing powders, washing-up liquids

---

The law differs from the first example $r_{ts} \doteqdot k r_t\, r_s$ – the duplication law – by already fitting in with other pieces of knowledge.[2] For example, it quantifies the common notion that people cannot effectively say what they want, except more of the same, and it seems to clash with various speculative consumer theories of advertising formulated as sequences of the awareness→intention →purchase kind.

At a more down-to-earth level, it is also known that current users of a brand virtually all say that they intend to buy it again,

2. But see Reading 6, p. 92. [Ed.]

and further that for current non-users such an intention varies with the recency or the frequency of their *past* usage, if any, of the brand. This additional empirical knowledge (Bird and Ehrenberg, 1966) explains the shape of the $I = k\sqrt{U}$ type of relationship. It also explains two systematic deviations from the $I = k\sqrt{U}$ norm which would otherwise appear quite paradoxical. These deviations occur within the average limits of fit of ± 3 per cent and apply to successfully launched new brands and to slowly dying old brands respectively, as follows:

1. *Fewer* people than the norm say they intend to buy successful new brands, but *more* people do in fact buy them subsequently.

2. *More* people than the norm say that they will buy dying old brands, but *fewer* people go on buying them in the long-run.

The explanation is that the 'tail' of past users for a new brand is necessarily short, relative to its current usage level, and it is this incidence of past users which essentially determines the level of expressed intentions-to-buy. Conversely, an old, slowly dying brand has a long 'tail' of past users, which is reflected in its relatively high level of expressed intentions-to-buy.

The purchasing constant 1·4

The third illustration of quantitative marketing laws takes the simplest possible form which any law can take, namely that of an absolute constant. This is one of two special points of interest. The other is that this constant is part of, or derivable from, a fairly advanced empirically-based theory or system of laws. The theory concerns consumer purchasing behaviour, as studied for example for Unilever and Cadbury's, Esso, ICI and J. Walter Thompson (Chatfield *et al.*, 1966). It deals with any brand of frequently bought consumer goods under stationary conditions, i.e. for the common situation where there is no trend from one time-period to the next. Consider p time-periods, and the proportion of the consumer population who buy r_i units in the ith time-period (of length T_i), and r_j units in the jth period, etc. It is then found empirically that this proportion can be represented by the coefficient of $(u_i)^{r_i}(u_j)^{r_j}$ ... in expanding the expression

$$\left\{ 1 + a \sum_{i=1}^{p} T_i (1 - u_i) \right\}^{-k}$$

23

in powers of the dummy variables u_i, u_j, etc., where a and k are two empirical parameters specific to the brand.

This simple descriptive device has in effect been found to model stationary purchasing behaviour for brands in all the thirty or so different product-fields so far studied, of both food and non-food types. The theory has generally been found to describe some thousands of different cases, covering a range of conditions summarized in Table 3.

Table 3 Empirical Conditions under which Various Aspects of the Stationary Purchasing Model are Known to Hold

---

Percentage of buyers ranging from almost 0 to 50% or more

The 4 to 6 leading brands in each product-field
Large, medium and small pack-sizes

Great Britain
Continental Europe
USA

From 1950 to 1966
Summer/winter

Different demographic sub-groups – size of household, etc.

Buying behaviour in periods of 1 week to 6 months or more

Different product-fields including bread, breakfast cereals, butter, canned vegetables, cat and dog foods, clothing, cocoa, coffee, confectionery, cooking fats, detergents, disinfectants, fruit drinks, household soaps, household cleaners, jams and marmalade, margarine, petrol, polishes, processed cheese, sausages, shampoos, soft drinks, soup, toilet paper, toilet soap

---

The model subsumes all quantitative aspects of stationary purchasing of any given brand. For example, the increasing penetration of any brand in longer time-periods is successfully described by it, and repeat-buying behaviour in successive equal time-periods. It also deals with the frequency distribution of the different amounts bought in any single time-period: thus, the proportion of a brand's total sales which is accounted for by buyers of more than r units in the time-period, r being any number, is given by a one-parameter expression. For it follows from the theory, and is found to be true in practice when the parameter k is small compared with a, that this proportion is simply q^r, where $q = a/(1 + a)$ in terms of the first of the two parameters a and k of the model.[3]

However, an even simpler specific law of stationary consumer purchasing behaviour is that the people who buy a brand in one time-period but not in the next will in that first time-period buy an average of about 1·4 units of it. This approximate constant can be theoretically derived from the model. Since this model of stationary purchasing generally holds in other respects, the constant deduced from it should in theory also hold, i.e. for any product-field, for a large brand or a small brand, for a brand with many repeat-buyers or one with few, and irrespective of the length of the two periods in question – weeks, months, quarters, etc. And in practice it does hold. Thus, for stationary brands it has been found (Chatfield *et al.*, 1966) that Britons who buy anything in one time-period but not in the next, buy on average about 1·4 units of it. And so do Americans. A re-analysis of some of the purchasing data for the Chicago Metropolitan Area published by George Brown (1952) has recently been completed.[4] American households who in 1951 bought a then-stationary brand of – to be specific – margarine like 'Parkay', 'Allsweet' 'Good Luck' and 'Nutley', or a stationary brand of detergents like 'American Family Flakes', 'Tide' and 'Rinso' (pack-sizes I and II) in one time-period but not the next, also bought on average roughly 1·4 units. Thus

Monthly: Buying in one month but not the next –
average amount bought $\doteqdot$ 1·5 units,
Quarterly: Buying in one quarter but not the next –
average amount bought $\doteqdot$ 1·4 units.

These data are subject to considerable sampling error since the number of such buyers in Brown's sample was only about 5 to 10 households per brand, but the fit seems good enough.

3. The condition $k \ll a$ refers to the so-called 'variance discrepancy': see reference cited. The parameter a can be estimated from w, the average amount bought per buyer in the time-period, by solving the implicit equation $w = a/\ln(1 + a)$ or the explicit approximate formula

$$\tfrac{1}{2}a \doteqdot 1\cdot23(w - 1)^{1\cdot23}.$$

4. See Reading 6, pp. 71–2. [Ed.]

Laws of inhibition

The above results illustrate that it is easy to find stable and simple laws in marketing. However, it would be disingenuous and indeed misleading to pretend that many such laws have yet been established. Very little integrated and generalised quantitative knowledge about marketing process exists so far. For this situation, four quite unnecessary laws appear to be causally responsible:

The law of personal pessimism: 'In *my* case, nothing ever remains the same.'

The law of empirical inaction: 'If still in doubt, just assume something.'

The law of perpetually promising psuedo-probabilistic paraphernalia: 'It is a well-known statistical procedure and may this time give a clearcut and lasting result.'

The law of the ignorant problem-solver: 'I know nothing of your subject-matter, but have techniques and will sub-optimize.'

For further reading on these four laws, the initial reference on page 13 and textbooks on 'modern' scientific methods and experimental design, on multivariate analysis, Bayesian theory and statistical analysis and inference generally, and on OR techniques, may be helpful.

The discussion following this talk has shown that there are three further laws of inhibition which had been prematurely pensioned-off. They are of course:

The law of the man of action: 'I am too busy pretending to solve today's problems to tackle tomorrow's before it is again too late.'

The law of the practical-minded manager: 'I cannot invest in basic research unless I know how to apply the results before you know what they are.'

The law of keeping secrets from oneself: 'We must keep the results from our competitors even if it means not getting them ourselves.'

These seven laws seem to account for most of the near-constant tendency to do virtually no long-term basic research into marketing phenomena. This particular finding holds in this country and elsewhere, and so far also across time.

Acknowledgement

This talk is largely based on some work which is being carried out for Research Bureau Ltd (Unilever) on regression analysis and the derivation of quantitative relationships.

References

BIRD, M., and EHRENBERG, A. S. C. (1966), 'Intentions-to-buy and claimed brand usage', *Operational Research Quarterly*, vol. 17, pp. 27–46 and vol. 18, pp. 65–6.

BROWN, G. H. (1952), 'Brand loyalty — fact or fiction?', *Advertising Age*, vol. 23, 9 June and 6 October.

BUZZELL, R. D. (1963), 'Is marketing a science?', *Harvard Business Review*, vol. 41, pp. 32–6.

CHATFIELD, C., EHRENBERG, A. S. C., and GOODHARDT, G. J. (1966), 'Progress on a simplified model of stationary purchasing behaviour', *Journal of the Royal Statistical Society*, *A*, vol. 129, pp. 317–67.

LANGHOFF, P. (ed.) (1965), *Models, Measurement and Marketing*, Prentice-Hall.

RAMOND, C. K. (1965), Editorial, *Journal of Advertising Research*, vol. 5, no. 4, p. 68.

2 George H. Brown

Brand-Loyalty

From George H. Brown 'Brand-loyalty – fact or fiction?',
Advertising Age, vol. 24, 1953.

One of the most intriguing of all marketing questions revolves around 'brand loyalty'. Do customers purchase a favourite brand time after time or do they shop around at random? Do the type of merchandise involved and the relative strength of brands have an important influence? How many customers stay with a single brand of a frequently purchased item for a considerable period of time? Just what is a 'brand loyal' customer? Can a brand develop enough consumer loyalty so that it can get a sizable share of the market from a relatively small group of steady purchasers, or must it make occasional sales to a large proportion of the families in the market?

Through the co-operation of the *Chicago Tribune*, *Advertising Age* has sponsored some basic research into the problems of brand loyalty at the University of Chicago. *The Chicago Tribune* has been operating a consumer-purchase panel covering a wide variety of grocery and drug items for four years.

The panel is a diary operation, perhaps the most extensive conducted on a local or regional basis by any private organization. It shows not only which items are purchased by the families in the panel, but the sequence of purchase. Thus, if a family makes ten purchases of coffee in a month, the panel data show not only the total purchases and the brands bought, but whether brand A, accounting for five of the ten purchases, was bought five consecutive times and then abandoned, or whether the five purchases of that brand were interspersed with purchases of one or more other brands.

The *Tribune* panel data used in the study covered the calendar year 1951. Although 610 families in the panel kept a complete record of their purchases for that year, only the purchases of 100 buyers of a particular product class were analysed in detail. Nine products, selected for assumed differences in brand loyalty patterns, were included in the study. Each of these has been separately reported during 1952 in an issue of *Advertising Age*.

During the study a method of 'direct classification' of families according to loyalty was developed. Any family making five or more purchases during the year was placed in one of four basic categories depending upon the purchase pattern shown. While this is not the place to discuss the method, the principle can be illustrated as follows:

1. Family showing *undivided loyalty* bought brand A in the following sequence: A A A A A A

2. Family showing *divided loyalty* bought brands A and B in the following sequence: A B A B A B

3. Family showing *unstable loyalty* bought brands A and B in the following sequence: A A A B B B

4. Family showing *no loyalty* bought brands A, B, C, D, E and F, in the following sequence: A F C B D E.

The results of the direct classification for the nine products studied can be summarized as in Table I.

On the basis of these findings, an effort will be made to answer

Table 1 Analysis of Classifiable Families According to Brand Loyalty
(All buyers = 100%)

Item	Undivided loyalty	Divided loyalty	Unstable loyalty	No loyalty
Margarine	21·1	13·8	27·5	37·5
Toothpaste	61·3	6·5	17·7	14·5
Coffee	47·2	18·1	29·5	5·2
All-purpose flour	73·2	7·1	14·1	5·6
Shampoo	44·0	10·4	12·3	33·3
Ready-to-eat cereal	12·5	22·7	18·2	46·6
Headache remedies	46·1	23·1	5·8	25·0
Soaps and sudsers	16·8	20·0	26·2	37·0
Concentrated orange juice	26·8	7·0	39·4	26·8

some of the basic questions posed at the outset of the study. The conclusions, obviously, are restricted to the data studied and cannot be generalized to other items without additional research. Within the limits of our resources, however, here goes.

Question 1 Do consumers purchase a favorite brand time after time or do they shop around at random?

Answer: On the basis of the nine products studied, the majority of consumers tend to purchase a favorite brand or set of brands. Only a minority divide their purchases over five brands or more or otherwise show evidence of buying brands at random. Brand loyalty is a fact, not a fiction.

Question 2 How many consumers stay with a single brand of a frequent-purchase item for a considerable time?

Answer: Somewhere between a fourth and a half of the buyers of a frequently purchased item stayed with a single brand during the twelve-month period under study. These statistics are based on our study of margarine, coffee, ready-to-eat cereal, soaps and sudsers, and concentrated orange juice. Interestingly enough, with the exception of all-purpose flour, the same generalization would apply to the other products included in the study.

The extremely low figure for ready-to-eat cereal is due in part to the fact that *family* rather than *individual* loyalty is reflected in the panel data. It is possible that some of the families classified as having divided loyalty are in truth loyal to a single brand in terms of the individuals in the family. By the same token, of course, consumer loyalty to all the other products may be higher on an individual basis than on the family basis shown in the table.

Question 3 Do the type of merchandise involved and the relative strength of brands have an important influence on brand loyalty?

Answer: The answer to this question is no and yes, i.e. the type of merchandise doesn't have very much influence on brand loyalty, but there is a definite relationship between strength of brands and nature of the loyalty shown.

Every effort I have made to group products by some simple classification shows no relationship to brand loyalty. Most food products have a lower loyalty than the non-food items, but coffee exceeds shampoo, and all-purpose flour heads the list for loyalty. The frequently purchased items show great variation in loyalty, but the same is true for headache remedies, flour and toothpaste, all of which are infrequently purchased. There does, however, seem to be a tendency for the less frequently purchased non-food items to show a somewhat higher degree of loyalty.

There is certainly no sharp difference between the 'personalized' products such as toothpaste, shampoo and, to a certain extent, coffee, and 'family use' products such as margarine, flour and concentrated orange juice in so far as brand loyalty is concerned, although here again the 'family use' products tend, or might be expected, to have a somewhat slightly lower degree of brand loyalty. Presumably the buyer has a stronger feeling towards a product he uses personally, although it might be argued that is easier to change the behaviour of a single individual than that of an individual representing the group. Actually, the dividing line between 'personal use' and 'family use' products gets very thin.

The most useful generalization seems to be that loyalty is high in well established products where little or no change in product has occurred in recent years, such as flour and coffee, while loyalty is low where product entries are frequent, such as margarine, ready-to-eat cereal, concentrated orange juice and shampoo. Toothpaste has a higher-than-expected loyalty on this basis, and headache remedies a lower-than-expected rating, but even so their loyalty is high relative to the more dynamic product classes.

The importance of brand strength to brand loyalty can be seen in Table 2, which compares the approximate market share of the two leading brands and the proportion of classifiable families showing undivided loyalty to a single brand. Although the 'new product' influence is discernible, the relationship between the two series is clear enough.

Question 4 Just what is a 'brand loyal' customer?

Answer: A brand loyal customer is one who tends to repurchase a particular brand because of some real or imaginary superiority attributed to that brand. The wording of this answer should be

31

studied with care since our experience has indicated that there are many types of loyalty existing in the market, of which brand loyalty is only one. For example, there is a loyalty towards a particular retail store which leads the person to buy the brands available in that store to the exclusion of brands stocked by other stores. There is a 'loyalty' towards the low-priced item which leads a person to repurchase a particular brand so long as it is the low-priced brand, but a switch will be made as soon as some other brand becomes lower in price. There is a 'loyalty'

Table 2 A Comparison of Brand Strength and Brand Loyalty

Item	Share of market going to the two leading brands	% of classifiable families showing undivided loyalty
Margarine	41·7	21·2
Toothpaste	56·3	61·3
Coffee	28·3	47·2
All-purpose flour	64·9	73·2
Shampoo	26·7	44·0
Ready-to-eat cereal	28·0	12·5
Headache remedies	48·8	46·2
Soaps and sudsers	33·5	16·8
Concentrated orange juice	33·0	26·8

that arises out of habit in that the buyer will always ask for or select a particular brand rather than go through the mental process of reviewing all the factors that affect the purchase decision. This type of loyalty cannot withstand the 'special offer' or 'out-of-stock' inducement to try another brand. True brand loyalty reflects a deliberate decision to concentrate purchase on a single brand due to some real or imaginary superiority of that brand. This type of loyalty can be held in varying degrees, depending upon the strength of the superiority, but it is a 'brand' loyalty rather than a store, price or convenience loyalty.

It should be obvious from this discussion that the measurement of 'brand' loyalty is complicated by the existence of 'store' loyalty, 'price' loyalty and 'habitual' buying, and by individual as opposed to family or spending-unit loyalty. What has been presented here as a measurement of brand loyalty is in reality a complex of all of these factors, of which, however, brand loyalty is by far the most important element. Future work in this problem should make the measurement more precise.

Question 5 Can a brand develop enough consumer loyalty so that it can get a sizable share of market from a relatively small group of steady purchasers, or must it make occasional sales to a large proportion of families in the market?

Answer: A brand can develop enough consumer loyalty so that it can get a sizable share of market from a relatively small group of steady purchasers; however, the ideal situation seems to be to avoid the extremes of loyalty or non-loyalty. While a sizable share of the market can be secured through high loyalty among a relatively small group of buyers – witness Squibb toothpaste with 4·8 per cent of the market from 3 per cent of the total toothpaste-buying families, or Rayve shampoo with 4·2 per cent of the market from 5 per cent of the shampoo buying families – the most successful brands combine a moderate degree of loyalty with wide market coverage. Table 3, which reports the proportion

Table 3 Proportion of Total Volume Coming from Families Concentrating Their Purchases on One Brand for the Leading Brand in the Nine Product Classes Studied

	Degree of concentration of purchase			
Brand	75–100%	50–74·9%	25–49·9%	0·1–24·9%
Allsweet (margarine)	53·0	14·5	18·7	13·8
Colgate (toothpaste)	63·7	27·8	6·0	2·5
Hills Brothers (coffee)	63·0	12·6	5·4	19·0
Pillsbury (flour)	66·0	23·8	7·2	3·0
Drene (shampoo)	30·7	42·8	17·4	9·1
Kellogg's Corn Flakes (cereal)	27·3	15·9	20·1	36·7
Bayer Aspirin (head-ache remedies)	43·6	28·2	17·7	10·5
American Family Flakes	34·1	10·1	38·1	17·7
Snow Crop (concentrated orange juice)	20·1	40·5	26·1	13·3

of business coming from 'loyal' customers – those giving 75 per cent of their volume to a single brand – shows that characteristically half to two-thirds of their volume comes from this group, with the remainder from less loyal buyers. Some brands, such as Kellogg's Rice Krispies, secure a good share of the market, approximately 6 per cent, even though almost 80 per cent of its volume comes from occasional purchasers. As a rule, however, brands with extremely high loyalty, e.g. Fij Oil shampoo, or extremely low loyalty, e.g. Keyko margarine, end up with a relatively small share of the total market.

Question 6 What bearing, if any, does a high or low degree of brand loyalty have on advertising decisions?

Answer: If brand loyalty is high, the advertiser has a good case for 'investment' expenditures where large amounts are expended over short periods of time to win new users in the knowledge that continued purchases after the advertising has been curtailed will 'amortize' the advertising investment. If there is a low degree of brand loyalty in the product class, advertising expenditures should be continued at a fairly steady rate on a 'pay-as-you-go' basis, or demonstrated returns in extra sales equal to or greater, than the extra advertising costs. Since the market is likely to be composed of both loyal and random purchasers, some combination of these approaches should be undertaken, with the advertising 'mix' dependent upon the loyalty to the brands in the product class under consideration.

It should be emphasized, however, that brand loyalty is a means to an end rather than an end in itself. The ultimate objective of a business organization is to serve the community by providing wanted goods and services. Sometimes a small segment of the community will want a particular kind of service, in which case brand loyalty will be high but a market share will be low. In other cases, a large segment of the community may want variety or may be constantly seeking for some impossible goal in which case brand loyalty will be low and market share may be high or low depending upon a variety of other circumstances.

An intelligent use of data on brand loyalty requires an understanding that the whole market will seldom be so homogeneous that everyone will agree to vote one single brand the favorite.

Long-run successful business operations can be achieved with any combination of high and low brand loyalty and small or large market share. The fundamental criterion is that a sufficiently large segment of the market support the product quality being promoted.

3 Ronald E. Frank

Socio-Economic Factors

From Ronald E. Frank, 'Correlates of buying behavior for grocery products', *Journal of Marketing*, vol. 31, 1967, pp. 48–53.

During the last three and one-half years we have had an unusual opportunity to do research on the extent of market segmentation in the grocery-product field. We have had the data, as well as the technical and financial resources, to conduct a series of five investigations on the extent to which household, socio-economic and purchase characteristics are correlated with customer buying behavior in a wide range of grocery-product categories. A technical report of each of these studies either has been or is about to be published. (Frank and Boyd, Jr, 1965; Frank, Green and Seiber, Jr, 1967; Frank, Massy and Boyd, Jr, 1967; Frank, Douglas and Polli, 1967; and Frank, Douglas and Polli, 1967). The purpose of this article is to present, in a concise and nontechnical form, a summary of the results.

Each of the studies was concerned with determining the extent to which households with different socio-economic and purchasing characteristics also exhibited differences in buying behavior. The five buying characteristics studied were: total consumption, private-brand-proneness, brand loyalty, package-size-proneness, and average price paid per unit of product purchased.

All five of the investigations are based on *Chicago Tribune* consumer panel data for 1961.[1] The purchasing histories for each of 491 households in a number of product categories, ranging from 31 to 57, depending on the study, are included. The products cover a wide range of items such as regular coffee, tea, all-purpose flour, margarine, frozen dinners, packaged desserts, ready-to-eat cereals, scouring cleansers, peaches, pork and beans,

1. The author wishes to thank N. Don Kline and Edward A. Luby of the *Chicago Tribune* for their willing co-operation in making these data available.

canned tuna, toilet tissue and canned milk. The sample is drawn from the Chicago metropolitan area – the third largest in the United States.

Socio-economic characteristics[2]

1. Number of persons in family.
2. Number of adults in family.
3. Age of female head.
4. Age of youngest child.
5. Does housewife work?
6. Income.
7. Occupation.
8. Education of household head.
9. Number of cars.
10. Number of TV sets.
11. Religion of household heads (Catholic–non-Catholic).
12. Race of household heads (White–Non-white).
13. Building size.
14. Housewife status (households with and without female head).

Purchase characteristics

15. Proportion of purchases made in A & P.[3]
16. Proportion in National.[3]
17. Proportion in Jewel.[3]
18. Proportion in Kroger.[3]
19. Proportion in Hillman's.[3]
20. Total weight of purchases.[3]
21. Proportion of purchases devoted to private brands.[4]
22. Proportion of purchases devoted to brand purchased most often.[5]
23. Proportion of purchases devoted to small package sizes.[6]
24. Average price paid per unit purchased.[7]

2. These variables were included in all five studies.
3. These variables were included in all of the studies except that of total consumption.
4. Included in all studies except two: total consumption and private branding.
5. Included in package-size study only.
6. Included in brand-loyalty and average-price studies only.
7. Included in brand-loyalty and package-size studies only.

For each purchase by a household, a record was made of the household's serial number, date of the purchase, brand, number of units, package size, price paid, store where purchased and type of deal involved, if any. The entire data base includes records of approximately 400,000 purchases.

Multiple regression analysis was used in all five studies. The steps followed in each of them were quite similar. A summary was made for every household for each product category. For example, in the case of the total consumption study, the consumption during 1961 of each of the 57 products was computed for every one of the 491 households. For each household a summary was made of 14 socio-economic variables. The socio-economic characteristics comprised the set of independent variables to be studied. The list above reports a complete set of independent variables included in the five studies.

Separate multiple regression analyses were run for each product. For example, in the case of the total consumption study, 57 regressions were run, each of which analyzed the net relationship between the set of independent variables chosen for inclusion and household consumption for a product.

The definitions of the dependent variables in each of the other four studies were as follows:

1. Private-Brand-Proneness (PBP): The proportion of purchases devoted to private brands by a household for a product.

2. Brand Loyalty: The proportion of purchases that a household made for a product which were devoted to the brand purchased most often.

3. Package-Size-Proneness (PSP): The proportion of purchases devoted to small package sizes by a household for a product.

4. Average-Price Paid Per Unit of Product Purchased: The average price paid by a household for a product.

The findings

Two statistics will be used to report results in the following section. They are the coefficient of multiple determination (the square of the multiple correlation coefficient) and the partial correlation coefficient. The coefficient of determination measures the proportion of between-household variation, in the particular dimension of purchasing behavior being used as a dependent variable, that is associated with *the full set of independent variables*. The partial correlation coefficient measures the degree of association between the dependent variable and *one particular independent variable* while holding the others constant. A 'zero' coefficient of multiple determination would occur if the independent variable were completely uncorrelated with the buying characteristics under investigation, whereas 'one' would represent perfect correlation. In contrast, the partial correlation coefficient ranges from a negative to a positive one. Thus the partial correlation coefficient provides a measure of both the direction and degree of association, whereas the coefficient of multiple correlation measures degree but not direction. Each regression in a study generates one multiple correlation coefficient and as many partial correlation coefficients as there are independent variables included in the analysis.

These regression results are based on a number of assumptions. Two of the most important are that the relationship between the dependent and each of the independent variables is *linear*, and that there are no *interactions* between the effect of one independent variable and the level of another. For example, it might seem reasonable that total consumption would increase less rapidly at high income levels than at low. Or it may be that the effect of income on consumption depends on a person's occupation. The model upon which the results are based assumes that neither of these types of phenomena exists among any of the variables involved. The model, for example, assumes that the effect of income is linear and that the effect of income in no way depends on the level of one's occupation. Extensive tests of *nonlinear and interactive* models were conducted in all five of the studies. Almost without exception they produced no improvement in our ability to predict buying behavior or in our insights into its determinants. Therefore, we choose to report results based on the least complicated model.

Total consumption

Do heavy buyers of a grocery product have different socio-economic characteristics than their lighter counterparts? Often media selection is based on the objective of disproportionately reaching

39

the heavy buyers of a particular product. Some media buyers attempt to match the assumed socio-economic profile of a product's heavy buyers with the same characteristics for the media being evaluated. The objective is to concentrate advertising dollars in those media which are read by socio-economic types that have an above-average number of heavy buyers per dollar of advertising expense. This practice has come under considerable criticism in recent years (see, for example, Garfinkle, 1963; and Twedt, 1964). *It is based on the assumption that socio-economic characteristics are reasonably highly correlated with a household's product consumption.*

Many analyses have been done as to the socio-economic correlates of *total grocery consumption*. These findings have virtually no relevance to a producer of one specific type of grocery product unless one is willing to assume that the relationship between socio-economic characteristics and consumption is the same for *both* total grocery consumption and the particular product(s) of interest.

An analysis of the socio-economic correlates of consumption was done for each of the 57 different grocery product categories. Each of the 57 coefficients of determination that resulted served as a measure of the validity of the above assumption. The full set of socio-economic characteristics appearing above served as independent variables.

The average coefficient of multiple determination across all 57 product categories is 0·11 with a range of 0·00 to 0·29. Of the 14 socio-economic variables included in the analysis, 11 have a statistically significant tendency to be either positively or negatively associated with consumption across products. As one might expect, the most consistent variable across products is number of persons in family. Next in importance are age of youngest child, number of adults in family and housewife status.

While of some interest as a test of the aforementioned assumption, the effect of any single socio-economic variable is of little importance. What is important is our conclusion that *socio-economic variables are not likely to be useful in deriving media strategies for these products.* Consumption rates must be linked directly to media so they can be used for the objective of reaching the heavy consumers of grocery products. Tremendous strides in this direction are being made by firms such as the Brand Rating Index Corporation (BRI) and the American Research Bureau (ARB). For each person in its sample BRI collects purchase data for a wide variety of products as well as a measure of exposure to specific television programs, magazines, newspapers and radio stations. ARB collects both information on television exposure and product consumption by respondent. Nonetheless there are still many grocery manufacturers who implicitly or explicitly base their attempts to reach the 'heavy buyers' on the assumption that socio-economic characteristics are correlated with the household consumption of specific grocery products – an assumption which at best seems virtually invalid.

Private branding

Are private-brand-prone (PBP) grocery customers really different?
The answer to this question is of importance to:

1. *Retailers.* During the last decade competition between supermarkets has increased. As competition has become more intense, retailers have become aware of the need to differentiate their offerings. One of the principal ways by which supermarkets attempt to accomplish this objective is by means of the development of a private brand program. The use of private branding as a basis for differentiating a retailer's offerings from manufacturers' as well as from competing retailers' offerings rests, in part, on the extent to which private-brand-prone customers constitute an identifiable market segment (for example, one with distinct socio-economic and consumption habits).

2. *Manufacturers.* The expected profitability of entering into the production of private brands depends, in part, on their estimated effect on total revenue. To the extent that private-brand-prone customers constitute a distinct market segment (the less the overlap in customers of private and manufacturer brands in a product category) the smaller will be the magnitude of any opportunity loss due to the substitution of private brands for manufacturer brands by consumers of the product (and, hence, the larger the expected profit).

The average coefficient of multiple determination across the products included in the PBP analysis is 0·18. The most important

41

variables contributing to the prediction of PBP are the store purchase variables. Customers who tend to shop in stores with well developed private brand programs have a higher propensity to buy private brands than do other consumers. When one deletes the five store purchase variables from the analysis the average coefficient of determination falls from 0·18 to only 0·04.

There are some relatively modest associations between PBP and household socio-economic and consumption variables. Large families have a higher expected PBP than do small ones. The greater a household head's education, the higher is the expected level of the household's PBP. The more cars that are owned, the higher the PBP. The higher the household's consumption rate for a product, the more it is apt to be PBP. While the direction of the effects of these variables does appear to be reasonably consistent across products, their magnitude is nonetheless quite modest. The highest average partial correlation coefficient for either a socio-economic or purchase characteristic was 0·26 (based on absolute value) which was for the proportion of purchases made in A & P stores.

Virtually no segmentation of the market for any of the 44 grocery products included in the study has been achieved by means of the development of private branding programs. *Private and manufacturer brands meet in head-on competition in the sense that they are consumed by households with virtually the same socio-economic and total consumption characteristics.*

Brand loyalty

Do brand-loyal customers constitute an identifiable market segment? Do they have different rates of consumption? Different income levels? Ethnic backgrounds? Shopping store habits?

The relevance of brand loyalty to the formation of a profitable program of market segmentation has stirred the imaginations of both practitioners and scholars. Research supports the notion that brand loyalty is a reliable, persistent phenomenon (Frank, 1967). In spite of this fact, little is known about the determinants of brand loyalty. If management could identify the types of customers that have a tendency to concentrate disproportionately their purchases on a single brand or on a limited set of

42

brands, it would be in a better position to attempt to attract this 'hard-core' type buyer to its brand.

There appears to be virtually no association between house-hold, socio-economic and purchase characteristics included in the analysis and the degree of brand loyalty exhibited by a household. The average multiple coefficient of determination for the 44 products included in the brand loyalty study is only 0·12. Though eight of the variables do exhibit a reasonably consistent tendency to be correlated with brand loyalty, the magnitude of their association is extremely modest. Based on absolute value, the highest average partial correlation coefficient was 0·10 for average price paid. Next came the percentage of purchases on private brands with an average of −0·084.

The socio-economic and purchase characteristics included in the analysis make only a modest contribution to understanding the process that led to the formulation of brand loyalty.

Package size

What is the relationship between household socio-economic and purchase characteristics and package-size-proneness? To the extent that differences between small and larger package-size users do exist, the size(s) in which a brand is offered will segment its market. Brands offering different package sizes will tend to draw somewhat different clientele. Though a considerable amount of attention is paid to package-size decisions, there is, to our knowledge, no published study of the effectiveness of package size as a basis for market segmentation.

The degree of association between PSP and the independent variables included in the equation appears at first glance to be relatively high. The average coefficient of determination for the 31 products included was 0·41. However, when one removes 'price-paid' from the equation, the average drops to 0·19. The relation between average price and package size accounts for a large part of the predictive efficacy due to the fact that most manufacturers charge higher prices per ounce for small package sizes.

Of the 23 variables in the equation, 11 exhibit a statistically significant tendency to go in a given direction. Excluding relative

43

price, the two most consistent variables across products are number of adults in family, which is positively associated with package size in 87 per cent of the products, and total weight of purchases, which is negatively associated with package size in 84 per cent of the products. *To some extent package size appears to be a useful basis for market segmentation.*

Average price

To what extent is there a relationship between the average price paid per unit of a product purchased by a household and its socio-economic and total consumption characteristics? Brands that are relatively inexpensive at any given point in time (as a result of a permanent policy of 'low' prices, or as a result of a short-run special offer) may tend to draw their market shares from different *segments* of the population (for example, heavy versus light buyers) than brands that are typically higher priced. To the extent that socio-economic and total consumption characteristics are associated with price paid per unit, the price of a brand at any given point in time will tend to segment its market.

Package size, store shopping habits, and percentage of purchases spent in private brands have an impact on the price a household pays for a product. This impact is clearly seen when one contrasts the average coefficient of determination for equations (with the full set of variables) with the average generated by a run of equations with socio-economic and consumption characteristics only. The average for the former set of 44 equations was 0·37 whereas for the latter it was 0·10.

Household income, occupation, religion, building size, store shopping habits for National, Jewel, Kroger and Hillman's, as well as percentage of purchase devoted to small package sizes are all positively associated with average price paid per unit for grocery products. Five variables are negatively associated with price paid. They are number of persons in family, number of cars, race of household head, total purchases, and percentage spent on private brands. Though these effects tend to be somewhat persistent across products, they are quite modest in magnitude. The average partial correlation coefficient was 0·10 or greater for only three of the 22 variables, namely, the proportion of purchases in National, 0·10, the proportion of private brands purchases, 0·17, and the proportion devoted to small package sizes, 0·36.

Though the degree of correlation between average price paid per unit for a product by households and their socio-economic and purchase characteristics is modest, nonetheless the direction of the effects for a number of characteristics is consistent among product categories. *To some extent, the price at which a brand is sold at a point in time does segment its market.*

Socio-economic characteristics contribute little to our understanding of household variation in such aspects of product purchasing behavior as total consumption, private-brand-proneness, brand loyalty, package-size-proneness, and average price paid. Nonetheless, these negative findings do have some positive value. For some of us they add to the weight of evidence favoring what we already believed, while for others they have had a somewhat greater surprise value.

References

FRANK, R. E. (1967), 'Is brand loyalty a useful basis for market segmentation?', *Journal of Advertising Research*, vol. 7, pp. 27–33.

FRANK, R. E., and BOYD, H. W., Jr (1965), 'Are private-brand-prone food customers really different?', *Journal of Advertising Research*, vol. 5, no. 4, pp. 27–36.

FRANK, R. E., GREEN, P., and SEIBER, H., Jr (1967), 'Household correlates of "purchase price" for grocery products', *Journal of Marketing Research*, vol. 4, no. 1, pp. 54–8.

FRANK, R. E., MASSY, W., and BOYD, H. W., Jr (1967), 'Correlates of grocery product consumption rates', *Journal of Marketing Research*, vol. 4, no. 2, pp. 184–90.

FRANK, R. E., DOUGLAS, S. P., and POLLI, R. E. (1967), 'Household correlates of "brand loyalty" for grocery products', mimeographed in February.

FRANK, R. E., DOUGLAS, S. P., and POLLI, R. E. (1967), 'Household correlates of "package size" for grocery products', *Journal of Marketing Research*, vol. 1, no. 4, pp. 381–4.

GARFINKLE, N. (1963), 'A marketing approach to media selection', *Journal of Advertising Research*, vol. 3, no. 4, pp. 7–15.

TWEDT, D. W. (1964), 'Some practical applications of the "heavy half" theory', Tenth Annual Conference, Advertising Research Foundation, New York, 6 October.

4 Daniel Yankelovich

Market Segmentation

From Daniel Yankelovich, 'New criteria for market segmentation',
Harvard Business Review, vol. 42, 1964, pp. 83–90.

The director of marketing in a large company is confronted by
some of the most difficult problems in the history of U.S.
industry. To assist him, the information revolution of the past
decade puts at his disposal a vast array of techniques, facts and
figures. But without a way to master this information he can
easily be overwhelmed by the reports that flow in to him inces-
santly from marketing research, economic forecasts, cost analyses
and sales breakdowns. He must have more than mere access to
mountains of data. He must himself bring to bear a method of
analysis that cuts through the detail to focus sharply on new
opportunities.

In this article, I shall propose such a method. It is called
segmentation analysis. It is based on the proposition that once
you discover the most useful ways of segmenting a market, you
have produced the beginnings of a sound marketing strategy.

Unique advantages

Segmentation analysis has developed out of several key pre-
mises:

1. In today's economy, each brand appears to sell effectively to
only certain segments of any market and not to the whole market.

2. Sound marketing objectives depend on knowledge of how
segments which produce the most customers for a company's
brands differ in requirements and susceptibilities from the
segments which produce the largest number of customers for
competitive brands.

3. Traditional demographic methods of market segmentation do
not usually provide this knowledge. Analyses of market segments

by age, sex, geography and income level are not likely to provide as much direction for marketing strategy as management requires.

Once the marketing director does discover the most pragmatically useful way of segmenting his market, it becomes a new standard for almost all his evaluations. He will use it to appraise competitive strengths and vulnerabilities, to plan his product line, to determine his advertising and selling strategy and to set precise marketing objectives against which performance can later be measured. Specifically, segmentation analysis helps him to:

Direct the appropriate amounts of promotional attention and money to the most potentially profitable segments of his market.

Design a product line that truly parallels the demands of the market instead of one that bulks in some areas and ignores or scants other potentially quite profitable segments.

Catch the first sign of a major trend in a swiftly changing market and thus give him time to prepare to take advantage of it.

Determine the appeals that will be most effective in his company's advertising; and, where several different appeals are significantly effective, quantify the segments of the market responsive to each.

Choose advertising media more wisely and determine the proportion of budget that should be allocated to each medium in the light of anticipated impact.

Correct the timing of advertising and promotional efforts so that they are massed in the weeks, months and seasons when selling resistance is least and responsiveness is likely to be at its maximum.

Understand otherwise seemingly meaningless demographic market information and apply it in scores of new and effective ways.

These advantages hold in the case of both packaged goods and hard goods, and for commercial and industrial products as well as consumer products.

Guides to strategy

Segmentation analysis cuts through the data facing a marketing director when he tries to set targets based on markets as a whole, or when he relies primarily on demographic breakdowns. It is a systematic approach that permits the marketing planner to pick the strategically most important segmentations and then to design brands, products, packages, communications and marketing strategies around them. It infinitely simplifies the setting of objectives.

In the following sections we shall consider non-demographic ways of segmenting markets. These ways dramatize the point that finding marketing opportunities by depending solely on demographic breakdowns is like trying to win a national election by relying only on the information in a census. A modern census contains useful data but it identifies neither the crucial issues of an election nor those groups whose voting habits are still fluid, nor the needs, values and attitudes that influence how those groups will vote. This kind of information, rather than census-type data, is the kind that wins elections – and markets.

Consider, for example, companies like Procter & Gamble, General Motors or American Tobacco, whose multiple brands sell against one another and must, every day, win new elections in the marketplace:

These companies sell to the whole market, not by offering one brand that appeals to all people, but by covering the different segments with multiple brands. How can they prevent these brands from cannibalizing each other? How can they avoid surrendering opportunities to competitors by failing to provide brands that appeal to all important segments? In neither automobiles, soaps, nor cigarettes do demographic analyses reveal to the manufacturer what products to make or what products to sell to what segments of the market. Obviously, some modes of segmentation other than demographic are needed to explain why brands which differ so little nevertheless find their own niches in the market, each one appealing to a different segment.

The point at issue is not that demographic segmentation should be disregarded, but rather that it should be regarded as only one among many possible ways of analysing markets. In fact, the key requirement of segmentation analysis is that the marketing director should never assume in advance that any one method of segmentation is the best. His first job should be to muster all probable segmentations and *then* choose the most meaningful ones to work with. This approach is analogous to that used in research in the physical sciences, where the hypothesis that best seems to explain the phenomena under investigation is the one chosen for working purposes

Seven markets

In the following discussion we shall take seven markets for consumer and industrial products and see how they are affected by seven different modes of non-demographic segmentation. The products and modes are shown schematically in Table 1. Of course, these segments are not the only ones important in business. The seven I have picked are only *examples* of how segmentation analysis can enlarge the scope and depth of a marketer's thinking.

Watches

In this first case we deal with a relatively simple mode of segmentation analysis. The most productive way of analyzing the market for watches turns out to be segmentation by *value*. This approach discloses three distinct segments, each representing a different value attributed to watches by each of three different groups of consumers:

1. *People who want to pay the lowest possible price for any watch that works reasonably well.* If the watch fails after six months or a year, they will throw it out and replace it.

2. *People who value watches for their long life, good workmanship, good material, and good styling.* They are willing to pay for these product qualities.

3. *People who look not only for useful product features but also for meaningful emotional qualities.* The most important consideration in this segment is that the watch should suitably symbolize an important occasion. Consequently, fine styling, a well-known

49

brand name, the recommendation of the jeweler, and a gold or diamond case are highly valued.

Table 1 Example of Segmentation in Different Industries (Extract)

| Market | *Mode of segmentation* | | | | |
	Value	*Suscepti-bility to change*	*Purpose*	*Aesthetic concepts*	*Individual needs*
Watches	√				
Automobiles	√	√		√	
Perfumes			√		
Bath soaps			√		
Hair care					√
Other packaged goods	√		√	√	
Retail soft goods	√				

In 1962, my research shows, the watch market divided quantitatively as follows:

1. Approximately 23 per cent of the buyers bought for lowest price (value segment no. 1).

2. Another 46 per cent bought for durability and general product quality (value segment no. 2).

3. And 31 per cent bought watches as symbols of some important occasion (value segment no. 3).

Defining and quantifying such segments is helpful in marketing planning – especially if a watch company's product happens to appeal mostly to one segment or if the line straddles the three segments, failing to appeal effectively to any. Without such an understanding, the demographic characteristics of the market are most confusing. It turns out, for example, that the most expensive watches are being bought by people with both the highest and the lowest incomes. On the other hand, some upper-income consumers are no longer buying costly watches, but are buying cheap, well-styled watches to throw away when they require servicing. Other upper-income consumers, however, continue to buy fine, expensive watches for suitable occasions.

Timex's timely tactics. The planning implications in value segmentation are very broad for the industry. For one thing, many of the better watch companies in the years between 1957 and 1962 were inadvertently focusing exclusively on the third segment described – the 31 per cent of the market that bought a watch only as a gift on important occasions – thus leaving the bulk of the market open to attack and exploitation.

The U.S. Time Company took advantage of this opening and established a very strong position among the more than two-thirds of America's watch buyers in the first two segments. Its new low-price watch, the Timex, had obvious appeal for the first segment, and it catered to the second segment as well. At that time, higher-price watches were making the disastrous mistake in their advertising of equating product quality with water-proof and shock-resistant features. The Timex also offered these low-cost features, at lower prices, thus striking at a vulnerable area which the competition itself created. When Timex pressed its attack, it was able within a few years to claim that 'Timex sells more watches than any other watch company in the world.'

Even the *timing* of Timex's watch advertising was involved. Much of the third segment was buying watches only during the Christmas season, and so most of Timex's competitors concentrated their advertising in November and December. But since buying by the other two segments went on all the time, Timex advertised all year-round, getting exclusive attention ten months of the year.

Thus, non-demographic segmentation in the watch industry has directly affected almost every phase of marketing, including the composition of the product line. Major watch companies know that they must plan product line, pricing, advertising and distribution within the framework of the three basic value segments of this market.

Automobiles

The non-demographic segmentation of the automobile market is more complex than that of the watch market. The segments

51

crisscross, forming intricate patterns. Their dynamics must be seen clearly before automobile sales can be understood.

Segmentation analysis leads to at least three different ways of classifying the automobile market along non-demographic lines, all of which are important to marketing planning.

Value segmentation. The first mode of segmentation can be compared to that in the watch market – a threefold division along lines which represent how different people look at the meaning of *value* in an automobile:

1. *People who buy cars primarily for economy.* Many of these become owners of the Falcon, Ford, Rambler American and Chevrolet. They are less loyal to any make than the other segments, but go where the biggest savings are to be found.

2. *People who want to buy the best product they can find for their money.* These prospects emphasize values such as body quality, reliability, durability, economy of operation, and ease of upkeep. Rambler and Volkswagen have been successful because so many people in this segment were dissatisfied.

3. *People interested in 'personal enhancement' (a more accurate description than 'prestige').* A handsomely styled Pontiac or Thunderbird does a great deal for the owner's ego, even though the car may not serve as a status symbol. Although the value of an automobile as a status symbol has declined, the personal satisfaction in owning a fine car has not lessened for this segment of the market. It is interesting that while both watches and cars have declined in status value, they have retained *self-enhancement* value for large portions of the market.

Markets can change so swiftly, and the size of key segments can shift so rapidly, that great sensitivity is required to catch a trend in time to capitalize on it. In the automobile market, the biggest change in recent years has been the growth in segment two – the number of people oriented to strict product value. Only a few years ago, the bulk of the market was made up of the other segments, but now the product-value segment is probably the largest. Some automobile companies did not respond to this shift in the size of these market segments in time to maintain their share of the market.

Aesthetic concepts. A second way of segmenting the automobile market is by differences in *style* preferences. For example, most automobile buyers tell you that they like 'expensive looking' cars. To some people, however, 'expensive looking' means a great deal of chrome and ornamentation, while to others it means the very opposite – clean, conservative lines, lacking much chrome or ornamentation.

Unfortunately, the same *words* are used by consumers to describe diametrically opposed style concepts. Data that quantify buyers according to their aesthetic *responses* – their differing conceptions of what constitutes a good-looking car – are among the most useful an automobile company can possess.

The importance of aesthetic segmentation can be pointed up by this example:

When Ford changed from its 1959 styling to its 1960 styling, the change did not seem to be a radical one from the viewpoint of formal design. But, because it ran contrary to the special style expectations of a large group of loyal Ford buyers, it constituted a dramatic and unwelcome change to them. This essential segment was not prepared for the change, and the results were apparent in sales.

Susceptibility to change. A third and indispensable method of segmenting the automobile market cuts across the lines drawn by the other two modes of segmentation analysis. This involves measuring the relative susceptibility of potential car buyers to changing their choice of make. Consider the buyers of Chevrolet during any one year from the point of view of a competitor:

At one extreme are people whose brand loyalty is so solidly entrenched that no competitor can get home to them. They always buy Chevrolets. They are closed off to change.

At the other extreme are the open-minded and the unprejudiced buyers. They happened to buy a Chevrolet because they preferred its styling that year, or because they got a good buy, or because someone talked up the Fisher body to them. They could just as easily have purchased another make.

In the middle of this susceptibility continuum are people who are predisposed to Chevrolet to a greater or lesser degree. They can be persuaded to buy another make, but the persuasion has to be strong enough to break through the Chevrolet predisposition.

The implications of this kind of a susceptibility segmentation are far-reaching. Advertising effectiveness, for example, must be measured against each susceptiblity segment, not against the market as a whole. Competitors' advertising should appear in media most likely to break through the Chevrolet predisposition of the middle group. In addition, the wants of those who are not susceptible must be factored out, or they will muddy the picture. Marketing programs persuasive enough to influence the uncommitted may make no difference at all to the single largest group – those who are predisposed to Chevrolet but still open enough to respond to the right stimulus.

If the marketing director of an automobile company does not break down his potential market into segments representing key differences in susceptibility, or does not clearly understand the requirements of each key segment, his company can persevere for years with little or no results because its promotion programs are inadvertently being aimed at the wrong people.

Perfume

A segmentation analysis of the perfume market shows that a useful way to analyze it is by the different *purposes* women have in mind when they buy perfume.

One segment of the market thinks of a perfume as something to be added to what nature has supplied. Another segment believes that the purpose of fragrance products is to help a woman feel cleaner, fresher, and better groomed – to correct or negate what nature has supplied. In the latter instance, the fragrance product is used to *cancel out* natural body odors; in the former, to *add* a new scent. To illustrate this difference in point of view:

One woman told an interviewer, 'I like a woodsy scent like Fabergé. It seems more intense and lingers longer, and doesn't fade away like the sweeter scents.'

But another woman said, 'I literally loathe Fabergé. It makes me think of a streetcar full of women coming home from work who haven't bathed.'

These differences in reaction do not indicate objective differences in the scent of Fabergé. They are subjective differences in women's attitudes; they grow out of each woman's purpose in using a perfume.

Purposive segmentation, as this third mode of analysis might be called, has been of great value to alert marketers. For instance·

A company making a famous line of fragrance products realized that it was selling almost exclusively to a single segment, although it had believed it was competing in the whole market. Management had been misled by its marketing research, which had consistently shown no differences in the demographic characteristics of women buying the company's products and women buying competitors' products.

In the light of this insight, the company decided to allocate certain lines to the underdeveloped segments of the market. This required appropriate changes in the scent of the product and in its package design. A special advertising strategy was also developed, involving a different copy approach for each product line aimed at each segment.

In addition, it was learned that visualizations of the product in use helped to create viewer identification in the segment that used perfume for adding to nature's handiwork, but that more subtle methods of communication produced better results among the more reserved, more modest women in the second segment who want the 'canceling out' benefits of perfume. The media susceptibilities of women in the two segments were also found to be different.

Thus, from a single act of re-segmentation, the advertising department extracted data critical to its copy platform, communication strategy and media decisions.

Bathing soap

A comparable purposive segmentation was found in the closely related bathing soap field. The key split was between women whose chief requirement of soap was that it should clean them

55

adequately and those for whom bathing was a sensuous and enjoyable experience. The company – a new contender in this highly competitive field – focused its sights on the first segment, which had been much neglected in recent years. A new soap was shaped, designed and packaged to appeal to this segment, a new advertising approach was evolved, and results were very successful.

Hair-care market

The Breck–Halo competition in the shampoo market affords an excellent example of another kind of segmentation. For many years, Breck's recognition of the market's individualized segmentation gave the company a very strong position. Its line of individualized shampoos included one for dry hair, another for oily hair, and one for normal hair. This line accurately paralleled the marketing reality that women think of their hair as being dry, oily, or normal, and they do not believe that any one shampoo – such as an all-purpose Halo – can meet their individual requirements. Colgate has finally been obliged, in the past several years, to revise its long-held marketing approach to Halo, and to come out with products for dry hair and for oily hair, as well as for normal hair.

Other companies in the hair-care industry are beginning to recognize other segmentations in this field. For example, some women think of their hair as fine, others as coarse. Each newly discovered key segmentation contains the seeds of a new product, a new marketing approach, and a new opportunity.

Other packaged goods

Examples of segmentation analysis in other packaged goods can be selected almost at random. Let us mention a few briefly, to show the breadth of applicability of this method of marketing analysis:

In *convenience foods*, for example, we find that the most pragmatic classification is, once again, purposive segmentation. Analysis indicates that 'convenience' in foods has many different meanings for women, supporting several different market segments. Women for whom convenience means 'easy to use' are reached by products and appeals different from those used to reach women for whom convenience means shortcuts to creativity in cooking.

In the market for *cleaning agents*, some women clean preventively, while others clean therapeutically, i.e. only after a mess has been made. The appeals, the product characteristics, and the marketing approach must take into account these different reasons for buying – another example of purposive segmentation.

In still another market, some people use *air fresheners* to remove disagreeable odors and others to add an odor. A product like Gladé, which is keyed to the second segment, differs from one like Airwick in product concept, packaging and type of scent.

The *beer market* requires segmentation along at least four different axes – reasons for drinking beer (purposive), taste preferences (aesthetic), price/quality (value), and consumption level.

Retail soft goods

Although soft-goods manufacturers and retailers are aware that their customers are value conscious, not all of them realize that their markets break down into at least four different segments corresponding to four different conceptions of value held by women. For some women value means a willingness to pay a little more for quality. For others, value means merchandise on sale. Still other women look for value in terms of the lowest possible price, while others buy seconds or discounted merchandise as representing the best value.

Retailing operations like Sears, Roebuck are highly successful because they project *all* these value concepts, and do so in proportions which closely parallel their distribution in the total population.

Conclusion

To sum up the implications of the preceding analysis, let me stress three points:

1. *We should discard the old, unquestioned assumption that demography is always the best way of looking at markets.*

The demographic premise implies that differences in reasons

57

for buying, in brand choice influences, in frequency of use, or in susceptibility will be reflected in differences in age, sex, income, and geographical location. But this is usually not true. Markets should be scrutinized for important differences in buyer attitudes, motivations, values, usage patterns, aesthetic preferences, or degree of susceptibility. These may have no demographic correlatives. Above all, we must never assume in advance that we know the best way of looking at a market. This is the cardinal rule of segmentation analysis. All ways of segmenting markets must be considered, and *then* we must select out of the various methods available the ones that have the most important implications for action. This process of choosing the strategically most useful mode of segmentation is the essence of the marketing approach espoused in this article.

In considering cases like those described, we must understand that we are not dealing with different types of people, but with differences in people's *values*. A woman who buys a refrigerator because it is the cheapest available may want to buy the most expensive towels. A man who pays extra for his beer may own a cheap watch. A Ford-owning Kellogg's Corn Flakes-eater may be closed off to Chevrolet but susceptible to Post Toasties; he is the same man, but he has had different experiences and holds different values toward each product he purchases. By segmenting markets on the basis of the values, purposes, needs and attitudes relevant to the product being studied, as in Table 1, we avoid misleading information derived from attempts to divide people into types.

2. *The strategic-choice concept of segmentation broadens the scope of marketing planning to include the positioning of new products as well as of established products.*

It also has implications for brand planning, not just for individual products but for the composition of a line of competing brands where any meaningful segment in the market can possibly support a brand. One explanation of the successful competing brand strategy of companies like Procter & Gamble is that they are based on sensitivity to the many different modes of market segmentation. The brands offered by P & G often appear very similar to the outsider, but small, marginal differences between them appeal to different market segments. It is this rather than intramural competition that supports P & G successes.

3. *Marketing must develop its own interpretive theory, and not borrow a ready-made one from the social sciences.*

Marketing research, as an applied science, is tempted to borrow its theoretical structures from the disciplines from which it derives. The social sciences offer an abundance of such structures, but they are not applicable to marketing in their pure academic form. While the temptation to apply them in that form is great, it should be resisted. From sociology, for example, marketing has frequently borrowed the concept of status. This is a far-reaching concept, but it is not necessarily the most important one in a marketing problem, nor even one of the important ones. Again, early psychoanalytic theory has contributed an understanding of the sexual factor. While this can sometimes be helpful in an analysis of buying behavior in a given situation, some motivation researchers have become over-sensitive to the role of sex and, as a result, have made many mistakes. Much the same might be said of the concept of social character, that is, seeing the world as being 'inner-directed', 'other-directed', 'tradition-directed', 'autonomous', and so forth.

One of the values of segmentation analysis is that, while it has drawn on the insights of social scientists, it has developed an interpretive theory *within* marketing. It has been home-grown in business. This may explain its ability to impose patterns of meaning on the immense diversity of the market, and to provide the modern marketing director with a systematic method for evolving true marketing objectives.

5 J. M. Agostini

Mass-Media

J. M. Agostini, 'How to estimate unduplicated audiences',
Journal of Advertising Research, vol. 1, 1961, pp. 11–14.

When several vehicles – magazines, newspapers, etc. – are used
in an advertising campaign, it is easy to sum their audiences.
But because of audience duplication, this sum A always exceeds
the audience C actually reached by the combination, and it is
precisely this unduplicated audience C which must be measured
in order to evaluate the coverage of the campaign.

Audience analyses sometimes give data on audience duplication
for vehicles taken two by two; seldom do they give data on
audience duplication for a combination of three or more. But
the size of the unduplicated audience of several vehicles depends
not only on the number of people simultaneously covered by two,
but also on the number simultaneously covered by 3, 4, . . ., n
vehicles. Analyses made in the US and in France have shown that
readership of three or more vehicles, particularly magazines, is
very common. Therefore, when more than two vehicles are to be
used, as usually happens, the unduplicated audience is rarely
known. However, the press readership survey made in France
by the Centre d'Etude des Supports de Publicité (CESP) in 1957
may be considered a remarkable effort in this field. Duplications
were obtained for 30 magazines taken two by two – as well as
for all possible combinations of 15 of the 30 magazines! Three
large books were required to present the results of the 32,767
combinations possible.

These data are obviously very useful, but refer only to half the
publications covered by the survey. They do not show the
unduplicated audience of any magazine combination which
includes a magazine not among the 15 chosen. The purpose of
this paper is to describe a short-cut method of estimating the
unduplicated audience of a higher order combination of vehicles –

trio, quartet, etc. – from data on the duplication of these vehicles taken two by two. When applied to the CESP results, the proposed method leads to a satisfactory evaluation of the unduplicated audience provided by any of the 1,073,741,793 combinations possible with the 30 magazines whose paired duplications are known.

Method

Let:

$a, b, c, \ldots n$ be the vehicles of the combination, $A_a, A_b, \ldots A_n$ be their respective audiences, and A the sum of these individual audiences. Thus,

$$A = A_a + A_b + \ldots + A_n. \qquad \qquad 1$$

Owing to duplication, the unduplicated audience C is smaller than the sum of the audiences of the vehicles, i.e.

$$C = zA, \qquad \qquad 2$$

where z is a coefficient between 0 and 1.

The proposed method consists in calculating z from the square table giving the duplication of media taken two by two. This table shows the audience duplicated by two vehicles at the intersection of their row and column: D_{ab} is the number of people simultaneously covered by a and b.

	a	b	c	$\ldots$ n
a	—	D_{ab}	D_{ac}	$\ldots D_{an}$
b	D_{ba}	—	D_{bc}	$\ldots D_{bn}$
c	D_{ca}	D_{cb}	—	$\ldots D_{cn}$
.	.	.	.	—
.	.	.	.	—
.	.	.	.	—
n	D_{na}	D_{nb}	D_{nc}	$\ldots$ —

For obvious reasons this table is symmetrical about its main diagonal, D being the half-sum of all the terms in the table.

$$
\begin{aligned}
D = D_{ab} &+ D_{ac} + \ldots + D_{an} + \\
&+ D_{bc} + \ldots + D_{bn} + \\
&\ldots \text{etc.}
\end{aligned}
\qquad 3
$$

Thus D represents the total of the two by two duplicated audiences. In the case of magazines, D represents the total of the double readerships. We have, on the other hand, the total duplicated audiences:

$$A = A_a + A_b + \ldots + A_n \qquad \textbf{1}$$

Suppose we let

$$x = \frac{D}{A}. \qquad \textbf{4}$$

Now x is a factor which can be easily calculated starting from data already in our hands: the total audience of all vehicles and their two by two duplications.

We shall establish that there is a relation between x and the factor z of equation **2**.

$$z = \mathrm{f}(x). \qquad \textbf{5}$$

We shall prove that this relation may be satisfactorily represented by a unique curve the tracing of which will be given.

Knowing x, the value of z will be found on the curve, and this equation **2** will give a fair estimate of the unduplicated audience C, which is the object of our endeavor.

The relation between x and z

Obviously the greater the duplication between media, the less will be the unduplicated audience. The higher the value of D, the lower the value of C.

Inasmuch as $x = \frac{D}{A}$ and $z = \frac{C}{A}$, when x increases z decreases. When there is no duplication between media, the unduplicated audience equals the sum of the audiences. In this case, when $D = 0$, $x = 0$, and when $C = A$, $z = 1$.

Therefore when $x = 0$, $z = 1$.

Results released by the CESP enabled us to calculate the values of x and z for any combination of the 15 magazines for which the special study on unduplicated audiences was conducted. To calculate x for a given combination, we divided the duplication between the magazines, as obtained from the two by two table, by the sum A of audiences of the magazines. To calculate z, we divided the unduplicated audience C of the same combination, as actually observed in the special study, by the sum A of audiences of the magazines.

Theoretically we are in a position to work out 32,767 pairs of values for x and z. Actually we calculated only 98, selected at random from all combinations studied.

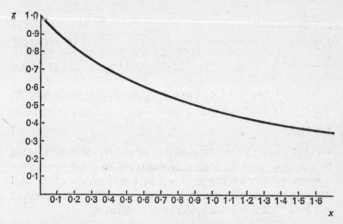

Figure 1 Observed relationship between unduplicated (z) and pair-wise duplicated (x) coefficients of the total audience

With x on the abscissa and z on the ordinate, we plotted 98 dots, the setting out of which clearly shows that the relation between x and z can be accurately depicted by a continuous curve (see Figure 1). Such a curve was traced through the 98 dots. The accuracy of the graphic tool thus obtained was very satisfactory. The difference between the value of z read from the curve and the true value was in 90 per cent of the cases less than 0·01 and never more than 0·02.

We then tried to translate this curve into an equation. The tracing of the curve looks like an equilateral hyperbola asymptotic to the x axis. Obviously when vehicles are added to a combination, the sum A may increase indefinitely while C must necessarily tend toward a limit, i.e. z must tend toward zero. The curve $z = f(x)$ must therefore have the x axis as its asymptote.

63

Accordingly we tried an equation of this form:

$$z = \frac{1}{Kx + 1}.$$

6

We found that when $K = 1 \cdot 125$, equation **6** represented perfectly the section of the curve traced on the chart up to $x = 1 \cdot 7$, the highest value of x observed in magazine combinations used to obtain the curve.

Practical example

Let us, for example, take four magazines, the unduplicated audience of which has been calculated in the CESP special study. This will enable us to judge the accuracy of the proposed graphic method.

Suppose we have to estimate the unduplicated audience of the following four magazines, knowing the individual audience of each:

	Readers (in thousands)
Selection	4741
Jours de France	1573
La Vie Catholique	2447
Nous Deux	4143

We also know their two by two duplications:

	S	JF	VC	ND
Selection	—	638	663	697
Jours de France		—	275	186
La Vie Catholique			—	283
Nous Deux				—

We calculate

$A = 4741 + 1573 + 2447 + 4143 = 12{,}904$
$D = 638 + 663 + 697 + 275 + 186 + 283$
$\quad = 2742,$

hence $x = \dfrac{D}{A} = 0 \cdot 21.$

On the curve we read the z value for $x = 0.21$, namely,

$z = 0.805$,

hence $C = zA = 0.805 \ (12{,}904) = 10{,}400$.

The true value of C given by the CESP special study was 10,468.

Other applications

The curve $z = f(x)$ on which the method is based was derived empirically from data on 15 French magazines. We have found that estimates obtained from the curve closely match the results actually obtained in the CESP special study. But this is no proof that the curve is valid for other media than those which served to build it. We therefore decided to test the proposed method beyond those 15 magazines.

The CESP survey tabulated the unduplicated audience of a few groups of media other than the 15 chosen magazines. When the two by two duplications are given as well, it is possible to apply our method and compare the estimate obtained with the actual result. We conducted three tests with:

1. Five women's magazines, of which only one was part of the 15.

2. Five general magazines, of which none was part of the 15.

3. Eleven Paris dailies.

In the three cases, the proposed method has led us to a fairly close estimate of the unduplicated audience:

	Estimated audience	Actual audience	Difference
1.	5,700,000	5,837,000	2·3%
2.	6,200,000	6,210,000	0·2%
3.	6,000,000	6,160,000	2·6%

All media previously mentioned are French publications the audiences of which were measured by this same CESP survey. It seemed advisable to test the proposed method with US magazines. This we were able to do thanks to the 1954 *Life* report, *A Study of Duplication*. In this study, audience duplications of five US magazines – *Life, Saturday Evening Post, Look, Ladies' Home Journal, This Week* – were analyzed.

Specifically, unduplicated audiences were given for all combinations of three, four and five magazines. In each case these audiences were analyzed according to sex and income. We thus have a total of 96 results regarding unduplicated audiences – 16 combinations for each of six groups (one over-all, two sexes and three income levels). The same audiences were evaluated by applying our method with the same constant, $K = 1.125$. Results:

In 82 cases, the difference between the actual audience and the estimated audience was less than 1 per cent.

In ten cases, this difference lay between 1 and 2 per cent.

In four cases, this difference exceeded 2 per cent (maximum 2.7 per cent).

It appears that the proposed method has a wide field of application.

Conclusions

If it is true that the only information required to estimate an unduplicated audience is the total audience and two by two vehicle duplications, then great economy of effort is possible. Instead of undertaking the fantastic amount of tabulation required to calculate the unduplicated audiences of all possible combinations of a restricted number of vehicles, it is preferable to set up, for all vehicles, a series of square tables of their two by two duplications, each table containing these duplications within one stratum. It should be noted that to evaluate the unduplicated audience of a combination of vehicles within a stratum, e.g. an age group, one must know the duplications *within this stratum*. Knowledge of duplications for the whole sample is not sufficient.

We feel that an analysis of the two by two duplications by strata for any individual audience analysis is much more efficient than a repetition of such voluminous work as the CESP special study. We must not forget, however, that if this tremendous enterprise had not been undertaken, we would not have found a method to save us from doing it in the future.

6 A. S. C. Ehrenberg

Some Coherent Patterns

A. S. C. Ehrenberg, 'Towards an integrated theory of consumer behaviour', *Journal of the Market Research Society*, vol. 11, 1969, pp. 305–37.

Something for theoreticians to work on and for practical men to think about.

1. Introduction
Empirically based theory

The aim of this paper is to draw together various relatively isolated laws of consumer behaviour for frequently-bought branded goods or services. Starting without formalized preconceptions of how or why people behave or feel as they do, the emphasis is on interrelating empirical patterns which are known to hold under wide ranges of observed conditions.

Consumer behaviour has been extensively examined during the last few decades. Bibliographies are given in review articles by Sheth (90) and Lawrence (81) from the marketing point-of-view, and by Ferber (58) from that of economics. The potential contributions of the social sciences have been documented by Britt's summarized readings (7).

In practice, most empirical studies of consumer behaviour have dealt with *ad hoc* market research problems by way of isolated data-collection exercises. As a consequence, it is known which brands are bought more often than others, that some people buy more than others, that more people have favourable attitudes towards the market-leader than towards a smaller-selling brand, and it is known how to measure these things routinely.

There has, however, been relatively little generalization or integration. There is very little empirically based theory. We do not know the relative importance of the various factors which affect consumer behaviour, nor how they are interrelated. We do not know whether consumer attitudes change before consumer behaviour (59), nor do we have generalizable theories of how to influence either consumer attitudes or behaviour (77–9, 82).

There has been little real understanding of how or why consumers make purchasing decisions, and it is often not even known what sort of decisions they make. The analysis in this paper is largely based on quantitative descriptive studies carried out in the last few years to try and reduce some of these gaps in our knowledge.

The scope of the analysis

The studies reported on here still do not say why some consumers buy a particular product, or why they choose one brand rather than another. Instead, if in a given time-period a certain number of people buy a particular brand, the results show *how* they do this, and with what other facts this ties in.

For example, the number of people who buy a particular brand at all in a given period is related to how *often* they buy it, to how many additional buyers of the brand there will be in some longer period, to how often these additional buyers will buy the brand, and to what *other* brands any of these people also buy, and how often. And we note how these patterns are interrelated for different brands, for different product-fields, and for different lengths of time-period.

Again, the extent to which people hold some particular attitude about a brand is related to their buying or usage patterns for this brand, to whether or not they also buy other brands, and to what *other* attitudes these people may also hold about these brands. The aim is to see how all these results can be predicted and understood.

The findings are given here in brief summary form, together with some illustrative tables. Leading manufacturers have some £100,000,000 worth of comparable market research data, and this acts as a check on the predictive validity and the practical usefulness of the findings. Fuller details and proofs are available in the original references cited.

In working towards a coherent theory, the paper is necessarily a review and summary of earlier work. However, for readers of this *Journal*, the degree of overlap with previous papers is small. For example, three earlier papers in the *Journal* have dealt with buyer behaviour, the topic of the following section. Two of these papers (35, 64) described some practical applications which are among the thirty-six application areas now listed in Table 10, and the third paper (22) gave an early version of a result which is implicitly referred to in the footnote on page 73. Otherwise, the results discussed here are new.

The broad topic of consumer behaviour is treated firstly in the narrow but central sense of people periodically buying branded products like non-durable household goods (§2) or using services like the mass-media (§3), and secondly as also embracing people's underlying attitudes (§4) and their appreciation of the inherent quality-factors of the product or service in question (§5). Since interest in analytic techniques is nowadays high, methodological considerations are also briefly summarised (§6).

The question of practical applications

There is a common feeling nowadays that research results should be of immediate practical value. However, basic research aimed at new knowledge and understanding must necessarily come first.

The technological gap can nonetheless be reduced by a deliberate policy of developing prototype applications. Early cases of such applications are therefore outlined at the end of each of the main sections of the present paper.

2. Buyer behaviour

The buying of a low-priced consumption item is usually quite a well-defined act and tends to be fairly easy to measure, e.g. by consumer panels or surveys. Buying is where consumer behaviour interacts most directly with the interests of producers and distributors and it is of particular importance to understand. In this section we therefore examine the patterns of repeat-buying and brand-switching which occur for frequently-bought branded consumer goods.

Repeat-buying

Repeat-buying is interpreted as any situation where a person buys more than one unit of a particular brand or product, either on the same purchase occasion or as several distinct purchase acts in a given time-period or in different time-periods. The question is what the patterns of repeat-buying are like, how they are inter-related, and on what factors they depend.

69

The NBD/LSD model. Suppose that some proportion b per cent of the population buy a given brand X in some particular time-period, such as a certain three-month period. Some people buy it just once in the period, some twice, some three times, and so on, the average number of purchases per buyer being w in the period. We therefore have two fundamental quantities:

b: the proportion of the population buying brand X at all in the period,

w: the average number of times these buyers of brand X buy it in the period.

Where necessary to avoid confusion, we use the symbols b_x, w_x with suffix X for brand X, and b_y, w_y for some other brand Y, and so on.

Suppose that in the next equal time-period brand X is bought by the same proportion of the population, b per cent, and at the same average frequency per buyer, w. There is therefore no trend in sales. This is the stationary or equilibrium situation for brand X.

Even under such simple equilibrium conditions, not all buyers of brand X in the first period buy it again in the second period. The following simple results hold:

The proportion of the buyers of brand X in the first period who buy X in the second period is approximately

$2 (w - 1)/(2 \cdot 3 w - 1)$.

Such repeat-buyers buy brand X in each period with an average frequency of approximately

$1 \cdot 23 w$.

The people who buy brand X in the first period but not in the second period, or vice versa, buy it in the period in question with an average frequency of approximately

$1 \cdot 4$, which is a constant.

The nature of period-to-period repeat-buying therefore generally depends on at most one quantity, namely the average frequency of buying the brand, w. Suppose for example that buyers of brand X in a given period buy it on average 3 times each in the

70

Table 1 Observed Repeat-Buying (o) in Successive Quarters and Theoretical NBD/LSD Estimates (t) (19 near-stationary cases – Chicago, Quarters 1 to 4, 1951)

Brand and size	Product	Quarters	Given data[1]		Repeat-buying					
			No. of buyers b (per quarter)	Purchases per buyer w	No. of repeat-buyers		Purchases per repeat-buyer		Purchases per one-quarter-only buyer[1]	
					t	o	t	o	t	o
Am. Fam. Flakes (20 oz)	Soaps	1 2	21	4·6	16	14	5·6	5·6	1·4	2·6[2]
Am. Fam. Flakes (½ lb)		3 4	19	4·2	15	14	5·1	5·2	1·4	1·4
All Sweet	Margarine	3 4	50	4·2	37	36	5·1	5·2	1·4	1·6
All Sweet	"	1 2	32	3·9	23	24	4·7	4·8	1·4	1·4
Hills Bros. (2 lb)	Coffee	2 3	12	3·3	8	8	4·0	4·3	1·4	1·3
Hills Bros.	"	3 4	13	3·3	9	8	3·9	4·3	1·4	1·5
Nutley (½ lb)	Margarine	1 2	18	3·0	12	12	3·6	3·7	1·4	1·4
Tide (52 oz)	Soaps	3 4	12	2·9	8	7	3·6	3·7	1·4	1·6
Hills Bros. (1 lb)	Coffee	1 2	22	2·5	14	15	3·1	3·2	1·4	1·2
Chase & Sanbourn	"	1 2	15	2·5	10	9	3·0	3·4	1·4	1·2
Parkay (½ lb)	Margarine	3 4	28	2·4	17	17	2·9	3·0	1·4	1·5
Eight O'clock (1 lb)	Coffee	3 4	18	2·3	11	10	2·8	3·2	1·4	1·5
Eight O'clock	"	3 2	17	2·3	10	9	2·8	2·8	1·4	1·4
Tide (52 oz)	Soaps	1 2	10	2·0	6	7	2·3	2·4	1·3	1·2
Pillsbury (5 lb)	Flour	3 2	27	2·0	16	14	2·4	2·8	1·3	1·3
Pillsbury (2 lb)	"	2 3	28	1·8	13	15	2·1	2·1	1·3	1·4
Pillsbury	"	3 4	13	1·8	7	7	2·1	1·8	1·3	1·4
Gold Medal (5 lb)	"	3 4	18	1·4	7	10	1·7	1·6	1·2	1·2
Gold Medal	"	2 3	18	1·3	6	10	1·3	1·5	1·2	1·2
Average			20	2·7	13	13	3·3	3·4	1·4	1·4

[1] Average of two equal or nearly-equal quarterly figures. Brands are arranged in decreasing order of w.
[2] A two-packs-banded-together promotion or the like occurred for American Family Flakes during Quarters 1 and 2.

period. Then under no-trend equilibrium conditions about $2(3 - 1)/(6\cdot9 - 1) = 0\cdot68$ (or 68 per cent) of them are found to buy X again in the next equal period, and they do so on average about $1\cdot23 \times 3 = 3\cdot7$ times each.

The empirical fit of these relationships is illustrated in Table 1 in terms of a re-analysis of the data in George Brown's pioneering papers on brand-loyalty (9, 65). These kinds of regularities occur for different brands and pack-sizes in a variety of product-fields, and for any time-period not less than a certain minimum length, usually a week, depending on the product-field. The range of conditions is summarized in Table 2 (12, 18, 22, 29, 38, 50, 57, 63, 76, 86).

Table 2 Summary of Empirical Conditions under which the NBD/LSD Theory of Repeat-Buying Generally Holds

---

Breakfast cereals, butter, canned vegetables, cat and dog foods, clothing, cocoa, coffee, confectionery, cooking fats, detergents, disinfectants, flour, food, drinks, household soaps, household cleaners, jams and marmalade, margarine, petrol, polishes, processed cheese, sausages, shampoos, soft drinks, soup, toilet paper, toilet soap

The leading brands in each product-field

Large, medium and small pack-sizes of the brand as a whole

Great Britain, Continental Europe, USA

1950–1968

Various demographic subgroups

Analysis periods ranging from 1 week to 1 year

The above repeat-buying formulae and many related results are simplifying approximations to a single mathematical formulation. This is the one-parameter LSD model of repeat-buying which is based on the Logarithmic Series Distribution (12, 50). For example, if we define the parameter a as a function of w by $w = a/\ln(1 + a)$, then the average number of purchases made by 'one-period-only' buyers is $a/(1 + a)\ln\{1 + a/(1 + a)\}$. The value of this theoretical quantity varies between only $1\cdot35$ and $1\cdot44$ for any value of $w > 2$, so that to one place of decimals it is constant at $1\cdot4$, as noted above.

The LSD model is in turn a simplification of the more general

NBD model, which is based on the multivariate Negative Binomial Distribution. This model derives from a stochastic theory where an individual consumer's purchases of a brand are regarded as following a Poisson distribution over time and the mean values for different consumers follow a Gamma-distribution (10, 12, 18, 50, 63).[1]

The NBD/LSD model does not necessarily apply to total product-field purchases, nor to new brands (69), nor to periods so short relative to the purchasing cycle for the product that little repeat-buying takes place (e.g. 54), nor yet to non-stationary situations where the sales or penetration level of the brand is changing (50, 63).

Again, if an appreciable number of people buy a given brand more often than once a week, the theory predicts more such very frequent buyers than actually occur (12, 18). This 'variance discrepancy' or 'shelving' phenomenon is highly regular and appears to involve only a single extra parameter for each product-field. It is often numerically negligible, but the incidence of *period-to-period* repeat-buyers can then be higher than the NBD value given by the *within-period* repeat-buying frequency w.

---

1. Repeat-buying of brand X in $i = 1$ to t time-periods of lengths T_i is described by the probability generating function of the multivariate NBD,

$$G(u) = \{1 + a \sum_i T_i (1 - u_i)\}^{-k},$$

where the u_i are dummy-variables and k and a are two parameters which are functions of the observed values of b and w in some time-period of arbitrary unit length. In a single unit period, the number of people making 0, 1, 2, 3, etc., purchases follows a negative binomial distribution (NBD) with mean ak (or bw). The proportion of people buying at all in the period is given by $b = 1 - (1 + a)^{-k}$. Results in a period of relative length T with parameter-value a_T are determined by $a_T = Ta$.

Putting $w = a/\ln(1 + a)$ and $k = 0$ gives the LSD model, in which b does not explicitly appear. The p.g.f. of the LSD is

$$G(u) = 1 - \ln \{1 + a \sum_i T_i (1 - u_i)\}/\ln(1 + a \sum_i T_i),$$

and purchases exclusive of non-buyers in a single period follow a logarithmic series distribution (LSD) with mean w. The proportion of the buyers in one period who also buy in the next equal period is $2 - \ln(1 + 2a)/\ln(1 + a)$, which for $2 < w < 20$ simplifies to about $2(w-1)/(2 \cdot 3w-1)$, while the average frequency of buying per repeat buyer simplifies to $1 \cdot 23w$, as mentioned in the main text. The LSD model is numerically almost identical with the NBD for any brand which in the analysis-period is bought by less than about 20 per cent of the population ($b < 0 \cdot 2$).

73

Conceptual and empirical reformulations arising from this discrepancy are being explored (e.g. 11, 89).

The quantity bought per purchase occasion. The average number of packs bought on a single purchase occasion does not seem to vary greatly by brand or by pack-size. In some product-fields, frequent buyers tend to buy slightly more per purchase occasion than do infrequent buyers, but the trend is very small. In general, the average number of units bought per purchase may therefore be regarded as a product-field constant. Only a limited number of systematic checks on this aspect of repeat-buying have so far been made, but any departure from this simple pattern is likely to be highly systematic.

The earlier stages of work on the NBD/LSD repeat-buying model were all expressed in terms of the number of units purchased (e.g. 12, 18). In some product-fields several units are often bought per purchase and only the purchase occasion can then serve as analysis-unit in the NBD/LSD theory. In most of the product-fields covered, people mostly buy one or perhaps two units per purchase; the distinction between the number of purchase occasions in a given period and the amount bought in the period is then numerically very small. In general, the purchase occasion formulation is, however, the more powerful one, since it also facilitates the analysis of buying patterns for brands sold in different pack-sizes, by aggregating purchase occasions irrespective of amount bought (55, 64, 66–8, 72, 76).

Brand rates of buying. The repeat-buying patterns of a given brand depend essentially on the average frequency w with which its buyers in the given period buy it. To interrelate the repeat-buying levels for the different brands in a product-field we therefore consider how the value of w varies from brand to brand.

We denote the average frequencies with which buyers of brands X, Y, Z, etc. in the period buy each brand by w_X, w_Y, w_Z, etc. Then the main finding is that the values of w_X, w_Y, etc. do not in fact differ very much, especially compared with the differences in the sales levels or market-shares of the brands (55, 67).

The values of w are, however, marginally higher for the leading brands, and we have the following relationship with the penetration levels b_X, b_Y, b_Z, etc.:

$$w_X (1 - b_X) = w_Y (1 - b_Y) = w_Z (1 - b_Z) = w.,$$

where $w.$ is a constant for the product-field, and can be thought of as the limiting value of the average frequency at which buyers of a brand buy it in the time-period as the number of such buyers tends to zero. The ratio of the buying frequencies w_X and w_Y therefore varies inversely with the ratio of the proportion of non-buyers of each brand,[2] namely:

$$w_X/w_Y = (1 - b_Y)/(1 - b_X).$$

The fit of the relationship is illustrated in Table 3 (67).

Table 3 The Near-Constancy of $w_X (1 - b_X)$ in a Half-Year Period (The five leading brands 1 to 5 in each of 5 product-fields, in decreasing order of market-share)

Brand	Product-field C	D	E	F	G	Average $w_X(1 - b_X)$	Average w_X
1	4·8	4·4	3·2	3·3	2·3	3·6	6
2	3·4	3·1	3·7	2·6	2·5	3·1	5
3	4·0	4·0	3·3	3·4	2·5	3·4	5
4	4·3	4·3	2·7	2·1	1·9	3·1	4
5	4·6	3·8	3·7	3·4	2·0	3·5	3
Aver.	4·2	3·9	3·3	3·0	2·2	3·3	5

Pack-size rates of buying. The approximate law $w (1 - b) =$ constant applies not only to each different brand in a product-field but also to any constituent pack-size. Thus suppose that w_x is the average frequency with which the 'small' pack-size x of brand X is bought by buyers of that pack-size of X, and that w_y is the corresponding rate of buying the small pack-size y of brand Y. Then the relationship

$$w_x (1 - b_x) = w_y (1 - b_y) = \text{constant}$$

2. If in numerical work b is expressed as a percentage rather than a proportion, the factor $(1 - b)$ should read $(100 - b$ per cent$)$.

holds empirically for the small pack-sizes of brands X and Y. The same form of relationship holds for any larger pack-size of the different brands (67).

Since the penetration for a pack-size of a brand is generally a good deal lower than the penetration for the whole brand (34), the factors $(1 - b)$ tend to be closer to 1 for pack-sizes than for brands as a whole, and so is the ratio $(1-b_x)/(1-b_y)$. The average frequency of buying a particular pack-size is therefore relatively constant across different brands.

Table 4 Half-Yearly Frequency of Buying a Pack-Size of a Brand per Half-Yearly Buyer of the Pack-Size of the Brand
(Average across the 5 leading brands in 5 product-fields; C to G)

| | Product-field | | | | | |
Buyers of	C	D	E	F	G	Average
Small pack of a brand	4·8	4·2	3·2	2·4	2·4	3·4
Large pack of a brand	3·8	4·1	4·4	3·1	2·0	3·5

An additional and quite separate finding is that the average frequency with which buyers of the small pack-size of a brand buy it turns out to be numerically very close to the average frequency with which buyers of a larger pack-size of the brand buy that, especially after allowing for different penetration levels b in terms of the factors $(1 - b)$. Table 4 briefly illustrates this extremely simple empirical result in terms of the straight rates w for the leading brands, across a number of different product-fields (67).

These rather powerful relationships deal with averages of very heterogeneous individual frequencies of purchase. Thus most buyers of a brand buy it just once in the period, some buy it twice, fewer three times, and there are a relatively small number of very heavy buyers. These distributions of light, medium and heavy buyers are, however, generally of the same NBD/LSD form, the numerical frequencies being predictable just from a knowledge of b and of w. Comparison of the values of w for different brands or pack-sizes such as in Tables 3 and 4 therefore effectively covers *all* aspects of the observed frequency distributions of purchases. However, in attempting to assess the deeper meaning of these relationships, the marked heterogeneity of the individual rates of purchases must be borne in mind.

Multi-brand buying

Turning from the frequencies with which people buy any given brand or pack-size, we now consider various aspects of how people buy *more* than one brand.

Duplicated buyers. Suppose b_{XY} stands for the proportion of the population who buy both brands X and brand Y in a given time-period. Then we have the empirical result that b_{XY} depends only on the penetrations b_X and b_Y of each brand in the period. In other words,

$$b_{XY} = Db_X b_Y,$$

where D is a number which is the same for all pairs of brands in the product-field in the given period. D can be thought of as the average of the ratios $b_{XY}/b_X b_Y$ for all pairs of brands, and is best calculated by $D = \Sigma b_{XY}/\Sigma b_X b_Y$.

This brand-switching law has been found to hold for a range of different product-fields and for different lengths of time-period (68, 72). Its degree of fit is illustrated by the residual deviations in Table 5 which are generally quite small.

Table 5 The Observed Duplications b_{XY} and the Theoretical Values $Db_X b_Y$*

(Five leading brands 1 to 5 of Product G in 24 weeks)
$b_1 = 29\%$, $b_2 = 17\%$, $b_3 = 19\%$, $b_4 = 26\%$, $b_5 = 9\%$

Brands $\begin{cases} X \\ Y \end{cases}$	1 4	1 3	1 2	3 4	2 4	2 3	1 5	4 5	3 5	2 5	*Average*
Observed b_{XY}	9·3	6·9	7·5	5·0	6·8	3·7	3·3	3·3	2·1	2·3	5·0
Theoretical $1 \cdot 3b_X b_Y/100$	9·8	7·2	6·4	6·4	5·7	4·2	3·4	3·0	2·2	2·0	5·0
Deviations $(b_{XY} - 1 \cdot 3b_X b_Y)$	−0·5	−0·3	1·1	−1·4	1·1	−0·5	−0·1	0·3	−0·1	0·3	0·0

*$D = 100 \Sigma b_{XY}/\Sigma b_X b_Y = 5020/3876 = 1 \cdot 3$

The relationship establishes in quantitative form the extent to which different brands are complementary or competitive with each other. In certain product-fields, systematic sub-patterns in the residual deviations have also been established. These relate to product-formulation or to factors like pricing and retail distribution. Again, for brands sold in different pack-sizes, the degree of brand-duplication seems to be related to certain systematic duplication patterns which operate at the pack-size level, i.e. duplication of purchase for different sizes of the same brand and for the same pack-size of different brands (34).

The value of the duplication-constant D tends to increase systematically the longer the analysis-period, the highest values found so far in half-yearly periods being about 1·5. In short time-periods D decreases almost to zero, except in some product-fields where the end-uses of different brands vary markedly and duplication of purchase remains consistently high. (High duplication levels in short time-periods have also been found in some unpublished results for duplication of purchase between different pack-sizes of a brand and for duplication between different varieties.)

Values of D less than 1 represent negative correlations. Purchase of one brand then actively inhibits purchase of another brand. This is a reflection of the 'dead-period' or 'consumption-period' effect which tends to occur between successive purchases of a product, and which also determines the minimum time-period for which repeat-buying of a brand follows the NBD/LSD repeat-buying model.

A value of D greater than 1 means that brand X is more likely to be bought by people who also buy brand Y in the period than by non-buyers of brand Y i.e. $b_{XY}/b_Y > b_X$, for $D > 1$. Suppose that $D = 1·3$ as in Table 4, and that brands 1 and 4 there are bought by 29 per cent and 26 per cent of the population in the half-year in question. Then the duplication law says that about $1·3 \times 29 \times 26/100 = 9·8$ per cent of the population should buy both brands 1 and 4, and this compares quite well with the observed duplication level of 9·3 per cent.

If buying of brands 1 and 4 were uncorrelated ($D = 1$), the percentage of duplicated buyers would be $29 \times 26/100 = 7·5$ per cent. The observed duplication of 9·3 per cent is therefore almost 30 per cent higher than this, and represents a highly systematic positive correlation which occurs for almost all pairs of brands. However, the actual correlation coefficient between buying or not buying one brand and buying or not buying another brand is low, about 0·06 for Brands 1 and 4. More generally, the correlations between buying one brand and buying another found so far range from +0·2 (for $D > 1$) to −0·1 (for $D < 1$).

This low correlation occurs because most buyers of one brand do not in fact buy the other brand. Knowing that a household buys one brand gives virtually no prediction of whether or not the household also buys another brand, even though the number of duplicated buyers differs substantially from the uncorrelated level.

Duplicated buyers' frequency of buying. We now consider the extent to which people's frequency of buying one brand, say X, is affected if they also buy another brand, say Y, in the same period. Let $w_{X \cdot Y}$ stand for the average frequency with which the duplicated buyers of the two brands buy brand X, i.e. the average frequency of buying X by people who also buy Y at least once in the period. This quantity is subject to several empirical relationships which are illustrated in Table 6 for the five leading brands of product G (72).

Firstly, the duplicated buyers of X and another brand buy brand X with an average frequency which is generally unaffected by just which other brand – say Y, or Z – is also bought, i.e.

$$w_{X \cdot Y} \doteqdot w_{X \cdot Z}$$

This can be seen in Table 6 by the near-constancy of the (non-diagonal) values $w_{X \cdot Y}$ in each column, particularly in the 'average' column $w_{\bar{X} \cdot Y}$.

Secondly, the duplicated buyers of X and any other brand Y buy brand X with an average frequency $w_{X \cdot Y}$ which tends to decrease with the proportion b_X of the population who buy brand X at all. This occurs in such a way that $w_{X \cdot Y}$ times the proportion of *non-buyers* of X is approximately constant for any X and Y, namely

$$w_{X \cdot Y} (1 - b_X) \doteqdot \text{constant},$$

thus echoing the relationships for the average frequency of purchase by *all* buyers mentioned above under the heading 'Brand rates of buying'. These results are shown in Table 6, where the values of $w_{X.\bar{Y}}(1 - b_X)$ in the last row show little variation and no trend.

Table 6 Half-Yearly Average Frequency $w_{X.Y}$ of Buying by Duplicated Buyers of Any Two Brands X and Y, and the Constancy of $w_{X.Y}(1 - b_X)$

(Five leading brands 1 to 5 of Product G, arranged in decreasing order of w_X)

		Brand $X =$					Average[2]
	Brands	*1*	*2*	*3*	*4*	*5*	$w_{\bar{X}.Y}$[3]
	1	$(3\cdot3)$[1]	$2\cdot6$[1]	$2\cdot3$	$2\cdot3$	$2\cdot4$	$2\cdot4$
	2	$2\cdot7$	$(3\cdot1)$[1]	$2\cdot8$	$2\cdot3$	$1\cdot3$	$2\cdot3$
Brand Y =	3	$2\cdot2$	$2\cdot9$	$(3\cdot0)$[1]	$2\cdot3$	$2\cdot1$	$2\cdot4$
	4	$2\cdot9$	$2\cdot7$	$2\cdot6$	$(2\cdot4)$[1]	$2\cdot0$	$2\cdot5$
	5	$2\cdot9$	$1\cdot9$	$2\cdot5$	$2\cdot4$	$(2\cdot2)$[1]	$2\cdot4$
Average[2]	$w_{X.\bar{Y}}$[3]	$2\cdot7$	$2\cdot5$	$2\cdot5$	$2\cdot3$	$2\cdot0$	$2\cdot4$
	$(1-b_X) w_{X.\bar{Y}}$[3]	$1\cdot9$	$2\cdot1$	$2\cdot0$	$1\cdot7$	$1\cdot8$	$1\cdot9$

Notes: 1. $w_{X.X} \equiv w_X$

2. Average of $w_{X.Y}$ across Y (i.e. $w_{X.\bar{Y}}$) or across X (i.e. $w_{\bar{X}.Y}$) for $X \neq Y$.

3. $w_{X.Y}$ = Average frequency of buying Brand X by those buyers of X who also buy Brand Y.

Thirdly, the average frequencies $w_{X.Y}$ of buying brand X by duplicated buyers is a little lower than the average rate w_X at which brand X is bought by *all* buyers of X. Thus $w_{X.Y}(1 - b_X)$ averages at $1\cdot9$ and $w_X(1 - b_X)$ averages at $2\cdot2$ (see Table 3), and both these averages of course closely reflect the values for the individual brands, since the expressions $w(1 - b)$ tend to be constant across the brands.

Buying the product. So far we have established how many buyers of one brand X also buy any specific other brand Y, and how much they buy of each of these two brands. We now consider the extent to which buyers of one brand, say X, buy *any* other brands. A simple measure of this is how often buyers of the particular brand X buy the product as a whole, i.e. any brand, including X. The basic result is that buyers of any one brand tend to buy the product equally as often as do buyers of another brand (55). This is illustrated by the average frequencies of buying the product shown in the first column of figures in Table 7.

Table 7 Half-Yearly Frequency of Buying the *product* per Half-Yearly Buyer of a Brand or Pack-Size of the Brand (Average across 5 product-fields, brands in decreasing order of market-share as in Table 3)

| Brand | Average frequency of buying the product by buyers of | | |
	the brand at all	the large pack	the small pack
1	15	16	16
2	15	15	15
3	15	16	17
4	15	16	16
5	16	16	17
Average	15	16	16

Furthermore, buyers of the *small* pack-size of the brand buy the product at almost the same average frequency as do buyers of the brand as a whole, and so do buyers of the *larger* pack-size of the brand (66, 67). This is also summarized in Table 7.

Combining these results with those illustrated in Tables 3 and 4 shows that different brands, or packs, do not differ in their overall degree of brand-loyalty, except for the numerically small and predictable $w(1-b)$ type of trend with market-share. Thus suppose that 20 per cent of the population buy brand X in the given period, at an average rate of 5 purchases each, and that these buyers of X buy the product, i.e. any brand, on average about 16 times each. Next, suppose that brand Y is bought by 10 per cent of the population in the period, i.e. that $b_Y = 0.1$.

Then the relationship in Table 7 tells us that buyers of Y will also buy the product on average 16 times each. The relationship $w(1 - b) =$ constant tells us that buyers of Y buy brand Y itself about $w_X(1 - b_X)/(1 - b_Y) = 5(0\cdot8/0\cdot9) = 4\cdot5$ times each. Buyers of brand X therefore buy brands other than X on average $16 - 5 = 11$ times, and buyers of brand Y buy brands other than Y about $16 - 4\cdot5 = 11\cdot5$ times, so that the overall degree of brand-loyalty is almost the same for each brand.

Sole buyers of a brand. An extreme form of brand-loyalty is that of the 'sole' buyer of a brand, who in the given time-period buys nothing else. His purchases of the brand therefore equal his total purchases of the product. We now consider firstly how many sole buyers occur for each brand, and secondly how often they buy.

The number of sole buyers of a brand, or of a pack-size of a brand, varies with its penetration level b. In other words, the proportion of buyers of a brand in a given period who are sole buyers in that period is approximately the same for different brands. This 'between-brands constant' varies inversely with the length of the analysis-period and this variation correlates with the time-period trend in the brand-duplication constant D mentioned above under the heading 'duplicated buyers', but no formal model for all this has yet been published.

The frequency with which sole buyers buy the brand in question does not vary significantly between one brand and another, as is illustrated in Table 8 (55). Sole buyers of a particular *pack-size* of a brand buy that pack-size with an average frequency which also does not vary significantly by brand. Furthermore, this average frequency is virtually the same for sole buyers of the *large* pack-size as for sole buyers of the *small* pack-size. This is again illustrated in Table 8. The figures in Table 8 are relatively variable because of small sample-sizes, but there certainly is no trend with market-share, and when the numbers of sole buyers are larger – as for example in shorter time-periods – the results are much more stable (66–7).

The sales importance of sole buyers varies by product-field. In one or two fields, sole buyers of any brand or pack of a brand tend to be rather *light* buyers of the product, and in one or two other fields they are relatively *heavy* buyers. But in the majority of fields studied so far, sole buyers buy rather more of the brand but somewhat less of the product than do all buyers of the brand (66).

A fundamental conceptual question about sole buyers – whose purchases of the brand and of the product are identical – is whether they act like product-buyers or like brand-buyers.

Table 8 Half-Yearly Frequency of Buying by Half-Yearly *sole* Buyers of a Brand or Pack-Size of a Brand
(Average across 5 product-fields, brands in decreasing order of market-share, as in Table 7)

Brand	Sole buyers of		
	the brand	the large pack	the small pack
1	10	7	7
2	8	5	5
3	8	6	6
4	8	3	3
5	9	6	6
Average	9	5	5

Repeat-buying and multi-brand buying. In general, the repeat-buying patterns for sub-groups of consumers defined by their *multi-brand* buying behaviour are not necessarily the same as those of *all* buyers of the brand, as summarized by the NBD/LSD repeat-buying model under the heading 'NBD/LSD model' above. To illustrate, consider the average number of purchases of a brand made per *sole* buyer of the brand in an analysis-period of length t, say w_{St}. Then the average number of repeat-purchases of the brand made in period t can be said to be $(w_{St} - 1)$, i.e. discounting the first purchase in the period which qualifies one as a 'buyer'. In a longer time-period, of length T, there will generally be fewer sole buyers of the brand. Their repeat-buying rate in the period is $(w_{ST} - 1)$. The empirical result then is that these repeat-buying rates vary about *pro rata* to the lengths of the time-periods (67), i.e.

$$(w_{ST} - 1) \doteqdot (w_{St} - 1)\,(T/t).$$

The corresponding result for the repeat-buying rates $(w_T - 1)$ and $(w_t - 1)$ by *all* buyers of the brand follows from the NBD/LSD model and is that they vary *less* than *pro rata*, i.e.

$$(w_T - 1) \doteqdot (w_t - 1)\,(T/t)^{0.82}.$$

This then is one difference between the purchasing behaviour of sole buyers and of all buyers of a brand.

Practical applications

The degree of consumer acceptance of any frequently-bought branded product is directly reflected by the extent of repeat-buying and brand-switching that occurs. To interpret some specific market condition or to build general evaluative or decision-orientated marketing models, the factors on which the observed repeat-buying and brand-switching patterns depend must therefore first be understood in generalizable terms.

Consider an example from the textile market. On the one hand, about 50 per cent of the women buying stockings in a given week will also have bought stockings the week before; on the other hand, only about 4 per cent of the people buying *socks* that week also bought socks the week before (54). This much lower repeat-buying level for socks can hardly mean that socks are on their way out, but without an interpretative background of the kinds of buying patterns which normally exist, it is not clear what such isolated figures really signify.

Applications to specific marketing problems. The most general use of the results in the sections headed 'repeat buying' and 'multi-brand buying' has in fact been to provide a general 'feel' for buyer behaviour: what are the repeat-buying and brand-switching patterns in my market actually like? Are 50 per cent week-by-week repeat-buying for stockings and 4 per cent for socks high, low or normal, good, bad or indifferent? Are there some specific exceptions to the product-field norms, and what are their implications? (70).

Apart from providing a general feel of the market, a common use of the results so far has been in interpreting trends of various kinds. The equilibrium model provides empirically-based predictive norms to show what repeat-buying and brand-switching would have been like in the *absence* of any positively effective marketing action or other dynamic market feature. This use of generalizable norms eliminates the need for controlled experimentation, which is usually very costly and often technically difficult. As an extreme example we consider a situation where controlled experimentation is altogether impossible, namely the analysis of a seasonal trend. Table 9 illustrates a case-history for a certain brand M (50, 63). Sales of this brand were a third higher in the peak-season than in the off-season.

Table 9 The Analysis of a Seasonal Trend for Brand M – Observed Repeat-Buying Levels and NBD/LSD No-Trend Norms (All figures rounded to nearest whole number for simplicity)

	Peak-season	
	Actual	Norms[1]
No. of buyers, b% of population	16%	12%
Av. no. of purchases per buyer, w	3	3
No. of repeat-buyers (had bought in off-season)	8%	8%
Av. no. of purchases per repeat-buyer	4	4
No. of extra buyers (had not bought in off-season)	8%	4%
Av. no. of purchases per extra buyer	2	1

1. Estimated by NBD/LSD formulae from off-season $b = 12\%$, $w = 3$.

Simple decomposition of sales into the number of buyers b and the average rate of buying w in each period showed that the sales increase came simply from having a third more buyers in the peak-season (16 per cent versus 12 per cent), with no change in the average rate of buying (3 purchases per buyer).

The next step was to break the peak-season buyers of brand M down according to whether or not they had also bought the brand in the preceding off-season. The resulting tabulation showed that only 8 per cent of the population had done so.

85

Seeing that only two-thirds of the off-season buyers bought at all in the peak-season, the main question now was not how repeat-buyers had contributed to the seasonal increase, but whether the brand was suffering a major sales decline which was temporarily covered up by some seasonal up-swing!

Comparison with the NBD/LSD norms, however, showed that the observed incidence of repeat-buying was in fact exactly in line with the degree of repeat-buying that would normally occur if there were no overall trend or other special disturbance in the market, i.e. $12 \times 2 (w - 1)/(2 \cdot 3w - 1) = 8$ per cent repeat-buyers, buying on average $1 \cdot 23 \times 3 \simeq 4$ times each. There was therefore neither any special *loss* of repeat-buyers not yet any special *gain* due to the seasonal trend. The degree of repeat-buying was just as if there had been no seasonal trend at all! The seasonal sales increase came solely from *extra* buyers in the peak-season, i.e. ones who had not bought brand M in the off-season. The NBD/LSD theory reflects how even without a trend one must expect about 4 per cent of the population to buy in the one period without having bought during the previous period, and that these 'new' buyers would buy on average about $1 \cdot 4$ times each. The additional sales therefore came from the greater number of such extra buyers, 8 per cent, buying at somewhat more than the normal frequency for 'new' buyers.

The occurrence of an above-normal influx of extra buyers of brand M in the peak-season may not seem very surprising, though it is an advance to be able to quantify how many extra buyers there are and that they are relatively heavy buyers. It had not, however, been expected that the off-season buyers buy no more in the peak-season than if there had been no seasonal trend at all. Indeed, even after the event this is not an 'obvious' finding: one still cannot predict, on the basis of this single case-history, whether the same seasonal effect will occur for brand M in other years, or for the other brands or other product-fields altogether.

This simple case-history illustrates the practical usefulness of the theoretical results. It is one of a wider range of specific practical problems that have so far been tackled, as listed in Table 10 (17–19, 22, 29, 34–7, 40–3, 50, 54–5, 57, 63–5, 69, 71, 76–9, 82, 86, 89).

Table 10 Some Practical Problems Tackled through Studies of Buyer Behaviour

Short-term versus long-term loyalty
Impulse versus habit-buying
Household versus individual brand-choice
The early development of brand-loyalty

The effect of house-names
Own label brands
The level of retail distribution

New brands
Test marketing
Relaunches
Life-cycle assessments
Long-term market forecasts

The growth of penetration
The leaky-bucket theory

Complementary versus substitute products or brands
Product-field definition
The profitable length of the product-line

The spacing of pack-sizes
Price differentials
Price changes

The way sales increase
Defending one's brand-share
Seasonal advertising
Launching an additional brand versus pushing one's existing brand

The relationships between attitude change and usage change
Response functions
Setting targets
Product/media data

Evaluating individual deals and promotions
Below-the-line generally
Deal-prone consumers

Estimating sampling errors
Biases in measuring buyer behaviour
Low-cost measuring techniques

International comparisons

General marketing models

Applications to marketing theory. Another major area of practical application of the empirical results here is in the further development and clarification of marketing theory itself. Generalizable empirical results in buyer behaviour have in the past been few. Apart from early empirical work such as that of Brown (9) and some recent experimental looks at how brand-loyalty develops (e.g. 84), most work on marketing theory has been *speculative*. Examples are endeavours to apply psychological learning theory to individual purchase sequences (e.g. 80), attempts to relate macro-measures of sales to promotional inputs (cf. 31, 60), recourse to abstract mathematical formulations of various kinds (cf. 53), and a concentration on forecasting the future without yet having developed an explicit understanding of the past (e.g. 88).

The most popular of these approaches has been to try to superimpose the theory of Markov processes on to purchasing behaviour (cf. 36, 51, 83). This appears, however, to have been done without much recourse to real data. The empirical results, summarized under the headings 'repeat-buying' and 'multi-brand buying' above, now flatly contradict the basic Markovian assumption that each brand has its intrinsic levels of brand-switching and that these remain the same irrespective of changes in the brand's market-share. Instead, different brands do not differ in their intrinsic repeat-buying and brand-switching properties, and these are predictable simply from each brand's penetration level b and buying-frequency w in a particular time-period.

The main theoretical consequence of all the empirical findings is in fact that under equilibrium conditions, buyer behaviour for different product-fields, for different brands and pack-sizes, and for any length of analysis-period greater than some minimum, is generally of the same simple form. The generality of this result is a *positive* reflection of the recent failures to find effective ways of 'segmenting' the markets for branded mass-production consumer goods (e.g. 43, 51).

The number of numerical parameters required to describe the equilibrium situation in the sections on repeat-buying and multi-brand buying appears to be near-minimal. Two or three general parameters are needed for each product-field as such, like the 'variance discrepancy' constant mentioned in the 'NBD/-LSD model' section, the duplication-constant D in $b_{XY} = Db_X b_Y$ in the section on duplicated buyers, and the limiting constants in the general relationships such as $w_X(1 - b_X) = w.$ in the sections on brand rates of buying and duplicated buyers' frequency of buying. These product-field parameters are not yet fully understood, but it is already clear that they are inter-related across different product-fields and time-periods and that they are functions of simple structural factors of the market like the mean inter-purchase time and the effective number of brands in the product-field.

Indeed, instead of being isolated findings, the various results are already beginning to be explicable in terms of each other. Thus from the empirical relationship $w_X(1 - b_X) = w_Y(1 - b_Y) = w.$, a constant (brand rates of buying), and from the fact that the average buyer of brand X and that of brand Y buy the *product* equally often (buying the product), it follows theoretically that buying of brands X and Y should be independent. This explains why the correlation implicit in the D-values in the section on duplicated buyers is low, and why $w_{X.Y}$ is not much lower than w_X in the section on duplicated buyers' frequency of buying.

Next, given the near-constancy of w implicit in $w(1 - b) = $ constant, it follows that the NBD parameter 'a' of the NBD/LSD model should be nearly constant for different brands. Together with the near-independence of buying X and buying Y it then follows that buying of the *aggregate* of X and Y should follow the NBD model to a close approximation. This is a very powerful result, and helps to 'explain' the fit of the NBD. (The more exact requirement is $w(1 - b/2) \simeq$ constant.) In particular, the equality of the pack-size rates of buying in the section on pack-size rates of buying explains why the NBD fits for brands as aggregates of the pack-sizes.

Again, a major puzzle about the NBD model has always been why people's repeat-buying of one brand, say X, can be summarized without taking account of what *other* brands, Y, etc., they may also be buying. The near-zero correlation of the duplicated buyers section between buying brands X and Y now explains why this can be so.

More generally, relationships such as $w_X(1 - b_X) = w.$ and $w_{X.Y}$

89

$(1 - b_{\mathrm{X}}) = $ constant are manifestations of the general law of 'double jeopardy' discussed by McPhee and Shuchman (85, 98), in that the fewer people buy a brand at all, the less often they buy it. The fundamental role of this relationship between b and w is perhaps best seen in terms of *sales*. Thus the sales volume of brand X can be effectively accounted for by its penetration level b_{X}, namely

sales of brand $\mathrm{X} = K b_{\mathrm{X}}/(1 - b_{\mathrm{X}})$,

where K is a constant, i.e. independent of the brand, which depends on w., on the population size, and on the average quantity or expenditure per purchase occasion (see section on quantity bought per purchase occasion).

This cross-sectional result appears to place a major constraint on the way sales can increase. Thus if brand X has a higher market-share than brand Y, it is because brand X has more buyers in any given period than does brand Y, rather than because brand X buyers buy this brand much more heavily than brand Y buyers buy that.

Media consumption

The periodic consumption of branded mass-media communications like TV programmes or printed newspapers and magazines has many similarities to the buying of branded non-durable consumer goods discussed in the last section.

Measurement problems

With mass media, the main emphasis is on measuring *consumption*, reading a newspaper, seeing a TV programme or a poster, etc. The purchasing act as such – buying a newspaper, paying for a cinema ticket – does not usually arise with television and posters. In any case, both for editorial or programme material and for advertising messages, the producers' and the consumers' interests interact at the point of consumption.

There has been a great deal of explicit concern over questions of the validity of audience measurement techniques, much more than in the case of buyer behaviour of consumer goods (cf. 19, 35, 54). However, despite a tendency to use small samples and some technical problems, a variety of radically different measurement techniques have in fact shown themselves capable of giving comparable results (20, 26, 28, 42, 99).

Consumption patterns

A good deal of work has been done in the 1960s on the consumption patterns for various mass-media in terms of the composition of the audience, degrees of attention, variations over time, and so on (cf. 1, 8, 13, 49, 99).

The most developed findings seem to occur in television and concern the proportion r_{st} of the population who view two programmes at times s and t on different days of the week. This proportion is directly related to the ratings r_s and r_t of the two programmes by the equation

$$r_{st} = kr_s r_t,$$

where k is a number which is the same for all pairs of programmes on the two days and on the channel or channels in question. In the form $r_{st}/r_s = kr_t$, this relationship says that:

The percentage of the audience of any TV programme on one day who watch any given TV programme on another day of the week is equal to the rating of the latter programme times a constant.

This duplication-of-viewing law has been found to hold for some 200,000 different pairs of programmes under a wide range of conditions in the UK and the US. It holds within average limits of ± 1 rating points which contain certain systematic sub-laws (38, 45, 47, 56, 62, 73–5, 99).

An extract of 49 cases in Table 11 illustrates the general fit of the law. The large positive deviation at about 6 p.m. in the two days is an instance of one of the main systematic sub-patterns established so far: this is a tendency for programmes near 6 p.m. on different days but on the same channel to have more viewers in common than is usual for any two programmes with the appropriate ratings. This 6 p.m. effect has occurred consistently over many years both in the UK and the US and appears to be a reflection of certain general social habits.

The duplication law $r_{st} = kr_s r_t$ is of the same mathematical form as the brand-duplication relationships $b_{XY} = Db_X b_Y$ in the section headed 'duplicated buyers'. In the latter, the level of

91

brand-duplication depends only on the penetration level b of each brand and not on the brands as such, and similarly, the level of audience duplication depends in general only on the rating r of each programme and not on programme-content or on any other specific factors.

Table 11 Duplication of Viewing: Observed Values (o) and Theoretical Values (t) Given by $r_{st} = kr_s r_t^1$
(Percentage of all housewives viewing, London, Monday and Thursday, 24 and 27 January 1966)

Monday ¼-hour starting & rating r_s	Thursday – ¼-hour starting and rating r_t													
	5 p.m. 8		6 p.m. 25		7 p.m. 43		8 p.m. 41		9 p.m. 34		10 p.m. 28		11 p.m. 18	
	o	t	o	t	o	t	o	t	o	t	o	t	o	t
5 p.m. 5	1	1	2	2	3	3	2	3	2	2	1	2	1	1
6 p.m. 24	5	3	17	8	14	14	12	13	10	11	10	9	6	6
7 p.m. 33	4	3	13	11	19	19	17	18	15	15	11	12	9	8
8 p.m. 43	4	5	14	14	23	24	22	23	19	19	16	16	9	10
9 p.m. 37	4	4	11	12	19	21	20	20	16	17	12	14	7	9
10 p.m. 38	2	3	8	9	15	16	14	15	14	13	10	10	8	7
11 p.m. 7	1	1	2	2	3	4	3	3	3	3	4	3	4	2

1. $k = \Sigma_{st}/\Sigma r_s \Sigma r_t = 0.014$

The duplication-constant k is given by the average value of the ratio $r_{st}/r_s r_t$ across all relevant programme-pairs. Goodhardt (62) has shown that k can also be calculated from quite different observable variables, namely each individual's total amounts of viewing on each of the two days, divided by the *average* individual's total amounts of viewing. Denoting these 'viewing intensities' by v_i' and v_i'' for the ith individual in a population of n, the duplication-law can be written as

$$r_{st} = \sum_i (v_i' v_i'')r_s r_t/n.$$

In this formulation it is free of any numerical constants or parameters.

The same duplication law can also be deduced theoretically from a certain type of stochastic process where the audience at time t is regarded as being generated by sampling the ith individual with a probability which is proportional both to his intensity of viewing v_i and to the rating r_t at this time t. Assuming that the sampling on different days is independent then leads again to the above relationship (62).

Practical applications

The fact that various different audience-measurement techniques give comparable results and are equally valid, as referred to above under 'measurement problems', makes it increasingly possible to concentrate on what *kinds* of information about mass-media audiences it is best to obtain, rather than on how precisely to measure audiences at all. There is however little evidence that the mass-communications industry has so far been guided by such rational considerations in its choice of measurement procedures (e.g. 44, 48). The general tendency is still to have continuous recourse to a stream of raw data rather than to any generalizable knowledge or empirically based theory, even though a substantial literature on using media data now exists, e.g. for media scheduling and assessment problems (cf. 8), or on the relation of advertising exposure and prior purchasing behaviour (cf. 43).

More positive use of the available knowledge is, however, being made in connexion with TV programming problems. One case already discussed in more detail in this *Journal* (74) concerns the 'inheritance effect', by which TV programmes on the same day are thought to 'inherit' exceptionally large parts of their audience from each other. Application of the duplication of viewing law has shown that this occurs only if the two programmes are not separated by more than one other programme. For programmes which are further apart, the observed duplication is the same as if the two programmes were on different days altogether, as is summarized in Table 12.

Another practical application of the duplication law has shown that there is a highly systematic degree of *channel-loyalty* across different days of the week. Thus somebody viewing BBC 1 at a particular time in May 1967 was about 40 per cent more likely to watch BBC 1 than ITV on the following day. The same applied the other way round. This is simply summarized by the fact that the within-channel duplication constants $100k$ were about 1·4 for any pair of days either on ITV or on BBC 1, and that the between-channel constant was 1·0 (73–5).

This channel-loyalty phenomenon occurs despite the lack of

93

any special addictive tendencies towards particular types or kinds of TV programmes, which is the main implication of the duplication law. The degree of understanding of viewing behaviour that is now being achieved has also allowed a beginning to be made on trying to establish to what extent people may not view what they say they like, or may not like what they view (74).

Table 12 Deviations of the Observed Duplications for Programme-Pairs on the *same* day from the Predictions of the *between-day* Duplication Law $r_{st} = 0.014\, r_s\, r_t$
(Housewives, London and North, 1 to 7 May 1967)

Programme-pairs	BBC 1	ITV	All
Adjacent	7	6	7
Adjacent-but-one	3	3	3
Excluding adjacent and adjacent-but-one	0	0	0

Consumer attitudes

Interest in people's *attitudes* generally centres on being able to understand or predict or influence their *behaviour*. It is, however, also accepted that people's attitudes towards a consumer good or service are themselves influenced by their usage behaviour. To understand attitudinal data we must therefore first understand the relationship between attitude and usage, or buying patterns, both with regard to general attitudinal measures such as brand awareness or expressed intention-to-buy and to more specific image variables.

Awareness and intention

For frequently-bought branded goods, a basic finding is that A, the proportion of the population who show spontaneous awareness of a given brand, is closely related to U, the proportion who currently use the brand. More specifically, the number of people who are *not* aware of a brand is directly proportional to the

94

number of people who are *not* using it, when both numbers are expressed on a logarithmic scale:

$$\log (1 - A) = Q \log (1 - U).$$

Q is a number which is constant across the different brands in a product-field; its value is to be estimated as the ratio of $\Sigma \log (1 - A)/\Sigma \log (1 - U)$, the summations being across the different brands of the product. This empirical relationship has been found to fit within a mean deviation of about $+0.03$, or 3 per cent, for about 100 brands in over 20 product-fields (3). Table 13 gives an illustrative example.

Table 13 Observed Brand Awareness A and Values Estimated from Usage Level U by $\log (1 - A) = 2.7 \log (1 - U)$
(Brands 1 to 5 of a non-food product)

Percentage of population spontaneously aware of the brand	Brand						Average
	1	2	3	4	5	6	
Observed 100A	48	48	18	12	10	8	24
Theoretical 100A	48	48	17	10	9	10	24
Discrepancy	0	0	1	2	1	-2	0

A similar log-log form of equation describes a relationship between I, the proportion of the population expressing an intention-to-buy a brand, and U, the proportion of people currently using it (4). This was initially established for some 200 brands in about 30 different product-fields in a closely equivalent form

$$I = K \sqrt{U},$$

where the K is again a number which is constant for the different brands in a product-field (2). The discrepancies $(I - K \sqrt{U})$ average at about ± 3 per cent on the 0 to 100 per cent Intentions scale. This residual variation circumscribes the size of any non-behavioural 'attitudinal' content which the intention-to-buy variable may have.

The only significant sub-patterns found so far are a tendency for old and slowly-dying brands, which fewer and fewer people buy, to have relatively *high* values of I compared with $K \sqrt{U}$, and for new successful brands, which more and more people buy, to attract relatively *low* values of expressed intentions-to-buy. These apparently paradoxical results are, however, explained by the fact that people's expressed intentions-to-buy are in fact determined by their current and by their *past* repeat-buying or usage patterns (2, 4, 38, 41).

In general, we note that if the sales of a brand are stationary, the percentage of people using the brand at a future point in time is obviously equal to U, the percentage using it currently. Since I is related to U by $I = K \sqrt{U}$, I will forecast the future usership level successfully, as by definition of 'intentions-to-buy' it ought to do. However, except in this trivial sense of the stationary case, the evidence is so far all negative: people's *changes* in (future) usership have been found to be unrelated to their currently expressed intentions-to-buy (2, 59).

Image variables

Consumer attitudes to specific 'image' aspects of a brand or product – e.g. whether they regard it as 'nourishing', or as giving 'value for money', or as 'kind to the hands' – are also strongly correlated with their buying or usage patterns (6).

For a broad usership classification like whether people are 'currently' using a brand, or have alternatively either used it 'formerly' or 'never tried' it, the numbers holding attitude 'a' about the brand tend to be systematically related by the equations

$$\log (1 - a_c) = F \log (1 - a_f)$$
$$= N \log (1 - a_n),$$

where a_c, a_f, and a_n are the proportions of 'current users' of the brand, of 'former users', and of 'never trieds' who hold attitude 'a' about the brand. The fit is generally to within mean deviations of about 0·05, or 5 per cent.

F and N are two numerical coefficients which are constant across all attitudes and all leading brands in the given product-field. The values of F and N generally vary by product-field, but F is usually about twice as large as N. An illustrative example of the fit of the equation is given in Table 14 for two brands and two attitudes in a product-field where $F = 4.3$ and $N = 2.4$ (6).

Table 14 Percentage of 'Former Users' a_f and 'Never Trieds' a_n of a Brand Who Hold an Attitude '*a*' about a Brand: Observed Values and Predictions from the Percentage of Current Users' a_c Holding Attitude a^1

(Two brands X and Y of a food product and two attitudes)

Brand X				Brand Y			
Attitude 'n': 'nourishing'							
	Obs.	*Pred.*	*(O–P)*		*Obs.*	*Pred.*	*(O–P)*
Current users	67	(67)	0	Current users	30	(30)	0
Former users	35	39	−4	Former users	18	14	4
Never tried	17	25	−8	Never tried	9	8	1
Attitude 'r': 'reasonable value'							
	Obs.	*Pred.*	*(O–P)*		*Obs.*	*Pred.*	*(O–P)*
Current users	42	(42)	—	Current users	28	(28)	—
Former users	19	21	−2	Former users	13	13	0
Never tried	7	11	−4	Never tried	6	7	−1

1. Predictions from
$$4.3 \log (100 - a_n)/100 = 2.4 \log (100 - a_f)/100 = \log (100 - a_c)/100$$

Holding the attitude about a brand is also correlated with the absolute usage levels of the brand. Thus for 'current users' of different brands, the percentage who hold attitude '*a*' about the brand tends to decrease with the absolute numbers of 'current users' of the brand, i.e. with the penetration levels *b* (5). Marked exceptions can occur for specific brands or attitudes, e.g. advertising replay, but the general relationship is another manifestation of the law of 'double jeopardy' (85, 91) already referred to in that the fewer the number of people using, or buying, a brand, the lower the proportion of such users who state that they *like* the brand.

Practical applications

Practical applications of these various attitudinal relationships are as yet few. This is partly because the findings are mostly very new, and partly because they appear to run counter to popular views about the nature of brand images. Thus it is usual to look for intrinsic image differences between brands, or for attitudinal changes over time, as diagnostic or prognostic marketing indicators. However, it is only the *residual* variation after allowing for usership patterns of each brand that is available for such interpretation. This remaining variability in the image data is not negligible, but it tends to be relatively small, as illustrated in Tables 13 and 14, and extensive work is needed to understand what it means (4).

The general finding here that attitudinal differences can largely be predicted from usage or buying behaviour, and the extremely uniform laws of buyer behaviour itself as discussed under the heading 'buyer behaviour' seem to link up with 'habit-buying' concepts (87) and with 'reinforcement' notions of how advertising works (e.g. 77–79). The data do not so far explain why one brand has a higher market-share or penetration level than another.

Quality factors

Both the differing penetration levels of one brand and another and some of the specific deviations from the laws discussed under the headings 'buyer behaviour' and 'consumer attitudes' may reflect differences in product-formulation as perceived by the consumer. The need is therefore to measure the factors which determine the consumer's sensory perception of the product. There is a corresponding need in the mass-media to identify factors by which to classify different TV programmes (74).

Sensory assessments

The feasibility of quantitatively measuring sensory-perceptible factors of quality has often been subjected to philosophical doubts but these need not inhibit practical progress (16). Highly consistent results can be obtained if personal likes or preferences are excluded from the objective description of the various possible sensorily perceptible states of the product and if different assessors are given common procedures and training to agree (11, 14–15, 92, 96–9).

Long-term reliability

The validity of such measuring techniques depends on their longer-term reliability, i.e. on establishing whether or not a score of x last year meant the same as a score of x does this year. This longer-term reliability can be established even for sensory assessments of quickly perishable food-stuffs. Such studies have also demonstrated the sensitivity of the measuring techniques, in that proof turned on observed *discrepancies* in certain experimental effects which were themselves only 3 per cent of the observable range of variation (97).

Practical applications

The practical use of product-testing procedures is a major preoccupation of producers of consumer goods, both in developing new products or brands and for quality-control and price-support purposes.

Once a reliable technique of assessment is established, it can be widely used. For example, the technique referred to in the previous section was for measuring the quality-factors of white fish. Technological applications have covered both intrinsic factors, such as the size, sex and sexual maturity of the fish, season and fishing ground, and extrinsic factors, e.g. methods of physical handling and stowage on board ship, chemical and bacteriological conditions of storage, variations in storage-temperatures, and quick-freezing and AFD. As an example we note that quite small but complex changes in the flavour F_m after m months' low-temperature storage were found to follow differential equations such as $dF_m/dm + 0\cdot032F_o = 0\cdot170$, and that F_m was consistently related to the texture T_m by the equation $F_m = 3\cdot2\ T_m - 2\cdot0$ and to certain chemical bases B present in the fish-muscle by $F + 7\cdot4 \log (1 + B) = 16$ (93–4, 97–8).

However, it still has to be established how the quality-factors of a product, including its packaging, pricing, image, etc., are related to consumer attitudes and to brand-choice and repeat-buying behaviour. On a single trial under artificial conditions, the consumers' *overall* preference for one product-formulation rather than another can be systematically related to their attitudes towards various *specific* attributes of the product (27) but the essential step of relating the results of product-testing to consumer acceptance in the market-place is still largely missing. The principal statistic here remains the saying that 'seven new products out of ten fail'.

Methodology

One approach to studying consumer behaviour is to try to bring order out of complex data by relying on modern statistical procedures. A more traditional approach is first to isolate some empirical regularities or constants by direct observation and simple analysis, and only then to synthesize these different relationships or laws into more complex theories. These two approaches can be judged by their results in practical application.

Sonking, or the scientification of non-knowledge

In the modern approach the emphasis is on formulating comprehensive mathematical 'models' at the beginning of the analysis, before any organized empirical knowledge has been established.

Such models usually contain stochastic elements and involve statistical 'best-fit' or other optimization procedures (32, 38–9, 45, 53, 64, 69, 72). The end-results characteristically are relationships which in each particular analysis contain many new numerical parameters (regression coefficients, etc). All these quantities need to be interpreted before the observed data can actually be understood (21, 23–5, 30, 46–7, 56).

Variable constants

The more traditional approach begins by searching for simple observable patterns which generalize and which can be summarized in isolation by straightforward descriptive relationships (40, 46). Relatively sophisticated mathematics are only called for subsequently, when integrating a number of such low-level laws. Integration turns on interrelating the numerical coefficients of the different laws. The more advanced models or theories then account for all the data with few, if any, unexplained numerical parameters. For example, while in physics the acceleration due to gravity near sea-level is approximately $g = 32$ ft/sec.^{2}, this isolated quantity (why is it 32?) is only a special case of the gravitational law $g = m_1 m_2/d^2$ which has no such numerical parameters.

Thus the numerical coefficients in scientific laws turn out to be 'variable constants', i.e. they are explained as functions of other variables; isolated numbers seem to occur mainly as extreme values, such as the velocity of light and the absolute zero of temperature. (Even in mathematical analysis, fundamental constants like π, e and i do not occur in isolation but are joined by relationships such as $i^i = e^{-\pi/2}$.)

Practical applications

The modern model-building approach referred to under 'sonking' has led to a sizeable literature but the results do not stand up to the basic test for scientific theories (e.g. 39, 45):

Take away the mathematical language and what generalized factual knowledge of the process in question remains? If the answer is none, the mathematical symbol for *that* is very simple.

Applying this test to the 'I sonk, therefore I am' approach has in fact left no tangible results – there appear to be no lasting and usable findings in marketing which have been derived by modern statistical or OR techniques. In contrast, the old-fashioned approach mentioned under 'variable constants' has led to the mathematical models outlined under all the major headings above. Their prime property is that they describe and interrelate various simple relationships which have been established as stable empirical generalizations. Furthermore, the number of unexplained numerical coefficients in these models is near-minimal.

Summary

Various aspects of consumer buying behaviour and attitudes are systematically interrelated.

Suppose that for any given brand X in a particular time-period

b_X is the percentage of the population who buy brand X,
w_X is the average number of times they buy brand X in the period.
Then under stationary equilibrium conditions, and with only three general product-field constants and a number of specific ones for item (1), we find that:

1. For any specific attitude about different brands, the percentage of current users, or buyers, of brand X who hold that attitude about brand X tends to be correlated with its penetration b_X.

101

2. For *past* users of brand X, the percentage who hold this attitude about the brand varies with the proportion of current users of X who hold the attitude about it, and hence depends on b_X.

3. For people who have 'never tried' brand X, the percentage who hold this attitude about the brand also depends on the proportion of current users who do so, and hence again on b_X.

4. For buyers of any other brand Y in the given period, the percentage who also buy brand X in the period depends on b_X. Correspondingly, for any two television programmes X and Y screened on different days of the week, the percentage of viewers of Y who also view X depends on the rating of X.

5. For people who buy both brands X and Y in the period, the average number of times they buy brand X depends on b_X and w_X.

6. The average number of times buyers of one brand buy the *product* in the period is the same as for buyers of any other brand, and hence does *not* depend on b_X.

7. For people who *only* buy brand X in the period, the average number of times they buy it is the same as for the sole buyers of any other brand, and hence is also independent of b_X.

8. The percentage of buyers of brand X who are sole buyers of the brand depends on b_X.

9. The number of buyers of brand X in the period who also buy this brand in another equal period depends on b_X and w_X.

10. The average number of times such repeat-buyers buy brand X in each period depends on w_X, and sometimes also on b_X.

11. w_X varies little between different brands and this variation depends on b_X.

12. However, it is *not* known how the penetration level b_X itself is determined.

These relationships can be expressed in quantitative form and hold under a wide range of conditions, generally within close limits of fit. Some of the residual deviations are, however, systematic, and some can already be interpreted.

These models of the *equilibrium* position now provide the basis for assessing and understanding *non-stationary* trends in consumer behaviour. The main theoretical need therefore is to establish a theory of consumer dynamics, by further observational analysis and by experimentation, so as to show what factors determine the major unknown that remains, i.e. the penetration level of each brand.

References

1. AGOSTINI, J. M. (1961), 'How to estimate unduplicated audiences', *Journal of Advertising Research*, vol. 1, no. 1, pp. 11–14.
2. BIRD, M., and EHRENBERG, A. S. C. (1966), 'Intentions-to-buy and claimed brand usage', *Operations Research Quarterly*, vol. 17, pp. 27–46 and vol. 18, pp 65–6.
3. BIRD, M., and EHRENBERG, A. S. C. (1966), 'Non-awareness and non-usage', *Journal of Advertising Research*, vol. 6, pp. 4–8.
4. BIRD, M., and EHRENBERG, A. S. C., 'Deviations between intentions and use', in preparation.
5. BIRD, M., and EHRENBERG, A. S. C. (1970), 'Consumer attitudes and brand usage', *Journal of the Market Research Society*, vol. 13, pp. 233–47.
6. BIRD, M., CHANNON, C., and EHRENBERG, A. S. C. (1970), 'Brand image and brand usage', *Journal of Marketing Research*, vol. 7, pp. 307–14.
7. BRITT, S. H. (ed.) (1969), *Consumer Behavior and the Behavioral Sciences*, Wiley.
8. BROADBENT, S. R. (1966), 'Media planning and models by 1970: a review', *Applied Statistics*, vol. 15, pp. 234–56.
9. BROWN, G. (1953), 'Brand loyalty — fact or fiction?', *Advertising Age*, vol. 24, January.
10. CHATFIELD, C. (1968), 'Discrete distributions in market research' *The 2nd International Symposium on Discrete Distributions*, Dallas, December.
11. CHATFIELD, C., and GOODHARDT, G. J. (1970), 'The beta-binomial distribution for consumer purchasing behaviour', *Applied Statistics*, vol. 19.
12. CHATFIELD, C., EHRENBERG, A. S. C., and GOODHARDT, G. J. (1966), 'Progress on a simplified model of stationary purchasing behaviour', *Journal of the Royal Statistical Society*, A, vol. 129, pp. 317–67.
13. COPLAND, B. D. (1961), 'Exposure and communication measures of outdoor advertising in Britain', *Journal of Advertising Research*, vol. 1, no. 3, pp. 13–17.
14. EHRENBERG, A. S. C. (1950), 'Estimation of heterogeneous error variances', *Nature*, vol. 166, p. 608.

15. EHRENBERG, A. S. C. (1950), 'Organoleptic tests in the food industry', *Chemistry and Industry*, vol. 4, p. 93.
16. EHRENBERG, A. S. C. (1955), 'Measurement and mathematics in psychology', *British Journal of Psychology*, vol. 46, pp. 20–29.
17. EHRENBERG, A. S. C. (1959), 'The relative merits of independent matched samples and of the panel technique for before-and-after studies', *Commentary* (now called *Journal of Market Research Society*), no. 1, pp. 1–7.
18. EHRENBERG, A. S. C. (1959), 'The pattern of consumer purchases', *Applied Statistics*, vol. 8, pp. 26–41.
19. EHRENBERG, A. S. C. (1960), 'A study of some potential biases in the operation of a consumer panel', *Applied Statistics*, vol. 9, pp. 20–27.
20. EHRENBERG, A. S. C. (1961), 'How reliable is aided recall of TV viewing?', *Journal of Advertising Research*, vol. 1, no. 4, pp. 29–31.
21. EHRENBERG, A. S. C. (1962), 'Some questions about factor analysis', *Statistician*, vol. 12, pp. 141–208.
22. EHRENBERG, A. S. C. (1963), 'Verified predictions of consumer purchasing patterns', *Commentary* (now *Journal of Market Research Society*), no. 10, pp. 16–21.
23. EHRENBERG, A. S. C. (1963), 'Some queries to factor analysts', *Statistician*, vol. 13, pp. 257–62.
24. EHRENBERG, A. S. C. (1963), 'On matching and experimental design', in *New Developments in Research*, Market Research Society, London.
25. EHRENBERG, A. S. C. (1963), 'Bivariate regression analysis is useless', *Applied Statistics*, vol. 12, pp. 161–79.
26. EHRENBERG, A. S. C. (1963), 'A review of 7-day aided recall', *Commentary* (now *Journal of Market Research Society*), no. 12, pp. 3–18.
27. EHRENBERG, A. S. C. (1964), 'Overall and attribute preferences in product testing – a pilot study', unpublished.
28. EHRENBERG, A. S. C. (1964), 'A comparison of TV audience measures', *Journal of Advertising Research*, vol. 4, no. 4, pp. 17–22.
29. EHRENBERG, A. S. C. (1964), 'Estimating the proportion of loyal buyers', *Journal of Marketing Research*, vol. 1, pp. 56–9.
30. EHRENBERG, A. S. C. (1964), 'A discussion on factor analysis', *Statistician*, vol. 14, pp. 47–61.
31. EHRENBERG, A. S. C. (1964), 'Some comments on the dynamic difference model', unpublished.
32. EHRENBERG, A. S. C. (1964), 'Description, prediction and decision', *Commentary* (now *Journal of Market Research Society*), no. 13, pp. 14–33.
33. EHRENBERG, A. S. C. (1964), 'What research for what problem', in *Research in Marketing*, Market Research Society, London.
34. EHRENBERG, A. S. C. (1965), 'Pack-size duplication of purchases' unpublished.

35. EHRENBERG, A. S. C. (1965), 'Knowledge as our discipline', *Commentary* (now *Journal of Market Research Society*), vol. 4, pp. 211–35.
36. EHRENBERG, A. S. C. (1965), 'An appraisal of Markov brand-switching models', *Journal of Marketing Research*, vol. 2, pp. 347–62.
37. EHRENBERG, A. S. C. (1966), 'Ten questions about consumer purchasing behaviour and some answers', *Advertising Quarterly*, vol. 9, pp. 3–8.
38. EHRENBERG, A. S. C. (1966), 'Laws in marketing – a tailpiece', *Applied Statistics*, vol. 15, pp. 257–67.
39. EHRENBERG, A. S. C. (1967), 'America and the rest – some comparisons', *Commentary* (now *Journal of Market Research Society*), vol. 9, pp. 12–21.
40. EHRENBERG, A. S. C. (1967), 'Where were you in the revolution? Marketing research in the future', *Admap*, vol. 3, no. 6, pp. 247–50.
41. EHRENBERG, A. S. C. (1967), 'The neglected use of data', *Journal of Advertising Research*, vol. 7, no. 1, pp. 2–7.
42. EHRENBERG, A. S. C. (1967), 'Surprise at poly-channel', *Admap*, vol. 2, pp. 562–7.
43. EHRENBERG, A. S. C. (1967), 'On not understanding media/product data', *Commentary* (now *Journal of Market Research Society*), vol. 9, pp. 203–12.
44. EHRENBERG, A. S. C. (1967), 'The next contract-but-two', *Admap*, vol. 3, pp. 118–9.
45. EHRENBERG, A. S. C. (1968), 'Models of fact: examples from marketing', in M. G. Kendall (ed.), *Mathematical Model Building in Economics and Industry*, Charles Griffin.
46. EHRENBERG, A. S. C. (1968), 'The elements of lawlike relationships', *Journal of Royal Statistical Society*, *A*, vol. 131, pp. 280–329.
47. EHRENBERG, A. S. C. (1968), 'The factor analytic search for programme types', *Journal of Advertising Research*, vol. 8, no. 1, pp. 55–63.
48. EHRENBERG, A. S. C. (1968), 'Media men don't want to know', *Journal of Market Research Society*, vol. 10, pp. 15–21.
49. EHRENBERG, A. S. C. (1968), 'The time and place for readership panels', *Journal of Advertising Research*, vol. 8, no. 2, pp. 19–22.
50. EHRENBERG, A. S. C. (1968), 'The practical meaning and usefulness of the NBD/LSD theory of repeat-buying', *Applied Statistics*, vol. 17, pp. 17–32.
51. EHRENBERG, A. S. C. (1968), 'On clarifying M and M', *Journal of Market Research*, vol. 5, pp. 228–9.
52. EHRENBERG, A. S. C. (1968), 'The great confidentiality nonsense' *Journal of Marketing Research*, vol. 5, p. 331.
53. EHRENBERG, A. S. C. (1968), 'Review of F. M. Nicosia's Consumer Decision Processes', *Journal of Marketing Research*, vol. 5, p. 334.

105

54. EHRENBERG, A. S. C. (1968), 'Repeat-buying of textile garments', *Operations Research Quarterly*, vol. 14, 421–32.

55. EHRENBERG, A. S. C. (1969), 'The discovery and use of laws of marketing', *Journal of Advertising Research*, vol. 9, no. 2, pp. 11–17.

56. EHRENBERG, A. S. C. (1969), 'Statisticians as their own customers', *Conference of Royal Statistical Society on Consumer Satisfaction*, April, Sheffield.

57. EHRENBERG, A. S. C. (1971), *Repeat-Buying: Theory and Applications*, North-Holland Publishing Co.

58. FERBER, R. (1962), 'Research on household behaviour', *American Economic Review*, vol. 52, pp. 19–23.

59. FOTHERGILL, J. E. (1969), 'Do attitudes change before behaviour?', *Proceedings of the 21st ESOMAR Congress*, Opatija, September, 1968, ESOMAR, Brussels.

60. FOTHERGILL, J. E., and EHRENBERG, A. S. C. (1965), 'The Schwerin analyses of advertising effectiveness', *Journal of Marketing Research*, vol. 2, pp. 298–306 and 413–14.

61. FRANK, R. E. (1967), 'Is brand loyalty a useful basis for market segmentation?' *Journal of Advertising Research*, vol. 7, pp. 27–33.

62. GOODHARDT, G. J. (1966), 'The constant in duplicated television viewing', *Nature*, vol. 212, no. 5070, p. 1616.

63. GOODHARDT, G. J., and EHRENBERG, A. S. C. (1967), 'Conditional trend analysis: a breakdown by initial purchasing level', *Journal of Marketing Research*, vol. 4, pp. 155–61.

64. GOODHARDT, G. J., and EHRENBERG, A. S. C. (1968), 'The amount bought by above-average buyers', *Journal of Market Research Society*, vol. 10, pp. 157–71.

65. GOODHARDT, G. J., and EHRENBERG, A. S. C. (1968), 'A comparison of American and British repeat-buying habits', *Journal of Marketing Research*, vol. 5, pp. 15–18.

66. GOODHARDT, G. J., and EHRENBERG, A. S. C. (1968), 'Competitive rates of purchasing: some initial results', *Admap*, vol. 9, pp. 157–68.

67. GOODHARDT, G. J., and EHRENBERG, A. S. C. (1968), 'Pack-size rates of purchasing', *Proceedings of the 21st ESOMAR Congress*, Opatija, September, ESOMAR.

68. GOODHARDT, G. J., and EHRENBERG, A. S. C. (1968), 'The incidence of brand-switching', *Nature*, vol. 220, no. 5764, p. 304.

69. GOODHARDT, G. J., and EHRENBERG, A. S. C. (1968), 'Repeat-buying of a new brand', *British Journal of Marketing*, vol. 2, pp. 200–205.

70. GOODHARDT, G. J., and EHRENBERG, A. S. C. (1969), 'Loyalty reports – a new analysis service', *Admap*, vol. 5, pp. 162–4.

71. GOODHARDT, G. J., and EHRENBERG, A. S. C. (1969), 'The evaluation of a consumer deal', *Admap*, vol. 5, pp. 388–93.

72. GOODHARDT, G. J., and EHRENBERG, A. S. C. (1969), 'A model of multi-brand buying', *Journal of Marketing Research*, vol. 6, pp. 77–84.

73. GOODHARDT, G. J., and EHRENBERG, A. S. C. (1969), 'Duplication of viewing between and within channels', *Journal of Marketing Research*, vol. 6, pp. 169–78.

74. GOODHARDT, G. J., and EHRENBERG, A. S. C. (1969), 'Practical applications of the duplication of viewing law', *Journal of Market Research Society*, vol. 11, pp. 6–24.

75. GOODHARDT, G. J., EHRENBERG, A. S. C., and HALDANE, I. R. (1968), 'The news in May', *WAPOR/AAPOR Conference*, Santa Barbara, May.

76. GRAHN, G. L. (1969), 'The negative binomial distribution model of repeat-purchase loyalty: an empirical investigation', *Journal of Marketing Research*, vol. 6, pp. 72–8.

77. HENDRICKSON, A. E. (1967), 'Choice behaviour and advertising', *Admap World Advertising Workshop*, Southampton, October.

78. JOYCE, T. (1967), 'What do we know about how advertising works?' *Proceedings of the ESOMAR Seminar on Advertising Research*, Noordwijk aan Zee, May, ESOMAR.

79. KING, S. (1967), 'Can research evaluate the creative content of advertising?' *Admap*, vol. 3, pp. 216–23.

80. KUEHN, A. A. (1958), *An Analysis of the Dynamics of Consumer Behaviour and its Implications for Marketing Management*, doctoral dissertation, Carnegie Institute of Technology.

81. LAWRENCE, R. J. (1966), 'Models of consumer purchasing behaviour', *Applied Statistics*, vol. 45, pp. 216–33.

82. LOWE WATSON, D. (1969), 'Advertising and the buyer/seller relationship', *Journal of Market Research Society*, vol. 11, pp. 125–45.

83. MASSY, W. F., and MORRISON, D. G. (1968), 'Comments on Ehrenberg's appraisal of brand-switching models', *Journal of Marketing Research*, vol. 5, pp. 225–9.

84. MCCONNELL, J. D. (1968), 'The development of brand loyalty: an experimental study', *Journal of Marketing Research*, vol. 5, pp. 13–19.

85. MCPHEE, W. N. (1963), *Formal Theories of Mass Behaviour*, Glencoe Free Press.

86. MORRISON, D. G. (1969), 'Conditional trend analysis: a model that allows for non-users', *Journal of Marketing Research*, vol. 6, pp. 342–6.

87. MURRAY, A. D., and GOODHARDT, G. J. (1963), 'Habit-buying among housewives', *New Developments in Research*, Market Research Society, London.

88. PARFITT, J. H., and COLLINS, B. J. K. (1968), 'The use of consumer panels for brand-share prediction', *Journal of Marketing Research*, vol. 5, pp. 131–95.

89. PYATT, F. G. (1969), 'A model of brand-loyalties', *Proceedings of the 1968 CEIR/Scicon Symposium on Model Building in Business and Industry*, M. G. Kendall (ed.), Griffin.

90. SHETH, J. N. (1967), 'A review of buyer behaviour', *Management Science, B*, vol. 13, pp. 718–56.

91. SHEWAN, J. M., and EHRENBERG, A. S. C. (1953), 'The objective approach to sensory tests of food', *Journal of the Science of Food and Agriculture*, vol. 4, pp. 482–90.

92. SHEWAN, J. M., and EHRENBERG, A. S. C. (1955), 'Volatile bases and ensory quality factors in iced white fish', *Journal of the Science of Food and Agriculture*, vol. 6, pp. 207–17.

93. SHEWAN, J. M., and EHRENBERG, A. S. C. (1957), 'Volatile bases as quality indices of iced North Sea cod', *Journal of the Science of Food and Agriculture*, vol. 8, pp. 227–31.

94. SHEWAN, J. M., and EHRENBERG, A. S. C. (1959), 'A comparison of certain Scottish and Canadian experiments in respect of grading fish for quality', *Journal of the Fisheries Research Board of Canada*, vol. 16, pp. 557–62.

95. SHEWAN, J. M., and EHRENBERG, A. S. C. (1959), 'A reliability study of sensory assessments', *Applied Statistics*, vol. 8, pp. 186–95.

96. SHEWAN, J. M., and EHRENBERG, A. S. C. (1960), 'The development and use of a taste panel technique – a review', *Occupational Psychology*, vol. 32, pp. 241–9.

97. SHEWAN, J. M., MACINTOSH, R. G., TUCKER, C. G., and EHRENBERG, A. S. C. (1953), 'The development of a numerical scoring system for the sensory assessment of the spoilage of wet white fish stored in ice', *Journal of the Science of Food and Agriculture*, vol. 4, pp. 283–98.

98. SHUCHMAN, A. (1968), 'Are there laws of consumer behaviour?' *Journal of Advertising Research*, vol. 8, pp. 19–28.

99. TWYMAN, W. A., and EHRENBERG, A. S. C. (1966), 'On measuring television audiences', *Journal of the Royal Statistical Society*, *A*, vol. 130, pp. 1–59.

Part Two **Consumer Attitudes**

The buying transaction is at the core of marketing, but the
pay-off to the consumer is in terms of the satisfaction he feels.
The measurement of attitudes and motives, and the search for
an understanding of how they can be influenced, have therefore
become increasingly popular.

The realization that more might be needed than a direct
question of what people think led in the 'fifties to a fashion
for motivation research, projective techniques, group
discussions and depth interviews. At its worst there was much
irresponsible borrowing of psychological techniques which had
not even been validated in their initial area of application, but
there is much that remains of lasting value.

The first reading in this part is something of a classic in the
field. In it Masón Haire of MIT showed in simple terms the
potential value and nature of indirect methods of
measurement. The reading also serves to emphasize the
dangers of too naïve an acceptance of the results. Male
motorists may regard saloon cars as 'wives' and sports cars
as 'mistresses', but in so far as most men do not have
mistresses, this attitude may perhaps not be really relevant
to their selection of a car to buy or drive. In reading 8,
Joyce of J. Walter Thompson discusses the wider range of
techniques of brand-image measurement.

In the following paper, the late Wroe Alderson of the
Wharton School – sometimes called the father of
marketing – gives a simple and clear summary of two opposing
psychological theories of consumer motivation in their relation
to advertising strategy. Both here and in the extracts from
Joyce's wider-ranging review of advertising in reading 10

we seem as yet to have reached no definitive view of how advertising affects consumer motivations, attitudes or behaviour. One reason may be the lack of explicit awareness that for established brands the main effect is *defensive* – to keep one's market-share rather than continually to gain extra buyers or extra sales. Irrespective of the deeper mysteries of the advertising process for frequently-bought branded goods, that is the effect which in practice it mostly has.

7 Mason Haire

Indirect Measurement

Mason Haire, 'Projective techniques in marketing research',
Journal of Marketing, vol. 14, 1950, pp. 649–56.

It is a well-accepted maxim in merchandising that, in many areas, we are selling the sizzle rather than the steak. Our market research techniques, however, in many of these same areas, are directed toward the steak. The sizzle is the subjective reaction of the consumer; the steak the objective characteristics of the product. The consumer's behavior will be based on the former rather than the latter set of characteristics. How can we come to know them better?

When we approach a consumer directly with questions about his reaction to a product we often get false and misleading answers. Very often this is because the question which we heard ourselves ask was not the one, or not the only one, that the respondent heard. For example, a brewery made two kinds of beer. To guide their merchandising techniques they wanted to know what kind of people drank each kind, and particularly, what differences there were between the two groups of consumers. A survey was conducted which led up to the questions, 'Do you drink — beer?' (If *yes*) 'Do you drink the Light or Regular?' (These were the two trade names under which the company marketed.) After identifying the consumers of each product, it was possible to find out about the characteristics of each group so that appropriate appeals could be used, media chosen, and so forth.

An interesting anomaly appeared in the survey data, however. The interviewing showed, on a reliable sample, that consumers drank Light over Regular in the ratio of 3 to 1. The company had been producing and selling Regular over Light for some time in a ratio of 9 to 1. Clearly, the attempt to identify characteristics of the two kinds was a failure. What made it miss so far?

111

When we say 'Do you drink Light or Regular?' we are at once asking which brand is used, but also, to some extent, saying 'Do you drink the regular run-of-the-mill product or do you drink the one that is more refined and shows more discrimination and taste?' The preponderance of 'Light' undoubtedly flows from this kind of distortion. When we ask questions of this sort about the product, we are very often asking also about the respondent. Not only do we say, 'What is — product like?' but, indirectly, 'What are you like?' Our responses are often made up of both elements inextricably interwoven. The answers to the second question will carry clichés and stereotypes, blocks, inhibitions and distortions whenever we approach an area that challenges the person's idea of himself.

There are many things that we need to know about a consumer's reaction to a product that he cannot tell us because they are to some extent socially unacceptable. For instance, the snob appeal of a product vitally influences its sale, but it is a thing that the consumer will not like to discuss explicitly. In other cases the consumer is influenced by motives of which he is, perhaps, vaguely aware, but which he finds difficult to put into words. The interviewer–respondent relationship puts a good deal of pressure on him to reply and to make sense in his reply. Consequently, he gives us stereotypical responses that use clichés which are commonly acceptable but do not necessarily represent the true motives. Many of our motives do not, in fact, 'make sense,' and are not logical. The question–answer relation demands sense above all. If the response does not represent the true state of affairs, the interviewer will never know it. He will go away. If it does not make sense it may represent the truth, but the respondent will feel like a fool and the interviewer will not go away. Much better produce a cliché and be rid of him.

The nature of projective tests

Still other kinds of motives exist of which the respondent may not be explicitly conscious himself. The product may be seen by him as related to things or people or values in his life, or as having a certain role in the scheme of things, and yet he may be quite unable, in response to a direct question, to describe these aspects of the object. Nevertheless, these characteristics may be of great importance as motives. How can we get at them?

Clinical psychologists have long been faced with a parallel set of problems. It is quite usual for a patient to be unable or unwilling to tell the therapist directly what kinds of things are stirring in his motivational pattern. Information about these drives is of vital importance to the process of cure, so a good deal of research has been directed toward the development of techniques to identify and define them. The development of projective techniques as diagnostic tools has provided one of the most useful means to uncover such motivations, and the market-researcher can well afford to borrow their essentials from the therapist.

Basically, a projective test involves presenting the subject with an ambiguous stimulus – one that does not quite make sense in itself – and asking him to make sense of it. The theory is that in order for it to make sense he will have to add to it – to fill out the picture – and in so doing he projects part of himself into it. Since we know what was in the original stimulus, we can quite easily identify the parts that were added, and, in this way, painlessly obtain information about the person. Examples of these tests come readily to hand. Nearly everyone is familiar with the Rorschach Test, in which a subject is shown a series of ink-blots and asked to tell what they look like. Here the stimulus is incomplete in itself, and the interpretation supplied by the patient provides useful information. This test yields fairly general answers about the personality, however, and often we would like to narrow down the area in which the patient is supplying information.

The Thematic Apperception Test offers a good example of this function. Let us suppose that with a particular patient we have reason to suppose that his relation to figures of authority is crucial to his therapeutic problem. We can give him a series of pictures where people are shown, but where the relationship of authority or the characteristics of the authoritarian figure are not complete. He is asked to tell a story about each picture. If in each story the subordinate finally kills the figure of authority, we have certain kinds of knowledge; if, on the other hand, he always

113

builds the story so that the subordinate figure achieves a secure and comfortable dependence, we have quite different information. It is often quite impossible to get the subject to tell us these things directly. Either he cannot or will not do so. Indirectly, however, he will tell us how he sees authority. Can we get him, similarly, to tell us how a product looks to him in his private view of the world?

A projective test in market research

Let us look at such an example applied to market research. For the purposes of experiment a conventional survey was made of attitudes toward Nescafé, an instant coffee. The questionnaire included the questions, 'Do you use instant coffee?' (If *No*) 'What do you dislike about it?' The bulk of the unfavorable responses fell into the general area 'I don't like the flavor.' This is such an easy answer to a complex question that one may suspect it is a stereotype, which at once gives a sensible response to get rid of the interviewer and conceals other motives. How can we get behind this facade?

In this case an indirect approach was used. Two shopping lists were prepared. They were identical in all respects, except that one list specified Nescafé and one Maxwell House Coffee. They were administered to alternate subjects, with no subject knowing of the existence of the other list. The instructions were: 'Read the shopping list below. Try to project yourself into the situation as far as possible until you can more or less characterize the woman who bought the groceries. Then write a brief description of her personality and character. Wherever possible indicate what factors influenced your judgment.'

Shopping List I
Pound and a half of hamburger
2 loaves Wonder bread
bunch of carrots
1 can Rumford's Baking Powder
Nescafé instant coffee
2 cans Del Monte peaches
5 lbs potatoes

114

Shopping List II

Pound and a half of hamburger
2 loaves Wonder bread
bunch of carrots
1 can Rumford's Baking Powder
1 lb. Maxwell House Coffee (Drip Grind)
2 cans Del Monte peaches
5 lbs potatoes

Fifty people responded to each of the two shopping lists given above. The responses to these shopping lists provided some very interesting material. The following main characteristics of their descriptions can be given:

1. Forty-eight per cent of the people described the woman who bought Nescafé as lazy; 4 per cent described the woman who bought Maxwell House as lazy.

2. Forty-eight per cent of the people described the woman who bought Nescafé as failing to plan household purchases and schedules well; 12 per cent described the woman who bought Maxwell House this way.

3. Four per cent described the Nescafé woman as thrifty; 16 per cent described the Maxwell House woman as thrifty. Twelve per cent described the Nescafé woman as spend-thrift; 0 per cent described the Maxwell House woman this way.

4. Sixteen per cent described the Nescafé woman as not a good wife; 0 per cent described the Maxwell House woman this way. Four per cent described the Nescafé woman as a good wife; 16 per cent described the Maxwell House woman as a good wife.

A clear picture begins to form here. Instant coffee represents a departure from 'home-made' coffee, and the traditions with respect to caring for one's family. Coffee-making is taken seriously, with vigorous proponents for laborious drip and filter-paper methods, firm believers in coffee boiled in a battered sauce pan, and the like. Coffee drinking is a form of intimacy and relaxation that gives it a special character.

On the one hand, coffee making is an art. It is quite common to hear a woman say, 'I can't seem to make good coffee,' in the same

115

way that one might say, 'I can't learn to play the violin.' It is acceptable to confess this inadequacy, for making coffee well is a mysterious touch that belongs, in a shadowy tradition, to the plump, aproned figure who is a little lost outside her kitchen but who has a sure sense in it and among its tools.

Coffee has a peculiar role in relation to the household and the home-and-family character. We may well have a picture, in the background, of a big black range that is always hot with baking and cooking, and has a big enamelled pot of coffee warming at the back. When a neighbor drops in during the morning, a cup of coffee is a medium of hospitality that does somewhat the same thing as cocktails in the late afternoon, but does it in a broader sphere.

These are real and important aspects of coffee. They are not physical characteristics of the product, but they are real values in the consumer's life, and they influence his purchasing. We need to know and assess them. The 'labor-saving' aspect of instant coffee, far from being an asset, may be a liability in that it violates these traditions. How often have we heard a wife respond to 'This cake is delicious!' with a pretty blush and 'Thank you – I made it with such-and-such a prepared cake mix.' This response is so invariable as to seem almost compulsive. It is almost unthinkable to anticipate a reply, 'Thank you, I made it with Pillsbury's flour and Borden's milk.' Here the specifications are unnecessary. All that is relevant is the implied 'I made it' – the art and the credit are carried directly by the verb that covers the process of mixing and processing the ingredients. In ready-mixed foods there seems to be a compulsive drive to refuse credit for the product, because the accomplishment is not the housewife's but the company's.

In this experiment, as a penalty for using 'synthetics,' the woman who buys Nescafé pays the price of being seen as lazy, spendthrift, a poor wife, and as failing to plan well for her family. The people who rejected instant coffee in the original direct question blamed its flavor. We may well wonder if their dislike of instant coffee was not to a large extent occasioned by a fear of being seen by one's self and others in the role they projected onto the Nescafé woman in the description. When asked directly, however, it is difficult to respond with this. One cannot say, 'I don't use Nescafé because people will think I am lazy and not a good wife.' Yet we know from these data that the feeling regarding laziness and shiftlessness was there. Later studies, reported below, showed that it determined buying habits, and that something could be done about it.

Analysis of responses

Some examples of the type of response received will show the kind of material obtained and how it may be analyzed. Three examples of each group are given below.

Descriptions of a woman who bought, among other things, Maxwell House Coffee.

1. I'd say she was a practical, frugal woman. She bought too many potatoes. She must like to cook and bake as she included baking powder. She must not care much about her figure as she does not discriminate about the food she buys.

2. The woman is quite influenced by advertising as she signified by the specific name brands on her shopping list. She probably is quite set in her ways and accepts no substitutes.

3. I have been able to observe several hundred women shoppers who have made very similar purchases to that listed above, and the only clue that I can detect that may have some bearing on her personality is the Del Monte peaches. This item when purchased singly indicates that she may be anxious to please either herself or members of her family with a 'treat'. She is probably a thrifty, sensible housewife.

Descriptions of a woman who bought, among other things, Nescafé Instant Coffee.

1. This woman appears to be either single or living alone. I would guess that she had an office job. Apparently, she likes to sleep late in the morning, basing my assumption on what she bought such as Instant Coffee which can be made in a hurry. She probably also has can [sic] peaches for breakfast, cans being easy to open. Assuming that she is just average, as opposed to those dazzling natural beauties who do not need much time to make up, she must appear rather sloppy, taking little time to make up in the morning. She is also used to eating supper out, too. Perhaps alone rather than with an escort. An old maid probably.

117

2. She seems to be lazy, because of her purchases of canned peaches and instant coffee. She doesn't seem to think, because she bought two loaves of bread, and then baking powder, unless she's thinking of making a cake. She probably just got married.

3. I think the woman is the type who never thinks ahead very far – the type who always sends Junior to the store to buy one item at a time. Also she is fundamentally lazy. All the items, with possible exception of the Rumford's, are easily prepared items. The girl may be an office girl who is just living from one day to the next in a sort of haphazard sort of life.

As we read these complete responses we begin to get a feeling for the picture that is created by Nescafé. It is particularly interesting to notice that the Nescafé woman is protected, to some extent, from the opprobrium of being lazy and haphazard by being seen as a single 'office girl' – a role that relieves one from guilt for not being interested in the home and food preparation.

The references to peaches are significant. In one case (Maxwell House) they are singled out as a sign that the woman is thoughtfully preparing a 'treat' for her family. On the other hand, when the Nescafé woman buys them it is evidence that she is lazy, since their 'canned' character is seen as central.

In terms of the sort of results presented above, it may be useful to demonstrate the way these stories are coded. The following items are extracted from the six stories quoted:

Maxwell House	*Nescafé*
1. Practical Frugal Likes to cook	1. Single Office girl Sloppy Old maid
2. Influenced by advertising Set in her ways	2. Lazy Does not plan Newly wed
3. Interested in family Thrifty Sensible	3. Lazy Does not plan Office girl

118

Items such as these are culled from each of the stories. Little by little, categories are shaped by the content of the stories themselves. In this way the respondent furnishes the dimensions of analysis as well as the scale values on these dimensions.

Second test

It is possible to wonder whether it is true that the opprobrium that is heaped on the Nescafé woman comes from her use of a device that represents a shortcut and labour saver in an area where she is expected to embrace painstaking time-consuming work in a ritualistic way. To test this, a variation was introduced into the shopping lists. In a second experiment, 150 housewives were

Table 1 Personality Characteristics Ascribed to Users of Prepared Foods

If they use	No prepared food (Maxwell House alone)		Nescafé (alone)		Maxwell House (plus pie mix)		Nescafé (plus pie mix)	
They are seen as	No.	%	No.	%	No.	%	No.	%
Not economical	12	17	24	32	6	30	7	35
Lazy	8	11	46	62	5	25	8	40
Poor personality and appearance	28	39	39	53	7	35	8	40
N =	72		74		20		20	

tested with the form given above, but a sample was added to this group which responded to a slightly different form. If we assume that the rejection in the first experiment came from the presence of a feeling about synthetic shortcuts, we might assume also that the addition of one more shortcut to both lists would bring the Maxwell House woman more into line with the Nescafé woman, since the former would now have the same guilt that the Nescafé woman originally had, while the Nescafé woman, already convicted of evading her duties, would be little further injured.

119

In order to accomplish this, a second prepared food was added to both lists. Immediately after the coffee in both lists the fictitious item 'Blueberry Fill Pie Mix' was added. The results are shown in Table 1.

It will be seen immediately, in the first two columns, that the group to whom the original form of the list was given showed the same kind of difference as reported above in their estimates of the two women. The group with an additional prepared food, however, brought the Maxwell House Coffee woman down until she is virtually undistinguishable from the Nescafé. There seems to be little doubt but that the prepared-food-character, and the stigma of avoiding housewifely duties is responsible for the projected personality characteristics.

Relation to purchasing

It is still relevant to ask whether the existence of these feelings in a potential consumer is related to purchasing. It is hypothesized that these personality descriptions provide an opportunity for the consumer to project hopes and fears and anxieties that are relevant to the way the product is seen, and that they represent important parts of her motivation in buying or not buying. To test this hypothesis, a small sample of fifty housewives, comparable in every way to the group just referred to, was given the original form of the shopping list (Nescafé only). In addition to obtaining the personality description, the interviewer, on a pretext, obtained permission to look at her pantry shelves and determine personally whether or not she had instant coffee of any brand. The results of this investigation are shown in Table 2.

The trend of these data shows conclusively that if a respondent sees the woman who buys Nescafé as having undesirable traits, she is not likely to buy instant coffee herself. The projected unacceptable characteristics go with failure to buy, and it does not seem unwarranted to assume that the association is causal.

Furthermore, these projected traits are, to some extent, additive. For instance, if a respondent describes the woman as having one bad trait only, she is about twice as likely not to have instant coffee. However, if she sees her as having two bad traits, and no good ones, for example, lazy, cannot cook, she is about three times as likely not to have instant coffee as she is to have it.

On the other hand, if she sees her as having two good traits, such as economical, cares for family, she is about six times as likely to have it as not.

Table 2

The woman who buys Nescafé is seen as	By women who had instant coffee in the house (N = 32)		By women who did not have instant coffee in the house (N = 18)	
	No.	%	No.	%
Economical**	22	70	5	28
Not economical	0	0	2	11
Cannot cook or does not like to**	5	16	10	55
Plans balanced meals*	9	29	2	11
Good housewife, plans well, cares about family**	9	29	0	0
Poor housewife, does not plan well, does not care about family*	5	16	7	39
Lazy*	6	19	7	39

* A single asterisk indicates that differences this great would be observed only 5 times out of 100 in repeated samplings of a population whose true difference is zero.

** A double asterisk indicates that the chances are 1 in 100. We are justified in rejecting the hypothesis that there is no difference between the groups.

It was pointed out earlier that some women felt it necessary to 'excuse' the woman who bought Nescafé by suggesting that she lived alone and hence could not be expected to be interested in cooking, or that she had a job and did not have time to shop better. Women who had instant coffee in the house found excuses almost twice as often as those who did not use instant coffee – twelve out of thirty-two, or 42 per cent, against four out of eighteen, or 22 per cent. These 'excuses' are vitally important for merchandising. The need for an excuse shows that there is a barrier to buying in the consumer's mind. The presence of excuses shows that there is a way around the barrier. The content of the excuses themselves provides valuable clues for directing appeals toward reducing buying resistance.

Conclusions

There seems to be no question that in the experimental situation described here, motives exist which are below the level of verbalization because they are socially unacceptable, difficult to verbalize cogently, or unrecognized; secondly, these motives are intimately related to the decision to purchase or not to purchase; and thirdly, it is possible to identify and assess such motives by approaching them indirectly.

Two important general points come out of the work reported. The first is in the statement of the problem. It is necessary for us to see a product in terms of a set of characteristics and attributes which are part of the consumer's 'private world,' and as such may have no simple relationship to characteristics of the object in the 'real' world. Each of us lives in a world which is composed of more than physical things and people. It is made up of goals, paths to goals, barriers, threats, and the like, and an individual's behavior is oriented with respect to these characteristics as much as to the 'objective' ones. In the area of merchandising, a product's character of being seen as a path to a goal is usually very much more important as a determinant of purchasing than its physical dimensions. We have taken advantage of these qualities in advertising and merchandising for a long time by an intuitive sort of 'playing-by-ear' on the subjective aspects of products. It is time for a systematic attack on the problem of the phenomenological description of objects. What kinds of dimensions are relevant to this world of goals and paths and barriers? What kind of terms will fit the phenomenological characteristics of an object in the same sense that the centimeter-gram-second system fits its physical dimensions? We need to know the answers to such questions, and the psychological definitions of valued objects.

The second general point is the methodological one that it is possible, by using appropriate techniques, to find out from the respondent what the phenomenological characteristics of various objects may be. By and large, a direct approach to this problem in terms of straight-forward questions will not yield satisfactory answers. It is possible, however, by the use of indirect techniques, to get the consumer to provide, quite unselfconsciously, a description of the value-character of objects in his environment.

8 Timothy Joyce

Brand Images

Excerpts from Timothy Joyce, 'Techniques of brand image measurement', in *New Developments in Research*, 1963, Market Research Society, London, pp. 45–63.

It is now an appreciable time since the term 'brand image' entered the day-to-day vocabulary of advertising and marketing people. While the theme was by no means a new one – at least to practitioners with some knowledge of psychology – its importance has been undeniable. By consenting to use the term, people engaged in the business of selling products have acknowledged that the impressions of a brand held by consumers do not necessarily correspond to reality, and that the success or failure of a product is therefore only partially dictated by its actual physical characteristics. True, it still comes as a shock to some advertisers that people may be influenced by non-rational considerations, and may not believe facts about the product which are self-evident to the advertiser. But, on the whole, the point has been taken. It has become fashionable to talk of advertising, for example, as 'adding psychological values to the product'. Moreover, it is easier for us as researchers to communicate with the advertiser about the need for research into people's attitudes and beliefs as well as their behaviour.

A parallel development which I do not think we should ignore is the introduction of the term 'image' into the vocabulary of the layman. Today everybody knows not only that advertisers are concerned about the images of their brands, but that companies, political parties, organizations, and even individual people, are concerned about their images. It has become a subject for cartoonists and satirists. The theme in non-commercial fields is an old one. [...]

This is an appropriate moment to consider the ways in which, in our own field, brand-image information is collected and used. The wide-spread popular use of the terms 'image' and 'brand

123

image' is to be approved, for it reflects an increased awareness of facts of human behaviour; but it obviously has its dangers, not least the danger of imprecision. I am going to start, therefore, by introducing 'brand image' as a technical term and defining it in a way which will differ in emphasis, at some points, from definitions which have been supplied in the past.

In my second section, I propose to classify alternative methods of brand-image measurement and to discuss their relative merits. I shall report on some experimental work showing how some of these methods differ in the results they produce. Finally, I shall pose two questions about the use of brand-image material and the future development of brand-image theory.

What is a brand image?

First, then, what is a brand image? I am going to introduce the term in the following way:

The brand image is the set of associations which a brand has acquired for an individual.

Certain features of this definition require further comment.

The image consists of associations

These may be associations with qualities, as where a washing product is associated with the quality of being mild or, perhaps, harsh. They may also, however, be associations with individual people or with kinds of people. A person may associate a brand of cigarette with older people and may perhaps think of individual elderly people of his acquaintance who smoke it. The association may also be with situations. For example, a housewife may associate a food product with a particular meal or time of day. All this shows that it is not going far enough to say that the image consists merely of beliefs about the product, unless we are speaking of beliefs in an unusually broad sense; the associations can be with remembered events or things of any kind and with abstractions from these events or things. Moreover, the beliefs which do enter into the brand image are not necessarily true beliefs. Finally, it will be obvious that the image does not imply the existence of mental pictures, any more than thought requires images in the sense of pictures.

124

The image consists of a set of associations

It would be wrong to think of the image as a collection of miscellaneous associations which are completely unrelated to each other in the individual's mind. The brand image is to a greater or less extent an integrated structure. Experimental psychological studies suggest that there is a tendency towards consistency within the image and also that the image, once formed, has some stability, as a result of perceptions which modify the image being suppressed or weakened unless they are exceptionally strong.

The implications of this for the brand image in practical life are easy to see. Firstly, the individual may deduce qualities of the brand from the associations which the brand has for him even though he has no direct experience of them. For example, a washing product which is considered to be a really effective cleanser may be thought to harm the hands, even by those who have not tried it; a food product which is thought of in connexion with poorer-quality outlets may be thought to be used by poor cooks. I say that the individual *may* deduce qualities in this way, not that he *will* do so in all circumstances, because it is easy to demonstrate that people do believe inconsistent things and that there is no more than a tendency towards consistency. However, some degree of integration can normally be presumed for a brand image and it is this which may cause us to search for the underlying factors in the image.

Secondly, so far as stability is concerned, it may be difficult to modify the image if there is a danger of the advertising (if this is the chosen means of image modification) being misperceived by those holding a contrary image. [...]

The image has been acquired over time

The associations which make up the image are based on experience or have been deduced from experience. It is, however, important to appreciate that they do not have to be based upon first-hand experience of the product. A brand may have an image before trial, and this image will be one of the factors determining whether the individual does eventually try the brand or not. It may be useful to remind ourselves about the many sources of the brand image, which include the following:

125

1. The brand name, and possibly the company name.

2. Advertising and other mentions in media. Hearsay.

3. Outlets in which available. Price. Pack. Use by other people.

4. Physical appearance and attributes of the product itself. Actual experience of the product in use.

An image may be derived from experiences which fall under only a few of these headings. In the extreme case, the consumer will merely have heard of the brand and the image, such as it is, will be based upon the associations which the name possesses *qua* name. That this can be important, of course, is one reason for care in name selection. The image suggested by the brand name may modify perception at the later stages of getting to know about a brand.

The brand image is held by an individual

So far, we have spoken exclusively about the associations which a brand has for an individual man or woman. However, products are usually sold within markets consisting of many individuals and it is natural therefore that the term 'brand image' should frequently be used to refer to the images, in the plural, held by many people. However, it is most important to appreciate the step which is being taken. It is psychologically, and logically, impossible for two people to have precisely the same image of a brand, in the sense in which we have defined it, for no two people have the same experiences; however, their respective images may have many of the same features, and it is this type of common feature which we are referring to, for example, when we say that a brand of beer has a sociable image. We mean that the associations which the brand has for a *number* of individuals can be classified in such a way that they will include experiences, real or imagined, which can be described as sociable. Of course, to establish that a beer has a sociable image, we can probably go about it more directly than by establishing all the associations which it has for everyone we interview and by classifying these associations; however, we should not forget the complexity of the situation we wish to summarize.

This, then, is the brand image. Naturally, in doing image research we are concerned primarily with the *key, operational features* of the images held by individuals, and we have to simplify and to restrict the field to *features of the image which can be shared by a number of individuals* if our conclusions are to be of practical value and can be grasped by human decision-makers. But the wealth of associations which a brand may have for a particular person and the wealth of patterns of these associations among different individuals make up the territory we are studying.

Brand-image measurement

I would like to turn now to the problem of brand-image measurement. First, a comment: it is striking how little there is in the literature on brand-image research on this subject. In particular, there are few discussions of alternative forms of question and methods for use in quantitative research into brand images. Individual methods are described in various papers but no systematic attempt to compare them has, so far as I know, previously been reported. This, therefore, is the field which I have primarily concentrated upon in this section.

First, however, the exploratory stages of research should be touched upon. The object of these stages will be to establish hypotheses about the images of the brands in the market to be studied, and about their probable influence upon consumer behaviour. The sources of these hypotheses may include free or semi-structured interviews, group discussions, and qualitative research making use of projective and other suitable tests, such as sentence completion tests. From these beginnings we have on occasion found it useful to draw up a hypothesized 'semantic map', showing the terms used in the product field to describe the products, the kinds of people who use them, and so on, and the apparent relationships between these terms and the brands. One useful result of this approach is that it helps to be sure that one is using descriptions which will be understood and which are without ambiguity.

The exploratory research, therefore, leads to a list of attributes which may be associated with the brands to a greater or lesser extent, and it is the purpose of the quantitative stage to show how strong or weak these associations are, and among which groups of the population they exist. A few points can be made about these attributes:

1. Firstly, in selecting the key, operational attributes one will usually find that they fit into a scheme such as the following, which can serve as a sort of 'check list':

(a) Access to the product: availability and price.

(b) The physical characteristics of the product and its pack.

(c) The job explicitly performed by the product.

(d) How well the job is performed, and what satisfactions or dissatisfactions are involved.

(e) The end result – which of the consumer's wants have been satisfied, how he feels, how he is seen by others.

(f) Situations or occasions for which the product is suitable or unsuitable.

(g) The supposed characteristics of the users of the product, their homes and possessions, their feelings and motives. Also, impressions of the dealer.

2. Secondly, the list of attributes can be shortened by removing the near-duplicates, usually on the basis of inspection of the results of a pilot survey. A more sophisticated approach might involve factor analysis of pilot results, retaining only those attributes needed to measure the presence of the main factors.

3. Thirdly, the attributes need not necessarily be expressed verbally. For example, illustrations of different people have been used and respondents asked to say for each one which product that person might use. While the use of non-verbal attributes may on occasion be dictated by a real difficulty found in putting the point verbally, or possibly by a need to keep the respondent interested, on the whole I would prefer verbal descriptions as less ambiguity may be involved. [...]

When we have our list of attributes and our list of brands, the problem becomes: how, in the quantitative stage of the research, can we most efficiently measure the associations between them? The following is a classification of the available methods.

Sorting (brand by brand or attribute by attribute)

1. Comparative (selection)

2. Absolute

(a) Free choice
  (i) Positive attributes only
  (ii) Positive and negative (opposite) attributes
(b) Forced choice

Scaling (brand by brand or attribute by attribute)

1. Comparative (ranking)

2. Absolute

(a) Verbal

(b) Numerical

(c) Spatial

The fundamental difference is between *sorting* techniques, in which the association beween a brand and an attribute for an individual is all-or-none, and *scaling* techniques where degrees of association are established. Within both sorting and scaling techniques, there are for *each* approach *two* alternative methods of presentation: either asking about the brands one by one, so that we ask all the questions we have to ask about brand A and then move on to the next, or about the attributes one by one, dealing with all the brands and then moving on to the next attribute.

Sorting

1. *Comparative*. The first sorting approach involves making *comparisons* either between brands or attributes. For example, if brands are being asked about one by one, the respondent might be asked which attribute was most appropriate to brand A. Alternatively, she might be asked to select two, three or any *given* number of attributes as appropriate to the brand. Vice versa, if *attributes* are being taken one by one the comparisons which the respondent makes are between *brands*. It should be made clear that the approach which we are now calling 'comparative' differs from the others in that the compulsions to compare brands is logical, following, as it were, from the rules of the game. It can be argued that all techniques involve psychological comparisons between brands or attributes to some degree.

2. *Absolute*. The second sorting approach is, at least logically, 'absolute' in that the respondent is not asked in so many words to compare the brands, or attributes.

(a) *Free choice*. In a *free choice* question, the respondent is asked to select the brands, or attributes, which are appropriate to the attribute, or brand. She can select as many or as few as she likes, none if she thinks that none is appropriate. This can either be done with positive attributes only, or with these together with the negative or opposite attributes. Thus, the respondent might be asked *both* which brands are modern *and* which are not modern, or which are old fashioned.

(b) *Forced choice*. The other absolute approach involves *forced choice*, i.e. the respondent is specifically asked for each brand, and for each attribute, whether it does or does not apply, or alternatively, which of *two* qualities applies – the attribute or its opposite. It is unnecessary to stress the importance of rotating orders of brands and attributes for any of these approaches.

Scaling

The *scaling* techniques available to market researchers are equally varied. Once again the main division is into (logically) comparative and absolute techniques.

1. *Comparative*. With the comparative technique, the respondent is asked to place a given number of brands or attributes, or all of them, in *order* of suitability for the attribute or brand which is being asked about. This is a form of measurement producing what is known as an 'ordinal scale'.

2. *Absolute*. The absolute methods of scaling may also yield an ordinal scale, with the difference that two or more brands or attributes may now be placed in the same scale position, i.e. the ordering is weak, not strong. Often, however, they are scored in a way which yields an 'interval scale', like measures of, e.g., time or longitude. This enables us to say, for example, that the difference between brands A and B on a given characteristic for an individual is twice as great as that between C and D.

(a) Of the absolute methods, *verbal* scales are well known. As an example, the respondent might be asked to say whether brand

A was 'one of the most efficient', 'very efficient', 'fairly efficient', 'not very efficient', or 'not at all efficient'.

(b) *Numerical* scales which have been used involve rating on a scale running from, say, $+3$ to -3, giving a product marks out of ten for possession of the quality, and so on.

(c) *Spatial* scales which have no numbers and words on them have the advantage that the intervals should be equal-appearing, which cannot be guaranteed for verbal scales at least without extensive testing. Scales which have been used include a ladder, the Stapel scale, and a simple straight line upon which the respondent has to place the brand. The best known spatial scale is probably the 'semantic differential' invented by Osgood, which in its usual application consists essentially of seven boxes and two opposite descriptions at each end, e.g., expensive, cheap. This is probably the best of the spatial scales, but, like all of them, it requires careful interviewer briefing and clear instructions to the respondents.

The experiment I now want to describe had as its aim a limited comparison of some of these techniques. I should make it clear that the technique finally chosen was intended to serve a rather specialized function. British Market Research Bureau runs for clients of the J. Walter Thompson Company a research service known as the Advertising Planning Index which is intended to measure some of the effects of advertising over time and, in particular, to determine how far goals which have been set are being reached. Along with measures of advertising recall, awareness, overall evaluation of the product and product use, image measures are included. The survey is syndicated in the sense that three product-fields appear on any given questionnaire.

Given this objective, therefore, it is easy to see that our requirement was a technique of brand-image measurement which would be easy and quick to administer, would provide a sufficiently accurate picture at a given point of time, making the right comparisons possible between brands; and, most important, making the right comparisons possible between images of the *same* brand at different points of time, by being both readily reproducible in the hands of the interviewers and sensitive to small actual changes in the image.

131

We decided to confine the experiment to 'absolute' methods, on the grounds that the 'comparative' methods would be unlikely to serve our purposes. If only one or a very few brands, or attributes, have to be selected or ranked using a comparative technique, there is clearly a danger of the most obvious brands or attributes being mentioned first by most people and of movements among the less obvious ones, which could be potentially important, being blurred or altogether lost. On the other hand, a complete ranking of all brands or attributes according to suitability could be very tedious to the respondent. On these grounds we did not consider it, for this purpose, though I would like to return to it briefly in a moment.

The first stage of the experiment was to select which of the remaining two sorting techniques, free-choice and forced-choice, would perform better than the other. The free-choice technique we used involved associating brands *both* with positive attributes *and* with their opposites. The object of this was to make it possible to take into account different levels of brand awareness and knowledge. For both the free-choice and the forced-choice techniques we tried each of the methods of presentation – asking about the brands one by one and about the attributes one by one – yielding four alternatives in all:

1. *Free-choice, attribute by attribute*: e.g. Which brands (LIST) are modern? And which are old fashioned?

2. *Free-choice, brand by brand*: Which of these qualities (LIST, including modern and old-fashioned) apply to brand A?

3. *Forced-choice, attribute by attribute*: Can you tell me for each of these brands (LIST) whether they are modern or not?

4. *Forced-choice, brand by brand*: Can you think of brand A and tell me for each of these qualities (LIST, including modern) whether it applies or does not apply?

For six brands in a single product-field, which in this case was toilet papers, and nine attributes, we split-ran the alternatives. Each version was administered to a national quota sample of 500 housewives at home, these samples being closely matched by age, class, region, and use of the products. The same interviewers interviewed each sub-sample and the four versions were administered over the same period. For each brand with respect to each attribute we computed two quantities: *image strength* i.e. the proportion of those interviewed who mentioned the brand; and *image favourability*, the proportion of those mentioning it who attributed the positive characteristic to it. The results were as follows:

1. First, the mean image strength and image favourability scores were as follows:

Method	Average image strength	Average image favourability
	%	%
(a) Free-choice, attribute by attribute	48·3	62·2
(b) Free-choice, brand by brand	60·2	74·8
(c) Forced-choice, attribute by attribute	86·5	70·0
(d) Forced-choice, brand by brand	85·3	76·6

Both forcing a choice, as one might expect, *and* asking about brands one by one led to an increase in image strength. However, it is clear also that the result of this appears to be that a higher proportion of the responses are favourable. The ratio of favourable to unfavourable responses is about 3 to 2 on method one, with a free choice; it can readily be seen that the *extra* mentions resulting from forcing a choice, method three, are favourable to unfavourable in the ratio 4 to 1.

Analysis shows that this tendency to give favourable responses if a choice is forced is particularly marked among non-users of the brand in question.

2. Secondly, did the different methods produce broadly the same picture in terms of the ranking in which the brands emerged in terms of favourability? The simplest way to test this is to calculate the relevant rank correlation coefficients. There were nine attributes and six pairwise comparisons between methods, i.e. 54 coefficients, of which 52 were found to be significantly positive, the mean of the 54 coefficients being 0·93. In other words, the results in these terms were remarkably close.

133

3. Thirdly, did the different methods discriminate between the brands to the same extent? To test this, the six brands were divided into two groups of three brands each which were very similar to each other in terms of their physical characteristics and their images. Pairwise comparisons were made within the groups and the differences tested for significance. This was therefore quite a severe test of discrimination. Again, 54 comparisons were made and the numbers of significant differences were as follows:

Method	Number of differences significant at 5% level
1. Free-choice, attribute by attribute	32
2. Free-choice, brand by brand	26
3. Forced-choice, attribute by attribute	24
4. Forced-choice, brand by brand	20

In words, the free-choice, attribute-by-attribute method was the best able to discriminate between these similar brands, and in general the ability to discriminate was inversely related to the overall favourableness of the response, as we might expect.

A further demonstration of the way in which the different methods gave the same overall pattern is provided by the fact that in only one case out of twenty-nine where a difference was significant for two or more methods was the result contradictory, i.e. with brand A having a significantly higher score than brand B with one method and vice versa for a second method.

This result does not fit some of the *a priori* grounds for defending forced-choice methods or brand-by-brand methods which have been urged, and it is perhaps worth considering why this should be. Firstly, it seems that compelling respondents to answer if they can tends to produce a high proportion of 'polite' responses or at least to respondents 'giving the brand the benefit of the doubt'. Secondly, it seems that to ask about brands one by one and to show the list of attributes causes a higher level of response than the other way round and, as a result, the same effect. This is probably due to the difficulty of taking in the whole list at a glance, and the consequential need for the respondent to work down the list, attribute by attribute. If a list of brands is shown and the attributes asked about one by one, on the other hand, the list can be taken in easily at a glance providing it is limited, say, to eight brands. It has, of course, been urged that brand-by-brand methods may be superior on the ground that they do not involve switching between psychological sets. I am not sure that this is justified. Either way, you are asking the respondent to make a large number of rapid decisions about the appropriateness of brands and descriptions to each other. And, particularly if the attributes are types of people or occasions, it may be more easy for the respondent to carry *them* in her mind than a *brand*.

4. Finally, it is perhaps relevant to report that a majority of the interviewers favoured method one as the easiest and quickest to administer.

The second stage in the experiment was to compare the chosen sorting technique – which on the above grounds was the free-choice, attribute-by-attribute technique – with a scaling method, and it was decided to split-run it against the semantic differential method. For administrative reasons, the questions were administered to national quota samples of 2000 and 1000 housewives at home respectively, on exactly the same basis as the previous experiment, six brands and seven attributes being asked about. The difference in sample size was taken into account in making the comparisons reported below. The semantic differential results were looked at in detail and were also scored in the usual way, responses in the spaces being given consecutive integral scores and weighted mean scores computed. The distributions obtained with the semantic differential question were all, incidentally, either J-shaped or symmetrical or evidently the sum of such distributions.

The results were as follows:

(a) Five of the attributes in this case were clearly evaluative, and mean image favourability figures were computed for these; in the case of the semantic differential scores, the scoring was adjusted so that if all of the responses had been at one end of the scale or the other the image favourability scores would have been 0 or 100 respectively. These were: 61·3 per cent for the semantic differential and 55·4 per cent for the free-choice question. Again,

135

forcing a choice, in effect, has led to rather more favourable responses, though not to the same extent as with a sorting technique.

(b) Again, rank correlation coefficients were computed for the two methods – seven coefficients in all. Five of these were significantly positive, the mean being 0·87. In other words, the two methods on the whole led to the brands being placed in the same order on each factor.

(c) Thirdly, pairwise comparisons between similar brands were made on exactly the same basis as that previously described, and the differences were tested for significance. Of the forty-two comparisons, twenty-seven yielded significant differences at the 5 per cent level using the free-choice technique, and twenty yielded significant differences using the semantic differential technique. Thus, the free-choice technique again proved to be the better discriminator.

(d) Fourthly, the semantic differential battery of questions took on average twice as long to administer in the field as the free-choice battery of questions.

So, once again, the free-choice technique has emerged as apparently superior. I believe, however, that the reasons for this are rather different from those adduced for its superiority over other sorting techniques. A clue is provided by some of the comments of the interviewers themselves, the following examples all referring to the semantic differential method:

'It definitely gives them the chance to reflect.'
'Although emphasizing that we want a quick impression only, most people try to give a considered opinion, even working out the answers in comparison with each other.'
'Some say it's not fair to rate a product you've not tried.'

The strong impression is given that the semantic differential leads to a cautious, considered response. It is at least arguable, I think, whether that is what one wants – and I believe it is definitely not what is wanted where sensitivity and responsiveness to image changes is required. The free-choice technique is far more like an association test and may be better able to perform this function on these grounds.

Does the apparent advantage which the free-choice technique enjoys at a given point in time extend to the measurement of brand images over time? One would expect it to do so, but we have at the moment only very scanty evidence of a comparison between it and the semantic differential, for two brands and three attributes only, at two points six months apart. Three of the six comparisons, between images of the same brand at different times, yielded differences significant at the 5 per cent level with the free-choice technique, and three yielded differences at this level with the semantic differential; but at the 1 per cent level the corresponding figures were three and one respectively, suggesting the better discrimination which we would expect.

I have assumed in the discussion so far that ability to show differences between similar brands, or between images of the same brand over time, is a test of the efficiency of a measuring technique, and it is perhaps necessary briefly to consider this assumption. While it is prima facie true, there are two dangers which might be suggested; first, that the selected method may exaggerate real differences, and second, that it might show differences which were not real ones at all. The first suggestion is not too worrying – it is tantamount to saying that we should, for example, raise our sights in setting brand image goals since it will be relatively easy to show a change.

The second suggestion would be more worrying, and here one has to argue about how far the results 'make sense' or, better, how far on the basis of them one takes decisions which over time prove to be right.

In practice, the free-choice technique has proved highly satisfactory as a means of measuring image changes. We have certainly been surprised by the sensitivity which it has shown. We have found a number of changes of 10 per cent – 20 per cent in image favourability over, say, a six-month period and our early assumption that images would change only slowly has not been borne out. Moreover the changes *have* mostly been plausible rather than baffling – a most desirable quality for research results in practice!

There are one or two things about using the free-choice technique in practice which we have discovered *ambulando* and it may be worth reporting them. Firstly, an introduction which makes it clear to the respondent what is wanted is vital [...] Secondly, the need to word the attributes carefully to avoid ambiguity is obvious. It is also necessary to be sure that the wording avoids a situation in which almost all responses are, say, favourable. [. . .] Thirdly, in some cases we have found that it is desirable to supplement the free-choice question by a *strictly* comparative method, i.e. where two brands have very similar images on a given point. It may then be possible to collapse the questions so that they might be, for instance, 'Which of these (one only) is the most soft? Which others are soft? Which of these are not quite so soft?' Indeed, in general it is most desirable to suit the question to the problem. Fourthly, image *strength* has proved to be a useful measure in its own right. It is obviously related to the experience that an individual could have had of the particular product in terms of the attribute in question.

I would not like to end this section by giving the impression that I regard the free-choice methods as always superior. A forced-choice or scaling technique may be more suitable for types of research quite different from the type we have been discussing. In particular, a scaling technique collects more information from each respondent about each brand, and for certain purposes, e.g. factor analysis, where product-moment correlation coefficients can be computed instead of tetrachoric coefficients, this may be desirable.

Future developments

Finally, I should like to conclude this paper by making two related pleas. First, the interpretation of brand image studies will not be satisfactory until consumers' wants can be studied and measured with as much precision as their brand images can be measured. Another way of stating the same thing is that we need to know the relative importance of the image attributes. And second, the brand image should be more firmly embedded than it has been in a theory of consumer choice. We need to relate it more closely to other influences upon behaviour, and to show just how it does influence purchasing decisions. [. . .]

9 Wroe Alderson

Motivation

Wroe Alderson, 'Advertising strategy and theories of motivation',
Cost and Profit Outlook, December 1956.

Motivation research undertakes to meet some of the needs of
advertising strategy. The strategist in advertising, as in any other
contest, is trying to out-guess his opponent by adopting a course
of action with a greater pay-off. Billions of dollars are spent every
year to influence consumer preference for products. There is
ample evidence of variation in the effectiveness of the advertising
dollar depending on how it is spent. Advertising has come to be
the major marketing expenditure for many companies, so that the
choice of an advertising strategy is a primary concern for marketing management. In a large company, even a small improvement
in the efficiency of advertising may be worth millions of dollars.
In a smaller company, it may not seem possible to advertise at all
unless some strategic advantage can be found which will give
greater effect to each dollar expended.

In trying to devise winning strategies, advertisers necessarily
rely upon some theory or explanation of how consumers can be
expected to react to products or to advertising appeals. Many
advertising experts are inveterate theorists themselves. Often the
theories propounded are created on the spot to persuade clients
to accept one campaign proposal or another. The great sums at
stake and the growing sophistication of both clients and agency
executives have created a demand for a more general theory of
motivation with foundations in psychology and the other social
sciences. Despite real progress in motivation theory and research,
the diversity of theoretical positions, particularly in psychology,
has created a confusion of counsel. Motivation research is an
essential aid to advertising strategy, but the advertising strategist
would be well advised to assay the long-range consequences of
some of the proposed theoretical positions.

For more than a generation the psychological foundations of advertising theory were relatively simple, consistent and widely accepted. The behaviorism of John B. Watson was distinctly an American product which seemed well adapted to the American scene and to advertising in particular. According to this view, a child entered the world with little except the capacity to receive impressions and to develop attitudes and habits implanted by its elders. Similarly, the consumer entering the market was like a clean slate on which the advertiser could leave whatever impressions he pleased. This view concerning the role of advertising spread rapidly after Watson himself left the university and entered the advertising field. Endless and massive repetition was regarded as the foundation for advertising success. Habits of buying particular products or brands were to be inculcated in millons of consumers, and constant repetition of simple and forthright messages became standard practice in advertising as in the classroom.

However inadequate this view of consumer psychology may seem today, it has a solid core of truth and continues to be manifested in advertising practice. In its extreme form, this doctrine makes the consuming public an inert and docile mass without the power of rational decision and subject to manipulation at the will of the advertiser. At the same time, it must be admitted that our daily lives are largely made up of useful habits which help us to avoid making an overwhelming number of decisions from moment to moment. A useful habit is not so much irrational as nonrational. It is not opposed to reason but can operate without the active intervention of reason. A rational being can properly make a decision to cultivate useful habits as a way of economizing psychic energy. There are some routines which have the force of habit but never become entirely automatic. This is certainly true of so-called 'buying habits'. Reminders through advertising, even though repetitious, can be of service to consumers in maintaining buying routines without really infringing on the prerogative of rational choice.

Motivation research today attempts to penetrate more deeply and to lay the foundation for strategies other than that of conditioning the consumer through massive repetition. This is an inevitable response to the pressures for advertising efficiency. Contemporary motivation research has drawn its inspiration from schools of psychology first developed in Europe as compared to the earlier commitment to the native American school of behaviorism. In fact, nearly all that now goes under the name of motivation research is derived from two great schools of European psychology, each with numerous variations and each now firmly established in the United States. These two schools are in such glaring contrast to each other that the only precept they really have in common is their opposition to behaviorism and its faith in the conditioned reflex. This article will attempt to say something about what these two schools are, about the implications for advertising strategy of adopting one view or the other, and about possible reconciliations between the two for motivation research, for advertising strategy and for management policy.

Contrasting views of motivation

The two principal schools of motivational theory are derived from Gestalt psychology and psychoanalysis. Gestalt psychology is associated with such names as Wertheimer, Kohler, Koffka and Lewin, all of whom came to the United States in their prime and published some of their most important work here. In fact, Gestalt scarcely became a psychology of motivation until it entered its American phase, having begun as a new approach to the psychological analysis of perception. Psychoanalysis is associated with such names as Freud, Adler, Jung, Rank, Sullivan and Fromm. Psychoanalysis has also gone through a major transition from the preponderantly biological interest of Freud and his followers to the social and cultural viewpoint of more recent writers such as Fromm, Sullivan, Kardiner and Horney. Gestalt as compared to behaviorism represented renewed interest in conscious mind and rational decision. Psychoanalysis invented and popularized such concepts as the unconscious or subconscious mind. Gestalt as a psychology of motivation is pre-eminently concerned with goal-directed behavior and rational use of the resources of the environment to attain conscious ends. Psychoanalysis, at least in its earlier versions, held that behavior is primarily determined by instinctive drives and

141

contended that we are unconsciously motivated to seek goals which we do not recognize or may be unwilling to acknowledge even to ourselves.

In a general way, one may be said to emphasize rational behavior and the other irrational behavior, even though it is not always possible to draw a sharp line between these two categories. One definition of rational behaviour would be the conscious and deliberate pursuit of goals that are consistent with the survival and well-being of the individual. Psychoanalysis would say that much of human behavior lies outside the area of rationality so defined, and that some of the most fundamental aspects of motivation are hidden below the level of consciousness. To the extent that this is true, it obviously complicates the problem of finding out what people really want or what motivates their behavior. It is also true, however, that rationality of goals or behavior would not necessarily mean that the task of motivation research would be easy. While psychoanalysis holds that ideas are repressed because the ego cannot accept them, people also forget because they have achieved a satisfactory adjustment and have had no reason to recall their original motivations. In case after case there seem to be perfectly practical and common-sense reasons why consumers should prefer one dishcloth, detergent or depilatory to another. If respondents seem vague when first challenged to explain, it is probably because they have had other things to think about, rather than because they are subject to any great inner tensions or anxieties connected with these everyday products.

One of the difficulties about the concept of rationality is that it is not always considered from the viewpoint of the subject whose behavior is under critical scrutiny. The inherent standards of rationality in a field of consumer use may be quite different from imputed standards of rationality existing in the mind of the outsider. All too often some producer assumes that users place a high value on certain technical characteristics of his product, only to find upon investigation that they have an entirely different conception of its principal virtues. It seems obvious after the fact, for example, that housewives might consider absorbency a valuable characteristic in a dishcloth. Nevertheless, the first draft of one survey questionnaire omitted this topic entirely, even though the manufacturer had made an exhaustive attempt to deal with every characteristic which could possibly interest the consumer.

The two leading schools of thought point to quite different conclusions about the development of personality. Gestalt in its original version pictured the rational mind as endowed with insights which enabled it to see a solution almost as soon as the problem situation was presented. Later versions make more allowance for learning from experience. The mature personality is one which has become progressively more skilled in the management of the resources of its environment. The mature personality, for psychoanalysis, is one which has finally achieved a degree of poise and balance after surviving nearly disastrous incidents along the way. Growing up, for psychoanalysts of biological bent, is the painful process of recovering from such traumatic experiences as birth, weaning, toilet training and puberty. Even those with social and cultural leanings picture the typical life history as a continuous battle to master the forces of a hostile environment. Obviously these two views have very different implications as to the way consumers will react toward goods or toward the various appeals presented in advertising. If the first view is correct, the consumer might be expected to regard a product as primarily an instrument for obtaining a given end and to judge it in terms of its instrumental efficiency. If the second view is correct, the consumer might be expected to be much more preoccupied with the symbolic aspect of goods, to utilize them as means of giving vent to suppressed desires, and to be more interested in symbols of mastery than in working tools.

Consequences of the instrumental view

If goods are working tools or instruments for gaining specific ends, advertising might be expected to take on an educational character. In a service magazine for housewives, for example, the tone of an advertisement might not be too different from that of an article describing a method for dealing with some household product. Like any other teacher, the advertiser might engage in repetition partly to make sure that each subject had learned the lesson and partly because there is a constant stream of new subjects who have not yet been exposed to the lesson. Advertising

143

from this viewpoint sees consumers in their social roles as members of households, as income earners and as purchasing agents for the household. It talks to them in terms which they can use in talking to their family and friends. Its appeals are made through public channels and are directed to what may be called the 'public' life of the individual, in contrast to what is peculiarly personal and private.

To proceed as if consumer behavior is fundamentally rational is to assume that behavior patterns will be convergent. That is to say, consumers with precisely the same problems will tend to adopt precisely the same solutions after some experience with the various alternatives. Rationality in the form in which it is generally available consists in being able to make comparative judgments among ways of accomplishing the same thing. Thus, at the level of consumer buying, it is reflected in a capacity to learn even when there is not enough creative insight to be right the first time.

Some advertisers who have themselves preferred rational appeals have sometimes been discouraged with the apparent results. Some years ago a leading dentifrice advertiser rebelled against what he considered the fantastic claims made by himself and his competitors. He decided to advertise that the sole function of a toothpaste was to clean teeth and that his product could do it as well as any other. About this time his brand began to suffer a serious decline in sales and he therefore soon returned to less factual and more colorful claims. Interestingly enough, the same manufacturer is today once more treating the consumer as a rational being and is presumably doing all right. Undoubtedly, consumers are steadily becoming more sophisticated, but it is also possible that the manufacturer misread the evidence as to consumer reactions on the first occasion.

It has already been pointed out that the supplier sometimes does not really know what the consumer's problem is. Even if he is familiar with the problem, he may not be clear as to the product features which are important to the user. There is also the possibility that, although there is a patent consumer need, there may not be a widespread conscious recognition of the need among consumers. Sometimes the advertiser must establish the fact that a problem exists before trying to show that his product offers a

144

solution. Emotionally colored language directed to this end is not inconsistent with the postulate of consumer rationality. Absorbed as we may be in our daily affairs, each of us may need to be startled into recognizing the urgency of some problem, the importance of being prepared for the eventuality which it represents or the frequency with which such occasions may be expected to arise.

Long experience in consumer research gives one considerable respect for the job done by the consumer-buyer. She must consider many things bearing on the well-being and happiness of herself and her family and in most instances must choose among a wide variety of products. Some consumers are more effective buyers than others or may have special buying skills in certain fields. These leaders of consumption tend to influence the buying decisions of other consumers. They are likely to talk in practical terms when they recommend a product to other consumers. Advertising that stresses rational reasons for purchase is more likely to be multiplied through word-of-mouth advertising. The consumer may have mixed motivations for purchase, particularly in the case of an item for her own personal use. Even here she may need rational reasons for justifying the purchase to other members of the household. Advertising that recognizes the postulate of consumer rationality would, therefore, seem to be a basic ingredient for most marketing programs. Such advertising recognizes the social role of the consumer-buyer, and is likely to create enduring values for the advertiser since it is consistent with basic trends in consumer attitudes and behavior.

Consequences of the symbolic view

Advertising that assigns a large place to the symbolic aspect of goods is related more to the remedial work of the clinic than to the educational task of the classroom. There may be some instances in which the advertiser can afford to play the role of the psychiatrist, but this is a difficult function to discharge through the media of mass communication. The psychiatric needs of the individual are highly personal and the effective symbols may be largely private. While Freud and others insisted that a study of dreams revealed universal symbols, it is common experience that the same symbol can mean many things to many people.

145

The symbolic approach tends to be divergent just as the instrumental approach is convergent. The very fact that a symbol might be recognized by others may make it less acceptable to the subject as an outlet for secret yearnings. When a product is regarded as an instrument, each user wants to get results as good as his fellows. When a product is regarded as a symbol, he may be more interested in characteristics which will help to set him apart from his fellows. A cherished symbol may either facilitate or delay maturation. It may help the individual to fit an aspect of experience into his life pattern. On the other hand, it may be a means of escape into the realm of fantasy. Thus the advertiser who is especially concerned with symbolic meanings is operating in a field of industrial poetry in which the impact on the audience or the future consequences for the advertiser are hard to predict.

Psychoanalysis divides people into types, but the typologies are almost as numerous as the analysts. Jung talks of extroverts and introverts; Rank, of the neurotic and creative man; Horney, of the compliant, aggressive and detached types. Fromm lists five orientations of personality including the marketing orientation and the productive orientation. There is still the orthodox classification which describes such character types as the oral, the anal and the genital. One great difficulty in applying such typologies is that no related classifications are available for families or households which, after all, are the fundamental purchasing units. In fact, it seems more reasonable that marketing should start from a study of the organization of household units and then deal with the personality traits which might make for good or poor household organization.

It would be hard to assess the outcome of advertising competition if the emphasis were to be primarily on symbolism. In one instance, a motivation study following the Freudian point of view indicated that consumers preferred vegetable shortening because animal fats were somehow related to a sense of sin. While this might be a consideration favoring vegetable shortening as such, it is hard to see how this point could be made effective for one brand rather than another. Similarly, if it be assumed that there is some symbolic value in lipsticks or cigarettes, all brands would presumably be equally potent symbols.

One justification for this type of approach might be the attempt

146

to achieve variety in advertising copy and presentation. In a given case, anything that can be said as to the instrumental value of a product may have been said many times over. The advertiser may suspect that his potential audience has become bored and inattentive so that these instrumental messages are no longer registering. He might use the Freudian approach as a way of developing new copy slants even though the grosser forms of Freudian symbolism were not actually apparent in the copy. His purpose might be to gain attention and to get new prospects to try his product, hoping that it could demonstrate its instrumental virtues upon trial. Overall advertising strategy in such a situation would presumably be that of continuing the repetitive messages but making them more palatable through a fresh approach. This type of advertising strategy would really rest upon Watsonian behaviorism even though it gave a passing nod to psychoanalysis.

Reconciliation in motivation research

I have attempted to describe the consequences of these two points of view, each on its own merits. My own preference is for Gestalt as the framework of motivational theory. More than one contemporary psychologist has demonstrated the capacity of the Gestalt position to utilize some of the basic insights of other schools without abandoning the postulate of essential rationality. One of the most successful is Carl Rogers, who has opened up new vistas in clinical practice through what he calls 'client-centered therapy'. The final chapter in his book by that name (Rogers, 1951) presents, in slightly over fifty pages, what is possibly the most useful synthesis to date of psychological theory for marketing and advertising.

This chapter contains nineteen propositions about human behavior and the processes of adjustment to the environment. The postulate of rationality is embodied in the fifth proposition which reads as follows: 'Behavior is basically the goal-directed attempt of the organism to satisfy its needs as experienced in the field as perceived.' The organism strives constantly to actualize, maintain and enhance itself. This seeking is accompanied by emotion, which facilitates the maintenance and enhancement of the organism.

The concept or image of the self arises out of experience and

147

helps to mediate the continual process of adjustment to the environment. Any experience which is inconsistent with the structure of the self image may be perceived as a threat. Maladjustment exists when the individual refuses to admit significant experience into consciousness or, as Rogers says, fails to 'symbolize and organize such experience into the Gestalt of the self structure.' Threats to the cherished self image bring anxiety and defensive behavior. Under favorable conditions, therapy can produce a reorganization of the value system and reduce the incongruity between experience and the structure of the self. In the normal course of maturation the individual replaces values which have been taken over from others and achieves an inner harmony through greater self-knowledge and acceptance.

This statement by Rogers affords a basis for reconciliation between the two major trends in motivation theory. It also makes a place for the theory of learning emphasized in the earlier behaviorism, but in more dynamic form. We do not learn by passive acceptance of impressions but by the continuous attempt to solve the problems posed by the environment. We make a more skillful use of our means as we learn more about the available instruments. We reshape our ends as we learn more about ourselves. Many achieve individual adjustment without professional counsel because of good family adjustment. A happy household is not only an end in itself but a fortunate setting for informal group therapy.

Marketing management solves its problems by helping consumers to solve their problems. While the good life demands an increasing variety of goods, it also draws on the realm of ideas and emotions. With becoming modesty the supplier of goods can recognize that some human problems are beyond his reach. He can well take account of the social and psychological setting in which his products will be used. Half-baked attempts to deal with the problems of disturbed personalities, however, are likely to end up being both poor therapy and poor selling.

A perspective such as that sketched by Rogers can provide some useful guideposts for motivation research. For the rational problem-solver, his own irrational impulses or defense mechanisms are part of the problem. We are learning how to devise experimental procedures which parallel the decision structure of real life problems. Ways can be found to introduce faulty self-knowledge as an element in these experimental designs. Progress in experimentation is a goal which might well attract the exponents of the nondirected interview as well as the advocates of massive sampling surveys. Advances in this type of motivation research should contribute substantially to advertising effectiveness.

Rogers calls his view 'phenomenological,' a designation shared with other writers such as Snygg and Combs. This means that the environment as perceived by the subject is taken as the behavioral field. Both the world image and the self image of the individual are keys to understanding his behavior. Kenneth Boulding, in his recently published essay 'The Image,' suggests the term 'eiconics' for a science of images cutting across economics, psychology and the other social sciences. Advertising, which is in the business of creating images, has a stake in the outcome of such a project.

Meanwhile, advertising strategy wisely shows some restraint in applying the results of motivation studies in the present state of the art. The psychoanalytic view in particular is marked by two quite distinct versions from Freud himself, followed by a profusion of free-wheeling speculation by his many disciples. So far the major impact has not been on the advertiser's claims concerning his products, but on the manner of their presentation. A new aura of interest for a product may be created by a fresh copy approach, but the product still has to compete with other instruments recommended for the same purpose.

There is some warrant in clinical lore for calling a spade a symbol of fertility, but it still belongs in the tool shed rather than the boudoir. Every copywriter knows that a man buys suspenders to hold up his trousers and not as a 'reaction to castration anxiety.' A woman buys a garden hose to water the lawn and not because of the 'futility of urethral competition for the female.' Possibly we are saved from the solemnities of Freud by the sanity of Rabelais. Any student of the gusty Frenchman will remember a chapter on toilet training that has never been approached in Freudian literature. The five-year-old Gargantua has some remarkable things to say in this chapter about product testing. As for urethral competition, who can forget Gargantua's

149

first visit to Paris and the flood which drowned 260,418 Parisians, not counting women and children. He may have been visiting the Madison Avenue of that day, since his protest concerned the gullibility of the great crowds which gathered to behold any spectacle from 'a mule with tinkling bells' to 'a blind fiddler in the middle of a crosswalk.'

Advertising strategy must take account of both gullibility and gumption, of human needs both instrumental and symbolic. In the long run the odds are in favor of a strategy which takes rational problem solving as a fundamental aspect of human behavior. Despite all the quirks and foibles revealed by motivation research, rationality and efficiency are universal goals of the maturing individual. For most products, the long-run advantage probably lies with the kind of advertising appeals that will still make sense to the mature and balanced personalities which most of us are trying to become.

Reference

ROGERS, C. R. (1951), *Client-Centered Therapy*, Houghton Mifflin.

10 Timothy Joyce

Advertising

From Timothy Joyce, *What Do We Know about How Advertising Works?*, 1967, J. Walter Thompson Co. Ltd, London.

The question 'how does advertising work?' seems to be raised more and more often in connexion with research into advertising. There is increasing awareness that a number of advertising research methods in common use imply very different assumptions about the way advertising works. Rarely – if ever – is evidence presented that the assumptions made are correct. Also, discussions of difficulties of communication which are experienced between creative and research people often seem to point to different assumptions about the functions of advertising made by the two sides concerned.

Let us first consider what the problem is and why it is a problem. To start with, what do we mean by 'advertising' and what do we mean when we say that it 'works'? In the interests of simplicity, it seems legitimate to limit consideration to:

1. *Advertising which consists of impersonal communication*: face-to-face selling is excluded.

2. *Advertising in the main mass media such as press, TV, cinema, poster, radio*: aspects of merchandising such as competitions, offers and gifts are excluded, as are other variables – which certainly affect sales, of course – such as the pack and characteristics of the product itself.

3. *Advertising for consumer products*: advertising for products or services not purchased by the ultimate consumer is excluded, for instance, advertising for industrial goods.

4. *Advertising for low unit-price, high frequency-of-purchase products, or, to put it a bit more elegantly, 'cheap goods bought often'*: advertising for durables is excluded.

5. *Advertising, the object of which is to get the consumer to buy the product, either in the short or long run, and so to influence sales*: 'corporate image' advertising with objectives other than, or additional to, sales objectives is excluded, for instance, advertising addressed to current or potential shareholders, suppliers, or customers.

In fact, it is likely that most of what is advertising on *any* reasonable definition, at any rate in Britain, is advertising in the limited sense I am concerned with for the moment. Anyway these restrictions enable us to ignore the rather different mechanisms which may be at work in the other cases.

We are interested, then, in media advertising which aims to sell inexpensive, frequently-purchased products to consumers; and I think it is safe to assume that such advertising *does* work, or at least that it *can* do so, in the sense that if the advertising had not happened, less of the product would have been sold.

Let us assume then that advertising *is* capable of 'working', in the sense of increasing sales above the levels at which they would otherwise be. Why is there a problem about *how* it works?

Firstly, there is an interesting intellectual problem in that there is not a direct link between the operation of placing the advertisements in the media and the behaviour of the consumer purchasing the product, in the sense in which there *is* a direct link between the consumer purchasing the product and the product leaving the factory. Retailers and wholesalers order and re-order as a result of, or in anticipation of, consumer purchases and in the markets we are considering there is not much more to it than that. However, placing advertisements in the media seems to be capable of bringing about a kind of 'action at a distance', an idea of some importance in the history of science.

Advertisements can in general only work by being seen or heard by consumers and operating on their minds, a process which in some way influences one aspect of their behaviour – the physical operations of purchasing. *In this sense it is true, though unfortunately trivial, to say that advertising works by comunicating.*

Secondly, there are important practical problems which we would be better able to solve if we knew something about how advertising worked. Since the link between advertising and sales is not direct, and since it is well-known that many other variables affect sales besides advertising, we have to make decisions about advertising with judgement which may be faulty. Such decisions are the basic ones of how much to spend, what to say, who to attempt to say it to and where to say it, and even more complex ones of scheduling, such as whether to have bursts or continuous advertising, and what combination of frequency or coverage to go for, which could only be satisfactorily taken out of the realm of judgement if we actually knew something about 'response functions'. Now, any advance in knowledge of how advertising works may help us in one or more of these areas, either by resolving problems directly, e.g. by showing that certain creative approaches are bound to be more successful than others, or by showing how we can use research to resolve them, e.g. *if* we found that advertising worked by getting people to remember slogans, we would test advertisements and campaigns to see which of their slogans were best remembered.

So knowledge of how advertising works may have definite practical value, as well as helping to resolve an intellectual problem of some interest. What *do* we know about it?

Common-sense models of advertising

Let us look first at some well-known formulations of models, or theories, of how advertising works. Some of them come from researchers and some from advertising and creative people.

Researchers' models of advertising

One of the oldest models is that of Daniel Starch (1925), who wrote over forty years ago that:

'An advertisement, to be successful:

(a) Must be seen.
(b) Must be read.
(c) Must be believed.
(d) Must be remembered.
(e) Must be acted upon.'

These assumptions relate explicitly to the advertisement itself, rather than the state of mind of the consumer with respect to the product. As such it is probably an unsatisfactory model, if only

153

because it implies that the effects of each individual opportunity to see an advertisement are independent, and does not allow for 'build-up'. In real life it seems very unlikely that successive impacts of the same advertisement or of different advertisements in the same campaign do not interact – at the simplest level, there may be increasing returns or diminishing returns.

A much more recent and widely-quoted model of advertising which does allow for 'build-up', though not in a quantitative way, is the DAGMAR model (Colley, 1961) which refers to the state of mind of the consumer:

'All commercial communications that aim at the ultimate objective of a sale must carry a prospect through four levels of understanding:

From unawareness to

Awareness   The prospect must first be aware of the existence of a brand or company.

Comprehension   He must have a comprehension of what the product is and what it will do for him.

Conviction   He must arrive at a mental disposition or conviction to buy the product.

Action   Finally, he must stir himself to action.'

While it is clear from the rest of the book that the definitions of these terms, especially 'comprehension' and 'conviction' are somewhat loose, 'comprehension' seems to refer in most cases to penetration or recall of the main message or messages, 'conviction' to belief in these messages and overall favourableness towards the product or desire to buy. However, both terms may evidently also refer to aspects of brand images.

The belief that advertisements nudge the consumer along a spectrum which extends from complete ignorance of the product on the one hand to purchasing on the other, rather than individually achieving, or failing to achieve results which owe nothing to previous exposures, is stated as follows:

'The purpose of advertising is to bring about a change in a state of mind toward the purchase of a product. Rarely is a single

154

advertisement powerful enough to move a prospect from a complete state of unawareness to a condition of action. . . . Advertising accomplishment should be measured in terms of the extent to which it moves people up the ladder from one level to another.'

A further example of a model is the well-known AIDA, the initials for attention, interest, desire, action. In so far as this is a serious attempt to sum up what advertising does, it could refer *either* to the response to the individual advertisement *or* to the consumer's state of mind with respect to the product, and it can from that point of view be regarded as intermediate between the Starch and DAGMAR models.

There are a number of other well-known formulations, some of which I have discussed elsewhere (Joyce, 1965), including the three-step model borrowed from psychology – 'cognition, affection, conation'. Cognition refers to the processes connected with knowing and thinking; affection to feeling or emotion; and conation to the desire for action. These models have not necessarily been put forward by researchers, but they have been widely used by researchers and have certainly greatly influenced the directions advertising research has taken. What are we to make of them?

The first thing that we notice is that they are put forward not on the basis of empirical evidence, but on the basis of an appeal to intuition or common-sense (Colley, 1961, p. 53: 'The concept of the Marketing Communications Spectrum . . . is applied common-sense'). To some extent each of them is true by tautology, and so this is what we would expect. For example, to take the first stage of Starch's model, a (press) advertisement *can* only have an influence if it is seen by the person concerned. Or again, there is a sense in which someone cannot comprehend a message concerning a brand (DAGMAR) unless he is aware of the brand. There is no harm in being reminded of the obviously true. However, at almost every stage in these models there are problems of definition, and if they are interpreted in such a way that they possess empirical content, the absence of empirical support must be worrying. Second, and now we shall restrict ourselves to the empirical content of these models, rather than their tautological

155

content, they generally imply that an important function of advertising is to implant factual messages – messages which are believed and remembered (Starch), or which are comprehended and lead to conviction (DAGMAR). In short, the object of advertising is to get the consumer to learn something. These assumptions, explicit or implicit, underlie research which establishes 'penetration' or 'impact', and which is very commonly used in pre-testing or campaign evaluation. We shall look at the evidence for and against these assumptions later, but meanwhile it is enough to bring them out into the open.

Again, the models, DAGMAR particularly, seem to me possibly to have empirical content in another way – they imply a rational consumer weighing up the arguments. The choice of the terms 'comprehension' and 'conviction' suggests this strongly. The object of advertising is seen as being to present persuasive arguments. Just *how* rational buying decisions, and reactions to advertisements, are, is therefore a matter we could explore with advantage.

Another feature of most of these models is that they appear to be concerned only, or at least mainly, with the business of turning non-buyers into buyers – or in a competitive field in which almost everyone buys one brand or another, turning a buyer of someone else's brand into a purchaser of one's own brand. This implies what might be called a redemptive view of advertising – that advertising works by conversion. It is certainly tempting to think of a purchaser of brand X becoming increasingly dissatisfied with it, and at the same time increasingly interested in brand Y and anxious to examine all the facts and arguments presented about it, until at some point he gives up brand X and switches to brand Y. However, how far this fits the known facts of consumer behaviour will be questioned shortly.

Advertising men's models of advertising

Just as the researchers' models often accompany and support a particular approach to advertising research, e.g. Starch, so – as we might expect – advertising men's models are often put forward by those who have a particular view of advertising they wish to promote. One of the best-known examples is the development by Rosser Reeves of the theory of the Unique Selling Proposition or

USP (Reeves, 1961). Reeves states: 'The consumer tends to remember just one thing from an advertisement – one strong claim, or one strong concept. . . . Each advertisement must make a proposition to the consumer. The proposition must be one that the competition either cannot, or does not, offer. The proposition must be so strong that it can move the mass millions, i.e. pull over new customers to your product'.

It is not altogether easy to pin down the meaning of the terms used, but the USP school seems to be saying that an advertisement works by *making a claim for the product* which is clearly related to the consumer's need, i.e. it promises a benefit, which is unique and true of the product concerned, and which will be recalled by the consumer and motivate him to action at the appropriate time.

Discussion of alternative approaches to advertising used largely to be concerned with the contrast between the USP school and the 'brand image' school which was often associated with David Ogilvy (1963). Again, it is not easy to distil from these sources a clear statement which will pass as a scientific judgement of how advertising works, but the 'brand image' school seemed to be more concerned than the USP school with non-verbal methods of communication, with the evocation of moods, and with investing a brand with additional favourable connotations which had nothing specifically to do with the product field concerned, e.g. connotations of prestige and quality such as Ogilvy's claim to 'give a brand a first-class ticket through life'.

Other views of advertising put forward in the literature on the subject have stressed the importance of emotion and of unconscious motivation. An eloquent statement of this view comes from Pierre Martineau (1957). His opinion is that virtually all human behaviour is some form of self-expression, and that everything we buy helps us to convey to others and to ourselves the kind of people we are. Therefore, in addition to the practical qualities of products, their 'user images' and other associations are all-important. 'A primary task of the advertiser is to invest his product or his institution with rich psychological overtones.' However, people need to think of themselves as rational, and even where the choice may be a matter of emotion and feeling, a *rationalization* is required which the consumer can believe to be

157

the reason for his choice. Therefore, the ideal advertisement is a blend of both logic and emotion, of realism and fantasy.

Comment

The comparisons between the models of advertising which have been most widely talked about and used in the research and advertising worlds are of some interest. They have certain features in common – thus, both DAGMAR and the USP view imply that advertising works by implanting verbal propositions. However, there are differences. Advertising people have perhaps laid more stress on the consumer's *needs*. The idea of a 'proposition' is that it promises that the product will be something or do something which the consumer wants. Also, the brand-image schools have brought out the importance of generalized connotations of products which, again, they relate to the consumer's non-rational needs.

It would, I believe, be wrong to say that in their published statements, with a few possible exceptions, not so far quoted, research men who have concerned themselves with the subject have been more receptive to psychological theory and the state of psychological knowledge than advertising men. Both sides have put forward points of view which make sense to them in the light of their particular experience. However, a great deal has been learnt in the last few years by psychologists and communication researchers which certainly appears to have potential applications to advertising. The sections which follow attempt to draw together this new knowledge and to relate it to standard advertising research methods. It is obviously impossible to get anywhere at all unless the subject-matter can be divided, and for this reason I start by making the minimum assumptions, subject to qualification, that advertising works like this: consumers react to advertisements, their attitudes to products are influenced, and this in turn influences their purchasing behaviour and therefore sales.

Purchasing behaviour

If we are going to re-open discussion of the traditional models, it is best to begin by reminding ourselves of their starting point. We believe that advertising can lead to more sales, i.e. more purchasing by consumers, than there would have been if it had not

158

taken place. How does it achieve this? Let us first look at purchasing behaviour itself. Since advertising evidently influences behaviour, we can usefully start by inspecting behaviour. Again, we restrict ourselves arbitrarily by considering just consumer purchasing rather than other forms of behaviour.

What does the study of purchasing behaviour tell us? We may sometimes be tempted to think of any market where a number of rather similar brands are in competition in terms which imply that a consumer is a 'buyer' of one or other of the brands. If a consumer is a buyer of brand X and we want to influence him in a way which will help the sales of brand Y, we must 'convert' him to the use of Y. Unfortunately, a study of actual data shows that in many markets things are not so simple:

1. Consumers buy varying amounts of the product, in a way that is not necessarily related to, e.g., household size or any other constant. This has the implication, of course, even on a 'conversion' model, that some people are worth more than others to the advertiser.

2. Many people buy more than one brand, even in the course of quite a short time period. For this reason the term 'buyer' is ill-defined. Some people indeed will buy brand X alone, in the sense that over a year or more they buy no other brand, but there are also people who buy two, three or more brands with some degree of regularity. The obvious implication of this is that one way to increase sales is to increase the proportion of purchases of the brand concerned made by people who are *already* buying it.

3. In some fields the drive for the consumer to remain 'in-stock' is considerable – when she has run out, she will buy more. It may then be a task of advertising to stimulate *use* rather than, or as well as, purchase.

It clearly is not an altogether simple matter to state what effects advertising may have on purchasing.

Two further points. Firstly, and this is true even in a 'conversion market', we cannot ignore our current users. They may switch to other brands, or buy more of them, especially if subjected to their advertising. Advertising has a defensive as well as an offensive role and may well be needed to minimize these losses. For some products this defensive role may be the more important of the two. Getting priorities right, and assessing which balance of roles will bring the greatest return, is obviously a key decision which cannot at present be helped much by research. A valid means of establishing the degree to which a person was a 'potential switcher' would be of great help.

The second general point is that we should remember that much of the work of advertising consists of preventing a decline in sales, i.e. in maintaining the situation. Sometimes a conclusion is drawn that advertising has had no effect, because sales have not gone up. This can be misleading. The true measure of the effect of advertising is the difference between sales actually achieved and what would have happened if there had been no advertising, and we rarely measure this directly since to do this requires a willingness to stop advertising on an experimental basis in certain control towns or areas. If there had been no advertising, sales might have gone down. Advertising may expend much of its effort in maintaining the situation, or at least in preventing it from deteriorating any faster.

It seems very likely that expanding our knowledge of how advertising works will depend greatly on expanding our knowledge of the nature of use and purchasing patterns. Studies such as those being carried out by Ehrenberg are likely to prove of considerable value here (see Chatfield, Ehrenberg and Goodhardt, 1966).

Choice and attitudes

What causes the consumer to buy one brand rather than another, or not to buy at all? The advertiser is interested in consumer behaviour, which essentially means the consumer's choice of certain courses of action rather than others. He assumes that this choice is affected by consumer attitudes, which in turn can be influenced by advertising. What links, if any, can we forge between attitudes and choice?

One thing is clear to start with: a powerful determinant of consumer choice is habit or inertia. It suits the consumer to treat much of her activity as a matter of routine. To indulge in a process of conscious deliberation at every purchase would take an enormous amount of time and mental effort which, not unnaturally, there is a strong drive to avoid. Any satisfactory model of consumer choice is bound to give a large weight to the brand previously purchased. The significance of various forms of promotion, e.g. free samples, coupons and offers, is that they afford a means of penetrating the barriers of habit and bring about a momentary change from 'usual behaviour'. On subsequent occasions the consumer has to decide whether to continue with the brand whose promotion she took advantage of, or to go back to the former brand. In these circumstances it seems very likely that attitudes, partly created by advertising, will settle the outcome.

Attitudes

What do we mean by 'attitudes'? Perhaps the least potentially confusing definition for those who are accustomed to the use of the term in the advertising context is 'the consumer's system of beliefs, associations, images and memories concerning the brand'. Also, I do not propose to make any distinction between 'brand attitudes' and 'brand image', which again I define in this rather general way.

Three significant points follow from this definition. Firstly, it does *not* refer to a propensity to act in a given way. Secondly, we mean *more* by 'attitude' than just the overall evaluation of the product by the consumer – though the evaluative element of attitudes is of course of great importance. Thirdly, we imply that attitudes can be inferred or measured by research methods which are different from establishing the consumer's choice in purchasing situations.

The important point is this: we have defined 'attitude' in such a way that attitudes do not *necessarily* influence behaviour – they may do so but this is a matter of empirical investigation.

What do we know about attitudes and their influence upon behaviour? Among the more important research findings which are relevant from social psychology are those concerned with 'balance', 'congruity', or 'dissonance'. For some time it has been generally recognized that there is a strong drive among human beings for consistency. A good review of the better-

161

developed theories on this subject is that of Zajonc (in his 1960 article in the *Public Opinion Quarterly*), who presents work done by Heider, Osgood and Tannenbaum, and Festinger.

Heider's work on 'balance' explored the ways people view their relations with other people and their environment. A typical experiment involved presenting subjects with hypothetical situations involving two persons, P and O, and an impersonal entity, X, to rate for pleasantness. 'Balanced' situations, e.g. P likes O, P dislikes X, and O dislikes X, were regarded as more pleasant than 'unbalanced' situations, e.g. P dislikes O, P likes X, and O likes X.

Osgood and Tannenbaum's principle of 'congruity' is concerned with direction of attitude change: it postulates that when changes in attitude occur, they are in the direction of congruity with the prevailing frame of reference. Experiments have shown, for example, that when individuals are presented with arguments in favour of a concept they value which are attributed to a source they do not value, they think worse of the concept and better of the source.

An even more sophisticated statement of the theory is Festinger's theory of 'cognitive dissonance', which is rapidly becoming well known in advertising circles and which is backed up by a good deal of ingenious experimentation. The theory states that two elements of knowledge are dissonant if they are contradictory, and that dissonance is uncomfortable, with the result that an individual will actively avoid situations and information which might increase dissonance. An attractive feature of dissonance theory is that it has a number of non-obvious, even surprising, consequences which experiments have shown, however, to be empirically well founded. For example, experiments show that people who are compelled, by reward or punishment, to do something they do not like or to express an opinion they do not hold have a more favourable view of the activity or opinion after doing so. A far from obvious prediction of dissonance theory is that they will become more favourable if compliance is brought about by a *small* prize than by a large once, since there is then a greater need to reduce dissonance, and this is borne out in practice.

Some experiments carried out by Festinger and others refer to exposure to information and attitudes held after a decision. For example, it was pointed out that most decisions involve dissonance, in that the alternative not chosen will have had some attractive features, and the alternative actually chosen will have had some unattractive features. It was therefore predicted that after a decision is made the attractiveness of the chosen alternative will increase, and the individual will also seek information justifying the choice. This is again borne out in practice. An example of the latter consequence is that new car owners were found to notice and read advertisements about the cars they had recently purchased more than advertisements about other cars.

Since these findings suggest that behaviour change may cause attitude change rather than the other way round, and that exposure to advertising may also be caused by purchasing rather than the reverse, the theory of cognitive dissonance is obviously important for advertising theory.

What, then, do these theoretical formulations suggest that is of relevance to advertising, and how far is this supported by experimental results? Clearly there are two aspects of this – the interrelationship of attitudes themselves, and the interdependence of attitudes and behaviour. Firstly, the principles of consistency suggest that there will be a drive towards integration of the set of attitudes held by an individual towards a brand, with the consequence that a change in one attitude, brought about, let us suppose, by advertising, may cause changes in other attitudes, so that contradictory beliefs are not entertained. Experienced advertising people certainly know that success in registering a given point may have consequences which extend far beyond that particular point. These consequences may be favourable or unfavourable and it is obviously very desirable to know the nature of this 'fallout'.

Secondly, what of the relationship between attitudes and behaviour? Obviously, there is no point in setting out to influence attitudes if they do not influence behaviour – but do they? Some people have been, in my view, unnecessarily frightened, especially by the cognitive dissonance experiments, into the belief that the truth is all the other way, i.e. that purchasing behaviour affects attitudes towards products and that the reverse is not true.

One prediction we may make from dissonance theory is that,

in certain circumstances, dissonance may be reduced *by fitting behaviour to attitudes*; we become increasingly dissatisfied with our usual brand, or think increasingly highly of an alternative, and an easy way of reducing the dissonance is to buy the alternative brand. Where dissonance theory can help us is in recognizing that rather than a single arrow,

attitudes $\longrightarrow$ behaviour

there is a double arrow

attitudes $\rightleftarrows$ behaviour

and it is helpful to think of a tug-of-war between the two; in situations where attitudes and behaviour are dissonant, one *or* the other may change.

Finally, there is considerable evidence that commonly-used general measures of attitude, such as intentions-to-buy questions and awareness questions, which provide a measure of the association between the brand and the product field, are closely related to frequency or recency of purchase and may perhaps be at least partly 'caused by' this frequency or recency.

Ehrenberg and Bird (1966a, 1966b) found that levels of intentions-to-buy measures were *less* than what would be predicted, from the relationship established for stationary markets, in the case of new brands or brands increasing their sales, and *more* than this for declining brands. However, the view that movements in intentions-to-buy precede sales movements would predict the opposite. They found similar relationships between awareness and purchasing, with the additional factor that brand awareness levels appeared to be influenced by weight of advertising as well.

Needs

Most models of consumer choice include a reference to consumers' needs. I use the term 'needs' to cover a wide variety of things – drives, desires, requirements and wants. This is not the place for a discussion of definitions, but it again seems least confusing to use the term in the widest sense.

What do we know about the basic human needs? Psychologists who have dealt with this question include Maslow, who postulated the hierarchy of physiological and psychological needs such that the satisfaction of one of them would bring the next one into play. The classification of products as either 'necessaries, comforts, or luxuries' would fit a scheme like this. Some psychologists have specifically studied the motives which may cause people to allocate money to purchases. Thorndike (1940) gives a classification of these motives and gives an estimate of expenditure allocated to each motive by a group of subjects over a period of time.

There are one or two general questions concerning needs which it is worth touching upon. It is obviously important to recognize that needs differ for different individuals. Are there needs which are common to all product-fields, or at least a number of them? Some needs are very specific, and may even define the product-field concerned, e.g. headache remedies, washing-up liquids, and so on. Are there other needs which affect the choice of brands but which are not specifically linked to given fields? Experience suggests that there are such needs, and that these reflect general attitudes to products which differentiate them and which may influence choice. Examples of such needs are:

1. Social prestige – leading to attraction to a brand thought to be 'up the market'.

2. Being thought 'with it' or modern, youthful.

3. Being 'in the swim', choosing a brand which more and more people are buying – a bandwagon effect.

4. Being thought a good housewife.

5. Being thought economical and a good judge of value.

The importance of these 'added values' is that they are relatively easy to influence by advertising. In a mass market, once the brand has been very widely tried and the advertising is well known, there is little work to be done in imparting information, except when and if the product is re-formulated.

Can advertising influence needs? In particular, can it create new needs? One sometimes hears these questions discussed and someone will usually say that advertising cannot do this – it can only build on the needs which are already there. It seems to me that this is somewhat obtuse. In many cases it seems straightforward to say that advertising has helped to produce a need, possibly by creating dissatisfaction, and suggested a product to satisfy it. One of the strongest points which can be made by the supporters of advertising is that the consumer's level of aspiration is continually being raised by advertising, which says to her, in effect, that life could be better. Of course, the critics of advertising would say that this creates needless discontent, or that the objects of aspirations are meretricious. Either side of the argument implies that advertising can influence needs, in the ordinary sense of the phrase.

Is choice rational?

So, if we believe that the consumer's choice of a brand is influenced by its image, i.e. the consumer's attitude towards it, together with the consumer's system of needs, we presumably believe that the better the two – image and needs – fit together, the more likely the brand is to be chosen. Is there any possibility of developing a more precise model relating them to consumer choice?

Interesting attempts to develop such a model have been made by Rothman and Tate (1964) and Smulian (1964). Both rely upon establishing the image of an 'ideal brand' for each consumer, about which I personally have considerable doubts.

Does the work carried out by economists on consumer choice hold out any hope of linking attitudes and images, needs and choice? The traditional view of the consumer has suggested that the consumer chooses in such a way as to maximize some quantity, which may be a theoretical construct such as utility, or may be happiness or pleasure. However, modern economists have tended to reject concepts such as utility and to talk instead in terms of conditions of consistency in choice. But whether the behaviour studied by economists is maximizing behaviour or merely consistent behaviour, the assumption is made that choices are rational, and observation alone suggests that real-life choices cannot necessarily be accounted for on these lines.

H. A. Simon (1957) has suggested that the individual decision-maker, or consumer, *may* be choosing rationally if the definition of rationality is amended in two ways. First, the choices have to be evaluated against his or her own beliefs and values, i.e. his

166

or her own conception of reality, which may depart at many points from the objective situation. We recognize this in talking of 'the brand image', and in recognizing that it may not bear much relationship to the real nature of the brand. Secondly, the consumer does not maximize so much as 'satisfy'. He has an idea of what is 'good enough', based perhaps on a limited search among the alternatives to see what standards might be regarded as reasonable, and then searches until a satisfactory alternative is found and settles for it.

This view is plausible – a rational consumer should presumably try every single brand on the market in order to optimize, but many do not. One idea which is common to all models based upon traditional economic theory is the idea of choice being determined by the supposed future benefits of the alternative chosen. It is certainly tempting to think that this might indeed be a large part of the explanation of consumer choice: after all, products are bought essentially for what they *do*, after purchase. However, we must beware of the 'intellectualist fallacy' of arguing from what people should rationally do to what they actually do. There is all too little in the way of empirical results in this important area.

The response to an advertisement

We have sketched the consumer as possessing interacting attitude, need and behaviour patterns. What happens to these patterns when the consumer is exposed to an advertisement? Does an advertisement change, or maintain, behaviour by changing, or reinforcing, *attitudes*? And are there *other* links between advertisements and behaviour?

We are again in a position of having to make certain assumptions in order even to be able to discuss the subject, and the sections which follow assume that it is at least possible to draw crude distinctions between attending to an advertisement, perceiving it, becoming involved with it, including acquiring attitudes towards it, and recalling it or its message after it is no longer in view. This classification may, of course, prove unsatisfactory and we may have to 'throw away the ladder' after climbing up it.

167

Attention

It is well known that we attend to only a small part of what in principle we can see or hear. This phenomenon can be illustrated in the following way so far as advertisements are concerned. Consider a person reading a newspaper. All parts of the page or pages open in front of him will be within his visual field – he can see all parts of them 'out of the corner of his eye', i.e. with peripheral vision, even if he is not looking at them directly. However, his attention is directed to whatever he is specifically reading or studying. When he finishes reading or studying this particular part of the page he may look at another part which has attracted his attention, and so on. It is clear that there is some mechanism which evaluates all that is in the visual field, operating, however, mostly below the threshold of consciousness, which classifies particular objects, headlines, pictures, etc., as worth conscious attention or not. This sort of screening process affects our attention to the input of all our senses.

Much of the same sort of considerations apply to other media as they do to the press, e.g. to TV and posters, though in these cases it is more a question of whether the attention is directed at the medium or at something else, e.g. at the TV set when a commercial is being transmitted, or at something else in the viewing room, rather than at one part of the medium instead of another, e.g. at an advertisement rather than editorial matter, in the press.

What causes people to attend to particular stimuli? It seems that an important factor is the recognition of some part of the stimulus as being relevant to the individual's interests and needs. The problem of gaining attention is a major one in creating an advertisement. Obviously, much will be lost if the attention of many of those at whom the advertisement is directed is never obtained. For this reason, the measurement of 'attention value' has been an important aspect of both pre-testing and post-testing systems.

One important question is whether there can be any value in exposure to an advertisement to which no attention is paid. For example, we may not look directly at a press advertisement and not even be consciously aware of its presence: can it convey information or affect attitudes? Common-sense suggests that this may happen. The fact that attention levels are highly associated with the respondent's interest in the product advertised suggests that enough information is often taken in about an advertisement, below the threshold of attention, for the respondent to recognize what product is being advertised and, in effect, to decide not to pay attention to it. It seems likely that other information could also be taken in below this threshold, e.g. visual symbols, which could affect attitudes. For some advertisements this could be important, especially the image of the brand. This may also be important where respondents are likely to have a number of opportunities to see an advertisement, such that exposures after the first may 'remind' the respondent – still below the attention threshold – of the first exposure. Attention, therefore, is not a necessary condition of effect; it may make effects such as information-transfer more likely, but how much more likely will depend on the advertisement. Experiments suggest that the brain 'takes in' a very great deal of information, much more than is consciously attended to, almost all of which, however, is very quickly forgotten.

Perception

Assuming for the sake of argument that an advertisement is being consciously attended to, what is perceived? Is what is *perceived* subjectively what is *there* objectively? If the view of the consumer that I am trying to build up is accepted, it will not be surprising that the answer is 'not necessarily'. And, indeed, there is a lot of evidence indicating that how people perceive advertisements depends to a great extent on their preconceptions and their interests. In extreme cases this can lead to misunderstanding and mistakes.

In some cases communications are subject to what is known as an 'assimilation' effect. If the recipient is able to perceive, or misperceive, an advertisement as representing exactly what he already believes, it may be rendered ineffective if the object was to persuade him to change his mind. However, over-shooting by presenting extreme arguments may involve the opposite risk of a 'contrast' effect, where the arguments used or implied are recognized as being quite opposed to the subject's prior beliefs and therefore flatly rejected. It appears that there may be an optimum degree of disagreement between the subject's point of view and that of the advertisement or communication – the difference being large enough to have effect, but not so large as to bring about rejection.

Involvement

The consumer attends, we trust, to the advertisement, and perceives it in the desired way; does she become involved with it? This rather loose term is best explored by considering some of the measures which have been used in pre-testing systems.

Firstly, *liking*. Does it matter whether an advertisement is liked or not? Evidence from several quarters, see, e.g. Treasure and Joyce (1967), suggests that liking is in general probably not positively associated with effectiveness, or, more strictly, it is not associated with attributes which one believes on much better ground to be *closely associated* with effectiveness, such as desire for the product after exposure to the advertisement. Equally, liking is not negatively associated with effectiveness either: there is no evidence that one has 'to offend to sell'. It seems that worthwhile involvement is a more complicated matter than overall favourableness to the advertisement.

Secondly, *interest*. A number of interest measures are in common use in pre-testing. For example, Audience Studies Limited in the United Kingdom obtain a second-by-second record of settings on an 'interest dial' from a sub-sample of those attending their tests of TV commercials. Apparatus such as the psychogalvanometer and cameras to measure pupil dilation have made use of the physiological correlates of interest. Some forms of copy test establish interest by covering up the copy and inviting respondents to choose one advertisement only which they wish to read.

More work is needed on the measuring of 'interest' and the nature of physiological responses. However, it seems in the light of such evidence as is available to be a more profitable aspect to study than, say, liking. Unpublished work by BMRB suggests that, in terms of verbal descriptions, of advertisements at any rate, there may be two aspects of 'interest' – the 'stimulation' side, represented by such descriptions as imaginative, startling, novel or exciting, and the 'enjoyment' side, represented by such descriptions as entertaining, pleasant or amusing. There is some evidence that the former group is more strongly associated with effectiveness than the latter, which has more to do with liking. This suggests that there is something in the view that advertisements should expect some contribution from the audience: if people can be brought to see things for themselves they are more likely to agree with them than if they are passive spectators. An advertisement which contains something slightly unexpected which the audience can get to grips with, *provided it is not misunderstood*, may achieve this. (See discussion of 'pitching the communication at the right level of difficulty' in Golby, 1963.)

Is it necessary that the consumer should identify herself with the people or situations shown? There is a good deal of evidence that *identification* greatly improves the chance of persuasion. If people can rationalize their rejection of an argument by saying 'that isn't how things are at all' or 'she doesn't have my problems', communication will be impeded. The measurement of identification is not, however, an entirely simple matter and will depend to some extent on the particular advertisement. Identification can be very effective at the level of fantasy as well as of realism, and this fact should make one cautious of possibly naïve research methods in this area.

'Identification' is a term in need of better definition. One of the ideas it implies is certainly that of 'conditioning agreement' (Golby, 1963), i.e. the use of statements or arguments with which the consumer will almost certainly agree in order to get her in the right frame of mind to receive new information or arguments. This certainly is a useful device. It is important that it should not misfire, however.

Next, is it necessary that an advertisement should be *believed*? Much advertising research has been based on the assumption that belief is a prerequisite of effectiveness. However, a good deal of evidence exists to suggest that this is not as simple as it may look. Work done by Maloney (1962, 1963) in particular suggests that belief in advertising claims contributes much less to effectiveness than 'curious non-belief', i.e. the view that 'I don't know whether the claim is true or not but I am interested to try the

171

product'. There is also evidence from unpublished B M R B work, that people look upon advertising to some extent as a 'game' in which descriptions and claims must be expected to be somewhat exaggerated, and cannot therefore be taken literally. What matters is that the game should not be played unfairly and that a false impression of the product, after normal exaggeration is discounted, should not be created. In other words, what matters is whether the consumer believes what it is intended she should believe *about the product*, not what the claims literally say.

Can advertising have any other effects apart from those already discussed? It seems likely to me that one function of advertising not so far touched on is persuasion by *suggestion*. People are all more or less suggestible and can often be induced to do what someone else wishes by suggestion alone, and there seems no reason why this should not extend to advertising media.

Advertising may at least, in certain circumstances, help the consumer to reach decisions by suggesting which brand she should buy. The mechanism of suggestion is something we know little about. It is possible, though admittedly this is speculation, that it works best if the advertisement creates some sort of tension which the purchase then discharges. Again this suggests that an advertisement may *not* benefit from being over-complete, i.e. leaving nothing to be deduced or imagined.

Recall

When the advertisement is no longer being seen or heard, and other stimuli take its place, possibly advertisements for other products, of course, what is remembered? There are three types of recall we could be concerned with: recall of the advertisement having been seen; recall of the content of the advertisement, especially slogans; and recall of the information or images that it communicated. The latter obviously are an addition to the stock of attitudes about the product. The first two, however, are related directly to the advertisement: are they important?

A large number of approaches to pre-testing are based on the assumption that they are. Recall, impact and penetration measures are in widespread use. The reasons why such measures are used are not as simple as they might appear:

1. Recall and recognition measures may, of course, be used to establish the degree to which the advertisement attracted attention on exposure.

2. Playback measures may be used to see whether the message was comprehended: misunderstandings may be picked up as a result of incorrect playback.

3. Apart from these considerations, however, the extent to which the advertisement or its content or slogans are recalled is thought to be of value *in its own right*.

Pursuing the latter point, while there is a large body of opinion favourable to such measures, there is also a large body which doubts the relevance of them. *In principle*, it certainly does not follow that an advertisement which is effective in persuading or influencing attitudes will be remembered better. It is also true that the object of advertising is more that of getting the product recognized and known than the advertising recognized and known.

Fortunately, the relationship between recall and effectiveness, in terms of attitude and behaviour changes, has been studied by Haskins (1964). He concludes on the basis of a number of studies, some of which were concerned with advertising and some with other forms of communication, that 'Learning and recall of factual information from mass communications occur. However, recall and retention measures seem, at best, irrelevant to the ultimate effects desired, the changing of attitudes and behaviour'. One reason for this is that 'recall of factual material is not necessary for absorption of connotative meaning. . . . Most learning taking place via the mass media is incidental learning, rather than intentional, motivated study such as occurs in the classroom. Perhaps the best usage of the mass media is not to communicate facts at all but some other kind of meaning'.

Common-sense suggests that there are occasions where recall measures serve a useful purpose – where, for example, for (supposed) good reasons it is explicitly seen as an advertisement's job to communicate a particular piece of information, it is worth measuring the extent to which it is known. There may also be reasons for using measures for establishing attention and comprehension, as pointed out above. However, in general there seems to be sufficient evidence available to lead one not to rely upon recall measures as overall measures of effectiveness, and this has an obvious bearing upon at least some interpretations of the Starch and DAGMAR models referred to at the beginning of this paper. In so far as they imply that advertising works by implanting facts or claims they do not appear to have experimental support.

One important function of some advertisements which should not be forgotten is the reminder function. In certain cases this may have the effect, when exposure to an advertisement takes place, of bringing to mind the content of the advertisement absorbed on a previous exposure. The original experience is 'reconstructed', even though the new exposure need not involve a high level of attention. Some campaigns make use of this 'reconstruction' effect by reducing the size or length of advertisements, while sticking to the overall theme and treatment, when it is judged that most people in the target audience will have been exposed sufficiently to the longer or larger version. In such a case the extent of recall of the original advertisement *is* important. However, research to measure such an effect would obviously need to be rather more sophisticated in design than most recall – penetration studies.

Apart from this consideration, my belief is that what matters is not that the advertisement should be familiar, but that the brand should be familiar. All other things being equal, a brand about which something is known is probably more likely to be chosen than a brand about which nothing is known. Mere familiarity is probably of some help; even the knowledge that the brand is advertised may do good as a result of the belief that advertised brands should be better or more reliable than others. But in addition to this, of course, we want to invest the brand with a wide range of favourable associations and attitudes.

Conclusions

To summarize some of the main points in this discussion:

1. The view that 'advertising works by converting more people to use the brand' is misleading in several ways. Advertising may

be working even though sales are level or even going down, by preventing (greater) loss of users. And in some markets at least, increasing the loyalty of people who are already users, and increasing the amount they buy, may be a better prospect than bringing over non-users.

2. It therefore seems to be true that in many situations advertising largely works by exploiting and reinforcing the already favourable attitudes of people who may be 'users' in at least a broad sense. However, in other situations it obviously has an important role in extending trial.

3. Attitudes influence purchasing, but purchasing influences attitudes as well. Using research to establish the precise links between the two may therefore be difficult.

4. Consumers' decisions cannot be fitted to a model of rational choice, at least not without extensive modification of such a model. The 'rational argument' model of advertising is therefore generally inappropriate.

5. Attention and perception are highly selective. Consumers bring preconceptions to advertisements and may misperceive or misunderstand them.

6. Involvement in an advertisement is a much more complex matter than such terms as 'liking' and 'belief' imply: it probably does not matter if an advertisement is not liked or not literally believed. However, interest in the sense of stimulation, and identification in the very broadest sense, are probably important.

7. Recall of the product, rather than the advertisement or slogan, is what counts.

8. Above all, the consumer is not passive, helpless advertising fodder. There is a strong drive for consistency and stability in the consumer's structures of needs, attitudes and behaviour. This may lead to a tug-of-war between the perception of an advertisement and attitudes, and a tug-of-war between attitudes and purchasing behaviour.

To summarize these conclusions in visual form, a diagram has been included near the end of the paper which shows 'how advertising may work'.

Consumer Attitudes

We might take as our starting point a simple model of advertising consisting just of two arrows joining the three boxes – an arrow from 'advertising' to 'attitudes', showing that advertising changes or reinforces attitudes by investing the product with favourable associations, and an arrow from 'attitudes' to 'purchasing' showing that favourable attitudes lead to interest in the product being aroused when there is an opportunity to buy it or to a reinforcement of a purchasing habit.

However, it seems that it would also be correct to put in arrows going the other way. Purchasing may influence attitudes, partly as a straightforward reflection of product experience, but partly by the drive to reduce dissonance, which leads to favourable attitudes in justification to oneself of the decision. Equally, the impact of advertising on the consumer is very much affected by preconceived attitudes: both attention and perception are selective and this selectivity is affected by them.

It also appears legitimate to put in arrows linking advertising and purchasing directly. We have considered the possibility that advertising may partly work by suggestion, a process in which attitudes need not necessarily function as an intermediary. Also, there is evidence that the fact of having bought a particular product may in some circumstances heighten attention to

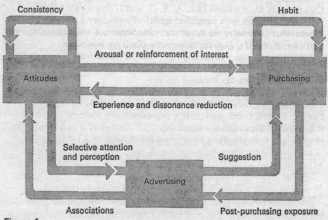

Figure 1

176

advertisements for that product, again as a part of the phenomenon of the drive to reduce dissonance.

Finally, it seems appropriate too to introduce two 'loops' in the system. We have considered a certain amount of evidence that there is a drive towards consistency among attitudes even when advertising stimuli and purchasing situations are absent, and we therefore put in a loop around 'attitudes'. Also, we have recognized that much purchasing is habitual and apparently unaffected by advertising or by attitude changes, at any rate below some sort of threshold level. This is represented by a loop around 'purchasing'.

The precise direction of the arrows and the labelling of arrows and boxes is perhaps less important than the general impression conveyed by the diagram, which is surely correct – that the advertising–attitudes–purchasing system is a complex system of interacting variables. The model itself is tentative, but this general conclusion seems unlikely to be overthrown.

References

BIRD, M., and EHRENBERG, A. S. C. (1966a), 'Intentions-to-buy and claimed brand usage', *Operational Research Quarterly*, vol. 17, pp. 27–46, and vol. 18, pp. 65–6.

BIRD, M., and EHRENBERG, A. S. C. (1966b), 'Non-awareness and non-usage', *Journal of Advertising Research*, vol. 6, pp. 4–8.

CHATFIELD, C., EHRENBERG, A. S. C., and GOODHARDT, G. J. (1966), 'Progress on a simplified model of stationary purchasing behaviour', *Journal of the Royal Statistical Society*, A, vol. 129, pp. 317–67

COLLEY, R. (1961), *Defining Advertising Goals for Measured Advertising Results*, Association of National Advertisers.

GOLBY, C. (1963), 'Towards a theory of persuasive communication' *Conference of Market Research Society*.

HASKINS, J. B. (1964), 'Factual recall as a measure of advertising effectiveness', *Journal of Advertising Research*, vol. 4, no. 1, pp. 2–8.

JOYCE, T. (1965), 'Model-building and advertising research', *Seminar of Market Research Society*.

MALONEY, J. C. (1962), 'Curiosity versus disbelief in advertising', *Journal of Advertising Research*, vol. 2, no. 2, pp. 2–8.

MALONEY, J. C. (1963), 'Is advertising believability really important?' *Journal of Marketing*, vol. 27, no. 5, pp. 1–9.

MARTINEAU, P. (1957), *Motivation in Advertising*, McGraw-Hill.

OGILVY, D. (1963), *Confessions of an Advertising Man*, Atheneum.

REEVES, R. (1961), *Reality in Advertising*, Knopf.

Consumer Attitudes

ROTHMAN, L. J., and TATE, B. (1964), 'Research techniques for minority or maniple marketing', *Conference of Market Research Society*.

SIMON, H. A. (1957), *Models of Man*, Chapman & Hall.

SMULIAN, P. (1964), *How to Know Your Product as the Consumer Sees It*, Maps Ltd.

STARCH, D. (1925), *Principles of Advertising*, Shaw.

THORNDIKE, E. L. (1940), *Human Nature and the Social Order*, Macmillan.

TREASURE, J. A. P., and JOYCE, T. (1967), 'As others see us', Institute of Practitioners in Advertising, occasional paper.

A general review of many of the findings of social psychology referred to in this paper will be found in Krech, D., Crutchfield, R. S., and Ballachey, E. L. (1962), *Individual in Society*, McGraw-Hill.

Part Three Durable Goods

The four papers in this section reflect something of the wide variety of techniques and approaches which have been adopted in investigations of the demand for, and ownership of, consumer durable goods. The scene is set in the first paper which reviews much of the literature contributing to this variety of approaches.

The next paper is the most empirical in this section. It is a statement of some basic ways of looking at the ownership of durable goods with a view to predicting future growth. The orientation is that of market research and of the need to consider alternative approaches in making forecasts. One of these emphasizes that the accumulation of durable goods involves consumers in ordering alternatives over time and in making choices, a theme which is to be found throughout much of the literature.

The paper by Stone and the late D. A. Rowe is a classic. It represents the highest levels of achievement which have been reached by the modification of the traditional economic theory of consumer behaviour so as to accommodate consumer durable goods. Over the years, Stone and Rowe have produced many papers on consumer behaviour, often in association with others, and especially with J. A. C. Brown. Theirs have been the outstanding contributions from the European side of the Atlantic and beyond. Indeed it is likely that a majority of the important contributors to empirical demand analysis throughout the world have at one time or another worked with Stone in Cambridge.

The final paper in this section, by Katona, develops another approach. This paper is concerned not only with durable goods but also with the role that attitudes and expectations play in consumers' more general expenditure patterns. Katona's work at the Survey Research Center at the University of Michigan is pioneering. Although not yet integrated into the main stream of economic thought, it is far too important to be ignored.

11 F. G. Pyatt

The Analysis of Demand

From F. G. Pyatt, *Priority Patterns and the Demand for Household Durable Goods*, Cambridge University Press, 1964, pp. 1–10.

Much attention has been given in recent years by econometricians to the problems of explaining and predicting consumers' demands for household durable goods. This interest has been motivated by two factors. Firstly, the growing importance of durable goods in advanced economies, both as an item of expenditure and in industrial production, has created a need for knowledge of the likely developments of this growth and its determinants. Secondly, the problems facing the empirical analyst in this field are, to a large extent, unsolved, and certainly there is no common body of theory to which the various studies undertaken to date may be related.

This latter point contrasts with the situation pertaining to analyses of the demand for non-durable goods. Here there is a well established body of theory upon which quantitative analysts may draw in formulating the relationships they investigate. Its most convenient expression has, perhaps, been given by Hicks (1950). The theory assumes that the extent to which a consumer derives satisfaction from consumption can be expressed as a general function of his rates of consumption of particular commodities, known as a utility function. According to the theory, the consumer endeavours to maximize his utility subject to the restraint set by his income on total expenditure. Admittedly, this theory is of limited usefulness in demand studies both on account of its static nature and because of its generality. Econometricians would undoubtedly be better served by a more restrictive theory. Even so, the classical value theory, and in particular Slutsky's equation, does provide a basis for studies of the demand for consumption goods.[1] Full use of this theoreti-

1. Slutsky's equation first appeared in his 1915 article. It is derived and

181

cal foundation has been made by Brown (1962) and Stone and Croft-Murray (1959).[2]

The main objections to transferring the conclusions of the classical value theory[3] to analyses of the demand for durable goods stem from the essential differences between perishable and durable commodities. Domestic durable goods are generally indivisible and, by definition, have a longer life than the basic period of account. Perishable goods are generally more nearly perfectly divisible, and their lives are less than the basic accounting period. Consequently saving up and stock-holding are important elements in the behaviour of households in relation to the accumulation of durable goods. This is not so for perishable goods, and the classical theory does not embrace them.

Rather than reject the classical theory because of these limitations, several authors interested in the empirical analysis of the demand for domestic durable goods have considered a reformulation of the classical theory in which stock-holding, rather than consumption, is the primary activity of households.

---

discussed in Hicks (1950, pp. 307–9). Broadly, it shows how the effect of an increase in the price of a particular product can be split into a substitution effect for one product versus others for a given standard of living, and an income effect due to the change in standard of living as a result of the price change.

2. Stone (1954) has shown that the most general linear system which preserves adding-up, homogeneity, i.e. no money illusion, and symmetry of substitution effects is given, in matrix notation, by

$e = b\mu + Bp,$

where e is a vector of expenditure on n commodities, μ is income and p is a vector of prices; b is a vector of parameters and B is a square matrix of parameters, the elements of which are subject to $n(n - 1)$ restraints. Use of this system in analysing time series of market data is justified by Stone and Croft-Murray (1959) in the following terms: 'It may be argued that a symmetric substitution matrix is not something that should be looked for in market equations. In theory this may be admitted, but in practice such a restriction of the parameters provides, in the present state of knowledge, a plausible way of simplifying demand equations to the point where there is some hope of reaching definite empirical results.'

3. Conclusions of this theory are, firstly, that the demand for each commodity is a homogeneous function of degree zero of income and the prices of all commodities, and secondly, that the substitution effects referred to in footnote 1 above are negative and symmetric as between pairs of commodities.

The first steps in this direction were made by Theil (1951) who has reconstructed the arguments of the classical demand theory under the assumption that the individual consumer's utility function depends both on consumption during a period and stocks held at the end of it. Farrell (1954) takes this argument a stage further by stating that the main characteristic of a consumer durable is that utility is derived from owning it rather than from consuming it. This is the philosophy underlying an interesting paper by Cramer (1957) in which he reformulates the classical theory starting from an indifference map defined over stocks of available commodities and which is independent of their rates of consumption. In doing this the author found it necessary to make certain restrictive assumptions in addition to those inevitably inherited from the classical analysis, including the assumption that stocks depreciate linearly over time. Cramer failed to establish short-term price elasticities of demand and expresses serious misgivings as to the validity of the assumption implied in his analysis that a consumer will make an instantaneous shift from one preferred set of stocks to another in response to a discrete change in prices.

Such a shift does not only imply instantaneous purchases, it also involves simultaneously the sale of some of the present stocks. But the price at which most commodities, once they have been acquired, can be sold by the consumer is usually far less than the purchase price of the same (Cramer, 1957, p. 85).

Cramer's analysis was successful, however, in obtaining some interesting results which depend only on the concept of stable positions. Firstly, he showed that his analysis implied that the stock of a particular commodity held is a function of prices and net worth, or wealth. Secondly, provided only stable positions are considered, savings should depend on the ratio of income to wealth. If the philosophy underlying these conclusions can be accepted then they are obviously most useful to demand analysts working in the field of consumer durable goods.[4]

Unfortunately the usefulness of Cramer's results is limited not only by the assumptions upon which they are based discussed

4. Cramer has conducted two empirical enquiries based on the conclusions of this analysis which are discussed below.

above; their usefulness is also restricted by the fact that they make no allowance for changes in the quality of existing durable goods and the innovation of new ones.

The implications of changes, typically improvements, in the quality of existing durable goods, and the innovation of new ones, have not been ignored by economic theorists. Duesenberry (1949) has noted that the innovation of new goods, and particularly of durable goods, may be a factor in explaining the stability of the savings ratio in the United States since 1909, whilst expressing doubts as to the importance of this factor in the earlier period, 1879–1909. Friedman (1957) has put forward an explanation of this phenomenon in terms of his permanent income hypothesis. He argues that the marginal propensity to save out of 'windfall' receipts is greater than that for permanent income. Thus a once-and-for-all increase in income, which is initially thought of as a windfall by consumers, results in a continuous trend in the propensity to save from an initially increased, to the original, level. Expenditure on durable goods plays an important part in this process, since Friedman includes such expenditure as a part of saving.

Friedman's hypothesis has proved to be a useful guide to the definition of the income variable which should enter into empirical analyses of the demand for durable goods.[5] But whilst there is a growing volume of evidence to support it, the Friedman hypothesis cannot yet be regarded as proven.[6] Even if it were, it is by no means a complete theory on which to base an analysis of the demand for a durable good.

In the absence of any well-established theory as to the nature and role of the various factors influencing the levels of demand for, and ownership of, domestic durable goods, empirical analysts have tended to proceed on an *ad hoc* basis, with each individual coming to his own conclusions as to which are the

5. For example, Burstein (1960) has found that the effect of changes in 'expected' income on changes in the consumption of refrigerator services is more like that of the effect between the absolute values of these variables than is the case if disposable income is used instead.

6. A recent test of one aspect of the permanent income hypothesis has been made by Bodkin (1960) whose results are opposite to those anticipated. They are given along with comments by Duesenberry and Friedman and a rejoinder by Bodkin in Friend and Jones (1960, vol. 2).

important factors and how they operate. Starting from common sense, conditioned by the classical value theory discussed above, this process has led to the formation of a general consensus of opinion in these matters without having yet reached the point where any particular author is conscious of his non-conformity in departing from it.

Two important factors in this development have been the limitations imposed on quantitative research by the available data and the statistical techniques for analysing it. As a preliminary to sketching out this development in terms of the principal contributions to it, it will be useful to consider first of all the essential nature of the phenomenon that is to be explained and predicted.

Domestic durable goods may be divided into two groups; those which are sufficiently cheap for anyone who wants to own them to do so, and those for which this is not the case.[7] At present the former group includes such items as cooking utensils, crockery, light bulbs, etc. The problem facing the consumer in purchasing these items is to decide what quality of item to buy and, therefore, how much to pay. The typical consumer is not exercised by doubts as to whether or not she can afford to buy these items at all. The market demand for such goods is, by definition, a replacement demand. This is not the case for items in the second group. For these items the process of innovation is not complete and consequently ownership of them has not yet reached its physical saturation level. Market demand for these commodities has, therefore, two components; a replacement demand from that part of the population which already owns them and an original demand from the remaining proportion of the population which does not own them as yet. Quite obviously, in a society in which standards of living are continuously rising, there is a tendency for all durable goods to start in the latter category and to move over into the former. When a durable good is first introduced, all demand for it is original demand. When it has been established for a long time all demand is replacement demand. The problems which will concern us here are those of explaining and forecasting original demands.

7. In practice this distinction would be extremely difficult to make in numerous instances.

Durable Goods

As we have already indicated, the existence of original demands for durable goods is inextricably involved in the process of their innovation, or more specifically, the process whereby the proportion of the population owning them tends from zero to its physical saturation level. In this context the notion of a physical saturation level requires some explanation. Everyone may own an adequate number of cups and saucers without their being of the Crown Derby design. Similarly, if and when everyone who wants to has the use of a motor car, not all the cars on the road will be Rolls Royces, and several people may have two motor cars. In general, the existence of a physical saturation level on the ownership of a particular durable good does not prejudice the possibility that the value of the stocks of that good held by households may be an increasing function of their standard of living. Expenditure on domestic cooking appliances has continued to increase despite the fact that most families have always possessed some such appliance.

Of equal importance to the distinction between the number of households owning a particular durable and the value of the stocks of the durable held by them, is the distinction between the monetary and physical saturation levels of ownership. The physical saturation level of ownership of a durable is the number of consumption units, or households, which would like to own that durable. The monetary saturation level is the number of households that would eventually own the durable if the monetary parameters of households' environments were to remain constant. Thus the monetary saturation level of ownership for a particular durable good may equal, but cannot exceed, the physical saturation level. For the initial stage, and a large portion of the subsequent stages of innovation of a major consumer durable, the monetary saturation level will be less than the physical saturation level.

The idea that there exists a monetary saturation level to which ownership will tend in a society with a stable economic environment has no counterpart in the classical demand theory. In that theory, purchases are uniquely determined by total expenditure and prices. Its introduction into the analysis of the demand for durable goods constitutes an assumption. It is, however, an assumption that has often found sympathy with workers in this field, particularly when expressed in the more general form that ownership of durable goods follows some increasing trend over time which is quite independent of monetary factors.

This trend may be described as a change in tastes, but it is probably more useful to give it the specific description of a learning process. When new commodities are first innovated there are, implicitly, only a few households which have experience of their use or consumption. Contact with such households informs other households of the qualities of the new commodity. Provided that some of these contacts are translated into purchases, an endemic growth process takes place until all households are fully aware of the new commodity and the number of households owning or using it is equal to the monetary saturation level of the commodity.

It was this aspect of the growth of ownership of durable goods which was considered by early workers in the field. They were obviously impressed by the similarities between the type of learning process described above and the process by which infectious diseases spread through closed populations. Biometricians had found that this latter type of process could be well described by a logistic growth curve. This curve is characterized by the differential equation

$$\frac{dy}{dt} = g(t)y\left(1 - \frac{y}{k}\right) \qquad\qquad 1$$

where y is the number of infected members of the population and k is the total number of members of the population who are not immune to the disease, i.e. the saturation level of diseased members; $g(t)$ is some arbitrary, non-negative, function of time. The general solution of equation 1 is

$$y = \frac{k}{1 + e^{-G(t)}} \qquad\qquad 2$$

where $G(t) = g(t)\,dt$.

Provided that $g(t)$ is non-negative, the function 2 has a sigmoid shape with an inflection point at $y = \frac{1}{2}k$ in the case $g(t) = $ constant.

In a study of the demand for bicycles in the Netherlands, Derksen and Rombouts (1937) described the logistic curve as 'the well-known form of a saturation curve' and fitted it (with $k = 1$ and $g(t) =$ constant) to time series data of the proportion of the Dutch population owning bicycles. In each of the following two years studies of the demand for automobiles in the United States appeared in the literature in which this same growth curve was used. The 1938 study, by de Wolff (1938), fits the logistic curve in its differential equation form to date on first purchases of passenger cars. The study by Roos and von Szeliski (1939) is essentially similar.

More recently, a study by Dernburg (1957) of the level of television ownership in various American cities in 1950, has made use of the logistic growth curve. His work is more sophisticated than that of the earlier workers, however, especially in its treatment of the function $G(t)$ entering in equation 2. In this study the arbitrary time function $G(t)$ is replaced by a linear function of the median income in an area (and its square), the length of time an area has been exposed to TV coverage, and a measure of the dispersion of incomes in the area, plus several variables measuring demographic and sociological characteristics.

An alternative approach is adopted by Bain (1961) in a study of the growth of television ownership in the United Kingdom. In this analysis the function $G(t)$ is affected only by seasonal factors in a given reception area but may differ between reception areas. Monetary and other factors are conceived of as influencing the saturation level, k.[8] Thus a monetary saturation level explicitly enters Bain's analysis, which is determined by the state of television reception and the median income in an area, and the prevailing hire purchase conditions.

Except in so far as the hire purchase variable used by Bain is a measure of the minimum proportion of the real price of a television set which must be paid under the prevailing restrictions, prices, and especially the price of a television set, do not enter into his model. The reason given by Bain for this omission is not that he considers prices to be unimportant. It is that, historically,

8. Since the saturation level in Bain's analysis is not constant, the type of growth curve he postulates is not strictly of the logistic form. Its characteristic equation is, however, equivalent to the form given above if k is written as a function of the exogenous variables income, hire purchase restrictions and the number of television signals transmitted.

prices have been so closely correlated with the level of ownership that a meaningful estimate of their importance was impossible to obtain.

The marked downward trend in the price of television sets since 1951 is not as apparent in a time series of the average price paid by households for television sets as it is in the constant quality price index which Bain considers. This is because there has been an improvement in the quality of television sets over this period.

Improvements over time in the average quality of a durable good may be generated either on the side of demand or on the supply side. Since there is a natural tendency for consumers' incomes to increase over time, it is only necessary to establish a positive relationship between income and quality purchased, as measured by price paid, to see how an improvement in the average quality of durables purchased may be generated over time by factors on the side of demand.

Such a relationship has been found in the first of two analyses by Cramer (1958 and 1962) designed to test the conclusions of his theoretical paper (Cramer, 1957), discussed above. In the first of these, which is based on the results of two sample surveys conducted by the Dutch Central Statistical Office, Cramer makes the following comments on the relationship between prices and income:

Some of the household appliances – refrigerators, washing machines, water-heaters – were comparatively recent innovations at the time. Ownership is restricted to the highest income groups and even there it occurs only rarely; unit prices show no systematic variation. For the other major durables, where ownership is well established in all income groups, we can go a little further. . . . No saturation is shown by unit prices. They go on steadily (if only slightly) increasing even among the higher income groups and are best described by the linear Engel curve used earlier (Cramer, 1958, p. 91).

These conclusions are illustrated for vacuum cleaners. In the illustration, as in the Engel curves referred to in the quotation above, unit prices are shown as a linear function of the value of households' total inventories of goods, and not of income. Free translation between inventory values and income is, however,

189

legitimate in this context since Cramer finds, from the same data, that the elasticity between these two variables is close to unity.

The observed values of income and inventory values on which Cramer's analysis is based are not only roughly proportional on average but also highly correlated. This is because, for both surveys, the published tabulations are of average values of these variables for a small number of income groups. Thus it is not possible to establish from them whether income or wealth, as measured by the total value of household inventories of goods, is the primary determinant of ownership. All that can be established is that sensible, and similar results are obtained whichever variable is used.

In the second analysis (Cramer, 1962), an attempt is made to determine which of the two variables income and net worth (wealth) is the more important determinant of ownership of durable goods. The analysis is based on the information collected in the 1953 Oxford Savings Survey and refers to the ownership of four major domestic durable goods – motor cars, refrigerators, washing machines and television sets. The total sample of roughly 1100 households is disaggregated separately for each durable good according to those socio-demographic characteristics which are revealed as significant determinants of ownership by a contingency table test of significance. The next, and most important, part of the analysis is to fit a bivariate lognormal distribution function defined over the income/net worth plane to the observed values of a dummy variable which is unity if a household owns the durable in question and zero if it does not. Such a plane is fitted for each of the sub-groups of the sample derived from the previous contingency table analysis.

The use of a bivariate distribution function distinguishes Cramer's analysis from the more conventional methods of profit analysis of the response to a (single) stimulus which is an (unknown) function of more than one variable.[9] In this respect it is more in keeping with recent developments in biometry.[10]

9. A detailed description of the conventional methods is given in Chapter 7 of Finney (1957). The use of a single stimulus defined as a function of income and net worth is considered by Cramer but rejected because such a function must be specified in advance of the empirical analysis.

10. The recent developments involving the use of bivariate distributions

The bivariate distribution function fitted by Cramer refers to the distribution over households of critical values of income and net worth. If y denotes income and w denotes net worth, then a household will own a particular durable good if both of the conditions

$$y > y_o \text{ and } w > w_o$$

are fulfilled, where y_o and w_o are the critical values of income and net worth respectively for the household.

The results of Cramer's analysis are disappointing. They do not permit him to say which of the two variables income and net worth is the more important determinant of ownership. Indeed, he finds that the aggregate income and net worth elasticities of ownership for the four durables he considers are very similar.[11] This rather negative conclusion may be partly due to the fact that the problems of choice facing a household in deciding which durable good to purchase next are ignored.[12] By making separate analyses for each durable good Cramer automatically assumes that the distributions of tolerance points (y_o, w_o) for different durable goods are independent. In fact, if households which own neither a washing machine nor a refrigerator intend to purchase the former first, then their tolerance points for washing machines will be nearer, in some sense, to their present income/net worth situations than is the case for their tolerance points for refrigerators. In Cramer's analysis this need not be the case.

The criticism of Cramer's analysis, that it ignores the problems of choice facing a household in accumulating durable goods, could equally well be made of the other empirical studies discussed above. The classical demand theory is essentially a theory about choosing. In deciding which durable good to purchase next, a household has to make a choice which is virtually irrevocable until such times as the durable dies. Common sense suggests

---

are due to Plackett and Hewlett. Their work is discussed by Finney (1957, pp. 215–28).

11. See Cramer (1962, Table 26).

12. We do not mean to suggest by these remarks that had a different model been used and questions of choice considered that a different result would necessarily have been obtained.

that the act of choice amongst durable goods is, therefore, the subject of more serious deliberations than the allocation of expenditure over consumption goods. This contention is supported by the measure of success achieved in field surveys of consumers' intentions to purchase durable goods.

Klein and Lansing (1955) analyse data collected in 1952 and 1953 for roughly 700 'spending units' which constituted part of the reinterview sub-sample of the 1953 Survey of Consumer Finances. The object of this exercise was to ascertain:

What (linear) combination of variables best discriminates between buyers and nonbuyers of consumer durables? (Klein and Lansing, 1955, p. 109.)

Two main conclusions are reached by the authors. Firstly, that: 'The dominant variables in the relation are age, marital status, and purchase expectations' (p. 119), and secondly:

All three of the broad types of variables which we considered – financial, demographic, and attitudinal – proved to be important. In our data, thus, there is support for the basic proposition that three classes of variables all should be investigated in analysing consumers' purchases of durables (p. 129).

In view of the important role played by buying plans, 'purchase expectations', in discriminating between buyers and non-buyers of durable goods, it is a pity that Klein and Lansing did not extend their analysis to the estimation of functions to discriminate between buyers and non-buyers of particular durable goods. Such an analysis is at present being undertaken by the National Bureau of Economic Research. Their first report on it (see Juster, 1959) gives detailed tabulations of the expectations and planned purchases of the members of the Consumers Union panel for each year from 1946 to 1958. It also gives information on their actual economic circumstances and realized purchases of durable goods. Very little analysis of the relationships between these two types of data is given and is reserved for a later volume.

A direct consequence of trying to build a model of the demands for durable goods which takes into account the problems of choice confronting a household is that it stresses the need for a

13. The durable goods considered, collectively, are automobiles, furniture, refrigerators, radios, television sets and other household appliances.

model which yields consistent estimates of the demands for individual durable goods. One model which can easily be generalized to meet this need is that developed in a series of papers over recent years by Stone and Rowe (1957, 1958, 1960; and Stone, 1960).

In the Stone and Rowe model, purchases of a durable good in any given year are divided into two parts; consumption, or use of the year, and net additions to stocks during the year. Consumption is simply related to opening stocks plus an element due to the depreciation during the year of the purchases of that year. Net additions to stocks are assumed to be some function of (i.e. proportional to, in the simplest case) the difference between desired and actual stocks. In the simplest case, with stocks depreciating at a constant rate over time, this model implies that both consumption and purchases are proportional to certain weighted averages of actual and desired, equilibrium, stocks. This model may be generalized in a variety of ways to allow, for example, for the influence of hire-purchase restrictions on the rate of stock adjustment and for alternative assumptions to be made about the life distribution of durable goods. These generalizations are discussed by Stone (1960).

This survey of empirical studies of the demands for domestic durable goods is by no means exhaustive either of the problems treated in the literature or of the techniques used for analysing them. The studies which have been discussed were chosen because they represent interesting approaches to the understanding of the influence of the economic parameters of the demand for, and ownership of, domestic durable goods. Many of the studies which are excluded from our survey are primarily concerned either with the use of statistical techniques, or with explanation, in the correlation sense, of the available data. These are important aspects of the analysis of the demand for durable goods, but not ones which will concern us greatly here.

References

BAIN, A. D. (1961), 'The growth of television ownership in the United Kingdom', *Cowles Foundation Discussion Paper*, no. 116.

BODKIN, R. (1960), 'Windfall income and consumption', in I. Friend and R. Jones (eds.), *Proceedings of the Conference on Consumption and Saving*, vol. 2, p. 175, University of Pennsylvania.

193

Durable Goods

BROWN, J. A. C. (1962), *The Demand for Dairy Products in Six European Countries*, O.E.C.D.

BURSTEIN, M. L. (1960), 'The demand for household refrigeration in the United States', in A. C. Harberger (ed.), *The Demand for Durable Goods*, Chicago University Press.

CRAMER, J. S. (1957), 'A dynamic approach to the theory of consumer demand', *Review Economic Studies*, vol. 24, p. 73.

CRAMER, J. S. (1958), 'Ownership elasticities of durable consumer goods', *Review Economic Studies*, vol. 25, p. 87.

CRAMER, J. S. (1962), *The Ownership of Major Consumer Durables*, Department of Applied Economics Monograph, no. 7, Cambridge University Press.

DERKSEN, J. B. D., and ROMBOUTS, A. (1937), 'The demand for bicycles in the Netherlands', *Econometrica*, vol. 5, p. 295.

DERNBURG, T. F. (1957), 'Consumer response to innovation: television', *Cowles Foundation Discussion Paper*, no. 121.

DE WOLFF, P. (1938), 'The demand for passenger cars in the United States', *Econometrica*, vol. 6, p. 113.

DUESENBERRY, J. S. (1949), *Income, Saving and the Theory of Consumer Behaviour*. Harvard University Press.

FARRELL, M. J. (1954), 'The demand for motor cars in the United States', *Journal of the Royal Statistical Society*, *A*, vol. 117, p. 171.

FINNEY, D. J. (1957), *Profit Analysis*, 2nd ed., Cambridge University Press.

FRIEDMAN, M. (1957), *A Theory of the Consumption Function*, Princeton University Press.

FRIEND, I., and JONES, R. (eds.), (1960), *Proceedings of the Conference on Consumption and Saving*, vols. 1 and 2, Pennsylvania University Press.

HICKS, J. R. (1950), *Value and Capital*, 2nd edition, Clarendon Press.

JUSTER, T. F. (1959), Consumer expectations, plans and purchases: a progress report', *National Bureau of Economic Research Occasional Paper*, no. 70, New York.

KLEIN, L. R., and LANSING, J. B. (1955), 'Decisions to purchase consumer durable goods', *Journal of Marketing*, vol. 20, no. 2, p. 109.

ROOS, C. F., and VON SZELISKI, V. (1939), 'Factors governing changes in domestic automobile demand', in *The Dynamics of Automobile Demand*, p. 21, General Motors.

SLUTSKY, E. E. (1915), 'Sulla teoria del bilancio del consummatore', *G. Economisti*, vol. 51, pp. 1–26; reprinted in an English translation by Ragusa, O. (1952), as 'On the theory of the budget of the consumer', in *Readings in Price Theory*, Irwin.

STONE, J. R. N. (1954), 'Linear expenditure systems and demand analysis: an application to the pattern of British demand', *Economic Journal*, vol. 65, no. 255, pp. 511–27.

STONE, J. R. N. (1960), 'A dynamic model of demand', *Przeglad Statystyczny*, vol. 7, no. 3; reprinted as no. 167 of *University of Cambridge Department of Applied Economics Reprint Series*, 1961.

STONE, J. R. N., and CROFT-MURRAY, G. (1959), *Social Accounting and Economic Models*, Bowes and Bowes.

STONE, J. R. N., and ROWE, D. A. (1957), 'The market demand for durable goods', *Econometrica*, vol. 25, no. 3, p. 423.

STONE, J. R. N., and ROWE, D. A. (1958), 'Dynamic demand functions: some econometric results', *Economic Journal*, vol. 68, no. 269, p. 256

STONE, J. R. N., and ROWE, D. A. (1960), 'The durability of consumers' durable goods', *Econometrica*, vol. 28, no. 2, p. 407.

THEIL, H. (1951), *De invloed van de Voorroden op het Consumentengedreg*, Poortpers, Amsterdam.

12 D. A. Brown, S. F. Buck and F. G. Pyatt

The Growth of Ownership

D. A. Brown, S. F. Buck and F. G. Pyatt, 'Improving the sales forecast for consumer durables', *Journal of Marketing Research*, vol. 2, 1965, pp. 229–34.

Introduction

It is customary for forecasters to employ a number of separate estimates of the forecasts they attempt. The purpose of this paper is to indicate two such methods which, although based on similar material, are to a considerable extent independent. The first method is relatively simple, and depends on the availability of specified data. The second is more complex and theoretical, and is introduced as a new approach promising considerable benefit. The methods have been developed to utilize data which are being accumulated from a large continuous sample survey (AGB Research Ltd).

The basic information

Both approaches require detailed information on consumer purchasing behaviour. Moreover, both involve the use of past purchasing behaviour to predict the future: they do not involve questions about purchasing intentions. The assumption underlying the first method is that socioeconomic breakdowns of purchasing information enhance the accuracy of a sales forecast. The smaller sample sizes in the market segments formed by the breakdown are offset by the homogeneity of the information within each segment. The same advantages are obtainable by the second method where the breakdown is carried out in terms of the collection of durable goods owned by different household groups.

Data on consumer purchases are better estimates of long- and short-term trends than are post-factory deliveries, since it is usually impossible to adjust the latter for any buildup of stocks in wholesalers and retailers. A dramatic illustration of this has been given (Saltmarsh, 1963), and the following tabulation is taken from that experience, relating to refrigerators:

Year	Deliveries	Consumer buying
1958	100	100
1959	215	122
1960	257	198
1961	204	235
1962	192	220

Source: Saltmarsh (1963).

From this it is clear that manufacturers' expectations, presumably based on dispatch data, far exceeded consumer buying in 1959 and that this continued into 1960. It was misleading in this case to infer consumer purchases from information about deliveries.

The first method

The first approach involves the use of consumer purchases in terms of brands, sizes, types, subsections, total market, and this must be capable of analysis by a wide range of breakdowns such as region, social class and age of buyer.

It is central to our argument that the detail indicated must be available if forecasting is to be accurate. In sophisticated markets there is usually a considerable degree of fragmentation in order to meet a range of consumer requirements, and a single aggregated result for a total market is useful only to a limited degree. For example, in the washing machine market, data about the total market are of interest, but what is *vital* is information about single-tub *v.* twin-tub *v.* automatic machines. Substantially different trends may be at work within these sectors and this is critical to a forecast; a single aggregated figure will mask these movements.

The importance of brand share as a predictor is to be stressed. Whereas a guarantee card system may reveal much useful marketing information, and even indicate share of *total* market but not of a particular subsection, it can reveal nothing about competitive trends of brand share – a factor of great importance, as the following indicates:

197

Table 1 Nature of Recent Acquisitions

| | Pene-tration | Acquisitions | | | |
		Initial	Replace-ment	Addi-tional	Total
Cookers	96%	28%	70%	2%	100%
Vacuum cleaners	76	42	53	5	100
Washing machines	49	61	37	2	100
Refrigerators	35	89	10	1	100

Source: AGB Research Ltd.

In most industries the key market indicator is not volume, but market share. A declining volume with an increasing market share is normally a more healthy sign than an increasing volume and a declining market share. In the latter case, the business is usually in for some horrible shocks at the next decline in the trade cycle (Catherwood, 1963).

The present approach may be subdivided into three broad sections:

1. The initial purchase market.
2. The replacement market.
3. The multiple-ownership market.

Durable goods markets are made of these three components in varying proportions. Because in the United Kingdom the multiple-ownership market is generally small in relation to total purchases, it will receive little attention.

The initial purchase market

The general basis of the approach is that by taking a broad overall trend and splitting it into components, the growth velocities of the individual components may be measured and thus we can obtain a more precise estimate of the total. A simple example will illustrate this approach.

In Figure 1, faced with only the historical information AA' it would be reasonable to predict A'B. However, had we known that these purchases consisted of purchases of two sections of the public, Classes I and II, and that their historical data was as shown in Figure 2, we should realize that Class I was rapidly approaching saturation, that Class II gave no signs of accelerating, and that grounds for assuming a continuation of a linear

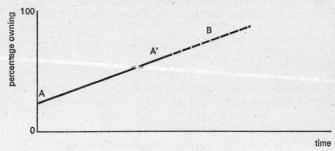

Figure 1 Prediction from the total penetration pattern

growth rate would be unjustified. This illustrates the approach – the search for the separate classes exhibiting different growth velocities so that we may more confidently construct our estimate of the total growth rate.

Examples. We will illustrate the approach by considering some data on four durables, each of which has yearly sales in Britain

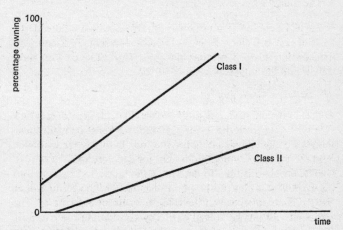

Figure 2 Penetration pattern in two demographic classes

of close to one million. These are cookers, vacuum cleaners, washing machines and refrigerators. The components describing the four markets are very different, as demonstrated in Table 1, which gives the total penetration and the initial replacement multiple-ownership nature of recent acquisitions (AGB Research Ltd).

The total cooker market appears to be a saturated one, with a penetration of 96 per cent. Its greatest component is thus the replacement market although the initial purchase market, which is a reflection of new homes and households, is a significant portion of the total. At the other extreme the refrigerator penetration is only 35 per cent, and recent data indicate that some 90 per cent of sales are initial purchases. For all four durables the multiple-ownership market is very small.

We will now consider the penetration figures more closely. Figure 3 contains the penetration patterns for each good from 1956 to mid-1963. The curves have been fitted to results of surveys during this period (AGB Research Ltd, and Report, 1961). Superimposed on the figure is a plot of a sigmoid curve whose equation is:

$$P = \frac{At^n}{1 + t^n}, \qquad\qquad 1$$

where P is the penetration and t the year, A and n being constants. The curve for a particular durable can be considered as a portion of the sigmoid curve which represents the complete penetration history of that durable. Thus, the cooker curve represents the upper asymptote of the cooker sigmoid, and the curve for vacuum cleaners is also approaching its upper boundary. The washing machine curve appears to correspond with the central portion of its sigmoid, while the refrigerator curve is just emerging from the lower asymptote. It must be made clear, however, that the sigmoids for the four durables are dissimilar and the values of A and n different for each durable.

The problem is then to determine the individual sigmoid and, in particular, to locate the point of inflection, the turning point on the curve, after which the rate of penetration decreases. This problem will not be solved easily by considering the curve for the total penetration of a durable. Rather it should be remembered that the total sigmoid is composed of a number of different sigmoids each relating to a segment of the market for that durable, and that these individual segments are at different stages in their sigmoid pattern.

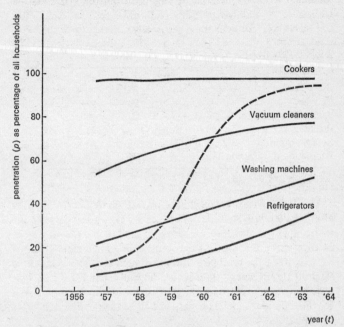

Figure 3 Penetration pattern in four durables

Knowledge of the individual time series for the important segments of the market will then give us a better forecasting estimate than the total trend. One significant way of segmenting the market is by social class, and Table 2 gives the penetration in each of the four social classes.[1]

Figure 3 shows that the penetration for cookers and vacuum

1. The four social classes can be described briefly as follows:
   AB Professional, managerial, businessmen, etc.
   C1 Supervisory and junior management, office workers
   C2 Skilled manual workers
   DE Laborers, pensioners, etc.

cleaners is close to saturation. Individual time series for the lower social classes would indicate whether the rate of vacuum cleaner sales was still increasing in these segments, or whether saturation was being reached at this apparent level. In this context it would be fruitful to separate from the DE class the economically inactive portions, e.g. old age pensioners, unemployed, and consider these separately.

Table 2 Penetration in the Four Social Classes

	Total	AB	C1	C2	DE
Cookers	96%	96%	98%	97%	93%
Vacuum cleaners	76	96	89	80	55
Washing machines	49	68	59	55	31
Refrigerators	35	77	51	33	15
Population distribution	100	8	24	36	32

Source: AGB Research Ltd.

The data for washing machines, in contrast to that for refrigerators, show relatively little differences in penetration between the three upper social classes. Is there a possibility that the saturation penetration in the upper classes is close to 70 per cent? If this is the case, then the total penetration curve is at a later stage in its sigmoid development than would appear from Figure 3. This possibility can be examined more closely with time series analysis for the individual social classes, as well as for the different types of appliance.

Large differences can be observed in the refrigerator penetration between classes. The market is capable of great expansion, as the total penetration figure of 35 per cent suggests, but 80 per cent of the expansion must take place in the lower social classes. Continuous data for more detailed breakdowns by type of durable within the lower social classes will indicate whether this expansion is possible. One further illustration of the differences in the four markets is given by a regional breakdown of the penetration figures in Table 3.

The penetration of cookers and vacuum cleaners does not vary significantly from area to area, but the contrast for the other two products is very marked. These data would suggest that the preferences and priorities in the south are different from those in the north and Scotland, and that different rates of expansion may well be expected in these parts of the country. The application of these different expansion rates will lead to sounder estimates of market growth than those we would obtain from dependence on national data alone. Analyses of this type will become possible with the accumulation of data from a large continuous sample survey of households.

Table 3 Penetration by Region

	Total	England and Wales		Scotland
	Total	South	North	Scotland
Cookers	96%	97%	95%	97%
Vacuum cleaners	76	76	75	74
Washing machines	49	38	59	51
Refrigerators	35	49	26	22

Source: AGB Research Ltd.

The replacement component

Our examples have dealt with an initial purchase market. There is usually a replacement component, and it is therefore necessary to measure the importance of replacements to construct the replacement model and to identify the most powerful factors in it.

We may regard the existing durables in the hands of consumers as the living population of goods. We can measure its age distribution and its average age. We can also measure the age at which death takes place and therefore estimate life expectancy.

Consider a durable whose existing age distribution is given by

$$Q_t(\theta) = \text{number whose age is } \theta \text{ in year } t. \qquad 2$$

By noting the ages at which replacements were made we can calculate

$$d(\theta) = \text{death rate at age } \theta. \qquad 3$$

Then the expected total deaths, D, leading to replacements in year t are given by

$$E(D_t) = \sum_{\theta=1}^{\infty} Q_{t-1}(\theta - 1)\, d(\theta). \qquad 4$$

203

This approach assumes that the death rates applicable in year $t - 1$ remain constant for year t; for more long-term forecasts careful watch should be kept on the development of the death rates over time. Two powerful determinants of the replacement market are the total population of goods, which itself is dependent upon the pattern of past demand, and the life expectancy of this population. A simple example will indicate their influence.

Table 4 Estimated Replacements for Two Populations of Durables

Age θ	Death rates $d(\theta)$	$Q_{t-1}(\theta - 1)$	
		Population 1	Population 2
1	0·1	100	124
2	0·2	90	94
3	0·4	72	60
4	1·0	43	27
Total population in year $t - 1$		305	305
D_t = replacement in year t		100	82

Table 4 considers two different populations of goods both subject to the same death rates, $d(\theta)$, where these are chosen so that no goods will last more than four years. It is of interest to note that Population 1 represents a constant purchasing rate of 100 items over the past four years, while Population 2 represents a purchasing rate which has increased linearly from 64 to 124 items over the past four years. It can be seen that the expected replacements in the following year are 100 in the first case and 82 in the second.

The second method

It is widely recognized that there are a great many durable goods which British households do not own, but which one day they hope to possess. The problem facing these households is that they cannot now afford to buy all the durables that they would like to own. Consequently, households must choose some particular durable as their immediate target and work toward acquiring it. For example, new households may first buy a cooker, then most likely a vacuum cleaner, and then set their sights on the acquisition of either a washing machine or a refrigerator. Thus, the choices which a household makes manifest themselves in an ordering, over time, of the durable goods it accumulates. The analysis that we introduce here follows from an examination of these choices.

The first point to note is that a market research survey, in which households are asked which of a collection of durable goods they own, provides a rich source of information on the sequence of acquisition which these households have followed. As an example, suppose that only two durable goods are considered, washing machines and refrigerators. A survey of 1000 households might reveal the following ownership pattern:

Own neither	200
Own washing machine only	500
Own refrigerator only	100
Own both washing machine and refrigerator	200
	1000

Thus, 70 per cent of the sample owns a washing machine and 30 per cent owns a refrigerator. However, the figures tell us far more; in particular they tell us that when a household owns one of the two durables in question, the odds in favor of that durable being a washing machine are 5 to 1. In addition, there are 200 households, or 20 per cent of the sample, that have, as yet, to make the choice between buying a washing machine and a refrigerator. If tastes are constant, then 167 ($= 5/6 \times 200$) of these households will buy a washing machine next and 33 will buy a refrigerator next, i.e. the demand of the 200 will split between washing machines and refrigerators in the observed ratio of 5 to 1. The assumption of constant tastes represents a simple but reasonable hypothesis for this type of market. Furthermore, all of the 500 households that own only a washing machine will be in the market for refrigerators, and all of the 100 that own only a refrigerator will be in the market for washing machines. Thus, among the households that own one of the two durables, demand will again be split in the ratio of 5 to 1, but this time in favor of refrigerators.

205

Table 5 Markets for Washing Machines and Refrigerators

| | In the market for | | Total |
Present situation	Washing machines	Refrigerators	number of households
Own neither a washing machine nor refrigerator	167	33	200
Own washing machine only	—	500	500
Own refrigerator only	100	—	100
Own both washing machine and refrigerator	—	—	200
Total	267	533	1000

This analysis suggests that the markets for washing machines and refrigerators can be built up as in Table 5. Consequently, if households which own neither a washing machine nor a refrigerator are just as likely to make a purchase in the next twelve months as those which own one of these two durables, then sales of the two durables can be expected to be in the ratio of 267 to 533, i.e. 1 to 2. Alternatively, if households owning neither durable are three times as likely to make a purchase as those which own one of the two durables, than sales of the two durables can be expected to be equal, since $(167 \times 3) + 100 = 600 = (33 \times 3) + 500$.

This suggests that considerable insight into the durable accumulation process can be gained by breaking down the probability, $P(A)$, that a household will acquire a particular durable, A, in the next twelve months into two components, $P(a)$ and $P(b)$. $P(a)$ is the probability that A is the most preferred of the durables not owned, given the particular collection of durables owned, and that an acquisition is made. $P(b)$ is the probability that a particular collection of goods is owned and an acquisition is made. Then

$$P(A) = \sum P(a).P(b), \qquad 5$$

the summation extending over all possible collections of durables.

$P(a)$ is a statement about household preferences, given a particular choice situation. By combining such statements for all possible choice situations, a picture can be built up of the priorities placed by households on different durables – a priority pattern. Thus, in the illustration above, the priority pattern is given in Table 6.

Table 6 The Priority Pattern

		Probability that the durable purchased next is	
Washing machine	Refrigerator	Washing machine	Refrigerator
Not owned	Not owned	5/6	1/6
Owned	Not owned	0	1
Not owned	Owned	1	0

$P(b)$ can in turn be dichotomized such that

$$P(b) = \sum P(c).P(d),\qquad\qquad 6$$

where $P(c)$ is the probability that an acquisition is made, given that the particular collection of durables is owned, while $P(d)$ is the probability that a particular collection of durables is owned.

Several methods can be used to estimate $P(c)$. The simplest is to assume that the probability of a household making an acquisition, given the collection of durable goods that it owns, remains constant. Thus, if 95 per cent of the households that owned nothing twelve months ago had made a purchase in the last twelve months, then the probability that an acquisition is made, given that nothing is owned, can be estimated as 0.95; $P(d)$ is known directly from observation.

Thus we see that all the components of the probability that a particular durable is acquired can be observed directly from sample survey information, under appropriate assumptions. Should these assumptions prove to be invalid, the formulation retains its validity but more subtle techniques for estimating its parameters from the available data can and must be invoked. It remains true, however, that the information in a sample survey can be analyzed in depth to establish not only how, but why new acquisitions of durable goods will vary one against the other in future.

So far, we have considered only an elementary statement of the possibilities of analysis using the concept of a priority pattern. Various sophistications are discussed by Pyatt (1964), and two of them are mentioned here. First, note that the relative number of households owning particular collections of durables depends in part on the preferences of households, and in part on the rates at which they move through different stages of the accumulation process. If preferences are constant, this dichotomy reduces to dependence of numbers of durables owned on rates of accumulation, and dependence of the selection of durables owned on tastes. Various models describing the relationships between the numbers of durables owned and the rates at which households accumulate can be fitted to the data.

According to one such model, each household is subject to a stimulus to own durables, the response to this stimulus being a probability statement of the number of durables owned. As the stimulus changes, the probability statement changes. Consequently, households can be aggregated according to the distribution of the stimulus between them, and so the ownership levels of durable goods can be expressed as functions of the parameters of the aggregate stimulus distribution. Techniques for discovering the extent to which these parameters depend on such factors as income, wealth and prices are described by Pyatt (1964).

Second, the analysis can be modified quite easily to take account of changing preferences. This facility is particularly important since new durable goods may be easily accommodated within the analysis. Briefly, if tastes are changing, the preferences by households expressed in their recent purchases reflect the difference between the stocks of durables they own and the stocks that they would like to own according to their current tastes. Since the stocks they own and the adjustments they have made in, say, the last twelve months are observable in a survey, it follows that the stocks they would like to own can be deduced. Thus, future demand can be predicted on the assumption that next year's sales will represent a further stage in the adjustment to the new preference structure. In other words, households are assumed to keep moving from where they are toward a fixed target. This can be further relaxed to allow for a moving target if a time series of surveys is available for analysis.

An implication of the methods used to allow for changing preferences is that the priority pattern model is a generalization of that proposed by Stone and Rowe (1957). In it, the demands for durables are expressed as linear functions of the differences between current ownership levels and the ownership levels desired after the next purchase has been made. One way of looking at priority pattern analysis is to regard it as a means of estimating the parameters of these linear functions from survey data, and of generating estimates of what desired ownership levels will be after the next purchase. All but one of the ingredients of the model can be estimated from survey material. This one is the change in the average stimulus over a period, and to the extent that it depends on the pace at which the economy is developing – the growth in incomes, credit restrictions, and so on, it must elude a purely cross-sectional study. Consequently, survey analysis cannot take us far beyond the estimation of the relative demands for different durables. However, as suggested by the analogy between priority pattern techniques and those of Stone and Rowe (1957), the grafting of the two types of analysis – time series and cross-sectional – is thoroughly practicable, and leads to a fully articulated model of future demand for individual durable goods.

Two final points illustrate the power of the techniques. By disaggregating households by type or region, variations in demand according to the criterion of disaggregation can be analyzed both in terms of the different preferences and rates of accumulation they represent. In particular, households can be grouped by media exposure, and hence demand can be predicted by media exposure groupings. Finally, the analysis extends readily beyond the field of durable goods and might, therefore, prove to be a useful complement to market research techniques over a wider field.

References

AGB RESEARCH LTD (n.d.), Report on the results of their 50,000-home audit continuous survey into durable goods.

CATHERWOOD, H. F. R. (1963), *The Director*, Institute of Directors.

PYATT, F. G. (1964), *Priority Patterns and the Demand for Household Durable Goods*, Department of Applied Economics Monograph 10, Cambridge University Press.

Durable Goods

REPORT ON DOMESTIC ELECTRICAL APPLIANCES (1961), *Women and the National Market*, Odhams Press.

SALTMARSH, J. A. (1963), *Electrical and Radio Trading*, NTP Business Journals Ltd.

STONE, R., and ROWE, D. A. (1957), 'The market demand for durable goods', *Econometrica*, vol. 25, pp. 423–43 (see Reading 13 below).

13 Richard Stone and D. A. Rowe

A Dynamic Theory

Richard Stone and D. A. Rowe, 'The market demand for durable goods', *Econometrica*, vol. 25, 1957, pp. 423-43.

Introduction

In this paper there are presented two studies in market demand which have been undertaken since the appearance of *The Measurement of Consumers' Expenditure and Behaviour* (Stone *et al.*, 1954). These analyses relate to durable and semi-durable goods and it is not to be expected that the demand for such goods can be described in terms of a static theory. Accordingly in the second and third sections a simple dynamic theory of demand is developed for use in the subsequent analyses. This theory recognizes a distinction between the actual stocks held at the outset of a period and the equilibrium stocks in a given income and price situation, and involves, for each commodity of any durability, an investment function designed to narrow and, under stable conditions, eventually to close the gap between the actual stock of the commodity in question and the corresponding equilibrium stock. Thus parameters associated with the durability of the commodity and the rate of attempted adjustment make their appearance in the demand functions along with the price and income parameters familiar in static theory. Short- and long-period elasticities of consumption and of purchases with respect to income and prices emerge as simple functions of this extended set of parameters.

For ease of reference the nature of the calculations made, which is the same for each commodity group, is summarized in the fourth section. The analyses themselves, based on British experience in the inter-war and post-war periods, are set out in the fifth and sixth sections. The conclusions reached are summarized in the final section.

In the applications which follow attention is concentrated on

211

the analysis of time series by single-equation methods. Some experiments have been made in the efficient combination of this material with budget data by means of an extension of Durbin's method (Durbin, 1953) and, in the case of clothing, in the introduction of a supply equation. It does not appear that these refinements would alter appreciably the results set out below but a full report on them must be deferred for the time being.

A dynamic theory of demand

The object of this section is to set out a simple dynamic theory of demand which is capable of being applied. The theory, which was designed in the first place for the analysis of demand for durables, is developed on general lines so that the demand for perishables appears in it as a special case in which one of the parameters assumes a limiting value.

The amount q represents total purchases of, or gross investment in, a commodity during a period, and is separated into two parts. One of these, net investment or v, represents an addition to the opening stock, s, while the other, u, corresponds to current consumption, that is to say to the amount of the available stock deemed to be used up in the period. Thus

$$q \equiv v + u. \qquad \qquad \mathbf{1}$$

It is assumed that the amount used up, u, can be expressed by a reducing balance depreciation formula with a depreciation rate per period of $1/n$. Thus in a period there will be used up $1/n$th of the opening stock, s, plus an equal or smaller proportion, $1/m$, of the purchases of the period, q, so that

$$u \equiv s/n + q/m$$
$$\equiv \frac{m}{n(m-1)} s + \frac{1}{m-1} v \qquad \qquad \mathbf{2}$$

from **1** where $m \geqslant n \geqslant 1$. If $n = 1$ the good in question is perfectly perishable. If $n > 1$ the good is, in greater or less degree, durable. If, in the latter case, $m = n$ then it is assumed that the purchases of the period are all concentrated at its outset. In general, therefore, it may be assumed that $m > n$ if $n > 1$. If the periods relate to the shortest interval for which data on q are available, it seems reasonable to assume that the purchases of any period are spread evenly through it. In this case m is a function of n, as shown in the fourth section, below, and its value rapidly approaches $2n - \frac{1}{3}$ as n increases.

The closing stock, Es, is identically equal to the opening stock, s, plus the net investment of the period, v. That is

$$Es \equiv s + v \qquad\qquad 3$$

where E is an operator such that $E^\theta x(t) = x(t + \theta)$. By combining 1, 2 and 3 it follows that

$$
\begin{aligned}
Es &= s + q - u \\
&\equiv \frac{n-1}{n} s + \frac{m-1}{m} q \\
&= \frac{m-1}{m} \sum_{\theta=0}^{\infty} \left(\frac{n-1}{n} \right) E^{-\theta} q \qquad\qquad 4
\end{aligned}
$$

or $s \equiv \dfrac{n(m-1)}{m(n-1)} \displaystyle\sum_{\theta=1}^{\infty} \left(\dfrac{n-1}{n} \right)^{\theta} E^{-\theta} q \qquad\qquad 5$

which enables the opening stock, s, to be calculated from a knowledge of past purchases, the rate of depreciation, and the manner in which purchases are assumed to be spread through the period. This in turn makes it possible to calculate u from 2 and then v from 1.

The crucial feature of the theory is a distinction between the opening stock, s, and the equilibrium stock, s^*, which is assumed to depend on consumers' incomes and prices. If these remained constant s would tend in time to s^*. This change would come about as a consequence of net investment, positive or negative. Since it cannot be supposed that, in general, any gap between s and s^* will be closed instantaneously, it will be assumed that net investment is undertaken so as to reduce the gap in a period by a certain proportion, mr/n. Thus

$$v = \frac{mr}{n} (s^* - s). \qquad\qquad 6$$

If a substitution for v is made from 6 into 2, it follows that

$$u = \frac{m}{n(m-1)} [rs^* + (1 - r)s], \qquad\qquad 7$$

and if **6** and **7** are added together it follows that

$$q = \frac{m}{n(m-1)} [rms^* + (1 - rm)s]. \qquad \textbf{8}$$

Thus both u and q are a certain proportion of certain weighted averages of s^* and s.

The investment equation, **6**, is suitable for combining with a linear relationship connecting s^* with income and the price structure. In practice it is often more appropriate to use a logarithmic relationship for this purpose and it is then convenient to write the investment equation in the form

$$v = \frac{ms}{n} \left[\left(\frac{s^*}{s} \right)^r - 1 \right] \qquad \textbf{9}$$

whence $u = \dfrac{m}{n(m-1)} [s^{*r}s^{1-r}]$ $\qquad \textbf{10}$

and $q = \dfrac{m^2}{n(m-1)} [s^{*r} s^{1-r}] - \dfrac{ms}{n}.$ $\qquad \textbf{11}$

Equation **10** differs from **7** in that the weighted arithmetic average of s^* and s is replaced by a weighted geometric average.

In equilibrium, since $v = 0$, consumption, u^*, is given by

$$u^* = \frac{m}{n(m-1)} s^*. \qquad \textbf{12}$$

Accordingly **6** through **11** can be expressed in terms of u^* and s or s^* and s indifferently. Thus, for example, **7** can be written in the form

$$u = ru^* + (1 - r) \left[\frac{ms}{n(m-1)} \right]. \qquad \textbf{13}$$

Goods become less durable or more perishable as n diminishes and perfectly perishable goods arise as the limiting case in which $n \to 1$. In this case the term in brackets in **13** reduces to $E^{-1}u$ as can be seen as follows. From **5**

$$\frac{ms}{n(m-1)} = \frac{1}{n-1} \sum_{\theta=1}^{\infty} \left(\frac{n-1}{n} \right)^{\theta} E^{-\theta}q \qquad \textbf{14}$$

$$= \frac{E^{-1}q}{n} + \frac{1}{n} \sum_{\theta=2}^{\infty} \left(\frac{n-1}{n} \right)^{\theta-1} E^{-\theta}q,$$

which gives $\lim\limits_{n \to 1} \dfrac{ms}{n(m-1)} = E^{-1}q.$ $\qquad \textbf{15}$

Richard Stone and D. A. Rowe

Similarly, from **3** and **4**,

$$\lim_{n \to 1} \frac{v}{m-1} = q - E^{-1}q \qquad\qquad \textbf{16}$$

whence, in this case, from **2** $u = q$. Thus for perfectly perishable goods **7** and **10** can be written as

$$u = ru^* + (1 - r)E^{-1}u \qquad\qquad \textbf{17}$$

and $u = u^{*r} (E^{-1}u)^{1-r}$ \qquad\qquad \textbf{18}

respectively. These results follow wherever $m = n$ as shown by Stone and Rowe (1956).

From either **7**, **10**, **17** or **18** it follows that if $r = 1$, the term in opening stocks, in **7** and **10**, and in the last period's consumption, in **17** and **18**, disappears so that in this case consumption is a static function of income and prices, the variables assumed to determine s^* and u^*. The assumption that $r = 1$ is not *prima facie* inconsistent in **17** and **18**, but in **7** and **10** it is since $m/n > 1$. This being so, if $r = 1$ net investment as given by **6** and **11** would always be more than sufficient to remove the gap between s^* and s, a result which is hardly plausible. Thus it is likely that $r < 1$. This is certainly so for durable goods and possibly also for perishables since if a community insists on a quick adaptation to rising equilibrium levels for perishables it will, to that extent, keep down its rate of saving and thereby reduce the rate at which it can reach equilibrium in the consumption of the services of durable goods.

It is convenient at this point to consider the relationship connecting s^*, or u^*, with income and the price structure. Since the applications which follow relate to the demand for durables and since the form of the equations used is logarithmic, attention will here be concentrated on the relationship

$$s^* = \frac{an(m-1)}{m} \rho^b (p/\pi)^c e^{gt} \qquad\qquad \textbf{19}$$

where ρ denotes real income, p/π denotes the relative price of the commodity and t denotes time. This equation, when combined with **10**, leads to the following equation for consumption

$$u = a^r \rho^{br} (p/\pi)^{cr} e^{grt} \left[\frac{ms}{n(m-1)} \right]^{1-r}. \qquad\qquad \textbf{20}$$

215

Durable Goods

If **20** is expressed in terms of logarithms to the base e and if first-differences are taken of the expression so obtained there results

$$\Delta u' = br\Delta\rho' + cr\Delta(p/\pi)' + gr + (1 - r)\Delta s' \qquad 21$$

where the primes denote logarithms. Given a value of n, the relation of m to n and a series of q, u and s can be calculated. Given, in addition, series of ρ and p/π, estimates of b, c, g and r can be made by regression analysis. With the addition of a disturbance term, assumed to possess the properties appropriate for least-squares estimation, **21** is the basic form of the relationship used in the following applications.

Some further developments

While **21** represents a fairly general form of adaptive behaviour, it is a simple matter to make it still more general in two distinct ways. Firstly, in **19** it is assumed that the stock level at which the community is aiming in any period is determined, apart from a trend factor, by the current level of income and prices. It may be, however, that adjustment is made to some average of recent experience rather than to current levels. This can be done by defining a new variable, ρ^* as

$$\rho^* = \rho^\eta \, (E^{-1}\rho)^{1-\eta} \qquad 22$$

and by replacing $\Delta\rho'$ in **21** by $\Delta\rho^{*'} = \eta\Delta\rho' + (1 - \eta)\Delta E^{-1}\rho'$. By adding together the estimates of $br\eta$ and $br(1 - \eta)$ estimates of br and thence of η are obtained. If $\eta = 1$ then $\rho^* = \rho$ and the community adjusts to current real income. If $0 < \eta < 1$ then the community adjusts to an average, with positive weights, of current income and the income of the previous period. If $\eta > 1$ then the community adjusts to an extrapolation of recent income experience. A similar refinement may be introduced into the treatment of prices.

Secondly, in **9** it is assumed that r, which controls the amount of adjustment to be attempted in a period, is constant. It may be, however, that it varies systematically. For example, it might happen that a greater rate of adaptation was undertaken when prices were rising than when prices were falling. If $\Delta s'$ is subtracted from both sides of **21** each remaining term on the right-hand side contains r as a factor. Suppose that in fact the rate of

216

adjustment is not constant but is proportional to a variable x so that r should everywhere be replaced by rx. If then each term on the right-hand side of the equation for $\Delta u' - \Delta s'$ derived from **21** is multiplied by x so that $x\Delta\rho'$, $x\Delta(p/\pi)'$, x, and $x\Delta s'$ replace $\Delta\rho'$, $\Delta(p/\pi)'$, 1, and $\Delta s'$, then the parameters in **21** can be estimated on the assumption that the rate of adjustment is proportional to x.

It is a simple matter to derive the short-period and long-period elasticities of consumption with respect to real income and relative prices since these are respectively the elasticities of u and u^* with respect to ρ and p/π. The two short-period elasticities can be seen from **20** to be equal to br and cr. Since equilibrium consumption, u^*, is proportional to equilibrium stocks, s^*, it follows from **19** that the two long-period elasticities are, respectively, b and c. Thus the long-period elasticities are equal to the short-period elasticities divided by r.

The corresponding elasticities for purchases can also readily be derived. Thus, since in equilibrium there is no net investment, $q = u^*$ and so the long-period elasticities are b and c, as before. By combining **11** and **19** it can be seen that the short-period elasticities of purchases with respect to real income and the price ratio are $brmu/q$ and $crmu/q$. Thus for small changes from an initial position of equilibrium, these elasticities are given approximately by brm and crm.

While the long-period elasticities are independent of the length of the unit time period considered, the parameter r and the short-period elasticities are not. This may be seen by considering the effect of aggregating over time on consumption in the linear model. For this purpose equation **7** may be rewritten more briefly as

$$u = \alpha s^* + \beta s \qquad \qquad 23$$

where, by comparing coefficients, it can be seen that

$$1 - r = \beta/(\alpha + \beta). \qquad \qquad 24$$

Similarly **3** and **6** may be combined to give

$$Es = \frac{mrs^*}{n} + \left(1 - \frac{mr}{n}\right) s$$
$$= \gamma s^* + (1 - \gamma)s, \qquad \qquad 25$$

say. If it is assumed that the equilibrium level of stocks remains unchanged through the σ periods of the aggregation: $E^\theta s^* = s^*$ $(\theta = 1, \cdots, \sigma - 1)$ it follows, by repeated substitution in **25** that

$$E^\theta s = \gamma \sum_{v=0}^{\theta-1} (1 - \gamma)^v s^* + (1 - \gamma)^\theta s$$

$$= [1 - (1 - \gamma)^\theta]s^* + (1 - \gamma)^\theta s. \tag{26}$$

Then by substituting from **26** into **23** and summing over time, there results

$$U = \sum_{\theta=0}^{\sigma=1} E^\theta u$$

$$= \left[\sigma\alpha + \sigma\beta - \beta \sum_{\theta=0}^{\sigma-1} (1 - \gamma)^\theta \right] s^* + \beta \sum_{\theta=0}^{\sigma-1} (1 - \gamma)^\theta s$$

$$= As^* + Bs, \tag{27}$$

say, an expression for aggregate consumption comparable with **23**. The relationship between r and the corresponding aggregate parameter, R, may be derived by writing the aggregate form of **24** and substituting from **27**; that is

$$1 - R = B/(A + B)$$

$$= \frac{\beta}{\sigma(\alpha + \beta)} \sum_{\theta=0}^{\sigma-1} (1 - \gamma)^\theta$$

$$= \frac{1 - r}{\sigma} \sum_{\theta=0}^{\sigma-1} \left(1 - \frac{mr}{n} \right)^\theta$$

$$= \frac{n(1 - r)}{mr\sigma} \left\{ 1 - \left(1 - \frac{mr}{n} \right)^\sigma \right\} \tag{28}$$

from which it may be seen that while the two rates are equal for $r = 0$ or 1, they will differ within this range for $\sigma > 1$. The inverse relation for r in terms of R cannot be directly determined.

Although it is only possible to carry out this aggregation for the linear form of the relationship, it is reasonable to assume that it will hold approximately for the logarithmic form also. For if s^* is constant, consumption as given by equation **10** may be regarded as a function of the level of the opening stock, $u = f(s)$, and therefore

$$u = f(s^*) + (s - s^*)f'(s^*) + \cdots$$

$$= \frac{m}{n(m-1)}\,[rs^* + (1-r)s] \qquad\qquad 29$$

approximately, the omitted terms of the expansion involving fractions of the first and higher powers of $(s - s^*)/s$.

It may be noted that there is a further approximation involved in the use of the relation 28 in practical applications. For simplicity in computing it is reasonable to assume that purchases are spread evenly through the unit period. It may be seen from the aggregation carried out above, however, that the distributions of purchases through the aggregate period will depend upon r as well as n and m. Furthermore it is not the case that the equilibrium level s^* remains unchanged throughout the aggregate period.

The nature of the estimates and calculations actually made

The data available on quantities relate in each case simply to a series for q. An assumption is then made about n in the light of any information, such as allowances for tax purposes, that may be available. Given n, m is calculated on the assumption that purchases are spread evenly through the period. On this basis the relationship of m to n is as follows.

Suppose the period is divided into a number, h, of equal small intervals. If q is purchased in the whole period, the amount purchased in any small interval is q/h. The written down value at the end of the period of the purchases made in a single interval is the quantity q/h depreciated over the remaining portion of the period. The written down value at the end of a period of all purchases in a period is the sum

$$\sum_{\theta=0}^{h-1} \frac{q}{h}\left(\frac{n-1}{n}\right)^{(h-\theta)/h} = \frac{q}{h}\sum_{\theta=1}^{h}\left(\frac{n-1}{n}\right)^{\theta/h}$$

$$= \frac{q}{hn\{[n/(n-1)]^{1/h} - 1\}}. \qquad\qquad 30$$

The amount of these purchases used up in the period is the difference between this sum and the total amount purchased, q. If the number of intervals is increased indefinitely

$$\frac{q}{m} = \lim_{h \to \infty} \left[1 - \frac{1}{hn\{[n/(n-1)]^{1/h} - 1\}} \right] q, \qquad 31$$

that is, $\dfrac{1}{m} = 1 - \dfrac{1}{n \log_e [n/(n-1)]}$ \qquad\qquad 32

which enables m to be calculated from n.

Since the series for q are available only back to 1900 it is necessary to guess a value for s in that year. This, together with the information just described, enables a series of s to be constructed from 5 and thence of u from 2 and of v from 1.

Since the series used in the analyses described in the following sections begin around 1920, the original assumption about s in 1900 is of minor importance. A more important question is the value assumed for n. Since there is not very much to go on in the cases examined in this paper, an attempt has been made to find out whether a choice can be made from the data themselves. In order to do this alternative calculations have been made with different values of n and the effect on the sum of squares

$$\sum [(q - q_c)/E^{-1} q]^2$$

has been examined.

With reducing balance depreciation and $n > 1$, no good is completely written off in finite time. In considering appropriate values of n it may be helpful to know the corresponding number of periods, n^*, taken to write down a purchase to 10 per cent of its value, that is, to consume 90 per cent of it. A convenient linear approximation for n^* in terms of n can be derived as follows:

$$n^* = -2 \cdot 3/\log_e [(n-1)/n]$$

$$= 2 \cdot 3 \left/ \sum_{\theta=1}^{\infty} (1/\theta n^{\theta}) \right.$$

$$= 2 \cdot 3n - 1 \cdot 2. \qquad\qquad 33$$

Thus, for example, if $n = 5$, $n^* = 10 \cdot 3$ so that if 20 per cent of a good is consumed in a year, 90 per cent of it will be consumed in approximately 10·3 years.

This information together with series of ρ and p/π makes it possible to estimate the parameters in **21**. Consideration of **9**, **10** and **11** shows that nothing further can be gained by the use of expressions for v or q. The first-difference form of **21** was chosen because the experience gained by Stone *et al.* (1954) suggests that this form leads to a rather satisfactory lack of serial correlation in the residuals of demand equations for perishables. Given this form of the demand equation, the calculated level, expressed in logarithms, u'_c, is obtained by adding the calculated year-to-year change, $\Delta_c u'$, to the actual level of the preceding year. Thus

$$u'_c = E^{-1}u' + \Delta_c u' \qquad\qquad 34$$

or $\quad u_c = \text{antilog } (E^{-1}u' + \Delta_c u'). \qquad\qquad 35$

From **35**, q_c, v_c, and Es_c are derived as follows:

$$q_c = mu_c - \frac{ms}{n}, \qquad\qquad 36$$

$$v_c = q_c - u_c, \qquad\qquad 37$$

$$Es_c = s + v_c. \qquad\qquad 38$$

It follows from **36** that in calculating q any error in the calculated value of u is multiplied by m. Accordingly u_c must be very close to u if the equations are to be of practical use in calculating q, the variable which is of most interest from the standpoint of forecasting.

In the following tables and sections the calculated levels are all obtained on the basis of a knowledge of the preceding year's actual level. It would always be possible, as indicated by Stone and Prais (1953), to base the estimates on the actual levels of λ years ago and the changes in the determining variables over the intervening period but, in the following analyses, $\lambda = 1$ in all cases.

The quarterly data, used here for the post-war period 1950–55, may be dealt with in a similar way. With a knowledge of the opening stock in 1950, obtained from the annual data, and the appropriate quarterly depreciation rate, quarterly series for s, u and v may be derived from the quarterly series of purchases.

221

Table 1 Actual and Calculated Values for Clothing (£(1938) per equivalent adult: annual rate)

	q	$q_c(1)$	$q_c(2)$	u	$u_c(1)$	$u_c(2)$	v	$v_c(1)$	$v_c(2)$	Es	$Es_c(1)$	$Es_c(2)$
1923	8·40	8·44	8·40	8·27	8·29	8·27	0·13	0·15	0·13	5·18	5·20	5·19
1924	8·43	8·37	8·38	8·39	8·35	8·36	0·04	0·02	0·02	5·23	5·20	5·20
1925	8·57	8·48	8·51	8·49	8·45	8·46	0·08	0·03	0·05	5·30	5·26	5·27
1926	8·47	8·42	8·34	8·50	8·48	8·44	−0·04	−0·06	−0·10	5·27	5·24	5·21
1927	8·90	8·92	8·94	8·69	8·70	8·71	0·21	0·22	0·23	5·48	5·49	5·50
1928	8·98	8·82	8·81	8·90	8·82	8·82	0·08	0·00	−0·01	5·56	5·48	5·48
1929	9·10	9·05	9·06	9·02	9·00	9·00	0·08	0·05	0·06	5·64	5·61	5·62
1930	8·92	9·07	9·07	8·99	9·07	9·07	−0·08	0·00	0·00	5·56	5·64	5·63
1931	9·00	9·03	8·99	8·97	8·99	8·97	0·03	0·04	0·02	5·59	5·60	5·58
1932	8·58	8·71	8·67	8·78	8·85	8·83	−0·20	−0·14	−0·16	5·38	5·45	5·43
1933	8·79	8·88	8·93	8·73	8·77	8·79	0·06	0·11	0·13	5·45	5·49	5·51
1934	8·81	8·98	9·02	8·79	8·87	8·89	0·02	0·11	0·13	5·47	5·56	5·57
1935	9·09	9·00	9·01	8·95	8·90	8·90	0·15	0·10	0·10	5·61	5·57	5·57
1936	9·32	9·28	9·28	9·18	9·16	9·16	0·14	0·12	0·12	5·75	5·73	5·73
1937	9·12	9·14	9·18	9·19	9·20	9·22	−0·07	−0·06	−0·04	5·68	5·69	5·71
1938	9·02	8·94	8·96	9·08	9·04	9·05	−0·07	−0·10	−0·09	5·62	5·58	5·59
1950 (a)	8·45	8·90	8·97	8·59	8·67	8·68	−0·14	−0·23	−0·29	5·32	5·42	5·43
(b)	8·78	8·46	8·42	8·60	8·54	8·53	0·19	−0·08	−0·11	5·36	5·30	5·29
(c)	9·44	9·01	8·90	8·78	8·70	8·68	0·67	0·31	0·22	5·54	5·44	5·42
(d)	9·45	9·18	9·20	9·01	8·96	8·96	0·44	0·22	0·24	5·63	5·59	5·60

1951	(a)	9·82	9·71	9·60	9·19	9·17	9·15	0·63	0·54	0·45	5·79	5·76	5·74
	(b)	8·29	8·45	8·68	9·13	9·16	9·20	−0·84	−0·71	−0·52	5·58	5·61	5·66
	(c)	7·42	7·74	7·83	8·71	8·76	8·78	−1·29	−1·02	−0·95	5·27	5·33	5·34
	(d)	7·15	7·33	7·36	8·24	8·27	8·28	−1·09	−0·94	−0·92	4·38	5·03	5·04
1952	(a)	7·70	7·70	7·60	7·96	7·96	7·95	−0·27	−0·27	−0·34	4·91	4·92	4·90
	(b)	7·78	7·67	7·72	7·88	7·86	7·87	−0·10	−0·19	−0·15	4·89	4·86	4·87
	(c)	8·07	8·07	8·05	7·90	7·90	7·90	0·17	0·17	0·15	4·94	4·93	4·92
	(d)	8·13	7·97	8·00	7·98	7·95	7·96	0·15	0·02	0·04	4·97	4·94	4·95
1953	(a)	8·04	8·25	8·20	8·00	8·04	8·03	0·04	0·21	0·18	4·97	5·02	5·01
	(b)	8·01	8·46	8·37	8·00	8·08	8·07	0·00	0·38	0·30	2·97	5·07	5·05
	(c)	8·04	7·83	7·88	8·01	7·98	7·98	0·02	−0·14	−0·11	2·98	4·94	4·95
	(d)	8·14	8·11	8·09	8·05	8·05	8·04	0·08	0·06	0·04	5·00	5·01	5·00
1954	(a)	8·13	8·02	8·04	8·06	8·04	8·04	0·07	−0·02	−0·01	5·01	4·99	5·00
	(b)	8·59	8·61	8·52	8·15	8·16	8·14	0·44	0·46	0·38	5·12	5·12	5·10
	(c)	8·42	8·58	8·58	8·27	8·30	8·30	0·15	0·28	0·28	5·17	5·19	5·19
	(d)	8·36	8·82	8·75	8·32	8·40	8·39	0·04	0·41	0·36	5·16	5·27	5·26
1955	(a)	8·32	7·88	8·00	8·31	8·23	8·25	0·01	−0·35	−0·25	5·16	5·07	5·10
	(b)	8·75	8·57	8·54	8·38	8·35	8·34	0·37	0·22	0·20	5·25	5·21	5·21
	(c)	8·73	8·89	8·89	8·50	8·53	8·53	0·22	0·36	0·36	5·32	5·34	5·34
	(d)	9·04	8·78	8·83	8·64	8·60	8·61	0·39	0·18	0·22	5·40	5·37	5·38

Note: In this table are shown the actual values of the variables and the calculated values for (1) the inter-war and post-war periods analysed separately, and (2) the combined regression for both periods taken together. The quarterly figures are seasonally adjusted values at annual rates. The calculated values in this table are obtained essentially by multiplying the actual value of the preceding year or quarter by the calculated proportionate change. Thus, for the inter-war analysis, the calculated change in u between 1936 and 1937 is 9·20–9·18 = 0·02 and not 9·20–9·16 = 0·04. The actual change is 9·19–9·18 = 0·01.

Table 2 Actual and Calculated Values for Household Durable Goods (£(1938) million: annual rate)

	q	$q_c(1)$	$q_c(2)$	u	$u_c(1)$	$u_c(2)$	v	$v_c(1)$	$v_c(2)$	Es	$Es_c(1)$	$Es_c(2)$
1923	166	170	170	135	135	135	32	35	34	483	487	486
1924	168	173	173	143	144	144	25	29	30	508	512	513
1925	176	175	175	150	150	150	26	25	25	535	533	533
1926	180	178	175	157	157	157	22	21	19	557	556	553
1927	196	194	196	165	165	165	31	29	31	588	586	588
1928	203	199	199	174	173	173	29	26	26	617	614	614
1929	212	210	210	182	182	182	30	28	28	648	645	646
1930	215	211	211	190	190	190	25	21	22	672	669	669
1931	218	217	216	197	197	196	21	20	19	694	692	692
1932	226	223	219	203	203	202	23	20	17	716	714	711
1933	235	232	233	210	209	210	26	23	24	742	739	740
1934	253	247	249	219	218	218	35	29	31	776	771	773
1935	267	269	270	229	229	229	38	40	41	814	816	817
1936	269	275	278	239	240	240	30	35	38	844	849	852
1937	257	254	257	245	244	245	12	10	12	857	854	856
1938	234	249	248	245	247	247	−11	2	1	846	859	858
1950 (a)	238	240	243	174	174	174	64	66	68	613	614	614
(b)	244	239	239	179	179	179	66	60	60	630	628	628
(c)	253	254	253	184	184	184	69	71	69	648	647	647
(d)	254	254	253	189	189	189	65	65	64	664	664	664

1951 (a)	274	267	265	194	194	194	194	80	73	71	684	682	682
(b)	253	242	244	199	198	199	199	54	43	46	698	695	695
(c)	216	232	234	201	202	202	202	14	30	32	711	705	706
(d)	211	205	206	202	202	202	202	8	3	4	703	702	702
1952 (a)	226	221	221	203	203	203	203	22	18	18	709	708	708
(b)	214	223	226	204	205	205	205	10	18	21	711	713	714
(c)	217	221	219	205	205	205	205	12	15	14	715	715	715
(d)	226	221	224	206	206	206	206	19	15	18	720	719	719
1953 (a)	233	233	234	208	208	208	208	25	25	26	726	726	726
(b)	256	256	259	211	211	211	211	45	45	49	737	737	738
(c)	254	250	252	214	214	214	214	40	37	38	748	747	747
(d)	254	260	258	217	217	217	217	37	44	41	757	759	758
1954 (a)	246	254	253	219	219	219	219	27	35	34	764	766	765
(b)	269	265	261	222	221	221	221	48	43	40	776	775	774
(c)	297	278	282	226	225	225	225	71	53	57	794	789	790
(d)	307	321	320	231	232	232	232	76	89	88	813	816	816
1955 (a)	286	292	289	236	236	236	236	50	56	53	826	827	826
(b)	282	295	292	239	240	240	240	42	55	52	836	839	839
(c)	299	291	290	243	243	242	242	56	48	47	851	849	848
(d)	311	303	301	247	247	247	247	64	56	54	867	865	865

Note: In this table are shown the actual values of the variables and the calculated values for (1) the inter-war and post-war periods analysed separately, and (2) the combined regression for both periods taken together. The quarterly figures are seasonally adjusted values at annual rates. The calculated values in this table are obtained essentially by multiplying the actual value of the preceding year or quarter by the calculated proportionate change. Thus, for the inter-war analysis, the calculated change in u between 1936 and 1937 is 244–239 = 5 and not 244–240 = 4. The actual change is 245–239 = 5.

The relation between the annual and quarterly rates of depreciation is simply

$$1 - 1/n = (1 - 1/n_q)^4 \qquad\qquad 39$$

where $1/n_q$ is the quarterly rate of depreciation. The corresponding value of m_q may be then derived from 32.

With the quarterly data it is also necessary to allow for the influence of purely seasonal factors in demand independent of income and prices. For this purpose it would be possible to introduce a further set of seasonal indicators into the basic regression equation 21. An equivalent procedure, which simplifies the computing, is to adjust each of the variables in 21 for seasonal variation before calculating the regression. A first-difference model was used (Stone, 1956) involving the dummy variables z_i $(i = 1, \ldots, 4)$ with a unit for the ith quarter in each year and zeros elsewhere, and a linear trend $l(t)$. For example, for the dependent variable the equation fitted is of the form

$$\Delta u' = \sum_{i=1}^{4} d_i z_i + l(t). \qquad\qquad 40$$

The residuals from this equation, $\Delta \bar{u}'$ say, were used for the basic regression equivalent to 21, which now takes the form

$$\Delta \bar{u}' = b r_q \Delta \bar{p}' + c r_q \Delta (\bar{p}/\bar{\pi})' + (1 - r_q)\Delta \bar{s}' \qquad\qquad 41$$

where b and c may be determined as before, and r may be derived from r_q by the relation 28.

The actual and calculated series for the quarterly data are shown in Tables 1 and 2 on the preceding pages in their seasonally adjusted form. Since these adjustments are based on the logarithms of the series, and are therefore multiplicative, not additive, the basic relations 1 to 3 cannot all be maintained for the 'actual' values. It may be seen that in the present case equation 3 is only approximately satisfied for the quarterly series of v and s.

Besides obtaining the results for the inter-war annual and post-war quarterly data separately, an attempt has also been made in the following sections to derive a single set of coefficients by combining both sets of data. Two methods have been used. The first simply treats the two sets of coefficients as different

226

Table 3 Annual Series for the Auxiliary Variables Used in the Analyses

Year	Relative prices (1938 = 100·0)		Total consumers' expenditure £(1938)m.	Number of equivalent adults m.
	Clothing	Household durable goods		
1921	108·1	105·7	3153	36 78
1922	97·2	95·8	3264	37·03
1923	96·8	92·2	3363	37·19
1924	99·3	91·6	3440	37·48
1925	100·9	90·9	3520	37·74
1926	97·5	88·3	3513	38·00
1927	96·0	88·5	3651	38·29
1928	97·3	88·4	3708	38·50
1929	97·9	88·3	3787	38·71
1930	97·9	89·9	3841	38·97
1931	94·6	89·6	3879	39·20
1932	93·7	85·1	3858	39·46
1933	93·3	86·9	3955	39·65
1934	94·8	88·1	4071	39·81
1935	94·6	87·3	4177	40·10
1936	94·3	89·6	4296	40·37
1937	98·4	97·3	4371	40·62
1938	100·0	100·0	4394	40·82
1949	115·1	121·4	4457	41·99
1950	112·9	121·6	4559	42·25
1951	118·9	130·8	4531	42·27
1952	110·8	126·3	4481	42·47
1953	106·5	118·3	4652	42·64
1954	106·2	114·0	4852	42·85
1955	104·8	112·1	5004	43·02

sample results which may be combined to give a best linear unbiased estimate. In the present case, as has been shown by Aitken (1934–5), this involves a knowledge of the whole variance matrix for each set of coefficients. Estimates of these variance matrices may be derived for this purpose from the regression data.

An alternative method is to calculate a single set of coefficients from a common regression using all the data after suitable transformation. This requires an iterative procedure which is an adaptation of the method suggested for dealing with a variable r in the third section above. If the basic, annual, equation **21** is rearranged by deducting $\Delta s'$ from both sides and then multiplied through by $x = r_q/r$, the coefficients on the right-hand side become directly comparable with those of the basic, quarterly, equation **41** similarly rearranged. For any given value of r_q the corresponding value of r, and therefore of the ratio x, may be determined by using **28**. Thus, starting with an assumed value $r_q^{(0)}$, the transformed data may be used to obtain a regression estimate $r_q^{(1)}$. The process may then be repeated starting with $r_q^{(1)}$. The iteration is carried on until a satisfactory convergence for r_q is obtained. Since only the dependent variable is changed for each regression the successive iterations are carried out fairly easily.

Clothing

A part of this series, denoted by q, is shown in Table 1 along with various other series relating to clothing quantities involved in this study. From this series, and an extrapolation of it into the nineteenth century, direct estimates of s, u and v were made for three assumed values of n. These estimates depend, of course, on the value of n assumed. In the following comments it is assumed that $n = 1.25$.

The actual values of the various derived series are of some interest and will be briefly described before the analyses are considered. It must, of course, be kept in mind that changes in varieties and qualities are important and that, with the information available, it is hard to avoid a superficial treatment of these characteristics.

The series of q and u rose slowly and irregularly over the inter-war years and even in the early part of 1951, the post-war peak, u did not surpass the level of the late 1930s. Investment fluctuated rather closely around zero in the inter-war years and, with much more variation, has shown a similar tendency in the 1950s after a succession of positive values after the war. The recessions of the 1930s and of the early 1950s are dwarfed by the catastrophic falls in purchases and consumption which took place during the war.

Equation **21** was applied over the period 1921–2 to 1937–8 with the following results as shown in Table 5.

It is clear from this table that the value of r and of the short-period responses br and cr are all rather sensitive to the value

Table 4 Quarterly Series for the Auxiliary Variables Used in the Analyses

Quarter	Relative prices (1938 = 100·0)		Total consumers' expenditure £(1938)m.	Number of equivalent adults m.
	Clothing	Household durable goods		
1949 (d)	114·5	121·4	1185	42·09
1950 (a)	112·6	119·0	1060	42·15
(b)	110·1	120·1	1112	42·22
(c)	113·2	121·8	1170	42·25
(d)	115·2	124·8	1217	42·26
1951 (a)	117·3	128·8	1115	42·26
(b)	118·2	131·9	1124	42·27
(c)	119·9	132·9	1133	42·30
(d)	121·5	131·0	1158	42·35
1952 (a)	116·4	129·6	1051	42·40
(b)	111·8	126·8	1096	42·45
(c)	108·1	126·9	1145	42·49
(d)	108·0	122·8	1189	42·53
1953 (a)	106·9	123·1	1078	42·58
(b)	105·0	116·7	1151	42·62
(c)	106·3	117·3	1185	42·67
(d)	107·7	116·8	1238	42·72
1954 (a)	106·7	117·8	1111	42·77
(b)	104·9	117·4	1190	42·82
(c)	105·7	113·3	1239	42·87
(d)	107·4	109·5	1312	42·91
1955 (a)	106·7	112·7	1160	42·96
(b)	104·5	112·6	1227	43·00
(c)	104·6	111·5	1281	43·04
(d)	104·0	111·8	1335	43·08

Table 5

n	br	b	cr	c	gr	g	r	R^2	$\sum [(q - q_c)/E^{-1}q]^2$ ($\times 10^4$)
1	1·94	1·66	−0·52	−0·45	−0·015	−0·013	1·17	0·93	16·70
	(0·23)	(0·22)	(0·12)	(0·12)	(0·004)	(0·004)	(0·06)		
1·25	0·95	1·52	−0·25	−0·40	−0·007	−0·012	0·62	0·89	18·10
	(0·12)	(0·25)	(0·07)	(0·14)	(0·002)	(0·004)	(0·05)		
1·5	0·75	1·48	−0·21	−0·41	−0·005	−0·011	0·51	0·90	20·26
	(0·10)	(0·28)	(0·06)	(0·15)	(0·002)	(0·004)	(0·06)		

of n and that they all decline as n increases. As a consequence of this similarity of movement, the long-period responses b and c and the residual trend coefficient, g, are in each case relatively little affected by the value chosen for n. From the last two columns of the table it can be seen that, in this case, the multiple correlation coefficient associated with 21, R^2, and the residual sum of squares, $\sum [(q - q_c)/E^{-1} q]^2$, combine in suggesting a very low value for n. From common observation, however, $n > 1$ in the case of clothing and so these indications cannot be taken as conclusive. It might seem appropriate to consider the possibility that $n = 2$ but even this value implies the assumption that, on the average, clothing is written down to 10 per cent of its value in approximately three and one-third years. With $n = 3$ the corresponding period is approximately five and two-thirds years which seems too high as an average figure. This example illustrates the difficulty of checking an assumed value of n by references to the available time series and the importance of trying to collect direct evidence on the value of n.

If it may be assumed that $n = 1.25$, implying that clothing is on the average written down to 10 per cent of its value in just under one year and a half, then the long-period total expenditure elasticity, b, could be taken as 1.5. This value compares with a total expenditure elasticity derived from the budget investigations of 1937–9 of 1.41 ± 0.08. The corresponding short-period consumption elasticity is found to be only a little under unity. The short-period total expenditure elasticity for purchases, however, is probably higher than the long-period value, for in this case $brm = 1.89 \pm 0.24$. The long-period price (substitution) elasticity, c, works out at -0.4 compared with a short-period elasticity for consumption of -0.25 and for purchases of -0.5. The residual trend coefficient for consumption is of the order of -0.01. This value may be due to gradual changes in the quality characteristics of clothing which are not properly reflected in the rather crude estimates of quantities and prices, especially for the earlier years of the period, on which the analyses are unavoidably based.

In addition to the 'actual' values of q, u, v and Es for $n = 1.25$, Table 1 also contains the corresponding 'calculated' values. In this table the calculated values are obtained, as explained in the preceding section, by adding the calculated year-to-year changes

231

on to the actual value of the preceding year. Actual values and the corresponding calculated values derived in this way were also obtained for the years 1950 through 1955, following the final de-rationing of clothing early in 1949. The annual changes in these years are more pronounced than for the pre-war period and the agreement between actual and calculated series is much less satisfactory. A considerable fall in q from 1950 to 1951 is estimated but it is not as large as the actual fall. From 1951 to 1952, q fell a little further but the calculated change was positive. It is only for the final period, 1954 to 1955, that the actual and calculated series come closely together again.

It is possible that the discrepancies in the post-war years are due not so much to extraneous factors 'peculiar to this period, or to changes in the response patterns, but rather to the failure of the annual model to reflect a series of marked short-term fluctuations. It is therefore of considerable interest to examine the quarterly data available for these years. With a knowledge of the level of opening stocks in 1950, obtained from the annual series, and the quarterly depreciation rate corresponding to $n = 1.25$, the quarterly figures of u, v and s could be derived from the recorded purchases in the same way as for the annual data. The series, seasonally adjusted, are shown in Table 1.

The results of applying equation 41 to these data are as shown in Table 6.

Table 6

n	n_q	br_q	b	cr_q	c	r_q	r	R^a
1·25	3·02	0·53 (0·10)	1·80 (0·47)	−0·05 (0·10)	−0·18 (0·36)	0·30 (0·07)	0·70 (0·08)	0·92

Although the estimates are subject to slightly wider margins of error, it is evident that for the comparable coefficients, b, c and r, there is a very fair degree of agreement with the results from the inter-war annual data. The values of r seem to be particularly close for the two periods. The long-period total expenditure, elasticity is somewhat higher for the post-war years while the long-period price (substitution) elasticity appears to be lower. In neither case, however, are these coefficients significantly different in the two periods.

232

In Table 1 the corresponding calculated values of q, u, v and *Es* are also shown for this equation. As before, they are obtained by adding the calculated quarterly change to the actual value of the preceding quarter. The advantages of the quarterly model are here clearly apparent. The course of the recession and recovery in clothing purchases in these years is closely reflected by the calculated series although the proportionate discrepancies tend to be larger than those found for the inter-war years.

In the absence of any significant difference in the results obtained for the inter-war and post-war periods, a single relationship may be postulated for the whole period. Combining the two sets of coefficients gives a long-period total expenditure elasticity $b = 1.58 \pm 0.22$, a long-period price (substitution) elasticity $c = -0.33 \pm 0.12$, and $r = 0.65 \pm 0.04$. These values are very much as might be expected and the reduction in the standard errors indicates the increased precision obtained by combining the data for the two periods. They may be compared with the results of calculating a single regression for the whole period by the iterative procedure described in the previous section. These are as follows as shown in Table 7.

Table 7

n	n_q	br_q	b	cr_q	c	r_q	r
1.25	3.02	0.42 (0.06)	1.52 (0.27)	-0.07 (0.05)	-0.26 (0.20)	0.28 (0.03)	0.67 (0.05)

Although the increased precision of the estimates is not here so apparent, the long-period coefficients are very similar. The average values themselves tend to conform more to inter-war levels, but they remain sufficiently close to those of the separate analyses for the calculated series from this equation to be very similar, as is shown in Table 1.

Household durable goods

This large and heterogeneous class of commodities includes furniture, furnishings, electrical goods, hardware, china and glassware. The analysis was conducted on the same lines and for the same periods as in the case of clothing except that consumption was expressed per family rather than per equivalent adult. For the series shown in Table 2 it was assumed that $n = 4$. This is equivalent to the assumption that, on the average, the constituents of this class of commodities are written down to 10 per cent of their value in approximately eight years.

In the inter-war period investment was positive and comparatively steady, with the result that stocks and therefore consumption rose from year to year. Purchases reached a peak in 1936 which was surpassed effectively only in 1954. Consumption was approximately stationary from 1936 to 1939 and then, with negative investment from 1938 through 1945, declined to a low point in 1945. Post-war investment levels have been somewhat higher on the average and somewhat more variable than in the inter-war years. By the year 1955 consumption, which had risen fairly steadily since 1945, was nearly back to the level of the late 1930s.

The results of the calculations for the period 1922–3 to 1937–8, which have been made for different values of n, are brought together in Table 8.

The values of n chosen, from 2 to 5, correspond to a range of from three and one-third years to approximately ten and one-third years for the time taken to write down a commodity to 10 per cent of its value. As n increases the values of r and of the short-period elasticities, br and cr, fall almost proportionately. The long-period elasticities are therefore much more consistent from one analysis to another. The value of the multiple correlation coefficient, R^2, attains a just perceptible maximum for $n = 4$. More significantly, the sum of squares

$$\sum [(q - q_c)/E^{-1} q]^2$$

is a minimum for this value. There is, then, in this case an indication from the analysis itself of the rate of depreciation, and the value indicated is certainly plausible on *a priori* grounds.

Though fairly stable with respect to variations in n, the long-period elasticities are only determined within a fairly wide margin of error in this analysis. From the pre-war budgets, however, the (long-period) total expenditure elasticity is estimated at 2.35 ± 0.27. Thus a substantial improvement in accuracy might be expected from the combination of the two

234

Table 8

n	br	b	cr	c	gr	g	r	R^2	$\sum[(q-q_c)/E^{-1}q]^2$ $(\times 10^4)$
2	0·73	2·64	−0·29	−1·05	−0·0003	−0·001	0·28	0·92	81·57
	(0·15)	(0·87)	(0·05)	(0·37)	(0·0028)	(0·010)	(0·08)		
3	0·49	2·39	−0·19	−0·95	0·0005	0·002	0·20	0·94	80·83
	(0·10)	(0·94)	(0·03)	(0·38)	(0·0026)	(0·012)	(0·08)		
4	0·37	2·42	−0·15	−0·97	0·0003	0·002	0·15	0·95	75·30
	(0·07)	(1·18)	(0·02)	(0·48)	(0·0024)	(0·015)	(0·07)		
5	0·30	2·76	−0·12	−1·09	−0·0002	−0·002	0·11	0·94	78·00
	(0·06)	(1·85)	(0·02)	(0·75)	(0·0023)	(0·022)	(0·07)		

sources of information. The long-period price (substitution) elasticity is seen to be approximately unity. In the short period, however, both price and income effects with respect to consumption are markedly inelastic; with $r = 0.15$ the short-period consumption elasticities are actually less than one-sixth of the corresponding long-period values. The short-period elasticities for purchases are more nearly of the same order of magnitude as the long-period values, for $brm = 2.83$ and $crm = 1.15$. The residual trend coefficient is always many times less than its standard error and is effectively zero.

The data in Table 2 show the extent to which the inter-war relationship succeeds in accounting for year-to-year changes. The movement in consumption is reproduced rather closely as may be expected when n is relatively large. There is, however, a tendency for u_c to be above or below u for several years in succession. These deviations are extremely small in this period and do not lead to any marked discrepancies between q and q_c.

The results obtained from the quarterly data for the post-war years 1950–5 were as shown in Table 9.

Table 9

n	n_q	br_q	b	cr_q	c	r_q	r	R^2
4	14.41	0.14 (0.03)	3.53 (4.39)	−0.023 (0.020)	−0.57 (1.02)	0.04 (0.05)	0.15 (0.17)	0.97

The corresponding calculated series are also shown in Table 2. The value of r obtained here is the same as for the inter-war annual data. However, the coefficient in the regression, r_q, is necessarily small and cannot be estimated very precisely from the number of observations available. As a consequence the estimates of the long-period elasticities are both subject to wide margins of error. As far as the evidence goes, there are no significant differences from the inter-war equation.

The explanation of the quarterly changes in consumption is clearly very good, and although in this case $m_q = 28.47$, it can be seen frome Tabl 2 that the calculated changes in purchases, q_c, are also very satisfactory.

If the coefficients for the inter-war and post-war periods are combined, the average long-period total expenditure elasticity is $b = 2\cdot02 \pm 0\cdot98$, the long-period price (substitution) elasticity $c = -0\cdot71 \pm 0\cdot34$, and $r = 0\cdot19 \pm 0\cdot05$. Though determined with increased precision it is noticeable that the values of both b and r are found to lie slightly outside the limits of the separate estimates. This result must be due to the effect of the covariance elements entering into the calculation. From the common regression for the whole period the results are as shown in Table 10.

Table 10

n	n_q	br_q	b	cr_q	c	r_q	r
4	14·41	0·12 (0·02)	2·94 (0·85)	−0·037 (0·007)	−0·88 (0·32)	0·04 (0·01)	0·15 (0·04)

A further reduction of the standard errors is obtained here and the coefficients are more clearly an average of the inter-war and post-war values. The calculated series from this equation are also shown in Table 2. It can be seen that a large part of the variations in demand for both the inter-war and post-war periods can be accounted for by this common pattern of response.

Summary and conclusions

The contents of this paper and the conclusions reached can be summarized as follows.

1. The second section contains a simple dynamic theory of demand expressed *ab initio* in aggregative terms. The theory employs a reducing balance depreciation formula with a depreciation rate that is constant over time, a concept of equilibrium consumption which depends, apart from a residual trend, on current income and the current price structure and an investment relationship designed to narrow and, under stable conditions, eventually to eliminate the difference between equilibrium and actual stocks.

2. For lack of direct information it has been necessary to assume not only the constancy of the depreciation rate but also its magnitude in different cases. Calculations are presented for

237

different assumed values of the depreciation rate but it is not always possible to make a choice on the basis of the observations alone. In the further application of the theory it is desirable to obtain direct information about the appropriate value of the depreciation rate in different cases.

3. The fifth and sixth sections contain applications of the theory to the determination of the demand for clothing and household durable goods in the United Kingdom. The basic consumption relationships are fitted to the first-differences of the logarithms of consumption. In each case about 90 per cent of the observed variance is accounted for by the fitted relationships. The theory could equally well be applied to t'.ie analysis of perishable goods and services but this has not been done.

4. In addition to a parameter reflecting durability and the usual parameters associated with income and prices, the theory also involves a parameter, r, associated with the rate at which adjustment to equilibrium is attempted. In terms of this set of parameters estimates of both long- and short-period elasticities can be made. Where comparison is possible the long-period total expenditure elasticities derived in this paper are remarkably close to alternative estimates based on budget data for the period 1937–9. Durbin's method for the efficient combination of time series and cross-section data has been extended to meet the present requirements by Aitchison but the necessary calculations have not yet been made. In the present case, the use of this method would not lead to any substantial change in the estimates but to a considerable reduction in their standard errors.

5. The parameters in the consumption relationships were estimated from annual data for the period 1921–2 to 1937–8 and from quarterly data for the post-war period 1950–5. For both commodities it was found that there was no significant difference in the basic response pattern of demand for the two periods and that a satisfactory single relationship could be obtained for the whole period. It was also evident that where a series of marked short-term fluctuations were encountered, as for clothing in the post-war years, an annual model could not provide a satisfactory explanation and the underlying relationships could only be determined from quarterly data.

References

AITKEN, A. C. (1934–5), 'On least squares and the linear combination of observations', *Proceedings of the Royal Society of Edinburgh*, vol. 55, pp. 42–8.

DURBIN, J. (1953), 'A note on regression when there is extraneous information about one of the coefficients', *Journal of the American Statistical Association*, vol. 48, pp. 799–808.

STONE, R. (1956), 'Models for seasonal adjustment', *Quantity and Price Indexes in National Accounts*, O.E.E.C.

STONE, R., and PRAIS, S. J. (1953), 'Forecasting from econometric equations: a further note on derationing', *Economic Journal*, vol. 63, no. 249, pp. 185–95.

STONE, R., assisted by ROWE, D. A., CORLETT, W. J., HURSTFIELD, R., and POTTER, M. (1954), *The Measurement of Consumers' Expenditure and Behaviour in the United Kingdom, 1920-38*, vol. 1: *Studies in the National Income and Expenditure of the United Kingdom*, Cambridge University Press.

STONE, R., and ROWE, D. A. (1956), 'Aggregate consumption and investment functions for the household sector considered in the light of British experience', *Nationalokonomisk Tidsskrift*, vol. 94, 1–2, pts 1–2, pp. 1–32.

14 George Katona

Attitudes and Expectations

From George Katona, *The Powerful Consumer*, McGraw-Hill, 1960, pp. 54–67.

In order to understand the effects which attitudes and expectations have on economic action, we must get acquainted with certain psychological considerations regarding the function of attitudes.

I turn a switch and the light goes on. In this case a mechanism reacts in the same way over and over again. For centuries many thinkers conceived of human behavior as if it were analogous with that of machines. They postulated that the same stimulus always brings forth the same reaction and proposed a mechanistic theory of human behavior, characterized by order and simplicity. They believed that to give up such principles would be to abandon all hope of understanding human behavior. Modern psychology does believe in determinism, law and order in human behavior. Yet it does not conceive of people as automata and does not posit a fixed, one-to-one relation between stimuli and responses.

Stimuli elicit responses; they present occasions for responses rather than fully determining them. It is not possible to predict the response by knowing the stimulus alone. Two persons may react differently to the same stimulus, and the same person may react differently to it on successive occasions. Human beings are capable of learning. Mechanistic or quasi-automatic reaction determined by immediate stimuli alone is extremely rare in the case of what psychologists call the higher mental processes, which include most of economic behaviour.

Intervening variables

The psychological field contains intervening variables. Between the stimuli and the responses is the organism. As the result of

240

past experience there exist habits, attitudes and motives which intervene by influencing how stimuli are perceived and how the organism reacts to them. The response then is a function of both the environment and the person.

Turning to economic behavior, level of income and financial assets function either as enabling conditions, if they are ample, or as constraints, if they are insufficient. Things that happen to the decision maker are precipitating circumstances or stimuli. A change in salary or the breakdown of one's car may serve as examples. News and information which reach the organism are a very important category of stimuli. Economic behavior in particular is most commonly stimulated by information received by consumers and businessmen.

Yet the same level of income or the same new information may be viewed differently by different people or by the same person at different times. Information transmitted is not identical with information received and with information which becomes salient. How we perceive changes in the environment depends to some extent on us, that is, on subjective or intervening variables. The most important function of intervening variables is to organize. What fits in or what is consistent with our predispositions has the best chance of influencing us. All intervening variables are learned through experience but some are relatively permanent as, for instance, sociocultural norms, well-ingrained motives and personality traits acquired early in childhood. Stability over fairly long periods also characterizes a variety of habits developed and sustained over many years. Other motives and attitudes change much more easily under the impact of situational factors and nevertheless influence our perceptions of the environment.

One important aspect of our behavioral environment is group belonging. It is the individual who feels, thinks and acts. But how he feels, thinks and acts is influenced by the group to which he belongs. Most of the time each of us is a member of a group, sometimes a member of several groups and at different times of different groups. Some groups are very powerful; then it appears justifiable to speak of group motives or group attitudes. One of the most powerful groups to which practically all of us belong is the family. What happens to other members of our family

241

affects us and we act in behalf of our family. But a person may shift from being a family member and acting as one to being a member of a business firm. What happens to the firm concerns him then and he acts in the name of the firm. Or a person may identify himself with a social group or with a political or national group. Submerging of the ego in a group – as in the case of soldiers on patrol, members of a basketball team in action or people in a mob – is one, but not the only, form of group influence. Weaker influences are much more common, as well as conflicts from belonging to several groups. One major principle applies to all these cases: swimming with the current is much easier than swimming against the current. What news and information reach us is at least colored by our group belonging; so is our interpretation of the news; and the principle of social facilitation says that action similar to the action of other members of our group is easy, while contrary action is difficult. We often act as we believe others act, who are either members of our group or of reference groups which we set as standards without really belonging to them.

Attitudes are generalized viewpoints with an affective connotation. The usual sharp distinction between cognition and affect or emotion must be abandoned when we turn to the sets or frames of mind which influence our perceptions and behavior. We are for or against innumerable things. Sometimes we may be able to give clear reasons why we favor or oppose an idea or development. But the underlying set of liking or disliking is not the same as the reasons occasionally presented. Attitudes, that is, emotionally colored points of view, may influence behavior irrespective of whether they are based on rational arguments or held without clear awareness of their reasons.

Expectations are a subgroup of attitudes. They, too, are intervening variables which influence behavior. They are those attitudes which represent an extension of the time perspective into the future. Expectations are, then, subjective notions of things to come colored by affect, approval or disapproval, satisfaction or dissatisfaction. Expectations – expressed intentions to act in a certain way as well as notions about what will happen to the person holding the expectations, or to the society

242

or the economy – are current data which represent attitudes held at the time they are expressed. To what extent expectations can be viewed as predispositions to future action and have a predictive value will be discussed later.

Enduring and variable attitudes

Frequently in the past, general and specific attitudes have been distinguished from each other. Optimism, irrespective of its specific content, would then represent a different kind of attitude from optimism regarding one's own immediate income prospects, for instance. This, however, is not a fundamental distinction but rather a matter of the degree of generalization. There exists a tendency toward generalization and toward consistency in attitudes. But consistency is not always achieved and often specific attitudes conflict with more deep-seated general attitudes. Thus it is possible for a person with optimistic personality traits to expect unfavorable economic conditions to prevail at a given time, as well as for a pessimist to expect business recovery. The basic distinction between different kinds of attitudes and expectations is that between stable and enduring attitudes on the one hand and variable attitudes on the other.

Some attitudes are acquired very early in life and may be viewed as permanent personality traits. Others depend on new experiences and information and may change in the short run. More correctly, all attitudes have situational determinants as well as a personality basis. In the case of some attitudes, however, either the situational or the personality aspect predominates. All attitudes tend to become habitual, reinforced by repeated action or reiteration. Yet some become deeply ingrained habits while others, held for a short time, may be changed easily. Honesty, punctuality or conservatism, for instance, are personality traits which give rise to attitudes in the former category. No doubt, such attitudes may be influenced by changing conditions or new experiences, but to a much smaller extent than other attitudes.

It has been demonstrated that some attitudes relevant, for instance, to political behavior and voting – such as conservatism or liberalism, favoring the Republican or Democratic party – are acquired early in life and may remain in force during an entire

243

lifetime. But obviously, with some people at least, the events that occur before an election or the personality of a candidate also give rise to attitudes which may influence their action.

In studying business behavior, enduring attitudes are found which have become part of the psychological make-up of practically all businessmen at a given time and country – honesty or concern with profits, for instance. Other attitudes differ from person to person – as, for instance, attitudes toward risk taking and speculation – though they, too, may be acquired in childhood or during early business experiences and may endure over long periods of time. Finally, there are attitudes which vary from time to time and develop in response to changes in environment.

Our concern is with attitudes which are variable because they are influenced by economic developments – both on a personal and on a national level – and which in turn influence our reactions to these developments. Expecting or not expecting inflation or recession belong in this category, even though they are associated with more enduring attitudes as well as such personality traits as being of a basically optimistic or pessimistic disposition.

The differentiation between relatively stable and relatively variable attitudes is a question for empirical research. To be sure, attitudes that are, in principle, variable may remain unchanged over several years, provided nothing important happens during those years to make for changes. Yet if the measurement of a variety of attitudes is repeated at times when the economic climate has undergone substantial changes, we should expect to find great differences in the degree of stability of different attitudes among a large number of people.

Such a study of the degree of stability in economic attitudes was carried out recently (Katona, 1959). Over a period of three years, 1954–7, the same attitudinal questions were addressed to the same representative sample of the urban population three times. The statistical measures developed for the measurement of the extent of homogeneity or repetitiousness in attitudes showed great differences. At the one extreme were the answers received when people were asked whether in their opinion their personal financial situation would be better or worse a few years from the time of questioning. Close to one-half of the sample gave identical answers three times in three consecutive years and most others gave the same answer twice and slightly different answers once; for instance, they said 'same' rather than 'better' but only a handful shifted from 'better' to 'worse'. Similarly, questions about satisfaction with standard of living or with amounts saved resulted in a relatively low degree of variability.

On the other hand, expectations about how business conditions or prices would change 'during the next year' showed great variability. Only one out of every five people gave the same answer three times when asked about their price expectations and most of these were people with little education who said three times, 'There will be no change'. The proportion of people who shifted from 'Prices will go down' to 'Prices will go up' was much higher than the proportion with stable attitudes.

These studies did not show that there existed two classes of attitudes, entirely independent of each other. They did show, however, that it is possible to designate the relatively variable attitudes. Thus it was possible to select the most promising candidates for studies of the relation between changes in attitudes and changes in consumer expenditures as reported in Chapter 3.

Selectivity and organization

We may recall the previous references to the substantial role of habits in economic behavior as well as to genuine decision making which commonly takes the form of deviating from habitual behavior. Situationally determined opinions, attitudes, and expectations are of primary relevance when habitual behavior is *not* followed. When no problem is seen and the stimuli elicit almost automatically the usual, oft-repeated responses, expectations are not aroused and do not intervene. But when the decision maker finds himself in a crossroad situation in which he is aware of different possibilities of action, attitudes and expectations serve the function of steering the decision in a certain direction. Expectations do not play a role in each and every form of economic behavior, and businessmen and consumers do not have expectations about each and every aspect of the future. But under certain circumstances expectations are of crucial importance.

Learned behavior is highly selective. In any given situation only certain aspects of the past and certain notions about the future become salient. Problem solving obtains direction through suppressing certain notions and being preoccupied with others which appear to fit. The organization of information according to affective predispositions helps in solving the problem – though of course not necessarily in attaining the best solution.

Evidence supporting these statements will be presented later when we shall show that at certain times, in the face of diverse news, the information of which people were aware remained highly consistent. In times of unfavorable attitudes and expectations, good business news frequently did not become salient; at other times good news only could make itself heard.

Further, in analyzing the expectations of managers of different kinds of business firms, a definite structuring of attitudes appeared.[1] Some business leaders, for example, were found to be preoccupied with marketing problems and to view all kinds of news and information exclusively from the point of view of the possible impact on their sales and sales prospects. With managers in other branches of industry, excess capacity or the problem of automation were so predominant that their thinking and their expectations revolved almost exclusively about those issues. In other industries or at other times, cost of production or, specifically, wage increases so dominated businessmen's thinking that all expectations were colored by it.

Organization of attitudes not only makes problem solving manageable but also serves to reduce uncertainty. Logically the problem of uncertainty may be formulated thus: the future is uncertain because such a multitude of factors may influence it that it becomes impossible to obtain a clear picture of each. When, however, only a few developments are viewed as relevant, or when the trend of business is seen as going on as it has been going except for one or two crucial question marks, businessmen and consumers may focus their attention on those few questions and arrive at a solution. This explanation is supported by the

1. These studies have been described in Katona (1958). Many other references to business expectations made later in this chapter are taken from the same essay. An earlier formulation of the theory of expectations is found in Katona (1951).

finding that for most people the term uncertainty does not have the meaning of simply not knowing what will happen in the future. Uncertainty has definite unfavorable connotations; it implies fear of adverse developments because the feeling of uncertainty arises only when problem solving has been attempted but has not been successful.

The representation of the future

Certain aspects of the future do, of course, appear fairly certain. Such aspects have been ruled out of our definition of expectations, which are conceived as representing subjective notions of things to come.

In the field of business it is fairly simple to distinguish between information about the future which is held with some certainty and the subjective notions about the future. Business data regarding future developments – which economists call '*ex ante* data' – may be classified into four categories, the first three of which are not included in our definition of expectations. They represent information which is customarily written into or available from business records in the same manner as such *ex post* data as past sales or profits.

Contracts. Contracts entered into represent the first category of *ex ante* data. Records of contracts already awarded represent information about future activity, information which is widely used for predictive purposes. To be sure, contracts may be cancelled, but this is a relatively rare occurrence except under catastrophic circumstances. New orders received by manufacturers and unfilled orders of manufacturers are further examples of this category of *ex ante* data which are found in business records and which represent information about the future.

Budgets. Corporation budgets prepared by business executives and approved by the board of directors are part of business records and yet reflect future activity. The same is true, of course, of government budgets. Budgets, in contrast to contracts, can be changed unilaterally. Budgets are often revised and represent a guide for future behavior rather than rigorous standards.

247

Durable Goods

Estimates. Various departments of business firms prepare a variety of estimates and forecasts of things to come. These estimates, usually recorded in business memoranda, serve as information for business management and may influence its decisions, but rarely determine them.

Opinions, notions, intentions and guesses of executives. This final category of *ex ante* data, in contrast to the preceding categories, is hardly ever recorded on paper and may nonetheless influence the firm's behavior. Information about such opinions can become available to the researcher through skillful personal interviewing. It is this category alone which we shall designate by the term expectations.

Many of the business anticipations data regularly collected by various government and private agencies during the last few years fall into other categories. Thus the Securities and Exchange Commission and the Commerce Department conduct mail surveys to collect information on business capital expenditures to be undertaken during the next quarter or year. Much of the information they collect represents contracts awarded or budgets approved. Information on sales expectations, collected for instance by Dun & Bradstreet, may often be classified as estimates, but sometimes also as opinions or guesses.

Turning to consumers, we may obtain some information on the contractual obligations of all consumers – for instance, on prospective repayments of mortgage and installment debt – from business records. We may also study the distribution of contractual obligations and of numerous other commitments through personal interviews with a representative sample of households. Consumer plans for the future fall overwhelmingly into the fourth category of *ex ante* data, and can be studied only through personal interviews. The sample survey alone can yield information on plans or intentions to buy houses, automobiles and other goods, as well as on a variety of other expectations. At any given time only a very small proportion of people have already contracted to buy a house or a car, or made a definite decision within their family about a future purchase. The difference between people who are committed to buy a car and people who have a notion that they might buy a car in a few months is related to

248

differences in the degree or confidence attached to expectations. No doubt, the subjective probability attached to expectations varies greatly. But, as we shall see, it would be a great mistake to restrict the study of expectations to those which are held with a high degree of confidence.

Expectations may refer both to matters on which the person who expresses the expectation may take action and to matters on which he has no influence whatsoever. In the field of business, expectations have sometimes been divided into those concerning the firm of which the person expressing an opinion is an executive, the industry to which the firm belongs, and thirdly the economy as a whole. The assumption was that opinions about future developments should be most reliable in the first and least reliable in the third category. It was assumed, for example, that an executive would know most about the future sales of his firm, somewhat less about the future sales of his industry, and least about the future Gross National Product representing the total of sales in the economy. When, however, executives were questioned about all three areas, it frequently appeared that the subjective degree of certainty of expectations did not correspond with this assumption. Often very confident judgments were made about next year's GNP or next year's trend of the cost-of-living index, while conditional answers were given about next year's sales of the executive's own firm or even about the prices to be charged by his firm. These differences could be attributed partly to the detailed knowledge available to the executive about his own business. He might be aware, for instance, of the great extent to which pending negotiations with one large customer could influence the firm's next year's sales. Furthermore, it was found that general expectations obtain much more frequent external confirmation than expectations regarding one's own activities. Reports and conversations often result in an executive's forming fairly definite opinions about the economy as a whole, but not about his own business. Finally, some people believe that the multitude of influences to which the entire economy is subject make for fairly small changes so that the total result is more easily foreseeable, while the single case, what happens to the individual, is subject to much uncertainty.

The same holds true of the public at large. People often have definite notions about the prospects of war or peace, prosperity or depression, inflation or deflation, while they are highly uncertain about what will happen to their own jobs or incomes. That the opposite may also occur is of no concern here. Our present concern is to refute the notion that the researcher should be concerned only with expectations held with great confidence, or with expectations about developments which the subject can influence.

How do a person's expectations about things that may happen to him compare with expectations of things he may do? In comparing income expectations, for instance, with expectations of spending on durable goods, we found a variety of situations. Sometimes income expectations are very definite and held with great certitude, while intentions as to savings or purchases are most indefinite. Sometimes just the opposite is true. Among business expectations it is quite difficult to find any which may be classified as referring exclusively to the executive's or firm's own decisions. Prices set by manufacturers on their products, or wages paid to their employees, are often felt by business executives to depend on circumstances over which they have no control. The extent of felt discretion in action varies greatly. Again the conclusion emerges: we would not be justified in refraining from inquiring about any kinds of expectations on the basis that they are uncertain or that they are irrelevant or outside the scope of the subject's possible knowledge. A person's opinions may be just as strong – or sometimes even stronger – in areas beyond his control as in areas determined by his own action. For a complete evaluation of the relationship between consumer expectations and the economy we must, therefore, collect information on the respondent's expectations, whether they be firmly or lightly held, about his own actions, about things which may happen to him, about things which may happen to groups to which he belongs – family, neighbors, people with the same occupation, or the industry – as well as about developments in the entire economy or society.

The questions should refer to the near as well as the more distant future. Even though few people have given thought to the business outlook during the next five years, their answers to such a question reflect their underlying sentiments. The questions about expectations must be supplemented by questions about the past and the present so as to determine the degree of satisfaction with what has been achieved.

Every question intended to elicit an attitude or an expectation is followed by a question about underlying reasons. We always ask, why do you think so? This serves, first, the elementary purpose of eliminating some reporting and recording errors. Then, an expectation for which a person has no explanation may not be held very firmly. This deduction is, however, open to doubt because of interpersonal differences in abilities to verbalize thoughts and opinions. The major value of the 'why' question may be in its enabling us to differentiate between periods in which different reasons are given for the same expectation. For example, it is most useful to note that at one time when the majority opinion is that 'prices will go up', the most common reason given for the belief is that 'the government is spending lots of money', while at another time the same majority opinion is most commonly explained by 'I don't know, but everybody says that prices will be higher next year than they are now'. Changes in the frequency with which different kinds of reasons are mentioned give us significant clues for understanding changes in people's sentiments.

Expressed intentions to buy

Is there really anything to be gained by studying such a great variety of attitudes and expectations? Even if they were to influence action, why should the student of economic trends be concerned with them? Being interested in predicting prospective purchases of consumer durable goods, should he not leave the resolution of the various motives, attitudes and expectations to the consumers themselves and simply ask them about their purchase plans? Is not each consumer himself in the best position to resolve the various influences to which he is subjected and come up with the most reliable prediction of his future actions?[2]

Studies of consumer buying intentions were, in fact, begun by the Survey Research Center and its predecessor organization somewhat earlier than studies of other expectations. The studies

2. Among others, Okun (1960) expressed the opinion that much greater reliance should be placed on buying intentions than on other expectations.

of buying plans did provide very useful information concerning purchases which are commonly planned ahead for a considerable length of time. But they provided no substitute for the study of other expectations. Buying intentions simply represent one of several ways in which attitudes may express themselves.

When we measure buying intentions, we intercept the decision-making process at a rather late stage, when the underlying sentiment has already become somewhat crystallized. Reliance on buying intentions alone, in place of studies of expectations about income and the trend of business does not suffice because changes in incipient, underlying tendencies are of paramount interest. The emphasis placed on studies of buying plans represents but another instance of some students' desire to neglect the less certain aspects of behavior in favor of supposedly definite aspects. Yet even buying plans are far from definite in the sense of ruling out the impact of the uncertainty of the future.

Like all other expectations, consumer buying intentions are attitudes held at a given time and not definite predictions of things to come. As said before, the proportion of consumers who at any given time have made definite decisions to purchase durable goods is quite small. When people are asked whether they expect to buy a car or a television set during the following six months or twelve months, they most commonly express their attitudes toward such a purchase rather than a definite plan. Vague opinions and guesses, or even indefinite statements, such as that the car is fairly old and it might be a good idea to replace it, may be put into definite categories by the researcher, who obtains a measure of change by using the same principles of classification in successive studies. But the researcher in doing so should not assume that the respondent has already resolved his conflicts and has made a final decision.

The planning period varies greatly for different goods. Certain inexpensive durable goods are often bought after consideration for a few days or a few weeks. Even automobiles and houses are sometimes bought without advance planning; sometimes, however, after many years of planning. In classifying answers to questions about buying plans as expressed attitudes, the researcher may disregard differences among individuals in the definiteness of plans and in the length of planning periods. His interest lies in finding out whether buying intentions are more or less frequently expressed in one survey than in the preceding one. His findings will then represent indications that consumer inclinations to buy have increased or decreased, rather than represent predictions of things to come.

Expectations and prediction

What is the relationship between changes in consumer attitudes and forecasts of economic trends? Can studies of attitude change serve to forecast forthcoming developments? This crucial question has been variously answered in the past. The first two answers, listed for the sake of completeness, are of course unacceptable since they contradict the psychological considerations presented here.

1. There are those who hold that attitudes and expectations originate in emotional or impulsive factors. Therefore they are not understandable and are so unstable that they can have no predictive value.

2. Some others contend that expectations are the results rather than the causes of economic and financial developments. Therefore they do not influence behavior, and information about them cannot add significantly to our knowledge.

3. Still others hold similarly that expectations originate in past developments but concede that they, in turn, influence behavior. People expect those things to happen which have happened in the past. An upward movement of prices or profits gives rise to expectation of a continued upward movement; generally prosperous economic conditions arouse the expectation of continued prosperity; prevailing unemployment, the expectation of further unemployment, etc. Therefore, even though expectations may influence behavior, it would be much simpler to measure the specific factors which generate the expectations and thus arrive at equally valid predictions.[3] As we have already seen in the last chapter, our surveys have revealed that occasionally, under certain circumstances, expectations may originate in past trends and indicate a continuation of those trends. But this is not generally true.

3. Some writers speak of 'proxy variables' when they substitute past changes in prices or incomes for price or income expectations.

4. The experience provided by fifteen years of survey research supports a fourth position which holds that a direct study of changes in expectations is scientifically feasible and can be used in forecasting economic trends. Expectations originate in a variety of economic, political, social or personal developments. The manner in which they are formed is a very complicated process. A study of the multitude of environmental 'facts' would not suffice to show in advance how these facts are perceived and what expectations they will produce. Therefore we have no recourse but to measure directly the prevailing expectations which help to shape business and consumer action.

Attitudes and expectations influence demand for certain goods at the time they are held. Information on changes in attitudes and expectations helps to explain changes in demand. The primary function of a study of attitudes and expectations is diagnostic. Good diagnosis of prevailing trends and their causes, of course, helps in making predictions. But forecasting remains a separate step, additional to the measurement of prevailing expectations.

Any forecast derived from attitudinal measurements obviously postulates endurance of the attitudes. Suppose we find in June that people are more optimistic than they were earlier in the year. In order to make any statement about consumer behavior in the third and fourth quarter of the year we must assume that new measurements in, say, July or October, would not contradict the findings of June. It is possible that expectations might undergo a change even shortly after their measurement. But attitudes and expectations of broad groups of people, not necessarily of each individual, hardly ever change abruptly except under the impact of major events. That major events would abruptly change attitudes is easily understood. If a war should break out unexpectedly soon after a study of attitudes was completed, one would hardly attribute any predictive value to the attitudes. Which events, of much lesser importance than war, may constitute unexpected major events is a question for empirical studies.

We must not forget, of course, that changes in consumer attitudes, and in consumer demand as well, do not depend on the consumers alone but are subject to influence by business and government action. Assume, for instance, that consumer surveys disclose a substantial trend toward a pessimistic and uncertain evaluation of the future; thereupon business or government or both introduce such new measures as price reductions, lowering of interest rates or of taxes. If then the prediction derived from the attitudinal measurements – that consumer demand for durable goods will decline – does not come true, should we assume that attitudes have no predictive value? Would it not be justified to contend that attitudinal measurements had been most useful and fulfilled their ultimate function? In either case, government or business action would no doubt constitute major, unexpected events which obviate the predictive value of the attitudes as they were originally determined.

Data on expectations are not forecasts but ingredients of forecasts. Major new developments which take place after the measurement of expectations are further ingredients which eventually will be known to the forecaster. He may also be aided by the fact that survey research can usually determine whether or not the people have anticipated the subsequent developments.

In the absence of major events, substantial changes in the attitudes of masses of people will not occur without casting shadows ahead. In other words, a reversal of observed attitudes is much less probable than a further accentuation of a trend. This is true, at least, for the period immediately following the determination of attitudes. No general rule can be made about the length of that period, but empirical studies, reported in the previous chapter, disclosed that most commonly the anticipatory value of attitudinal data extended over a period from six to nine months.

In summary, attitude change has both an explanatory and a predictive function. Attitude change is defined as a finding that at a given time a significantly higher or lower proportion of the population holds certain attitudes than at an earlier time. To explain the double function of such a finding let us say, for example, that at time point 3 a significantly higher proportion of a representative sample is found to be optimistic, confident, and secure than at a preceding time point 2 and a still earlier time point 1. Under such circumstances we would expect to find that more people had bought durable goods during the period

255

between time points 2 and 3 than between time points 1 and 2. Therefore we would conclude that the change in attitudes had contributed to our understanding of the increase in demand. Secondly, we would expect the demand for durable goods to rise after time point 3, which means that we assign predictive value to the change in attitudes.

Both the explanatory and the predictive function of attitude change has then been related to a change in the *direction* of demand for durable goods. How about the *magnitude* of the change in demand? In a certain sense the two questions are closely related. If attitudes remain unchanged – in other words, if differences between two successive measurements are not significant – we conclude that demand will either increase or decrease slightly but will not change greatly. If the attitude change is substantial, not only are we more confident that demand will change but we shall expect the change to be of significant magnitude in the direction indicated by the attitudes. Nevertheless, there is a great difference between predicting direction and predicting magnitude of a forthcoming change. Although it is possible to devise a scale for measuring attitudes, it is hardly possible to correlate attitude measurements with such others as dollar sales of durable goods and thus to say, for example, that a '10 per cent improvement' in attitudes would indicate a 10 per cent increase in sales. There exists a second reason why this kind of prediction of the magnitude of change is not justified: the magnitude of consumer demand is much more susceptible to the influence of external developments than is the direction of demand. The latter, as we said, is subject to change only as the result of major new events. The former, on the other hand, is influenced by a variety of less important developments and therefore may change more frequently. Furthermore, there exist 'feedback' effects which may in turn serve to cause still more change in magnitude – but not direction – of demand. To illustrate, an increase in demand for durable goods, initiated by an improvement in attitudes, may serve to spur consumer confidence and thus result in still further increase in consumer demand.

That studies of consumer attitudes serve primarily to enable us to understand and predict the direction, rather than the magnitude, of changes in demand does not detract greatly from the value of such studies. It is indeed the question of what direction the economy will take that is of prime importance to students of business cycles and to policy makers both in business and in government. Will the prevailing trend continue, or will there be a change? If there is a change, will it be upward or downward? These are the questions of primary interest and precisely the ones which studies of changes in attitudes help to answer.

References

KATONA, G. (1951), 'Expectations and decisions in economic behavior', in D. Lerner and H. Lasswell (eds.), *The Policy Sciences*, Stanford University Press, pp. 219–32.

KATONA, G. (1958), 'Business expectations in the framework of psychological economics', M. J. Bowman (ed.), *Expectations, Uncertainty and Business Behaviour*, Social Science Research Council, pp. 59–73.

KATONA, G. (1959), 'Repetitiousness and variability of consumer behavior', *Human Relations*, vol. 12, pp. 35–49.

OKUN, A. M. (1960), 'The value of anticipations data in forecasting national products', in G. Katona (ed.), *The Quality and Economic Significance of Anticipations Data*, National Bureau of Economic Research, p. 455.

Part Four **Economic Factors**

The economics literature on consumer behaviour is large
and growing. The first paper in this section is a major review.
Here Robert Ferber, currently president of the American
Marketing Association, covers all the main aspects of
economic research in the field, including research into savings
behaviour and the aggregate expenditure of households.

The second paper, by Stone, Brown and Rowe, exemplifies
the level of difficulty in the techniques used in contemporary
analysis. Only excerpts from the original paper are presented
here: the excluded sections relate to computational and other
technical problems which are of less concern initially.

Stone's paper is built on the traditional economist's model
of consumer behaviour. However, two alternative models are
in process of development and have reached a stage at which
it is well worth drawing attention to them in the two final
papers. One approach owes much to the work of Orcutt at
Wisconsin, and the paper by Goldberger and Lee is in this
tradition. In it they attempt to explain the probability that
households take particular actions. The second formalizes
the notion that consumers have wants to be satisfied by
goods, but do not desire goods for their own sake. The ideas in
this paper have been current for some time, but their
development in Lancaster's paper takes us further and perhaps
provides a bridge between the traditional theory of economics
and the notions of product-field dimensions and brand images
which are familiar in marketing.

15 Robert Ferber

A Review

From Robert Ferber, 'Research on household behaviour'
American Economic Review, vol. 52, 1962, pp. 19–63.

The purpose of this article is to survey the main empirical research of recent years on household behavior. Although the emphasis is on empirical work, principal theoretical developments are also reviewed, partly because of their relevance to an understanding of current thinking in the field and partly to place the empirical studies in proper perspective.

It should be stressed that this article relates to consumer behavior at the microeconomic level. Although various parts touch on problems of aggregation and of macroeconomic relations, comprehensive coverage of these areas is outside the present scope. Furthermore, the focus is on spending and saving behavior rather than on the income or other economic or non-economic behavior aspects of the consumer. At the same time this article necessarily transcends the usual boundaries of economics in view of the growing importance of other disciplines to this area, particularly marketing, sociology and psychology.

Virtually all of the developments covered in this article relate to the period since the Second World War. This hardly constitutes much of a limitation considering the tremendous amount of research that has taken place during this period. As it is, this material is so extensive and diversified that only the highlights can be covered in a relatively short article such as this.

The great bulk of studies of household behavior in the past fifteen years have dealt with one or more of the following aspects of the subject:

1. Theories of spending, or saving, behavior.

2. Influence of variables other than income on spending and saving.

3. Determinants of asset holdings.

4. Determinants of specific expenditures.

5. Decision processes.

This classification accordingly serves as the framework for this article. Admittedly, it focuses entirely on the determinants of household behavior, and ignores the two other basic aspects of this subject, namely, the effects of household behavior on other sectors of the economy, and the measurement of household behavior. The fact remains, however, that relatively little work has been done in these areas, despite their great importance.[1] Excluded also are those studies dealing with the purchase behavior of a particular population, or reference group, and studies dealing with the choice of brands or of shopping locations. Some of these studies are covered in connexion with the determinants of specific expenditures. To cover all of them, however, is too much for this article, aside from the fact that these studies are primarily of a more routine nature.

General theories of spending or saving behaviour

Three general theories currently exist on the determinants of total consumer spending: the *absolute income hypothesis*, the *relative income hypothesis*, and the *permanent income hypothesis*. Though radically different in interpretation, they nevertheless possess certain properties in common. One such property is their purported generality. Each has been used on time series as well as on cross-section data and to derive macro- as well as micro-relationships.[2] Each was advanced originally in terms of individual behavior and then generalized to aggregate behavior,

1. Omitted also is the normative aspect of how households *should* behave. Hardly any empirical research has been devoted to this question, with the possible exception of exploratory studies in the measurement of utility. In its more pedestrian aspects, the normative question falls within the realm of home economics.

2. In the latter case, the application has often been to groups of households rather than to individual households, particularly in the case of the permanent income hypothesis, on the ground that the importance of erratic factors is so great for individual households as to obscure more basic relationships.

sometimes with explicit recognition of the aggregation problem, and at other times largely ignoring it on the apparent presumption that nonlinearities or distributional effects are relatively unimportant.

Each hypothesis postulates a relationship between consumption and income, though the concepts underlying these terms may vary substantially. In other words, the primary concern is to isolate the influence of income, and occasionally of wealth, on consumer spending, holding constant the effect of other possibly relevant, less important variables – age, family composition, location of residence, education, etc. Each is the subject of wide controversy, receiving support from some empirical studies but not from others. Finally, each when first presented appears deceptively simple, at least in theory, but when it comes to implementation, proponents of the same hypothesis often disagree with each other on appropriate definitions and approaches. This will become clear from a consideration of each hypothesis in turn.

Absolute income hypothesis

'... men are disposed, as a rule and on the average, to increase their consumption as their income increases, but not by as much as the increase in their income' (Keynes, 1936, p. 96). Whether or not this is the original statement of the absolute income hypothesis, there is no doubt that this statement by Keynes stimulated much empirical work to test this hypothesis and to derive 'the consumption function'. Many of these studies were carried out on time series, the general practice being to correlate aggregate consumption expenditures over time with aggregate disposable income and various other variables. They need not concern us here except to note that invariably they 'corroborated' the hypothesis, producing very high goodness of fit, adjusted correlation coefficients of 0·98 or more, with current income accounting for the bulk of the variation in consumption, the average and marginal propensities being less than unity, and with the marginal propensity less than the average propensity.[3]

3. For a summary of these studies to 1950, see Ferber (1953). An extensive bibliography of these earlier studies has been compiled by Orcutt and Roy (1949).

One early modification of the absolute income hypothesis was brought about by a theoretical controversy regarding the existence of any automatic force to assure full-employment equilibrium. Keynes took a negative position, but others showed that a full-employment equilibrium position could exist if consumption expenditures depended on wealth as well as on income, the 'Pigou real balance effect' (Pigou 1943).[4] It was only in the postwar period that data became available to test the relevance of a wealth variable. Such tests as were made did tend to show that aggregate consumption was influenced by this variable, though nowhere to the extent of the influence of current income (see Hamburger, 1955 and Klein, 1951b). It is pertinent to note, however, that the early postwar years were characterized by high asset–income ratios, low stocks of durables and relatively little debt.

At the micro level, many studies had been carried out prior to the advent of the *General Theory* but their focus invariably was on ascertaining budget relations for different groups of families or deriving Engel curves for particular components of expenditure.[5] In retrospect, such of these studies as were applicable appeared to corroborate the absolute income hypothesis. Indeed, it was this hypothesis that served as the basis for the derivation of estimates of aggregate expenditures for different population groups in 1935–6, namely, by 'blowing up' average consumption observed at each income level in the 1935–6 Consumer Purchases Study (US National Resources Planning Board, 1941).[6] The absolute income hypothesis also served as a basis for the derivation of aggregate forecasts of postwar consumption patterns, particularly the consumption patterns that might be expected under full employment (Cornfield *et al.*, 1947).

In its empirical applications the absolute income hypothesis has generally followed one of two forms. One form has been to express the level of saving, or of consumption expendi-

4. For a somewhat different interpretation, see Hansen (1961).

5. These are reviewed in Stigler (1954). A fairly comprehensive listing of these studies will be found in Williams and Zimmerman (1935).

6. The actual aggregation procedure was more complicated, but was based on this principle.

tures,[7] as a function of income and of other variables, i.e.

$$S = a + bY + cZ + u \qquad\qquad 1$$

where S represents saving, Y is income, Z is a conglomeration of other variables, u is a stochastic term, and the other letters represent parameters.[8]

The second form involves expressing the saving *ratio* as a function of the same independent variables, i.e.

$$\frac{S}{Y} = a' + b'Y + c'Z + u'. \qquad\qquad 2$$

Each of these forms has advantages and limitations. Thus, in equation 1 the marginal propensity is a constant and, if logarithms of the variables are used, the income elasticity is also constant, namely, b. Equation 2 does not possess this convenient property but may be more realistic for this reason. Parameter estimates based on equation 1 are subject to the danger of bias from two sources: the parameter estimates may be dominated by extreme values, and u is not likely to be independent of S. Expressing dollar variables in logarithms, assuming absence of negative values, removes this tendency somewhat, but not altogether. In actual practice, both forms have been used.[9]

Questions about the adequacy of the absolute income hypothesis arose because of its apparent inability to reconcile budget data on saving with observed long-run trends. Estimates of national saving and other aggregates derived by Kuznets (1946, 1952) and later by Goldsmith (1955, vol. 1, pp. 75–87) indicated that the aggregate saving ratio had remained virtually constant

7. It is perhaps needless to note that consumption functions and saving functions are the same, in theory, one being the complement of the other. However, substantial differences can be obtained in empirical work according to which term is being measured.

8. We shall follow the usual distinction between *saving* and *savings*, the former representing a flow, that is, the difference between income and consumption during a particular period, and the latter representing a stock as of a certain point in time. Unless otherwise specified, saving is defined as the amount set aside out of current income rather than as the net increment in wealth.

9. For applications of these functions at the microeconomic level, see Mendershausen (1940), Klein (1951a, 1954), Fisher (1962).

since the 1870s. Yet budget studies showed that the saving ratio rose substantially with income level. Since incomes have risen tremendously since the 1870s by almost any standard, this would suggest, according to the absolute income hypothesis, that the aggregate saving ratio should have moved up noticeably over time.

Relative income hypothesis

An answer to this apparent inconsistency is provided by the relative income hypothesis, which seems to have been first propounded by Dorothy Brady and Rose Friedman (1947). Its underlying assumption is that the saving rate depends not on the level of income but on the *relative position* of the individual on the income scale, i.e.

$$\frac{s}{y} = a + b\frac{y}{\bar{y}} \qquad\qquad 3$$

where s and y represent individual saving and income respectively, and $\bar{y}$ represents average income.

Much additional theoretical and empirical support of this hypothesis was provided by the work of Modigliani (1949) and of Duesenberry (1949), carried out at about the same time. On a theoretical level, Duesenberry supplied psychological support for this hypothesis, noting that a strong tendency exists in our social system for people to emulate their neighbors and, at the same time, to strive constantly toward a higher standard of living. Hence, once a new, higher standard of living is obtained, as at a cyclical peak, people are reluctant to return to a lower level when incomes go down. In other words, people seek to maintain at least the highest standard of living attained in the past.

On the basis of this reasoning, Duesenberry inferred that from an aggregate time-series point of view the relative income hypothesis could be transformed into one expressing the saving rate as a function of the ratio of current income to the highest level previously reached, i.e.

$$\frac{S}{Y} = a + b\frac{Y}{Y_0} \qquad\qquad 4$$

where Y_0 represents the highest level of income previously attained, after deflation for changes in prices and population.

The implication of this hypothesis is that the saving ratio in the long run is constant, independent of the absolute level of income, although in the short run, from one cycle to another, the rate depends on the ratio of current income to previous peak income.

One variation of this approach has been the suggestion by Davis (1952): that previous peak consumption be substituted for previous peak income. The rationale for this suggestion is that people become adjusted to a certain standard of *consumption* rather than to a certain level of income, so that it is past spending that influences current consumption rather than past income. An additional argument for the substitution of consumption for income is that current income, referring to a period of one year or less, is likely to be less stable and less representative of a family's living standard than is current consumption (Vickrey, 1947, pp. 280–95).

The empirical support for the relative income hypothesis has proceeded along two lines. One consisted of showing that the aggregate relations of a form similar to 4 provide at least as good explanations and statistical 'fits' to fluctuations in national personal saving over time as the various forms of the absolute income hypothesis (Davis, 1952; Duesenberry, 1949, pp. 89–92; Modigliani, 1949, pp. 379–99). Noteworthy in this respect was the finding of an independent evaluation that these functions yielded greater predictive accuracy outside of the period of observation than did various forms of the absolute income hypothesis (Ferber, 1955c).[10] In addition, of course, there was the constancy of the aggregate saving ratio over time which fitted in with the relative income hypothesis.

Secondly, a number of instances were demonstrated in which the relative income hypothesis was, and the absolute income hypothesis was not, able to explain differences in saving or consumption patterns observed in budget data. Thus, Brady and Friedman (1947) by this approach were able to reconcile the higher saving rates of village than city families at the same levels of income in 1935–6, and again in 1941; the similarly higher saving rates of farm families than nonfarm families in 1935–6,

10. However, the most accurate predictions of all were obtained when the functions were transformed into first-difference form, and it was then of little consequence which functional form was used.

and also in 1941; and various geographical differences in saving rates in 1935–6. Duesenberry (1949, chs. 4–5) used this hypothesis to reconcile the fact that dissaving at a given level of income was less frequent in 1941 than in 1935–6, that Negro families saved more than white families in 1935–6 at the same level of income, as well as to explain geographic differences in saving rates. Brady (1952) showed that family saving varied not only with family income but also with the income level of the community in which it resided.

Findings such as these do not necessarily serve to rule out the absolute income hypothesis, and it is still very much of an open question whether the facts do indeed conflict with the absolute income hypothesis or whether the hypothesis has been misinterpreted. A basic tenet of the hypothesis is the *ceteris paribus* assumption for all variables other than (current) income. Yet, data availability in empirical studies has been too restricted to allow other principal relevant variables to be held constant; and if such variables are indeed not constant, failure of saving, or the saving rate, to fluctuate with income may represent simply the effects of these omitted variables. Thus, Tobin (1951, pp. 145–9), shows that the apparent failure of the absolute income hypothesis to explain Negro–white saving differentials at the same level of income can be reconciled if allowance is made for the smaller financial resources available to Negro families than to white families. Because of this difference in wealth, Negro families are unable to dissave as frequently or as much as white families at the same income level, and therefore require extra financial reserves to tide them over emergencies.

In a similar manner Tobin shows that wealth differentials may explain geographic differences in saving rates, and even the historical constancy of the saving ratio. The latter is based on the presumption that the substantial growth in asset holdings over time may have reduced the need for saving out of current income and contributed to raising the propensity to consume as real income increased. Admittedly, the evidence is rather sketchy, as is noted by Tobin (1951, pp. 154–6) and is stressed by Milton Friedman (1957, pp. 173–82). However, if a variable such as wealth could be shown to have influenced the secular propensity to consume, the absolute income hypothesis could be vindicated.

The permanent income hypothesis

This most recent hypothesis on consumer behavior grew out of the rising concern regarding the adequacy of current income as the most appropriate determinant of consumption expenditures.[11] Particularly among nonwage-earner families income receipts vary substantially from period to period, while consumption outlays exhibit much greater stability. This led to the belief that people geared their expenditures to average actual and anticipated income over a number of periods rather than only to income received in the current period. The central idea is as follows:

Consider a large number of men all earning $100 a week and spending $100 a week on current consumption. Let them receive their pay once a week, the pay days being staggered, so that one-seventh are paid on Sunday, one-seventh on Monday, and so on. Suppose we collected budget data for a sample of these men for one day chosen at random, defined income as cash receipts on that day, and defined consumption as cash expenditures. One-seventh of the men would be recorded as having an income of $100, six-sevenths as having an income of zero. It may well be that the men would spend more on pay day than on other days but they would also make expenditures on other days, so we would record the one-seventh with an income of $100 as having positive savings, the other six-sevenths as having negative savings. Consumption might appear to rise with income, but, if so, not as much as income, so that the fraction of income saved would rise with income. These results tell us nothing meaningful about consumption behavior; they simply reflect the use of inappropriate concepts of income and consumption. Men do not adapt their cash expenditures on consumption to their cash receipts, and their cash expenditures on consumption may not be a good index of the value of services consumed – in our simple example, consumption expenditures might well be zero on Sunday (Friedman, 1957, p. 220).

As is often the case with developments of this sort, a theoretical foundation for this hypothesis was developed more or less independently by two different people: by Milton Friedman and by Franco Modigliani, the latter with the collaboration of R. E. Brumberg and Albert Ando. The two versions are similar in

11. For example, see Margaret Reid (1952a), Milton Friedman and Simon Kuznets (1945).

principle, though different in certain respects. Whether it is because of its deceptively simpler formulation or because of its more provocative interpretations and assumptions, the Friedman form has gained wider attention. In what follows both forms are presented, with greater emphasis on the Friedman formulation.

The permanent income hypothesis of Friedman may be said to rest on three fundamental tenets. Firstly, a consumer unit's measured (observed) income, y, and consumption, c, in a particular period may be segregated into 'transitory' and 'permanent' components, i.e.

$$y = y_p + y_t, \qquad\qquad \textbf{5a}$$
$$c = c_p + c_t. \qquad\qquad \textbf{5b}$$

Permanent income, say, in a given year, is the product of two factors: the wealth of the consumer unit, estimated as the discounted present value of a stream of future expected receipts, and the rate, r, or weighted average of a set of rates, at which these expected receipts are discounted (Friedman, n.d.).

The second tenet is that permanent consumption is a multiple, k, of permanent income:

$$c_p = k y_p \qquad\qquad \textbf{6}$$

where k depends only on the interest rate, i, the ratio of non-human to total, nonhuman plus human, wealth, w, and a catchall variable, u, of which age and tastes are principal components. In other words, $k = f(i, w, u,)$, but k is independent of the level of permanent income. It should be noted that consumption here is defined in the physical sense rather than in the monetary sense, i.e. as the physical consumption of goods and services. Durables purchased in a current period are considered as saving to the extent that they are not used up in that period.

Thirdly, transitory and permanent income are assumed to be uncorrelated, as are transitory and permanent consumption, and transitory consumption and transitory income:

$$r_{y_t y_p} = r_{c_t c_p} = r_{y_t c_t} = 0 \qquad\qquad \textbf{7}$$

As a result, a consumer unit is assumed to determine its standard of living on the basis of expected returns from its resources over its lifetime. These returns are expected to be constant from year to year, though in actual practice some fluctuation would result over time with changes in the anticipated amount of capital resources. The expenditures of the consumer unit are set as a constant proportion, k, of this permanent level of income, the value of k varying for consumer units of different types and of different tastes.[12] Actual consumption and actual income deviate from these planned, or permanent, levels to the extent that transitory factors enter in, e.g. a crop failure in the case of farm-family income or unexpected medical bills in the case of spending. However, these transitory factors are essentially random and independent of each other, with the primary result of serving to obscure the true underlying relationship between the permanent components of income and of consumption.

The Modigliani–Brumberg–Ando (MBA) formulation is essentially a 'permanent wealth' hypothesis rather than a 'permanent income' hypothesis, though in practice the two approaches converge. In its most recent formulation, the household or consumer unit is assumed to determine 'the amount available for consumption over life, which is the sum of the household's net worth at the beginning of the period . . . plus the present value of its non-property income . . . minus present value of planned bequests' (Modigliani and Ando, 1960, p. 78). The amount allocated to consumption, defined in the same manner as by Friedman, is a certain proportion of these resources. Actual consumption, however, differs from this allocated amount by transitory expenditures and by certain stochastic factors, v, i.e.

$$c_r = k_r{}^* x_r + v_r.\qquad 8$$

Thus, this relationship is essentially the same as that derived by Friedman (by substituting 6 into 5b, with k^* in 8 corresponding to the product of r and k). Note, however, that the variables in equation 8 have time subscripts whereas those of Friedman's do not. In the MBA formulation, k^* is assumed to vary explicitly with the age of the consumer unit, as is x, and possibly with other

12. A very similar formulation is provided by William Hamburger (1954–5). He postulates total current expenditures of consumers to depend principally on tastes, the interest rate and the discounted value of lifetime resources, the last being determined by the sum of wealth and a multiple of his current wage rate.

factors, such as family size. In the Friedman formulation, k is a constant for the same consumer unit over time.[13]

The MBA formulation is also more flexible in that the possibility is considered that transitory income and transitory consumption may be related to each other. In that event, Modigliani and Ando show that equation 8 turns into the following form:

$$c_r = f(k'_\tau, x_\tau, y_\tau) \qquad\qquad 9$$

so that current income as well as permanent income enter into this relation as determinants of current, observed, consumption. In their empirical work, however, Modigliani and Ando do not seem to have tested this relation.

In either formulation the central tenet is the assumption that the proportion of permanent income saved by a consumer unit in a given period is independent of its income, or its resources, during that period, and furthermore that transitory incomes may have no (Friedman) or little (MBA) effect on current consumption.

Clearly, from an empirical point of view, this is a very difficult hypothesis to test, because of the difficulty of measuring permanent income and permanent consumption. Nevertheless, the permanent income hypothesis is analytically a very rich one and lends itself to a number of significant inferences regarding individual and aggregate behavior. This is not the place to develop these inferences, particularly since they have been developed elsewhere (Friedman, 1957, chs 3 and 7; Modigliani and Ando, 1957; Modigliani and Ando, 1960, esp. pp. 74–109). However, one theoretical inference of this hypothesis deserves special mention because of its basic importance to the empirical tests. Under the permanent income hypothesis, the slope of the relation between observed consumption and observed income, namely, assuming linearity, b in: $c = a + by$, can be shown to be equivalent to kP_y, where P_y is the ratio of the variance of the permanent component of income to the total variance of income, i.e.

$$P_y = \frac{\sum (y_p - \bar{y}_p)^2}{\sum (y - \bar{y})^2}. \qquad\qquad 10$$

13. Although k may vary among consumer units, as noted previously, i.e. $k = f(i, w, u)$.

Since k is constant, by assumption, this means that fluctuations in the slope of measured income reflect fluctuations in the relative importance of the permanent component of income. Furthermore, P_y is equivalent to the income elasticity of consumption, if the elasticity is estimated at the sample means and if the transitory components of both income and consumption average zero. The significance of this becomes clear when we list the principal empirical results and observations advanced to support the permanent income hypothesis:

1. From time series aggregates, Friedman (1957, ch. 5) notes that the following findings are in accord with the hypothesis.

a. The marginal propensity to consume is invariably less than the average propensity to consume.

b. The ratio of permanent consumption to permanent income, k, appears to have been constant since at least 1897, after allowance for variability in the observed consumption–income ratio due to transitory factors.[14]

c. The income elasticity of consumption tends to rise as the period of observation to which a consumption function is fitted increases, thus confirming that transitory factors become less important over longer time spans.

d. Marginal propensities estimated from data deflated for price or population changes are less than those estimated from the corresponding undeflated data: permanent components are more important in the latter case because of the general positive correlation among output, prices and population.

2. From cross-section budget data, Friedman (1957, ch. 4) notes that:

a. Despite observed inequality of income distributions on a cross-section basis, long-run trends indicate that the income distribution is becoming, if anything, more equal – thereby suggesting that measured income is not a valid measure of wealth.

b. The average propensity to consume has been relatively

14. The allowance is rather arbitrary – seeing whether most of the annual points fall within 5 percentage points of a line going through the origin of the consumption–income graph and the long-run average of this ratio, 0.877. On the other hand, as Friedman notes, secular constancy of k is not an integral part of the permanent income hypothesis.

constant in budget studies covering different times and different groups. Furthermore, the stability in the average propensities, and the values of less than unity of the income elasticities, contradict the stability of these cross-section relations – suggesting that the consumption–income ratio declines as income rises, which is inconsistent with the time-series aggregates.

c. Income elasticities are less for the United States than for Great Britain or Sweden, suggesting that transitory factors are more important in the United States, as one might expect.

d. The income elasticity, as well as the marginal propensity and k, are all lower for farm families, and for nonfarm and own-business families, than for other nonfarm families, in accord with the hypothesis.

e. Consumption–income regressions for groups of families classified by income change have steeper slopes than the overall regression: the transitory component is smaller for income-change classes.

3. Turning to work other than Friedman's, P_y estimated from income data for the same consumer units over time yields consistent results for different groups and different time periods. Such estimates also correspond with estimated income elasticities from budget data, which also estimate, independently, P_y (Reid, 1952b).

4. Classification of families by income change appears to result largely in a manifestation of transitory income, rather than expenditure lagging behind changes in permanent income; the consumption–income ratio varies most between years for families with substantial income change (Reid and Dunsing, 1956).

5. The estimated income elasticity for all households exceeds the weighted average of income elasticities for relatively homogeneous groups of households – variation due to transitory factors is less important in the former case (Eisner, 1958; Modigliani and Ando, 1960, pp. 123–66).[15] Furthermore, no systematic association is apparent between mean income and the con-

15. 'Relatively homogeneous groups' means households classified by characteristics unrelated to transitory factors, and for which permanent and transitory incomes are uncorrelated. Classifying criteria used were city size, education, occupation, age, tenure.

sumption–income ratio for most critera; education is a notable exception.

6. Increasing the importance of transitory income by classifying families by current income categories reduces income elasticity estimates – transitory components are more important among these presumably more homogeneous subgroups (Dunsing and Reid, 1958).

7. Groups with the more variable incomes have higher saving ratios (Fisher, 1956, pp. 229–63).

8. The effect of age, or life cycle, is supported by the fact that the observed saving ratio is low for young age groups, highest in the later earning stages, and negative or very low in retirement (Modigliani and Ando, 1957).

Despite these seemingly impressive arguments, the permanent income hypothesis is by no means established. Indeed, the evidence to the contrary seems at least as impressive. This opposing evidence, like the arguments for the theory, covers both theoretical and empirical considerations. On a theoretical plane, question is raised regarding the validity of the two central tenets of the theory, namely, the independence of k of the level of income, and the lack of correlation between transitory consumption and transitory income. Thus, Friend and Kravis (1957a, p. 538) note that the permanent income hypothesis implies 'that low-income families will have no greater preference for purchase of future goods than will high-income families', while Duesenberry (1960, pp. 188–91) makes a similar criticism. Such a concept they find to be seriously deficient on purely deductive grounds because of the very different kinds of pressures and motivations acting on families at different income levels.

In a similar fashion, the assumption of a zero marginal propensity to consumer out of transitory income is questioned, partly on the basis that low-income families are under strong pressures to spend any unexpected income to meet current needs (Friend and Kravis, 1957a, pp. 539–41), and partly because of the very unequal distribution of wealth which mitigates against dissaving by low-income families to maintain consumption in the face of temporary declines in income (Tobin, 1958, p. 451).

275

Criticism of the permanent income hypothesis on empirical grounds has followed two lines. One line has been to note that much of the evidence advanced is either inconclusive or is not inconsistent with other principal hypotheses. Thus, under the absolute income hypothesis one would also expect the marginal propensity to consume to be less than the average propensity, groups with more variable incomes to have higher saving ratios, and consumption–income regressions for groups of families classified by income change to have steeper slopes than the over-all regression. In addition, as was noted previously, Tobin has suggested how the constancy of the long-run propensity to consume might be reconciled with the absolute income hypo-thesis. Furthermore, the interpretation given by Friedman to many of his test results is not the only possible interpretation and is at times subject to considerable doubt (Friend, 1958; Hou-thakker, 1958; Tobin, 1958), though some of the evidence can apparently be interpreted only in terms of it (Reid, 1952b).

From a more direct point of view, various test results have been advanced as contradicting the permanent income hypothesis. Thus, Friend and Kravis (1957a, pp. 544–5) show that the same variation in the saving rate occurs when families are classified by constancy of three-year income as by constancy of one-year income, based on recall data obtained in one-time interviews; in addition, they show that saving rates of different occupational groups appear to be closely correlated with the average income of these groups (p. 546; Friend and Kravis, 1957b, pp. 272–3).

To test the zero propensity to consume out of transitory income, Bodkin (1960) analyzed by correlation methods the extent to which consumption expenditures were made out of unexpected dividends paid in early 1950 out of National Service Life Insurance. This study yielded not only a statistically significant propensity but a propensity to consume out of these dividends much higher than out of regular income.[16] On the other hand,

16. Friedman attempts to reconcile the results with the permanent income hypothesis, on the assumption that these dividend receipts might have been anticipated and/or they created expectations of future dividend receipts, so that this windfall becomes a proxy for permanent income (Friedman, n.d., pp. 191–206). In view of the circumstances surrounding the payment of these dividends, however, such an assumption is highly questionable. A more likely explanation is one offered by Margaret Reid, unpublished,

Kreinin (1961b) obtained a low marginal propensity to consume out of restitution payments made by Germany to former citizens in Israel. However, these payments could hardly have been unexpected.

Admittedly, these negative findings are themselves subject to question. For example, the reliability and representativeness of budget data collected in a partial wartime period such as 1950 is a matter of doubt (Oxenfeldt, 1957). In any event, the permanent income hypothesis is far from proven. However, whether or not the permanent income hypothesis turns out to be valid, there is little doubt that, to quote Tobin (1958, p. 447), 'This is one of those rare contributions of which it can be said that research and thought in its field will not be the same henceforth'. Most of all, it has led to widespread recognition of the possible effects of variability in income on consumption patterns and has provided a theoretical basis for measuring these effects as a springboard for a more realistic theory of consumer behavior.[17]

Influence of variables other than income

A number of studies have been undertaken in recent years to ascertain the effect of particular variables entering into the *ceteris paribus* assumption of the consumption, or saving, function. These studies have focused generally on three sets of variables: socio-economic characteristics of the household, particularly age and life cycle; financial characteristics; and attitudes and expectations. Principal work in each of these sub-areas is reviewed in this section.

Focus on the *ceteris paribus* assumption does not necessarily abstract from the effect of income, for two principal reasons. Firstly, most socio-economic as well as other variables are related to income. Since most of these 'ceteris paribus studies' are carried out either by cross tabulation or by some multivariate method such as analysis of variance or multiple regression, part of the effect attributed to the particular variable may actually be due to

---

that the receipts may have stimulated purchase of homes, thereby setting off a long-run program of saving but a short-run program of spending.

17. For an interesting application of the permanent income hypothesis to analyzing consumer behavior, see the study by Jacob Mincer (1960) relating labor activity to family income and consumption.

income, particularly when interactions and other nonlinear effects are present. Secondly, to the extent that the permanent income hypothesis is valid, even holding constant the effect of current income, the only basis on which income data are available, means that these other variables act to some unknown extent as proxies for permanent income, thereby leading to biased estimates of the effect of these other variables. The fact remains, however, that the *ceteris paribus* variables are of interest in their own right, and even biased effects can be useful.

Socio-economic characteristics

Virtually every budget study presents breakdowns of expenditures and data on such characteristics as age, education, family size, etc. However, the isolation of the effects of these variables on total expenditures or on total saving has received relatively little attention until recently. The availability of the Surveys of Consumer Finances and the various BLS consumer expenditures studies, particularly the 1950 study, and the advent of the relative income and permanent income hypotheses have spurred new interest in these variables. As a result of the latter interest, various studies have attempted to derive saving–income ratios for different population groups. One such study, by Harold Watts (1958), ascribes a central role to occupation and education in the determination of expenditures. Watts attempts to explain expenditures on the basis of a person's expected future income, which is related to a 'cross-section profile' holding occupation, education and age constant. Among other things, he finds that, at a given level of income, those with more education expect higher incomes and spend more.

An attempt by James Morgan (1954) to isolate the effects of soci-economic factors on the saving ratio – in this study, saving is defined as changes in net worth, including purchases of durable goods – uses residuals from regressions of saving on income to examine the effect of a large number of additional socio-economic variables, partly by further regressions and partly by application of analysis of variance.[18] Among other things, these results show

18. Aside from purely statistical considerations, the validity of this methodological procedure depends on whether the absolute income hypothesis or the permanent income hypothesis is correct. If the latter is

that the self-employed, including farmers, had very different saving patterns from other families, that home owners saved more than renters, that dwellers in open country areas saved more than metropolitan dwellers, and that life cycle was highly relevant to understanding saving patterns.

In the case of family size, considerable attention has been given to the problem of allowing for variations in expenditures due to differences in family size, either by deflating by a family-size variable or by including family size as a separate factor. The principal work in this area has been concerned with converting family size into an equivalent-adult unit basis. This problem goes back many years, and an extensive literature has grown up around it, with more recent emphasis on the incorporation of this adjustment within a multivariate framework (see, for example, Prais and Houthakker, 1955, ch. 9; Friedman, 1952).

Attention has also been given to the effect on saving and spending of owning an unincorporated business. Various studies in recent years have thrown considerable light on the saving habits of unincorporated business families, as well as on aggregate saving trends in this area (Friend and Kravis, 1957b; Klein and Margolis, 1954). Thus, both Klein–Margolis and Friend–Kravis show that such families have much larger than average negative saving at low incomes and much higher than average positive saving at high incomes than other families, and that the same is true of both farm and nonfarm entrepreneurs. Friend–Kravis show that the self-employed exhibit much the same consumption pattern as that of other families; though another study by Klein (1960, pp. 331–5) suggests that the self-employed are more frequently home-owners and tend to spend less for rental costs and more for household operations than families of salaried professionals and officials. Klein also shows that the self-employed save more than other families principally because of their business saving; they do not save appreciably more in other forms.

Age and the life cycle. Perhaps the main analytical work in recent years relating to socio-economic characteristics has been with

---

the case, the procedure is a biased one because, as noted previously, only measured income is then held constant while the effect of permanent income is intermingled with the other socio-economic variables. See Friedman (1957, pp. 86ff.).

279

age and the life cycle. Although various early budget studies were concerned in part with the influence of age in one or more of these respects, it was primarily the 1935–6 Consumer Purchases Study with its extensive tabulations that served as a springboard for analysis of the influence of the age factor on consumption. In that study, attempts were made to examine variations in income and in consumption not only by different age groups but by different family types, reflecting to a large extent different stages of the family life cycle (US Department of Agriculture, 1939–41; US Bureau of Labor Statistics, 1938–41).

The substantial variations observed in income and consumption by age and family composition led to further study of these variables in the postwar years. The initial studies focused primarily on the effects of age or of family composition. Many of these studies were carried out at the Survey Research Center of the University of Michigan, based on data collected in the Survey of Consumer Finances. Using these data, Janet Fisher (1962, 1952, 1955) was able to develop much useful information on the role of the age factor in consumer behavior. These studies provide empirical data on the manner in which income increases from youth to about middle age and then declines thereafter, though with considerable variation by occupation and wealth; on the manner in which liquid assets rise from youth through middle age and decline thereafter; and on the different purchasing patterns of families in different age levels. Especially notable in the last category is the tendency for younger families to be heavy purchasers of durable goods even though they may have to dissave to do so, whereas older families with the necessary assets make relatively few durable goods purchases.[19]

In a very interesting exploratory study of the determinants of saving, Dorothy Brady (1956, p. 193) finds that to a large extent age comparisons of saving rates are confounded with the effects of income changes, so that 'the variation among the age groups in expenditures and saving within the current income bracket will

19. Of particular interest from this point of view is the article by Dorothy Brady (1955) on the influence of age on saving and spending patterns. More recently, a wealth of descriptive data on the consumption patterns of the aged will be found in the study by Sidney Goldstein (1960).

accordingly be a reflection of changes in the direction and magnitude of income . . .'. Holding income constant, saving is found to increase uniformly as the age of the wife rises. In addition, Brady shows that family saving is influenced not only by socio-economic variables such as age, family size and occupation, but may also be influenced substantially by the general level of income in the community where the family resides.

These and other results on the effect of family composition on spending and saving have brought into focus the importance of a life-cycle variable, a variable which would reflect the simultaneous influence of a number of different socio-economic characteristics.[20] This interest led, among other things, to the convening in 1954 of a conference by Consumer Behavior, Inc., on the life cycle as related to economic, marketing and sociological behavior of consumer units. The volume that grew out of this conference provides a wealth of data on the subject (Clark, 1955), ranging from provocative discussions of the role of age and US culture on consumer purchases, by David Riesman and Howard Rose-borough, to the first really thorough empirical study of consumer finances over the life cycle, by John B. Lansing and James N. Morgan. The latter study is particularly noteworthy because it uses as the basis for the analysis a classification of consumer units by stage of life cycle rather than by age alone, as was the case for virtually all of the previous studies. The article demonstrates the analytical values of such a classification and presents empirical data on the manner in which income, spending and assets vary over the life cycle. Related studies in this volume present information on the manner in which purchasing interest and purchasing trends vary by the life cycle, and on the possible impact of the life cycle on advertising (Barton, 1955; Miller, 1955, pp. 61–5).

Some studies have also been conducted on the effect of the life cycle on consumer behavior in Great Britain. Thus, Harold Lydall (1955) has traced the life-cycle pattern in income receipts

20. Actually, life cycle as a variable had for some time previous been a principal topic in the study of the sociology of the family, and had also been of interest in studying the spending patterns of farm families. For example, see Kirkpatrick (1934), Glick (1947).

in savings and in net worth, finding the pattern roughly similar in Great Britain to that in the United States.[21] At the same time, net worth does not appear to decline as much in Great Britain after income has turned down. In addition, a comparative study by Janet Fisher (1955, pp. 33–5) shows that durable-goods purchases were much more prevalent in the United States than in Great Britain for the same age groups, and that incomes began to decline at an earlier age in the United States than in Great Britain.

Financial factors

Income change. A number of studies of the effects of income change have been made in the postwar years. The findings of these studies are generally similar, but the interpretation of the findings has differed at times substantially, as noted in the discussion of the permanent income hypothesis. Thus, in several studies based on data collected in the Surveys of Consumer Finances, high saving rates are found to be associated, at the same income level, with recent increases in income while those whose incomes have fallen tend to save less. Dissaving was more common among those whose incomes had either declined or risen substantially than among consumer units with relatively stable incomes. Furthermore, an inverse correlation was found between the purchase of durable goods and saving, consumer units having major outlays for durable goods being much more likely to dissave (Katona, 1949a, 1949b; Katona and Fisher, 1951; Klein, 1955b; Morgan, 1954), Morgan notes that the effect of income change varies with asset ownership: among those with small amounts of liquid assets, saving does not vary so much with income change (Klein, 1954, p. 124).

Similar findings on the effect of income change on spending behavior were obtained by Ruth Mack (1948) in analyzing budget data of 600 farm families; and she suggests that the effect of changes in income is likely to differ for different expenditure categories. On the other hand, Margaret Reid shows that the same data can be interpreted as highlighting the importance of transitory income in distorting expenditure–income relationships.

21. Although life cycle is the focus of this study, only age is used as a classifying variable.

The incorporation of income-change as a variable in multiple regressions explaining household saving rates leads to mixed results. Studies by Klein (1951a, 1954), Morgan (1954) and Katona (1949a) indicate that the effects of this variable may interact partly with income expectations and partly with liquid assets. Furthermore, the effect may be asymmetrical, being more pronounced for income decreases than for income increases. Households experiencing income decreases and who expect further decreases appear to save more, at the same level of income, than households experiencing decreases but expecting an upturn in the near future (Klein, 1951a, p. 446).

In a unique study of short-run effects of income change upon saving, savings and expenditures in a relatively isolated New England community, George Brinegar (1953a, 1953b) finds that household behavior serves to amplify rather than to dampen the effects of income change upon purchases of goods and services. Thus, following a sharp income decrease milk purchases first declined, then rose above the earlier level, and finally leveled off. In addition, correlations between payrolls and bank balances indicated greater stability between payrolls and savings-account balances than between payrolls and saving in these accounts, thus providing some support for the Pigouvian analysis of income determination.

Wealth. The relevance of wealth to consumption and saving has been recognized in the theoretical literature for some time. As noted earlier, Pigou (1943) as well as Lerner in a different sense (1943, pp. 44–9), had stressed the importance of increases in wealth in maintaining full employment by causing the consumption–income schedule to shift to the right. Tobin has suggested that increases in wealth may be responsible for the constancy of the aggregate propensity to save over time. Ackley (1951) has ascribed a crucial role to wealth in the determination of the cyclical consumption function. In addition, wealth, it will be recalled, plays a central role in the permanent income hypothesis: in the Friedman formulation the ratio of permanent consumption to permanent income is assumed to rise with increases in the ratio of wealth to income; in the MBA formulation, wealth serves as the basis for estimating permanent income. However, empirical work has been, and continues to be, hampered by lack of data. This has been particularly true with regard to wealth and individual behavior, since data on liquid assets have been available only since the Second World War.

Although not conclusive, the weight of empirical evidence points to a positive, though erratic, relationship of liquid assets to consumption and saving, at least in the postwar years. Under the much less prosperous prewar conditions it is doubtful whether liquid assets exerted much influence on the consumption–income reationship, at least in the aggregate (Cohen, 1954); on a cross-section basis there do not seem to be any data. In the postwar years, the effect of liquid assets appears to have varied with time. A strong positive relationship with durable-goods expenditures existed in the late 1940s and a much weaker effect in the early 1950s (Klein, 1954).

As a general rule, the saving rate for individual households appears to vary inversely with the ratio of liquid assets to income, and the influence of liquid assets on saving tends to diminish as the level of income rises (Klein, 1951a; 1951b, pp. 210–27). Households with a given amount of liquid assets that experience a decline in income tend to save less than households with the same income decline but with less liquid assets, or than households with the same amount of liquid assets but no income decline.

In his study, Morgan (1954) found the liquid-asset effect to interact with income change, the saving rate increasing with liquid assets for those experiencing a substantial income increase, and the saving rate varying inversely with liquid-asset holdings among those experiencing substantial income declines.

Various students of the problem have suggested that net worth is a more relevant concept than liquid assets (Lydall, 1958; Tobin, 1952). This concept is also much closer to the definition of wealth in the MBA formulation of the permanent income hypothesis, in which wealth plays a basic role. Unfortunately, data on net worth are difficult to collect, and hypotheses based on net worth or on total resources have yet to be subjected to direct examination.

Expectations and intentions-to-buy

Although the role of expectations in consumer behavior has been discussed in the economic literature for many years, empirical research in this area has been purely a postwar development, and is attributable largely to the activity of one man, George Katona. His interest in economic behavior supplemented by a strong psychological background led him to stress, in the 1940s, the importance of expectations and attitudes in a high-level economy. He noted the importance of studying the factors underlying decision processes in economic behavior as well as the growing discretionary aspects of consumer spending, in the case of which attitudes and expectations might be expected to exert a dominant role (Katona, 1947). Such factors influence *willingness* to buy, which for spending and saving other than that which is habitual would seem to be about as important as *ability* to buy.[22] With the aid of data collected under his supervision in the annual Surveys of Consumer Finances, he has been able to present considerable support for this point of view, showing that durable goods purchases were related to a number of individual attitudes as well as to an index of attitudinal variables (Katona and Mueller, 1956, pp. 91–106).

On the basis of such analyses, Katona and his associates at the Survey Research Center were able to conclude that 'motives, attitudes, and expectations often change at about the same time and in the same direction among large groups of consumers. Such changes commonly occur prior to changes in the rate of postponable spending and of saving' (Katona, 1955, p. 67), and hence attitudinal data were valuable for predicting consumer spending and saving behavior. As a result of these studies, the Survey of Consumer Finances has been collecting such data every year and using them as a basis for analyzing and also predicting consumer behavior.

Data on intentions-to-buy were also collected in the annual Surveys of Consumer Finances, as part of the attitudinal section. It soon became evident, however, that not only did these data differ conceptually from that obtained with the other attitudinal

22. The main theoretical arguments are presented in his early volume (Katona, 1951, pp. 63–8). Also, see the study by George Katona and Eva Mueller (1953).

questions – representing in effect an *ex ante* expression of consumer purchases – but exhibited at times a marked relationship to actual purchases apart from the attitudinal data. Such relationships were apparent both over time and on a cross-section basis, even though these intentions referred to a year or more ahead (Lansing and Withey, 1955, pp. 405–40). In addition, experimentation with the collection of plans-to-buy data on a quarterly basis showed that meaningful quarterly data could be collected and, furthermore, that an even more marked relationship existed between plans to buy reported quarterly and later purchases (Ferber, 1954).

Considerable additional support for the value of plans-to-buy data has been provided by a project of the National Bureau of Economic Research under the direction of F. T. Juster, to analyze the value, as a forecasting tool, of buying plans as reported by Consumers Union subscribers. Although Consumers Union subscribers are not typical of the total population, and although buying plans were collected on an annual basis, year-to-year changes in buying plans for selected major durable goods were found to foreshadow closely corresponding changes in actual purchases for the postwar years (Juster, 1960b, 1957). In addition, these studies indicated that plans-to-buy data made a net contribution to predictive accuracy even after income was taken into account (Juster, 1960a).

Partly as a result of these findings and partly because of the inter-correlation between plans to buy and attitudinal variables, a lively controversy has arisen regarding the relative superiority of these two types of data for forecasting purchases. Katona and some of his associates at Michigan maintain that attitudinal data provide insight into underlying motives and buying forces apart from soci-economic factors – age, income, wealth, etc – and that such information can help improve forecasts. Others feel that plans-to-buy, though perhaps not as fundamental in a psychological sense, is the relevant overt variable for forecasting purposes, and that once such data have been taken into account, no net additional contribution can be expected from information on expectations or attitudes.[23]

23. An excellent source for recent arguments and evidence pro and con is Eva Mueller (1960).

To date, the empirical tests provide strong evidence in favor of the second hypothesis. After reviewing the evidence then available, the Federal Reserve Consultant Committee on Consumer Survey Statistics under the chairmanship of Arthur Smithies concluded, in 1955, that 'buying intentions, properly interpreted, appear to have predictive value. . . . Other attitudes are highly correlated with buying intentions, both over time and as among spending units, and there is so far no convincing evidence that they make an independent contribution to ability to predict, . . .' (US Federal Reserve Board, 1955, pp. 137–8). Klein and Lansing (1955, pp. 115–26) found plans-to-buy to help significantly in multiple regressions discriminating between buyers and nonbuyers of durable goods – in addition to age, income and marital status – while other attitudinal variables were either not effective or much less effective. In a fundamental test, Tobin (1951) showed by regression analysis that plans-to-buy, in addition to socio-economic variables, made an appreciable net contribution to explaining durable goods purchases whereas this was not true of an attitudinal index; and, when combined in the same equation, plans-to-buy was significant, but not the attitudinal index. Similar results were obtained by Okun (1960).

Eva Mueller (1960), though espousing the other side, shows that buying intentions but not an attitudinal index contribute significantly to multiple regressions explaining major durable-goods purchases. The only evidence to the contrary presented so far is also in this study, which shows that an attitudinal index contributes more than buying plans, or than the same index including buying plans, to explaining aggregate semi-annual fluctuations in durable goods expenditures from 1952 to 1957. However, this test is not as comprehensive as Tobin's, including only income as an independent variable and making no allowance for heteroscedasticity.

The findings regarding the value of buying intentions as a predictive tool have been impressive enough that such data are now collected on a continuing, short-run basis. Consumer spending plans for major durables and other large expenditures have been collected bimonthly by telephone by the National Industrial Conference Board since 1958 (Cohen and Gainsbrugh, 1958), while the Federal Reserve Board in conjunction with the

US Bureau of the Census has been collecting quarterly buying intentions data on a much more comprehensive basis since 1959 (Weiss *et al.*, 1960).

Attitudinal data have not been ignored. Indeed virtually everybody is agreed that 'the primary reason for collecting data on psychological factors influencing behavior is to improve the diagnosis of the prevailing situation' (Katona, 1960a, p. 455). Many of the studies reviewed here, particularly those of Katona and Mueller, have shown how expectations and attitudes are related to buying plans and to economic events, and have thrown light on their nature and characteristics.[24]

Determinants of asset holdings

The growing stock of consumer assets has led to investigation not only of the influence of assets on saving behavior but also on the factors associated with holding particular assets. With these more recent studies, the focus shifts from flows out of income to the investment decisions of the household and to explaining differences in the total stock of assets and their distribution among households and over time.

Reasons for holding particular types of assets have been discussed in the theoretical literature for some time (e.g. Keynes, 1936, ch. 16). More recently, Katona (1951, pp. 98–107) has attempted to merge these reasons with motivational and other psychological factors as a basis for empirical study.

Empirical studies are, as yet, relatively few. In a comprehensive study of the factors influencing the composition of the 'capital account' of the household – essentially financial assets, durables, business capital – Watts and Tobin concluded that 'households tend to maintain some sort of balance in their capital accounts both between assets yielding direct service and financial assets, and between liquid funds and liabilities' (Watts and Tobin, 1960, p. 48). Ownership of different assets was positively correlated, while assets and debts were negatively correlated: apparently as households moved up the economic status scale,

24. In the former respect, see in addition to the previously cited publications, Katona (1960b) and Calla Van Syckle (1954). In the latter connection, see Ferber (1955b) and Katona (1958).

more of all kinds of assets were acquired and debt was reduced.

By means of a series of multiple regressions on the 1950 Consumer Expenditures data, Watts and Tobin find the composition of particular portfolios to be influenced by a number of 'fundamental but unobserved measures of social, economic, and environmental characteristics' (Watts and Tobin, 1960, p. 48). In particular, households headed by people with more education tended to have larger stocks of assets and lower debt, with income and other relevant variables held constant. Older households had less invested in durables and less debt as well. Occupational differences are pronounced, though erratic. Larger families generally had more in durables and less cash than other households. Regional and city-size differences were also apparent. Higher-income households had more in financial assets and less in durables.

Despite the large number of significant relationships, however, in most instances less than 10 per cent of the variation in the dependent variable was explained.

In a study of factors influencing the holding of liquid assets by British households, Lydall (1958) finds total wealth, measured as net worth, rather than income level to be the primary determinant, of such holdings.[25] Applying multiple regressions to data from the Surveys of Consumer Finances, Harold Guthrie (1960) shows that liquid assets relative to income tend to rise with age and fall as the size of the consumer unit increases. In addition, the liquid-assets ratio is higher for those who appear to have permanently depressed incomes and is less for those anticipating income increases.

Two other US studies found that the proportion of total assets held in liquid form declined substantially as wealth increased. The proportion of assets in liquid form also declined with income level, but a multiple regression study including both income and total assets indicated, as in the case of Lydall's study, that wealth was by far the dominant factor (Claycamp, 1961, ch. 4).

25. It is not clear, however, to what extent this finding is affected by the fact that liquid assets averaged overall about one-fourth of net worth, but over 100 per cent in the lower net-worth classes.

Economic Factors

Using data from the Consumer Savings Project,[26] Claycamp applied multiple regression analysis to test the relevance of a wide range of socio-economic and psychological variables to the proportion of total financial assets held in variable-dollar form, that is, assets whose value fluctuates with changes in prices – common stocks, marketable bonds, real estate, etc. Age, home ownership, total assets and occupation were significantly related to various forms of this variable-dollar ratio. Attitudinal variables, such as price expectations and other economic expectations, were not significant.

A major part of Claycamp's work was the investigation of the apparent lack of substitution between different types of assets. Such a lack of substitution had been noted by Guthrie (1960, p. 478) between liquid assets and equity in homes; and he had suggested that 'consumers do not shift between asset forms while maintaining some normative level of security in total wealth'. Tobin and Watts (1960) had also advanced the same idea with their hypothesis that consumers, in the handling of their capital accounts, attempted to balance assets and debts against each other; while in a more recent study Phillip Cagan (1961) found an absence of substitution between pension contributions and other savings.

Claycamp's investigation (1961, p. 1) of the frequency of different asset holdings provided strong support for this phenomenon, extending it to different combinations of thirteen assets and debts, two or more at a time, using ownership frequencies and dollar amounts in turn. The results led to the so-called 'independence hypothesis,' namely, that 'there is no significant difference between the actual proportion . . . owning a combination of holdings and the expected proportion which is found by multiplying each of the proportions in the combination'. Confirmation of this hypothesis would have major implications for economic analysis.

Various studies have been made by Kreinin (1957, 1959, 1961a) with Survey Research Center data of the factors influencing ownership of specific assets, notably, liquid assets, life insurance

26. Sponsored by the Inter-University Committee for Research on Consumer Behavior with financial assistance from the Ford Foundation and the US Department of Agriculture.

and common stock. In these studies, which were carried out by analysis of variance, a number of socio-economic factors were found to be associated with ownership of these assets, particularly income and occupation. In the case of liquid assets, age and region were also significant; while education and liquid assets appeared to influence stock ownership. In the latter case, an optimistic outlook and willingness to take risk also showed some relationship to the dependent variable. In all of these studies, however, price expectations were not significantly related to the dependent variable, though other attitudinal variables were significant.[27]

Determinants of specific expenditures

Two different lines of approach have been used to ascertain the factors influencing the consumption of specific consumer products, reflecting the conceptual equality between purchases of goods by consumers and sales of these goods by retailers or manufacturers. One approach has attempted to explain static differences in product purchases of different households in terms of household characteristics, largely to the exclusion of prices and other market variables; while the other approach has attempted to explain temporal differences in aggregate sales in terms of market variables, largely to the exclusion of household characteristics, though aggregate income does appear in such functions.

Paralleling the consumption function, the first approach has been characterized by the search for so-called Engel curves – relationships between specific expenditures – or forms of saving – and income level, holding other relevant variables constant. The

27. Unfortunately, the method used in these studies is subject to serious question. In each case, the analysis of variance was carried out by treating the cell means as the unit of observation rather than the individual consumer unit. Since the cell sizes in consumer surveys are decidedly unequal, such a procedure is an immense time saver. However, the procedure is also likely to distort seriously the significance of different factors, particularly of interaction effects, since the variance among the cell means is treated as equivalent to the random sampling variance. Some experimental computations made by the writer indicate that such an assumption is clearly unjustified, and that the use of the individual consumer unit as the unit of observation is likely to produce very different results, especially bringing out unexpected significant variables and interaction effects.

second general approach has utilized sales data and related information from industry sources. This approach has necessarily had to be aggregative in nature and, for this reason, has generally focused on the derivation of time-series relationships; it is exemplified by the search for demand curves, to ascertain how sales fluctuate in response to changes in price, holding other relevant factors constant.

Empirical work on both approaches had its beginning about the mid-nineteenth century, with the work of Engel on household budgets and, some time later, with the work of a number of US and British statisticians on demand relationships.[28] Since then empirical studies in both areas have multiplied enormously, spurred by the growing interest in statistical methods, and the ease with which a demand study can be used as the basis for a thesis. With both approaches, the past two decades have witnessed numerous empirical studies of specific commodities – and, more recently, of services – which have added considerably to knowledge of the effect of different variables on purchases, or sales. At the same time, this period has witnessed a growing emphasis on methodological improvements, and it is here that the principal developments in this area have taken place. For this reason, the present review is relatively brief and, in view of the orientation of this paper, focuses primarily on the use of household budget data.

In the area of demand analysis, considerable progress has been made in the specification and estimation of relationships. Recognition that price and possibly other relevant variables are not always independent of quantity led to more careful specification of demand relationships and to the development of more appropriate methods of estimation. Interdependence was taken into account by the equation-systems approach, using limited-information or reduced-form methods of estimation (e.g. Tintner, 1951). For situations where the interdependence was not instantaneous, the simpler recursive method of estimation was developed and has been shown to yield highly effective results (Wold and Jureen, 1953). Although least squares is still probably the most widely used method of estimating the parameters of demand functions, in many instances justifiably so, and the controversy on the relative efficiency of the different estimation

28. For a brief description of these early studies, see G. J. Stigler (1954).

methods is by no means settled (e.g., Christ *et al.*, 1960), a wide variety of effective estimation procedures are currently available. Perhaps the most recent innovation is the use of both income and total expenditures as instrumental variables in deriving Engel Curves (Liviatan, 1961).

Considerable progress has also been made in specifying the *ceteris paribus* of demand functions. A major innovation has has been the introduction, and the significance revealed, of quality as a determining variable (Stone, 1954, pp. 388–9). Another innovation has been the attempt to allow discontinuity in reaction to changes in income and prices. One such attempt is exemplified by the 'ratchet effect' of Modigliani and Duesenberry, according to which people continually adjust upward their living standards in response to peak standards attained in the past. A somewhat different approach has been that of Farrell (1952), who allows for the possibility that demand relationships may be irreversible over time, that responses to a given change may depend not only on the amount of the change but also on the direction of change.

Further realism has been added through the use of lagged reactions, which have been shown to aid considerably in explaining fluctuations in demand (Chow, 1957, pp. 49–74; Suits, 1958). Distributed lags, and the so-called quasi-accelerator, in which demand is assumed to depend upon the rate of increase, as well as upon the prevailing level, of income), have also been introduced successfully in demand analysis (Nerlove, 1958).[29]

Attempts have been made to derive demand functions not only for a single commodity at a time but for a large range of commodities. This technique has been used by the US Department of Commerce as well as by Richard Stone in explaining fluctuations in consumer demand (see Paradiso and Winston, 1955, and Stone, 1954). Unfortunately, the use of a standardized equation for a wide range of commodities serves to place the demand function essentially in a statistical straitjacket, and at least one experimental study suggests that biased estimates of income elasticities may result (see Clark, 1955, pp. 410–13).

29. A general description of these and other innovations in demand analysis will be found in the recently published book by Robert Ferber and P. J. Verdoorn (1962, chs. 8, 9).

Turning to the use of household-budget data, Engel's 'Law' – that the proportion of household expenditure on food declines as household income rises – has by now been verified literally hundreds of times.[30] Generally, most studies also provide strong support for what is known as Schwabe's Law, namely, that the per cent of income spent for housing declines as income rises, although using permanent income concepts Margaret Reid (1952a, 1958) alleges that high-quality housing in reality is one of the main luxuries of consumers. Further support for both laws was obtained in a study by Houthakker (1957) in which he derived Engel curves for four expenditure groups based on data from each of forty surveys from seventeen countries. It is interesting that the function used in this study, as in many others, was essentially the same as used by Engel in his original paper, namely, a log-log relationship between the specific expenditure and total expenditures.

Recent studies reflect a growing interest in ascertaining the determinants not only of food expenditures but of a wide range of household purchases, such as housing, clothing, house furnishings and services.[31] These studies show that these consumer purchases are influenced by a wide variety of socio-economic characteristics; but, nevertheless, the proportion of variance in individual household purchases explained by these numerous factors is small, often the order of 0.3 or less. In addition, these studies tend to bear out earlier findings on income elasticity, yielding low elasticities close to unity for clothing and education, and higher elasticities for various types of recreation, personal care, home operation and other services.[32]

Special attention has been given to the relationship between durable-goods expenditures, financial saving and other variables;

30. For a partial list of studies, see the bibliography by James N. Morgan (1958a). There has also been an abortive tendency to mangle the principle by refuting its applicability with time-series data, something that would make Engel turn over in his grave.

31. On clothing, see Dorothy S. Brady (1960) and Morris Hamburg (1960); on house furnishings, see Vernon Lippitt (1959); on services, see Robert Ferber (1960) and on housing, see Sherman Maisel and Louis Winnick (1960).

32. For a summary of these earlier studies, see the review article by Ruth P. Mack (1952).

and strong evidence now exists that to a large extent purchase of durables is a substitute for financial saving (Friend and Jones, 1960a, pp. 336–59; Klein, 1955a; Maynes, 1959). All of these studies find purchase of durable goods related to a variety of socio-economic characteristics, particularly age, income change, size of consumer unit and various expectations. Studying the characteristics of a host of such purchases combined into 'consumer investment' expenditures – purchases of cars, other durables, household equipment, and additions and repairs to houses – Morgan (1958b) finds this category to have constituted a relatively constant proportion, between 12 and 16 per cent, of disposable income at all income levels, except the lowest and the highest, during each of the postwar years, 1947–56.[33] Such expenditures are found to be influenced, as in other studies, by a variety of demographic and attitudinal variables, and are found to be sticky downward and flexible upward with respect to changes in income.

As in the area of demand analysis, linear – in some cases, logarithmic – single-equation forms have been used to derive from the same data marginal propensities and income elasticities for a wide range of consumption categories. This was the approach used by Prais and Houthakker (1955) on English data, and by Crockett and Friend (1960, pp. 1–92) on American data. The Friend–Crockett study analyses by multiple regression analysis the effects on all major consumption categories of a large number of family characteristics including income. Among other things, their results indicate that family size and age, next to income, appear to exert the main influence on family consumption, particularly through the influence of family size on food expenditures and of age on durable goods purchases. The study also finds that income elasticities are reduced substantially once variables reflecting other family characteristics are introduced into the relationships.[34]

33. Morgan suggests that this proportion might have been constant at the highest income level too, if purchases of such items as summer homes, motor boats and fur coats had been included.

34. A basic question underlying many of these studies is whether they do provide reasonably accurate estimates of the income effect on particular expenditures. To the extent that the permanent income hypothesis is correct, income effects estimated by relating current expenditures to current

At the same time, dissatisfaction has been expressed over the rigid assumptions inherent in this approach. This dissatisfaction was crystallized to some extent by the findings of Prais and Houthakker (1955, pp. 87–103) that a semi-logarithmic form is preferable for necessities and a log-log form is preferable for luxuries; and by Stuvel and James (1950) that the use of only one form of equation to explain variations in food expenditures over the entire range of incomes and social classes is unsatisfactory.

One result of this dissatisfaction has been some interesting attempts to modify the Engel-curve approach. One approach has been to introduce nonlinearities into the expenditure–income relationship to allow for the possibility that a commodity may behave as a luxury in one range of income and as a necessity in a different range (Prais, 1952–3). A Sigmoid response curve, which has an upper asymptote and at the same time passes through the origin, appears to yield realistic results in such instances (Aitchison and Brown, 1954–5).

Another approach, one that uses linear equations, has been to explain consumer purchases of specific goods on the basis of relationships between stocks and wealth rather than between income and expenditure. Quasi-Engel curves relating inventories to a measure of wealth have been derived by Cramer (1958) for a wide variety of household goods based on two Dutch surveys, and by Houthakker and Haldi (1960) for automobiles based on panel data for US families. The latter study is particularly interesting, showing that at a given level of income gross investment in automobiles varies inversely with beginning-of-the-year inventory, and that at a given level of beginning inventories, gross investment rises with income level.[35]

income can be understated substantially. Thus, in the case of housing, Margaret Reid (1958) obtains income elasticities of close to 2 by using average incomes for groups instead of data, for individual households. On the other hand, as noted earlier, Friend and Kravis (1957a) obtained much the same income elasticities using three-year averages of household income as from one-year figures.

35. It might be noted that a somewhat similar approach was used by Hans Brems (1956) on time-series data to predict the long-run equilibrium demand for automobiles based on a model relating stock of automobiles to the equilibrium rate of growth and the average age at which cars are scrapped. An extension of this model, incorporating time lags, has been presented by Marc Nerlove (1957).

Dissatisfaction with the linear-equation approach has also led to the use of variance analysis rather than multiple regression to ascertain the net effect of different variables on household expenditures. Variance analysis offers a more flexible approach to the estimation of relationships, since no assumption is necessary regarding the form of the functional relationship. As a result, studies using this technique do not always give the clear-cut simple results yielded by multiple regression, but in many ways appear to be more realistic, bringing out effects of various characteristics not only singly but in combination with each other, (e.g. Crockett, 1957; Ferber, 1960, pp. 436–60; Lippitt, 1959). Unfortunately, as noted previously, several of these studies have utilized group averages rather than individual families as the unit of observation, thereby greatly reducing the chances of detecting interaction effects.

Another postwar development has been emphasis on obtaining and analyzing the expenditure and saving behavior of the same households over time. Popular for many years in marketing and advertising circles, the value of the consumer panel technique to economic analysis, and as a connecting link between time-series aggregates and cross-section budget surveys, has only recently been recognized, stimulated in part by the emphasis of the permanent income hypothesis on the life history of the household. Panel studies undertaken so far have clearly demonstrated their value. In addition to studies discussed earlier (Ferber, 1955a; Katona and Fisher, 1951),[36] Houthakker and Haldi, in their automobile investment study, which was based on panel data, were able to isolate family taste as a separate variable. In another study based on panel data, Jean Crockett (1957) showed that income elasticities based on continuous panel data were much closer to time-series elasticities than the usual cross-section elasticities.

The introduction of panel data in budget studies highlights the growing interest in recent years in integrating the techniques of demand analysis and of household budget analysis. Time-series aggregates have serious disadvantages because of the frequently unstable estimates of income and of demand elasticities obtained

36. Another study still being analyzed is a food purchase panel operated by Michigan State University; see Quackenbush and Shaffer (1960).

as a result of the high correlation between income and prices. On the other hand, cross-section data are essentially static and are difficult to use as a basis for prediction. Hence, a combination of the two types of data would seem to offer a much more powerful technique for understanding consumer behavior.

Initial efforts made to integrate these two sets of data have been directed toward deriving independent estimates of income elasticities from budget data, inserting these estimates into an aggregate time-series demand relation, and estimating the parameters of the other variables from the time-series data (Farrell, 1954; Tobin, 1950; Stone, 1954, esp. ch. 18). An alternative approach has been to search for cross-section functions that might be expected to remain stable over time. This approach was used by Eleanor Snyder (1958) in a study finding a cross-section consumption relationship for food to yield essentially the same estimates of the parameters when applied to eight different cross-section studies between 1888 and 1950. A more elaborate variation of this same general approach is the Crockett–Friend attempt to derive a complete set of consumer demand relationships (see Crockett and Friend, 1960, pp. 1–92). Derivation of stable relationships of this sort could be used for prediction *if* distributional changes in these variables could be anticipated and *if* stability were assured.

This general approach has been carried one step further by Vernon Lippitt (1959). He applied analysis of variance to measure the effect of relevant cross-section variables on the particular item of expenditure. Estimates of the aggregate effects of these variables were derived for years for which the necessary cross-section data were available; estimates for intervening years were obtained by interpolation. These aggregate effects were then incorporated into a time-series function relating expenditures to these variables as well as to other pertinent time-series variables. Although details of the procedure may be questioned, and although this procedure still requires an independent estimate of distributional effects for predictive purposes, Lippitt demonstrates convincingly that this procedure is practicable and, in, particular, that the distributional effect exerts a pronounced influence on estimated expenditures.

Household decision-making

The household can be viewed as a decision-making organization engaged in much the same activities as is a business firm. From this perspective, the household becomes a separate organization that receives income and other money receipts and that dispenses this money in accordance with certain criteria. Entering into these criteria are the wants and desires of different household members, the structure of the household and the interpersonal relationships existing among the different family members, all subject to various economic restraints. The explanation of consumer behavior then becomes a matter of identifying and measuring the relative importance of the factors that enter into the decision processes.

To borrow an analogy advanced by March and Simon (1959, pp. 178–82) in organization theory, the decision process can be subdivided into three distinct stages:

1. The manner in which the possibility of a particular action, e.g. purchase, comes to the attention of the household.

2. Specification of, and deliberation among, alternative forms of action.

3. The actual choice.

To illustrate, before a car is purchased, its desirability must first somehow come to the attention of the household. Then, different types of cars, brands, body-styles, etc., as well as different forms, cash $v.$ borrowing, and times of making the purchase must be specified, however implicitly, and a certain amount of deliberation among these alternatives must take place. Finally, one alternative is selected as best and the decision is made to purchase, or not to purchase.

The usual consumer surveys and budget studies reflect the last stage of this process, namely, decisions in the form of actual purchases. Past empirical research on household behavior, as reviewed in the preceding sections, has been concerned with the measurement of these purchases and with the extent to which they appear to have been influenced by socio-economic characteristics of the household and, to a lesser extent, by its attitudes and

299

expectations. In the latter sense, empirical research may be said to be reaching back into the second stage of the decision process. Nevertheless, from the point of view of decision theory, such results are of limited interest because no light is thrown on the dynamics of the decision process and, clearly, no knowledge is provided about decisions that were *not* consummated as purchases.

In recent years, an increasing amount of activity has focused on the second stage of the decision process, particularly on the extent of deliberation entering into consumer purchases. Thus, the previously cited works by Juster, Ferber, and Katona and his associates serve to reinforce the notion that many durable-goods purchases are planned and thought out carefully in advance. Particularly interesting in this respect is a study by Katona and Mueller on the extent of deliberation entering into decisions of four major household durables – TV, refrigerator, washing machine, and stove (Katona and Mueller, 1954). This study found considerable variation in the extent of advance deliberation among households. The actions of only about one-fourth of the group appeared to conform with the idea of the economic man, who considers a purchase very carefully and investigates numerous possibilities before making a final decision. An almost equal proportion were found to have made these purchases with virtually no advance deliberation, largely as a result of some fortuitous event. Extent of deliberation was more frequent among those with higher education, higher income, older people and those in professional occupations, as well as among people expressing a liking for shopping. Deliberation was less frequent when the product was inexpensive relative to the buyer's income, when a special deal was offered, or when the product was needed urgently – as when the currently owned model broke down. Families under some financial stress did not appear to consider alternatives any more thoroughly than other families.

Attempts have also been made to explain the decision process in terms of accumulation of desires for and against making a particular purchase, based on the approach to social psychology of Kurt Lewin. This approach has been used by Warren Bilkey (1953, 1957) on consumer panels to obtain periodic measures from the same families of the psychic tensions arising at various stages of the purchase decision. Intensity of desire for and against a particular purchase is measured in terms of positive and negative 'valences' registered by the household; the more the excess of positive valences over negative valences, the closer is the decision to action.

More recently, this theory has been extended into a general model of household buying-decisions by Joseph Clawson (1961), who represents such decisions as the quantitative interplay of different motivations, status dimensions and intensities. Except for isolated experiments, no general application has yet been made of such a model. Indeed, it remains to be shown that such an approach adds anything more to the explanation of the decision process than could be obtained from more straightforward data on buying intentions, attitudes and preferences.[37]

Very little empirical work has been carried out on the attention-directing stage of the purchase process. This is not surprising in view of the more ephemeral nature of the problem. However, two interesting studies can be mentioned. One study, by Eva Mueller (1958), attempts to ascertain the role of innovation in household purchases. Among other things, it finds that innovators, defined as those who are among the first to purchase new types of appliances, are scattered throughout the population but, as a rule, are generally found among the young, among the well-educated, among married couples with children and among those who are financially optimistic. People who already own similar appliances are more likely to be attracted to the new products, though this may reflect the interaction effect of assets and incomes.

The other study, carried out from a sociological point of view, traces how people through interpersonal contact become interested in purchasing air conditioners (Whyte, 1954). Based on block observations, this article shows rather strikingly how air conditioner purchases spread by means of neighborhood communication – among neighbors on the same block, over back alleys and over fences. The study suggests that this pattern of

37. The little work that has been done on the subject indicates that preferences may be very similar to purchase intentions, and that preferences are related to later purchases, at least as far as brand selection is concerned; see Seymour Banks (1950).

communication, particularly if catalyzed by the presence of a 'leader', accounts for differences in ownership rates of air conditioners among blocks of the same socio-economic status. In addition, the study stresses the importance of the group in motivating people to purchase new products, inferring that 'it is the group that determines when a luxury becomes a necessity' (Whyte, 1954, p. 117).[38] Other sociological studies have also affirmed the importance of the group, and of leaders, in influencing purchase behavior (Bourne, 1957; Katz and Lazarsfeld, 1955).

References

ACKLEY, G. (1951), 'The wealth-saving relationship', *Journal of Political Economy*, vol. 59, pp. 154–61.

AITCHISON, J., and BROWN, J. A. C. (1954–5), 'A synthesis of Engel curve theory', *Review of Economic Studies*, vol. 22, no. 1, pp. 35–46.

ALDERSON, W. (1961), 'Comments on "Decision-making regarding allocation and spending"', in N. N. Foote (ed.), *Household Decision-Making*, New York University Press, pp. 184–5.

BANKS, S. (1950), 'The relationship between preference and purchase of brands', *Journal of Marketing*, vol. 15, pp. 145–57.

BARTON, S. G. (1955), 'The life cycle and buying patterns', in L. H. Clark (ed.), *The Life Cycle and Consumer Behavior*, New York University Press, pp. 53–7.

BILKEY, W. J. (1953), 'A psychological approach to consumer behavior analysis', *Journal of Marketing*, vol. 18, pp. 18–25.

BILKEY, W. J. (1957), 'Consistency test of psychic tension rating involved in consumer purchasing behavior', *Journal of Social Psychology*, vol. 45, pp. 81–91.

BODKIN, R. (1960), 'Windfall income and consumption', in I. Friend and R. Jones (eds), *Proceedings of the Conference on Consumption and Saving*, University of Pennsylvania, vol. 2, pp. 175–87.

BOURNE, F. S. (1957), 'Group influences in marketing and public relations', in R. Likert and S. P. Hayes (eds.), *Some Applications of Behavioral Research*, UNESCO, pp. 205–57.

BRADY, D. S. (1952), 'Family saving in relation to changes in the level and distribution of income', in *Studies in Income and Wealth*, National Bureau of Economic Research, vol. 15, pp. 103–30.

BRADY, D. S. (1955), 'Influence of age on saving and spending patterns', *Monthly Labor Review*, vol 78, pp. 1240–44.

BRADY, D. S. (1956), 'Family saving 1888–1950', in R. W. Goldsmith, D. S. Brady and H. Mendershausen, *A Study of Saving in the United States*, Oxford University Press, vol. 3, pp. 139–276.

38. Much the same conclusion on the importance of community effects is reached by Dorothy Brady (1952, 1956) using an economic approach.

BRADY, D. S. (1960), 'Quantity and quality of clothing purchases', in I. Friend and R. Jones (eds.), *Proceedings of the Conference on Consumption and Saving*, University of Pennsylvania, vol 2. pp. 137–42.

BRADY, D. S., and FRIEDMAN, R. (1947), 'Savings and the income distribution', in *Studies in Income and Wealth*, National Bureau of Economic Research, vol. 10, pp. 247–65.

BREMS, H. (1956), 'Long-run automobile demand', *Journal of Marketing*, vol. 21, pp. 379–84.

BRINEGAR, G. K. (1953a), 'Short-run effects of income change upon expenditure , *Journal of Farm Economics*, vol. 35, pp. 99–109.

BRINEGAR, G. K. (1953b), 'Income, savings balances and net saving', *Review of Economics and Statistics*, vol. 35, pp. 71 1.

CAGAN, P. (1961), *Pension Plans and Aggregate Saving*, unpublished manuscript.

CHOW, G. (1957), *Demand for Automobiles in the United States*, North-Holland Publishing Co.

CHRIST, C., HILDRETH, C., LIU, T-C., and KLEIN, L. R. (1960), 'A symposium on simultaneous equation estimation', *Econometrica*, vol. 28, pp. 835–71.

CLARK, L. H. (ed.) (1955), *The Life Cycle and Consumer Behavior*, New York University Press.

CLAWSON, J. W. (1961), 'Family composition, motivation, and buying decisions', in N. N. Foote (ed.), *Household Decision-Making*, New York University Press, pp. 200–217.

COHEN, M. (1954), 'Liquid assets and the consumption function', *Review of Economics and Statistics*, col. 36, pp. 202–11.

COHEN, M., and GAINSBRUGH, M. R. (1958), 'Consumer buying plans: a new survey', *Conference Board Record*, vol. 15, pp. 449–67.

CORNFIELD, J., EVANS, W. D., and HOFFENBERG, M. (1947), 'Full employment patterns, 1950', *Monthly Labor Review*, vol. 70, pp. 163–90.

CRAMER, J. S. (1958), 'Ownership elasticities of durable consumer goods', *Review of Economic Studies*, vol. 25, pp. 87–96.

CROCKETT, J. (1957), 'A new type of estimate of the income elasticity of demand for food', *Proceedings of the American Statistical Association*, Business, Economics and Statistics Secretariat, pp. 117–22.

CROCKETT, J. (1960), 'Population change and the demand for food', in *Demographic and Economic Change in Developed Countries*, Universities – National Bureau Commercial and Economic Research, pp. 457–83.

CROCKETT, J., and FRIEND, I. (1960), 'A complete set of consumer demand relationships', in I. Friend and R. Jones (eds.), *Proceedings of the Conference on Consumption and Saving*, University of Pennsylvania, vol. 2, pp. 1–92.

DAVIS, T. E. (1952), 'The consumption function as a tool for prediction', *Review of Economics and Statistics*, vol. 34, pp. 270–77.

DUE, J. M. (1956), 'Postwar family expenditure studies in Western Europe', *Journal of Farm Economics*, vol. 38, pp. 846–56.

DUESENBERRY, J. (1949), *Income, Saving and the Theory of Consumer Behavior*, Harvard University Press.

DUESENBERRY, J. (1960), 'Comments on "General Saving Relations"', in I. Friend and R. Jones (eds), *Proceedings of the Conference on Consumption and Saving*, University of Pennsylvania, pp. 188–91.

DUNSING, M., and REID, M. G. (1958), 'Effect of varying degrees of transitory income on income elasticity of expenditures', *Journal of the American Statistical Association*, vol. 53, pp. 348–59.

EISNER, R. (1958), 'The permanent income hypothesis: comment', *American Economic Review*, vol. 48, pp. 972–90.

FARRELL, M. J. (1952), 'Irreversible demand functions', *Econometrica*, vol. 20, pp. 171–86.

FARRELL, M. J. (1954), 'Demand for motor cars in the United States', *Journal of the Royal Statistical Society*, part 2, vol. 117A, pp. 171–201.

FERBER, R. (1953), 'A study of aggregate consumption functions', *National Bureau of Economic Research*, technical paper no. 8.

FERBER, R. (1954), 'The role of planning in consumer purchases of durable goods', *American Economic Review*, vol. 44, pp. 854–74.

FERBER, R. (1955a), *Factors Influencing Durable Goods Purchases*, Bureau of Economic and Business Research, University of Illinois; reprinted in L. H. Clark (ed.), *The Life Cycle and Consumer Behavior*, New York University Press, pp. 75–112.

FERBER, R. (1955b), 'On the stability of consumer expectations', *Review of Economics and Statistics*, vol. 37, pp. 256–66.

FERBER, R. (1955c), 'The accuracy of aggregate savings functions in the postwar years', *Review of Economics and Statistics*, vol. 37, pp. 134–48.

FERBER, R. (1958), 'A statistical study of factors influencing temporal variations in aggregate service expenditures', in L. H. Clark (ed.), *Consumer Behavior: Research on Consumer Reactions*, Harper Brothers, pp. 394–414.

FERBER, R. (1960), 'Service expenditures at mid-century', in I. Friend and R. Jones (eds.), *Proceedings of the Conference on Consumption and Saving*, University of Pennsylvania, vol. 2, pp. 436–60.

FERBER, R. (1961), 'Making less and saving more', *Illinois Business Review*, vol. 18, no. 2, p. 8.

FERBER, R., and VERDOON, P. J. (1962), *Research Methods in Economics and Business*, Macmillan, New York.

FISHER, J. (1952), 'Postwar changes in income and savings among consumers in different age groups', *Econometrica*, vol. 20, pp. 47–70.

FISHER, J. (1955), 'Family life cycle analysis on research on consumer behavior', in L. H. Clark (ed.), *The Life Cycle and Consumer Behavior*, New York University Press, pp. 28–35.

FISHER, J. (1962), 'Income, spending, and saving patterns of consumer units in different age groups', in *Studies in Income and Wealth*, National Bureau of Economic Research, vol. 15, pp. 75–102.

FISHER, M. R. (1956), 'Explorations in savings behavior', *Bulletin Oxford University Institute of Statistics*, vol. 18, pp. 201–78.

FOOTE, N. N. (ed.) (1961), *Household Decision-Making*, New York University Press.

FRIEDMAN, M. (1952), 'A method of comparing incomes of families differing in composition', in *Studies in Income and Wealth*, National Bureau of Economic Research, vol. 15, pp. 9–20.

FRIEDMAN, M. (1957), *A Theory of the Consumption Function*, National Bureau of Economic Research.

FRIEDMAN, M. (n.d.), 'Windfalls, the "horizon" and related concepts in the permanent income hypothesis', unpublished memorandum.

FRIEDMAN, M. (1959), 'Comments on windfall income and consumption', in I. Friend and R. Jones (eds.), *Proceedings of the Conference on Consumption and Saving*, University of Pennsylvania, vol. 2, pp. 191–206.

FRIEDMAN, M., and KUNZETS, S. (1945), *Income from Independent Professional Practice*, National Bureau of Economic Research, New York.

FRIEND, I. (1958), 'Discussion of Milton Friedman's *A Theory of the Consumption Function*, in L. H. Clark (ed.), *Consumer Behavior: Research on Consumer Reactions*, Harper Brothers, pp. 456–8.

FRIEND, I., and KRAVIS, I. B. (1957a), 'Consumption patterns and permanent income', *American Economic Review, Proceedings*, vol. 47, pp. 536–55.

FRIEND, I., and KRAVIS, I. B. (1957b), 'Enterpreneurial income, saving and investment', *American Economic Review*, vol. 47, pp. 269–301.

FRIEND, I., and SCHOR, S. (1959), 'Who saves?', *Review of Economics Statistics*, part 2, vol. 41, pp. 213–48.

FRIEND, I., and JONES, R. (eds.) (1960a), *Proceedings of the Conference on Consumption and Saving*, University of Pennsylvania, vol. 2,

FRIEND, I., and JONES, R. (1960b), 'The concept of saving', in I. Friend and R. Jones (eds.), *Proceedings of the Conference on Consumption and Saving*, University of Pennsylvania, vol. 2, pp. 336–59.

GLICK, P. (1947), 'The family cycle', *American Sociological Review*, vol. 12, pp. 164–74.

GOLDSMITH, R. (1955), *A Study of Saving in the United States*, Oxford University Press.

GOLDSTEIN, S. (1960), *Consumption Patterns of the Aged*, Philadelphia University.

GUTHRIE, H. W. (1960), 'Consumers' propensities to hold liquid assets', *Journal of the American Statistical Association*, vol. 55, pp. 469–90.

305

Economic Factors

HAMBURG, M. (1960), 'Demand for clothing', in I. Friend and R. Jones (eds), *Proceedings of the Conference on Consumption and Saving*, University of Pennsylvania, vol. 1, pp. 311–58.

HAMBURGER, W. (1954–5), 'The determinants of aggregate consumption', *Review of Economic Studies*, vol. 22, no. 57, pp. 23–35.

HAMBURGER, W. (1955), 'The relation of consumption to wealth and the wage rate', *Econometrica*, vol. 23, pp. 1–17.

HANSEN, A. H. (1951), 'The Pigouvian effect', *Journal of Political Economy*, vol. 49, pp. 535–6.

HOUTHAKKER, H. S. (1957), 'An international comparison of household expenditure patterns, commemorating the centenary of Engel's law', *Econometrica*, vol. 25, pp. 532–51.

HOUTHAKKER, H. S. (1958), 'The permanent income hypothesis', *American Economic Review*, vol. 48, pp. 396–404.

HOUTHAKKER, H. S., and HALDI, J. (1960), 'Household investment in automobiles: an intemporal cross-section analysis', in I. Friend and R. Jones (eds.), *Proceedings of the Conference on Consumption and Saving*, University of Pennsylvania, vol. 1, pp. 175–225.

INTER-UNIVERSITY COMMITTEE FOR RESEARCH ON CONSUMER BEHAVIOR (1961), *Anticipation of Saving Behavior*, Interim Report no. 6.

JUSTER, F. T. (1957), 'Consumer expectations, plans, and purchases: a progress report', *National Bureau of Economic Research*, occasional paper no. 70.

JUSTER, F. T. (1960a), 'Predictions and consumer buying intentions' *American Economic Review*, *Proceedings*, vol. 50, pp. 604–17.

JUSTER, F. T. (1960b), 'The predictive value of Consumers Union spending-intentions data', in *The Quality and Economic Significance of Anticipations Data*, National Bureau of Economic Research, pp. 263–89.

KATONA, G. (1947), 'Contribution of psychological data to economic analysis', *Journal of the American Statistical Association*, vol. 42, pp. 449–59.

KATONA, G. (1949a), 'Effect of income changes on the rate of saving' *Review of Economics and Statistics*, vol. 39, pp. 95–103.

KATONA, G. (1949b), 'Analysis of dissaving', *American Economic Review*, vol. 39, pp. 673–88.

KATONA, G. (1951), *Psychological Analysis of Economic Behavior*, McGraw-Hill.

KATONA, G. (1955), 'The predictive value of data on consumer attitudes', in L. H. Clark (ed.), *The Life Cycle and Consumer Behavior*, New York University Press, pp. 66–74.

KATONA, G. (1958), 'Attitude change: instability of response and acquisition of experience', *Psychological Monograph*, vol. 72, no. 10.

KATONA, G. (ed.) (1960a), *The Quality and Economic Significance of Anticipations Data*, National Bureau of Economic Research.

KATONA, G. (1960b), *The Powerful Consumer*, McGraw-Hill.

306

KATONA, G., and FISHER, J. A. (1951), 'Postwar changes in the income of identical consumer units', in *Studies in Income and Wealth*, National Bureau of Economic Research, vol. 13, pp. 61–122.

KATONA, G., and MUELLER, E. (1953), *Consumer Attitudes and Demand, 1950–52*, Survey Research Center, University of Michigan.

KATONA, G., and MUELLER, E. (1954), 'A study of purchase decisions', in L. H. Clark (ed.), *Consumer Behavior: The Dynamics of Consumer Reactions*, Harper Brothers, pp. 30–87.

KATONA, G., and MUELLER, E. (1956), *Consumer Expectations, 1953–6*, Survey Research Center, University of Michigan.

KATZ, F., and LAZARSFELD, P. F. (1955), *Personal Influence*, Free Press, New York, pp. 234–47.

KEYNES, J. M. (1936), *The General Theory of Employment, Interest, and Money*, Harcourt, Brace & World.

KIRKPATRICK, E. L. (1934), 'The life cycle of the farm family'' *Wisconsin Agricultural Experimental Station*, research bulletin no. 121.

KLEIN, L. R. (1951a), 'Estimating patterns of savings behaviour from sample survey data', *Econometrica*, vol. 19, pp. 438–54.

KLEIN, L. R. (1951b), 'Assets, debts, and economic behavior', in *Studies in Income and Wealth*, National Bureau of Economic Research, vol. 14, pp. 195–227.

KLEIN, L. R. (1954), 'Statistical estimation of economic relations from survey data', in G. Katona, L. R. Klein, J. B. Lansing and J. N. Morgan, *Contributions of Survey Methods to Economics*, Columbia University Press, pp. 189–240.

KLEIN, L. R. (1955a), 'Major consumer expenditures and ownership of durables', *Bulletin Oxford University of Statistics*, vol. 17, pp. 387–414.

KLEIN, L. R. (1955b), 'Patterns of savings', *Bulletin Oxford University Institute of Statistics*, vol. 17, pp. 173–214.

KLEIN, L. R. (1960), 'Entrepreneurial saving', in I. Friend and R. Jones (eds), *Proceedings of the Conference on Consumption and Saving*, University of Pennsylvania, vol. 2.

KLEIN, L. R., and LANSING, J. B. (1955), 'Decisions to purchase consumer durable goods', *Journal of Marketing*, vol. 20, pp. 109–32.

KLEIN, L. R., and MARGOLIS, J. (1954), 'Statistical studies of unincorporated business', *Review of Economics and Statistics*, vol. 36, pp. 33–46.

KREININ, M. E. (1959), 'Factors associated with stock ownership', *Review of Economics and Statistics*, vol. 41, pp. 12–23.

KREININ, M. E. (1961a), 'Analysis of liquid asset ownership', *Review of Economics and Statistics*, vol. 43, pp. 76–80.

KREININ, M. E. (1961b), 'Windfall income and consumption', *American Economic Review*, vol. 51, pp. 388–90.

KREININ, M. E., LANSING, J. B., and MORGAN, J. N. (1957), 'Analysis of life insurance premiums', *Review of Economics and Statistics*, vol. 39, pp. 46–54.

Economic Factors

KUZNETS, S. (1946), *National Product Since 1869*, National Bureau of Economic Research.

KUZNETS, S. (1952), 'Proportion of capital formation to national product', *American Economic Review*, vol. 42, pp. 507–26.

LANSING, J. B. (1961), *An Investigation of Response Error*, Bureau of Economic and Business Research, Studies in Consumer Savings no. 2, University of Illinois.

LANSING, J. B., and WITHEY, S. B. (1955), 'Consumer anticipations: their use in forecasting behavior', in *Studies in Income and Wealth*, National Bureau of Economic Research, vol. 17, pp. 381–453.

LERNER, A. P. (1943), 'Fiscal finance and the Federal Debt', *Social Research*, vol. 10, pp. 38–51.

LIPPITT, V. (1959), *Determinants of Consumer Demand for Housefurnishings and Equipment*, Oxford University Press.

LIVIATAN, N. (1961), 'Errors in variables and Engel curve analysis', *Econometrica*, vol. 29, pp. 336–62.

LYDALL, H. (1955), 'The life cycle in income, saving, and asset ownership', *Econometrica*, vol. 23, pp. 131–50.

LYDALL, H. (1958), 'Income, assets, and the demand for money', *Review of Economics and Statistics*, vol. 40, pp. 1–14.

MACK, R. P. (1948), 'The direction of change in income and the consumption function', *Review of Economics and Statistics*, vol. 30, pp. 329–58.

MACK, R. P. (1952), 'Economics of consumption', in B. F. Haley (ed.), *Survey of Contemporary Economics*, Irwin, vol. 2, pp. 39–78.

MAISEL, S., and WINNICK, L. (1960), 'Family housing expenditures: elusive laws and intrusive variances', in I. Friend and R. Jones (eds), *Proceedings of the Conference on Consumption and Saving*, University of Pennsylvania, vol. 1, pp. 359–435.

MARCH, J. G., and SIMON, H. A. (1959), *Organizations*, Wiley.

MAYNES, E. S. (1959), 'The relationship between tangible investment and consumer saving', *Review of Economics and Statistics*, vol. 41, pp. 287–93.

MENDERSHAUSEN, H. (1940), 'Differenees in family saving between cities of different sizes and locations, Whites and Negroes', *Review of Economics and Statistics*, vol. 22, pp. 122–37.

MILLER, D. L. (1955), 'The life cycle and the impact of advertising', in L. H. Clark (ed.), *The Life Cycle and Consumer Behavior*, New York University Press, pp. 61–5.

MINCER, J. (1960), 'Labor supply, family income and consumption', *American Economic Review, Proceedings*, vol. 50, pp. 574–83.

MODIGLIANI, F. (1949), 'Fluctuations in the saving-income ratio: a problem in economic forecasting', in *Studies in Income and Wealth*, National Bureau of Economic Research, vol. 11, pp. 371–443.

MODIGLIANI, F., and ANDO, A. (1957), 'Tests of the life cycle hypothesis of savings', *Bulletin Oxford University Institute of Statistics*, vol. 19, pp. 99–124.

308

MODIGLIANI, F., and ANDO, A. (1960), 'The "permanent income" and the "life cycle" hypotheses of saving behavior: comparison and tests' in I. Friend and R. Jones (eds.), *Proceedings of the Conference on Consumption and Saving*, University of Pennsylvania, vol. 2, pp. 49–174.

MODIGLIANI, F., and BRUMBERG, R. E. (1954), 'Utility analysis and the consumption function: an interpretation of cross-section data', in K. K. Kurihara (ed.), *Post-Keynesian Economics*, North-Holland Publishing Co., pp. 388–436.

MORGAN, J. N. (1954), 'Factors relating to consumer saving when it is defined as a net-worth concept', in L. R. Klein (ed.), *Contributions of Survey Methods to Economics*, Oxford University Press, chs 3 and 4.

MORGAN, J. N. (1958a), 'A review of recent research on consumer behavior', in L. H. Clark (ed.), *Consumer Behavior: Research on Consumer Reactions*, Harper Brothers, pp. 93–219.

MORGAN, J. N. (1958b), 'Consumer investment expenditures', *American Economic Review*, vol. 48, pp. 874–902.

MUELLER, E. (1958), 'The desire for innovations in household goods', in L. H. Clark (ed.), *Consumer Behavior: Research on Consumer Reactions*, Harper Brothers, pp. 13–37.

MUELLER, E. (1960), 'Consumer attitudes: their influence and forecasting value', in *The Quality and Economic Significance of Anticipations Data*, National Bureau of Economic Research, pp. 149–75.

NERLOVE, M. (1957), 'A note on long-run automobile demand', *Journal of Marketing*, vol. 22, pp. 57–64.

NERLOVE, M. (1958), *Distributed Lags and Demand Analysis*, US Department of Agriculture.

OKUN, A. M. (1960), 'The value of anticipations data in forecasting national product', in G. Katona (ed.), *The Quality and Economic Significance of Anticipations Data*, National Bureau of Economic Research, pp. 411–28.

ORCUTT, G., and ROY, A. D. (1949), *A Bibliography of the Consumption Function*, Dept Applied Economics, Cambridge University, mimeographed.

ORCUTT, G., *et al.* (1961), *Micro-Analysis of Socio-Economic Systems: A Simulation Study*, Harper & Row.

OXENFELDT, A. R. (1957), 'Comments on the article by Friend and Karavis', *American Economic Review, Proceedings*, vol. 47, pp. 571–4.

PARADISO, L. J., and WINSTON, C. (1955), 'Consumer expenditure–income patterns', *Survey of Current Business*, vol. 35, pp. 23–32.

PIGOU, A. C. (1943), 'The classical stationary state', *Economic Journal*, vol. 53, pp. 343–51.

PRAIS, S. J. (1952–3), 'Nonlinear estimates of the Engel curve', *Review of Economic Studies*, part 2, vol. 20, pp. 87–104.

PRAIS, S. J., and HOUTHAKKER, H. S. (1955), *The Analysis of Family Budgets*, Cambridge University Press.

309

QUACKENBUSH, G. G., and SHAFFER, J. D. (1960), 'Collecting food purchase data by consumer panel', *Michigan State University Agricultural Experimental Station*, technical bulletin no. 279.

REID, M. G. (1952a), 'Effect of income concept upon expenditure curves of farm families', in *Studies in Income and Wealth*, National Bureau of Economic Research, vol. 15, pp. 133–74.

REID, M. G. (1952b), 'The relation of the within-group transitory component of income to the income elasticity of family expenditure', unpublished paper.

REID, M. G. (1958), 'Capital formation in residential real estate', *Journal of Political Economy*, vol. 66, pp. 131–53.

REID, M. G. (1960), 'Comments', in I. Friend and R. Jones (eds.), *Proceedings of the Conference on Consumption and Saving*, University of Pennsylvania, vol. 1, pp. 143–55.

REID, M. G., and DUNSING, M. (1956), 'Effect of variability of incomes on level of income-expenditure curves of farm families', *Review of Economics and Statistics*, vol. 38, pp. 90–95.

SNYDER, E. M. (1958), 'Impact of long-term structural changes on family expenditures, 1888–1950', in L. H. Clark (ed.), *Consumer Behavior: Research on Consumer Reactions*, Harper & Row, pp. 359–93.

STIGLER, G. J. (1954), 'The early history of empirical studies of consumer behavior', *Journal of Political Economy*, vol. 42, pp. 95–113.

STONE, R. (1954), *The Measurement of Consumers' Expenditure and Behaviour in the United Kingdom*, Cambridge University Press.

STUVEL, G., and JAMES, S. F. (1950), 'Household expenditures of food in Holland', *Journal of the Royal Statistical Society*, A, vol. 113, part 1, pp. 59–80.

SUITS, D. B. (1958), 'The demand for automobiles in the United States, 1929–56', *Review of Economics and Statistics*, vol. 40, pp. 273–80.

TINTER, G. (1951), 'Static econometric models and their empirical verification', *Metroeconomica*, vol. 2, pp. 172–81.

TOBIN, J. (1950), 'A statistical demand function for food in the USA', *Journal of the Royal Statistical Society*, series A, vol. 113, part 2, pp. 113–41.

TOBIN, J. (1951), 'Relative income, absolute income, and saving', in H. G. Johnson (ed.), *Money, Trade and Economic Growth: Essays in Honor of John Henry Williams*, Harvard University Press, pp. 135–56.

TOBIN, J. (1952), 'Asset holdings and spending decisions', *American Economic Review*, vol. 42, pp. 109–23.

TOBIN, J. (1958), 'Discussion of Milton Friedman's *A Theory of the Consumption Function*', in L. H. Clark (ed.), *Consumer Behavior: Research on Consumer Reactions*, Harper & Row, pp. 447–54.

TOBIN, J. (1959), 'On the predictive value of consumer intentions and attitudes', *Review of Economics and Statistics*, vol. 41, pp. 1–11.

US BUREAU OF LABOUR STATISTICS (1938–41), *Family Income and*

Expenditures (*in selected areas*), US Department of Labor Bulletin nos. 642–9.

US DEPARTMENT OF AGRICULTURE (1939–41), *Family Incomes and Expenditures* (titles vary), miscellaneous publications between no. 339 and no. 489.

US FEDERAL RESERVE BOARD (1955), *Report of Consultant Committee on Consumer Survey Statistics*, July.

US NATIONAL RESOURCES PLANNING BOARD (1941), Family Expenditures in the United States.

VAN SYCKLE, C. (1954), 'Economic expectations and spending plans of consumers', *Review of Economics and Statistics*, vol. 36, pp. 451–5.

VICKREY, W. S. (1947), 'Resource distribution patterns and the classification of families', in *Studies in Income and Wealth*, National Bureau of Economic Research, vol. 10, pp. 260–329.

WATTS, H. W. (1958), 'Long-run income, expenditure and consumer savings', *Cowles Foundation Paper*, no. 123.

WATTS, H. W., and TOBIN, J. (1960), 'Consumer expenditures and the capital account', in I. Friend and R. Jones (eds.), *Proceedings of the Conference on Consumption and Saving*, University of Pennsylvania, vol. 2, pp. 1–48.

WEISS, G. S., SMITH, T., and FLECHSIG, T. G. (1960), 'Quarterly survey of consumer buying intentions', *Federal Reserve Bulletin*, vol. 46, pp. 977–1003.

WHYTE, W. H., Jr (1954), 'The web of word of mouth', *Fortune*, November; reprinted in L. H. Clark (ed.), (1953), *The Life Cycle of Consumer Behavior*, New York University Press, pp. 113–22.

WILLIAMS, F. M., and ZIMMERMAN, C. C. (1935), *Studies of Family Living in the United States and Other Countries*, US Department of Agriculture Miscellaneous Publication, no. 223.

WOLD, H., and JUREEN, L. (1953), *Demand Analysis*, Cambridge University Press.

16 Richard Stone, J. A. C. Brown and D. A. Rowe

Aggregated Time-Series

Excerpts from Richard Stone, J. A. C. Brown and D. A. Rowe,
'Demand analysis and predictions for Britain: 1900–1970',
Europe's Future Consumption, North-Holland Publishing Co., 1963.

Introduction

Our work at present is based entirely on the analysis of time series; its main ingredients can be outlined as follows:

1. We possess annual estimates of consumers' expenditure per head of the population, divided into thirty categories, and the corresponding price index-numbers from the beginning of this century. For the purpose of this paper we have grouped these categories into eight main classes. The sources of this information are set out in the following section.

2. We use a model which enables a complete set of demand equations to be analysed simultaneously. In this model each class of expenditure is a homogeneous linear function of total expenditure and of the price index of each of the classes. The parameters of this system are not constants but linear functions of time. Thus each demand not only depends on total expenditure and the price structure but does so in a way which gradually changes over time. These changes can be extrapolated to yield a system of demand equations for 1970. Thus shifts associated with changes in tastes and new commodities form an integral part of the model. Various forms of the model are described in a subsequent section.

3. We use a two-stage iterative computing program to estimate the parameters in the model. We stop the calculations when the change made by the latest cycle to the values of a particular set of parameters is, in some sense, small. Experience shows that convergence is difficult to achieve and depends, in part at least, on adopting a suitable set of starting values. Since there appears

to be very little mathematical theory of convergent processes except in the simple case of two variables, there is evidently ground here for mathematical exploration.

4. The combination of 1, 2 and 3 gives us a consistent system of quantitative demand equations and the next thing to do is to see how well they describe the past. This is done in the section before the conclusions which also contains some comments on the changing pattern of demand which emerges from the analysis. [...]

The sources of information

The data on prices, quantities and expenditures used in this paper are based on four main sources depending on the period covered: for 1900 to 1919, the work of Prest and Adams (1954); for 1920 to 1938, the work of Stone and Rowe (1966), and Stone *et al* (1954); for 1939 to 1945, UK Central Statistical Office (1951); and for 1946 to 1960, the official Blue Books on national income and expenditure (1961, and annually). The first two of these sources belong to a series which has as its purpose the carrying back of the Blue Book picture of the British economy to the beginning of this century. As we work backwards, the available information becomes, on the whole, less complete and less reliable. We have, however, succeeded in building up reasonably comparable series for thirty categories of expenditure which for the purpose of the present paper we have grouped into eight main classes.

In order to obtain series of expenditure at constant prices we have constructed index-numbers with 1938 as a base. We are now moving over to a postwar base, but the calculations with this new material will not be ready for some time.

The model

The linear expenditure system, which is the basic form of the model used here, has already been described on a number of occasions (see Cambridge, Dept Applied Economics, 1962; Stone, 1954, 1961; Stone and Croft-Murray, 1959) but a little must be said about it here if this paper is to be reasonably self-contained. In matrix form, the system of equations can be written as

$$\hat{p}e = b\mu + (I - bi')\hat{c}p$$
$$= \hat{p}c + b(\mu - p'c). \qquad\qquad 1$$

In **1**: p denotes the price vector of the commodities or groups of commodites we are studying and $\hat{p}$ denotes a diagonal matrix formed from p; e denotes a vector of the quantities bought and so $\hat{p}e$ denotes a vector of expenditures; μ denotes total expenditure and so $\mu \equiv p'e$, where the prime denotes transposition; I and i denote respectively the unit matrix and the unit vector; and b and c denote vectors of parameters restricted by the fact that $i'\,b \equiv 1$.

From the first row of **1** we see that each element of $\hat{p}e$, that is each expenditure, is a linear function of total expenditure μ and of each of the prices, the elements of p. This system of equations is free from money illusion and is additive. The particular form of the matrix $(I - bi')\hat{c}$ which multiplies the price vector p is dictated by the fact that a plausible way to keep the number of parameters small is to impose on the system the Slutsky condition, that is, the condition that the matrix of elasticities of substitution be symmetric. With n commodity classes and these restrictions there are only $2n - 1$ independent parameters to be estimated.

From the second row of **1** we can give a simple interpretation of the consumers' behaviour which the model represents. The total expenditure on a commodity class, an element of $\hat{p}e$, is made up of two parts. Firstly, the average consumer buys a fixed quantity, an element of c, at whatever prices happen to be ruling, and the total cost of these purchases is $p'c$ which we call committed expenditure. Secondly, the average consumer looks to see how much money he has left and distributes this over the commodity classes in proportion to the elements of b, which sum to 1. The amount of money left over after committed expenditures have been paid for, $\mu - p'c$, we call supernumerary income.

We shall now summarize a number of properties of the model, some of which are advantageous, others restrictive.

1. As has been shown by Samuelson (1947–8) and Geary (1949–50) the preference field, or utility function, v say, is given by

$$\log v = b'[\log(e - c)] \qquad\qquad 2$$

or by any monotonic transformation of this expression. Thus the utility level can be calculated for any given set of purchases but the discovery that $v_1 > v_0$ could only tell us that the utility level in period 1 was greater than the utility level of period 0; it could not tell us by how much it was greater.

2. As has been shown by Klein and Rubin (1947–8), the system enables a constant-utility index-number of the cost of living to be constructed. This index is measured by the ratio μ_1^*/μ_0 where

$$\mu_1^* = p_1' c + (\mu_0 - p_0' c)\pi_b. \qquad\qquad 3$$

In 3 π_b denotes a geometric index of the price ratios – period 1 divided by period 0 – with the elements of b as weights. Thus the minimum amount of money needed in period 1 to enable the average consumer to remain on the same indifference surface as in period 0 is equal to committed expenditure at the prices of period 1 plus the supernumerary income of period 0 changed by a geometric index of the price ratios.

3. The system can only describe a world of substitutes from which complementary and inferior classes of commodity are excluded. This can be seen by deriving the elasticity of substitution, s_{jk} say, between commodities j and k. This elasticity takes the form

$$s_{jk} = \frac{(b_j - \delta_{jk})b_k\mu}{p_j e_j p_k e_k}(\mu - p'c) \qquad\qquad 4$$

where $\delta_{jk} = 1$ if $j = k$ and is zero in other cases. Assuming that supernumerary income is positive, the fact that all own-elasticities s_{jj} must in theory be negative means that $0 < b_j < 1$. This rules out inferior goods. In this case $b_j b_c$ is necessarily positive and so all s_{jk}, $j \neq k$, must be positive. This rules out complementary goods.

4. The Engel curves of the system, that is the relationships between e_j and μ for fixed p, are linear. The slope of the line is b_j/p_j and so varies with p_j; the intercept is $c_j - b_j(p'c)/p_j$.

5. The ordinary price-quantity demand curves of the system, that is the relationships between e_j and p_j for fixed μ and for fixed values of the remaining elements of p, are hyperbolas. With positive c_j they cannot be elastic.

6. The price-quantity demand curves calculated on the assumption that real income is held constant can be derived as follows. Writing p_{j1} for the price of commodity j in period 1, suppose $p_{j1} = p_{j0}$ for $j = 2, 3, \ldots, n$. Then 3 implies that

$$\mu_2^* = p_1' c + (\mu_0 - p_0' c)(p_{11}/p_{10})^{b_1}. \qquad 5$$

From 1 it follows that in this case

$$e_{11} = (1 - b_1)c_1 + b_1 (\mu_1^* - \sum_{j=2}^{n} p_{j1}c_j)/p_{11}. \qquad 6$$

If a substitution is made for μ_1^* from 5 into 6, it follows that

$$e_{11} = c_1 + b_1 (\mu_0 - p_0' c)/p_{10}^{b} \, p_{11}^{(1-b_1)} \qquad 7$$

which gives e_{11} as a function of p_{11} when real income is held constant.

The model which has just been described can be generalized so as to remove two fairly obvious defects. In the first place, the vectors b and c are constant and this implies that the average consumer never changes the quantities he feels committed to buying and never changes the way he allocated his expenditure out of supernumerary income. But, as the standard of living rises, one would expect committed quantities to rise and allocations to change. We can allow for these possibilities by making b and c depend on any variables which take preassigned values and, as was indicated by Stone (1954, 1955), this change in the model will not destroy its basic properties. In this paper we shall make use only of the simplest possibility, namely that b and c are linear functions of time. Thus at time θ, $\theta = 1, 2, \ldots, t$,

$$b_\theta = b^* + b^{**} \theta \qquad 8$$

and $c_\theta = c^* + c^{**} \theta.$ \qquad 9

With this generalization, it is necessary that $i'b^* \equiv 1$ and $i' b^{**} \equiv 0$ and so in place of the original $2n - 1$ independent parameters we now have $2(2n - 1)$.

In the second place, the model implies that adjustments are instantaneous: if total expenditure changes, the components immediately assume new equilibrium values. But in many cases one would expect that adjustment would take time because, for example, the average consumer may be faced with a financing problem in the case of such durable goods as cars, washing machines and television sets, or he may at first not know what to think of a new product that is put on the market and so take some time to make up his mind about it. A dynamic form of the model which takes account of such considerations has been described (see Cambridge, Dept of Applied Economics, 1962; Stone, 1961; Stone and Croft-Murray, 1959). We shall not discuss it here because, while dynamic adjustments are certainly important, we shall ignore them in this paper and concentrate on the kind of changes that can be reflected in the changing parameters described in the preceding paragraph. [...]

An application of the model

The application discussed in this section relates to the eight commodity groups set out in Table 1. The period covered is 1900 to 1960 and, in estimating the parameters, the years 1914 through 1919 and 1940 through 1947 were left out because of the abnormal conditions of war periods. We thus have $n(t - 14) = 376$ observations from which to determine $2(2n - 1) = 30$ independent parameters.

If we let θ range from $- 60$ to 0 so that $\theta = 0$ in 1960, the estimates of the parameters are as shown in Table 1. In this table the elements of b^* and c^* relate to 1960 and all are subject to fairly considerable trends: those shown in the column b^{**} are equally divided between positive and negative; while those shown in the column c^{**} are all positive. Thus, for example, the proportion of supernumerary income spent on food fell at the rate of 0·39 per cent each year until in 1960 it was as low as 8·05 per cent. At the same time committed purchases per head of food measured in 1938 prices rose each year by £ 0·332 until in 1960 they reached £ 33·73. In 1960 supernumerary income was £ 38·32 per head and committed expenditure on food at 1960 prices was £ 93·1 per head. Thus, according to the model, food expenditure per head in 1960 should have been

317

£ [(93·1 + (38·32 × 0·0805)] = 96·2 compared with the observed value of £ 95·8. In this case the error is rather less than one-half of 1 per cent.

Table 1 Parameters for Eight Consumption Groups, 1900–1960

	b^*	b^{**}	c^*	c^{**}
1. Food	0·0805	−0·0039	33·73	0·332
2. Clothing	0·1569	0·0021	9·26	0·043
3. Household	0·2263	0·0021	24·59	0·154
4. Communications	0·0023	−0·0004	1·13	0·026
5. Transport	0·2342	0·0016	8·97	0·165
6. Drink and tobacco	0·0956	−0·0019	10·20	0·058
7. Entertainment	−0·0143	−0·0008	5·05	0·075
8. Other	0·2186	0·0012	9·99	0·064
Total	1·0001	0·0000	102·92	0·917

The performance of the model over the sixty-one years is shown in the Figure 1. For comparative purposes the different series are drawn on a common logarithmic scale, though it must be remembered that the model is a linear one and that it is the sum of the absolute discrepancies that is being minimized. The general impression is that on the whole the fit is reasonably good. The postwar years appear to come out particularly well, but this is due to the use of a logarithmic scale. Let us now look at the series one by one.

Food. This is the largest commodity group and the fit is good throughout. Although the two war periods were left out in estimating the parameters, the series shown in the figure include all the years. The effect of food rationing in the second war in holding expenditure below the level given by the model is clearly shown. This is not, of course, the whole effect of rationing since μ represents total expenditure, not disposable income.

Clothing. In this case the fit is also good, though not quite as good as for food. In particular, through the 1950s the model reproduces the trend of the observations well but does not fully reproduce their sinuosities.

Household. Here it seems just possible to detect some systematic errors due to the assumption of trends in the parameters which are common to all periods. Before the first war these trends seem slightly too strong and in the interwar period they seem not quite strong enough. But on the whole the discrepancies are small and in the 1950s the fit is distinctly good.

Communications. This is a very small group which rises particularly rapidly, The fit is good, however, in the 1950s.

Transport. This is a heterogeneous series made up of public and private transport of all kinds and includes expenditure on private vehicles. Here the use of a common trend in all periods has well-marked bad effects: what is required is an accelerating trend. This is not surprising because the series is dominated by the rise of the motor car. In the 1900s cars were a novelty, during the interwar period they became generally accepted by the middle classes and since the last war they have begun to appeal to a mass market. A revised program which allows the trends to be parabolic rather than linear would probably remove most of the systematic discrepancies in the earlier part of the period. It would not however enable the halt in 1956 to be reproduced but that could hardly be expected since it was due to the effects of the Suez crisis, a specific event that cannot be reflected in a general model.

Drink and tobacco. Although the fit is good in the 1900s and the 1950s, the course of expenditure in the years between the wars is badly reproduced. It is not very easy to see why this should be so since the analysis for the interwar years alone given in Stone *et al.* (1954) was reasonably successful. In the war periods we can see the opposite of a rationing effect, namely expenditure well in excess of the level given by the model.

Entertainment. This is a small and heterogeneous group which is made up of expenditure on public entertainment, reading matter and sports and travel goods. As with transport, there seems to be a case here for an accelerating trend.

319

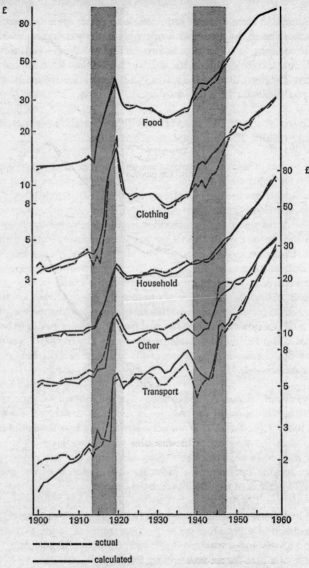

Figure 1 Expenditure per head in Britain at current prices

- - - actual
——— calculated

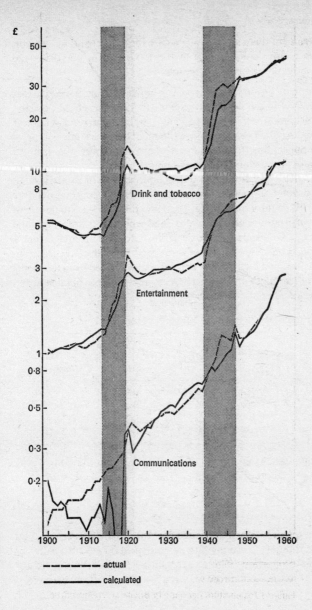

£

50
30
20

10
8

Drink and tobacco

5

3
2

Entertainment

1
0·8

0·5

0·3

Communications

0·2

1900   1910   1920   1930   1940   1950   1960

- - - - actual
———— calculated

Other. Here there seems to be a case for a decelerating trend or, at least, for smaller trends in the 1900s and in the 1920s and 1930s than in the postwar period.

Our conclusion from this survey of the individual series is that the model is usable for projections to 1970 but could be significantly improved by introducing parabolic in place of linear trends. Another way to assess the model is to examine some of its implications for consumers' behaviour over the last six decades. Let us look at two examples.

Firstly, it is well-known that the proportion of total expenditure devoted to food has remained remarkably constant over the last half century and that at the same time budget studies show total expenditure elasticities for food which tend to fall through time. This appears paradoxical but it follows from the model provided that the element of b for food has a negative trend. In fact it has, and furthermore the elasticities derived from the model at different times are in close agreement with those obtained from budget studies.

Table 2 Total Expenditure Elasticities for Food

| | $b_{j\theta}$ | $\dfrac{p_{j\theta} e_{j\theta}}{\mu_\theta}$ | Elasticities from | |
			Model	Budgets
1900	0·314	0·327	0·96	—
1938	0·166	0·292	0·57	0·59
1955	0·100	0·343	0·29	0·30
1960	0·080	0·309	0·26	0·25

The elasticity at time θ of expenditure on commodity j with respect to total expenditure is, from **1**:

$$\frac{\partial(p_{j\theta}e_{j\theta})}{\partial\mu_\theta} \cdot \frac{\mu_\theta}{p_{j\theta}e_{j\theta}} = \frac{b_{j\theta}\mu_\theta}{p_{j\theta}e_{j\theta}} = \frac{\partial e_{j\theta}}{\partial\mu_\theta} \cdot \frac{\mu_\theta}{\partial_{j\theta}}. \qquad \textbf{10}$$

From the first row of **10** we see that this elasticity is equal to the proportion of supernumerary income spent on j at time θ divided by the proportion of total expenditure devoted to j at time θ, and from the second row we see that the expenditure elasticity is equal to the corresponding quantity elasticity. The value of this elasticity at selected dates is shown in Table 2 together with similar estimates derived from budgets.

The similarity of the figures in the last two columns is striking and, further, the information derived from budgets taken in the early years of the century suggests an elasticity of about one. The same budget estimates for 1938, reached by different methods, can be found in Aitchison and Brown (1954–5) and Stone *et al.* (1954). The budget estimates for 1955 and 1960 are taken from UK Ministry of Agriculture (1962). The latter are strictly *income elasticities* and are restricted to total food consumed at home. For both these reasons they are probably a little on the low side but, as the compilers note, they are in themselves probably a little on the high side because 'the tendency to understate incomes, common to all budget surveys, is relatively greater among households with higher incomes'. Accordingly, we have not attempted any adjustment of the published figures.

A falling income elasticity can be given an interesting interpretation in the light of the log-normal-integral Engel curves developed in Aitchison and Brown (1954–5, 1957). These Engel curves imply a relationship between the elasticity and the saturation level so that if we know the actual level of expenditure at

Table 3 Food Saturation in £ Per Head

	Observed food expenditure	Per cent of saturation	Implied saturation
1900	21·3	0·39	54·7
1913	21·7	0·51	42·6
1924	23·9	0·59	40·5
1938	27·4	0·65	42·2
1950	31·5	0·78	40·7
1960	34·7	0·86	40·4

constant prices associated with a given elasticity we can calculate the corresponding saturation level. This is done for selected years in Table 3. The implication of this table is that in the early years of this century the level of food consumption aimed at by the average consumer fell by about 20 per cent and after that remained practically constant. From a casual knowledge of the

323

history of food habits a fall in the saturation level between the nineteenth and twentieth centuries seems plausible and so does a constancy of the saturation level over the last generation.

We conclude that the success of the comparison of food elasticities, and the general attitude to food implied, provide additional reasons for accepting the model in spite of the limitations to which we drew attention in the third section above. The second implication, which we shall now discuss, is less conclusive though equally interesting. It concerns the history of committed expenditure in relation to total expenditure. This relationship is set out for selected years in Table 4.

Table 4 Committed Expenditure in Relation to Total Expenditure

(£ Current Per Head and Ratios)

	Committed expenditure	*Total expenditure*	*Ratio*
1900	23·9	39·5	0·61
1913	35·7	45·1	0·79
1924	76·9	85·6	0·90
1938	82·8	93·8	0·88
1950	179·2	182·2	0·98
1960	271·9	310·2	0·88

This table shows that at all dates the proportion of expenditure committed has been higher than 50 per cent and that in the last generation is has normally been as high as 85 to 90 per cent. During war time it has usually risen to, and even above, 100 per cent only to fall again as more normal conditions return. Its very high level since the 1920s implies that for the broad groups of commodities considered here, the pattern of purchases is dominated by the gradual increases in committed purchases which reflect a basic standard of living that has been achieved and is not lightly to be given up. This picture of the consumer, hemmed in by his aspirations and achievements, and incapable of altering his consumption pattern radically in response to price movements seems to us very convincing, especially in a world which exploits far more than it used to the persuasive powers of advertising and the financing easements of hire purchase.

So, again, this implication of the model seems to us to tell in its favour, though such a conclusion is bound to be highly speculative in the present state of knowledge. It is, of course, a conclusion that relates to broad groups of consumption and not to its fine structure. If we wanted to include different brands of orange juice as separate commodities, we should have to modify the model. In fact, as was pointed out in Stone (1954), it is possible to replace $\hat{c}$ by pD where D is a symmetric matrix; but for our purposes we did not think it necessary to consider this generalization. [...]

Conclusions

In this section we shall bring together a number of comments on the model and its use which are scattered through the earlier sections. We can set out our conclusions under a number of heads, as follows.

1. The main strength of the model is that it enables us to analyse the demand for all groups of commodities over a comparatively long period within a single conceptual framework. We do not have to consider commodity groups one at a time nor do we have to treat postwar demand functions as though they were unrelated to the demand functions of earlier periods. From the point of view of projections this is a great advantage because it means that we are getting a consistent picture based on a considerable span of the past rather than a series of partial pictures based on only a short span.

2. Since this is the first analysis of its kind, it is naturally not in a very finished form. We have seen that, for some commodity groups, the assumption of linear trends introduced avoidable errors and that there were groups which could have been better approximated by accelerating or decelerating trends. On the assumption that all growth is fundamentally sigmoid in character, this is very much what one would expect. The simple thing to do to meet this difficulty is to replace linear trends by parabolic ones, and this we propose to do. We do not, however, feel very easy about parabolic trends and we hope eventually to be able

to introduce sigmoid trends into the model or to make the trends dependent on the past values of consumption. This last possibility is particularly important when projections are based on abnormally high growth rates and when, as a consequence, consumers' behaviour may be expected to undergo unusually rapid change.

3. We attach importance to the results obtained from the model conforming with other independent results such as those obtained from budget studies. In the case of food we have shown that they do conform, and we intend to see what happens with other commodity groups.

4. We intend to experiment with the dynamic version of the model because it allows for the fact that consumers' adjustments take time. This is particularly important in the case of durable goods which are becoming of much greater importance than they were in the past. First, however, we must solve the computing problems of introducing trends in the parameters of the dynamic model.

5. We intend to use the decomposable property of the model to subdivide the small number of commodity groups analysed in this paper. As we make our groups smaller we shall have to pay more attention to the nature of these groups than we did here, because we must avoid groups that are complementary or inferior to the others. When we do this we may have to consider the version of the model in which committed purchases are a function of the price structure.

6. From a statistical point of view the chief weakness of the model probably lies in the assumption of a scalar variance matrix. We should, therefore, try to replace this assumption by something more realistic.

7. We have seen that the model gives rise to considerable computing difficulties largely because of the problem of choosing initial values which will ensure convergence. In view of the more sophisticated models now being proposed in econometrics this problem seems to provide a useful field for research in applied mathematics.

Richard Stone, J. A. C. Brown and D. A. Rowe

References

AITCHISON, J., and BROWN, J. A. C. (1954–5), 'A synthesis of Engel curve theory', *Review of Economic Studies*, vol. 22, pp. 35–46.

AITCHISON, J., and BROWN, J. A. C. (1957), *The Lognormal Distribution*, Cambridge University Press.

CAMBRIDGE, DEPARTMENT of APPLIED ECONOMICS (1962), *A Computable Model of Economic Growth*, Chapman & Hall.

GEARY, R. C. (1949–50), 'A constant-utility index of the cost of living', *Review of Economic Studies*, vol. 18, pp. 65–6.

KLEIN, L. R., and RUBIN, H. (1947–8), 'A constant-utility index of the cost of living', *Review of Economic Studies*, vol. 15, no. 38, pp. 84–7.

PREST, A. R., assisted by ADAMS, A. A. (1954), *Consumers' Expenditure in the United Kingdom, 1900–1919*, Cambridge University Press.

SAMUELSON, P. A. (1947–8), 'Some implications of "linearity"', *Review of Economic Studies*, vol. 15, no. 38, pp. 88–90.

STONE, R. (1954), 'Linear expenditure systems and demand analysis: an application to the pattern of British demand', *Economic Journal*, vol. 64, no. 255, pp. 511–27.

STONE, R. (1955), 'Transaction models with an example based on the British national accounts', *Accounting Research*, vol. 6, no. 3, pp. 202–26.

STONE, R. (1961), *Input-Output and National Accounts*, OEEC.

STONE, R., and CROFT-MURRAY, G. (1959), *Social Accounting and Economic Models*, Bowes & Bowes.

STONE, R., *et al.* (1954), *The Measurement of Consumers' Expenditure and Behaviour in the United Kingdom, 1920–1938*, Cambridge University Press, vol. 1.

STONE, R., and ROWE, D. A. (1966), *The Measurement of Consumers' Expenditure and Behaviour in the United Kingdom, 1920–38*, Cambridge University Press, vol. 2.

UK CENTRAL STATISTICAL OFFICE (1951), *Statistical Digest of the War*, HMSO and Longmans.

UK CENTRAL STATISTICAL OFFICE (1961 and annually), *National Income and Expenditure: 1961*, HMSO.

UK MINISTRY OF AGRICULTURE, FISHERIES AND FOOD (1962), *Domestic Food Consumption and Expenditure: 1960*, HMSO.

17 Arthur S. Goldberger and Maw Lin Lee

Disaggregated Demand

Arthur S. Goldberger and Maw Lin Lee, 'Towards a micro-analytic model of the household sector', *American Economic Review*, vol. 52, 1962, pp. 241–51.

In his paper, 'Microanalytic Models of the United States Economy: Need and Development', Guy Orcutt has sketched out a framework for a microanalytic model of the United States. The present paper is concerned with the empirical implementation of the household sector of the model. The first section points out some of the principles guiding this work. The second section surveys a range of estimated operating characteristics currently available for inclusion in the sector model. Most of these are based upon single cross sections. We are currently analyzing a set of successive cross sections and report on this work in the third section.

Guidelines to empirical implementation

What are the data requirements for the empirical implementation of a microanalytic model of the household sector? The distinctive feature of such a model is its disaggregatedness: it uses individual household units – persons, families, spending units, etc. – as components, and it uses operating characteristics formulated in terms of rather narrowly defined variables of the household units.

One might dream of an ideal sample consisting of a continuous panel of US household units, which would keep detailed records permitting of fine cross classification – and which could be subjected to controlled experiment. But it is clear that this dream – or nightmare – is unlikely to be realized. In reality, we will be relying on a large variety of samples, surveys, censuses, along with aggregate time series. We will be faced with serious problems of combining and reconciling data drawn from different sources and employing different concepts. Nor do we propose to work

328

directly with the original data in all cases. Rather we are drawing upon the studies of many other researchers who have estimated empirical relationships – or 'operating characteristics'. Nor, finally, do we propose to wait until ideal pieces have been constructed for all parts of the model. At many points, no doubt, we will rely upon stopgap relationships – often derived from aggregate time series.

Similarly, the approach to estimation methods will be an eclectic one. Of course, we have no choice over estimation methods when we adopt operating characteristics prepared by others. In our own research we have found it useful to work within the framework of classical regression while trying to exploit the full power of this model. Thus, we interpret regression relationships as estimates of the conditional expectation of the regressand for given values of the regressor variables. We have often employed fairly free functional forms, using a dummy variable formulation for continuous as well as for categorical variables. The troublesome problem of dependent variables which are categorical has been handled by linear probability functions. The related problem of dependent variables which are bounded and/or concentrated at zero has been handled by a combination of linear probability and conditional amount functions. Recent work by our colleague, Arnold Zellner, has suggested some refinements for dealing with such relationships more satisfactorily.

It should be recognized that our objective is to have operating characteristics which generate individual observations for simulation runs rather than mere expected values or averages. It is clear that the assumption of normality of disturbances which would simplify the problem of generating individual observations is simply inappropriate in many cases. Therefore we expect to rely upon detailed examination of the pattern of sample residuals to provide information on the form and parameters of the distributions from which individual observations are to be generated.

Catalogue of available operating characteristics

Econometric research on the demographic and economic behavior of household units has been both extensive and intensive, so that there are now available many estimated relationships suitable for incorporation into our microanalytic model of the household sector. It is a task in itself – and a worthwhile one – to prepare a catalogue of such relationships. The catalogue could include a description of the sample data, a definition of the type of unit sampled, and a listing of the inputs – 'explanatory variables' – and of the outputs – 'dependent variables'.

Space limitations preclude the presentation of such a catalogue here. In a preliminary version of this paper, distributed by the Social Systems Research Institute, an illustrative catalogue was presented. It included such studies as those by Crockett and Friend, Watts and Tobin, and Miner, reported on in *Consumption and Saving* (University of Pennsylvania, 1960). The following comments were based upon a survey of that catalogue.

What is apparent from the survey is the wealth of operating characteristics available from past and current econometric research on household units. We do not contend that all that remains to be done is to slap the operating characteristics together into a model; considerable work is required to ensure consistency in splicing together these estimated relationships. Annual results must be converted to the monthly basis utilized in the model. This work should not be viewed as distortion of the estimated relationships, but rather as an attempt to fit them into an integrated model within which their full predictive power can be realized.

Also made apparent from this brief catalogue are blind spots in our picture of the household sector. For example, rather little is available on the determinants of occupation, education and location of residence. Since our model will be utilizing occupation, education and location of residence as inputs, we require some means of generating these characteristics of the units. A possible stopgap device is to utilize past trends in the marginal distribution of these characteristics to project future trends. Individual units would be assigned these characteristics randomly, or rather in accordance with a few obvious determinants, parent's occupation and education, so that the marginal distribution of these characteristics matches the projected trends.

Now, one cannot be content, permanently, with the estimated relationships for the outputs which they do generate. With a few exceptions, each of the operating characteristics has been estimated from a single cross section of units at a given point in time. Such a cross section typically provides little information on the past histories of the units which are, after all, important determinants of both current status and current behavior. Therefore, relationships estimated from the typical cross section contain ambiguous measures of the dependence of current outputs upon current status and inputs and have unnecessarily high unexplained variances. The attack upon this problem will be via more searching interviews and via continuing panel studies.

Another familiar fault of a single cross-section survey is that it suppresses the effect of the current environment – of 'market variables' like prices, interest rates, national unemployment rates, which are constant, or taken to be constant, over the given cross section but which may be expected to vary over time, and to influence the development of individual behavior over time. An attack upon this problem will be via the study of successive cross sections in conjunction with time series of market variables. We now report on a study of this type in which we are currently engaged.

Analysis of successive cross-sections

Since 1946 the Surveys of Consumer Finance have collected data early in each year on the demographic characteristics, financial situation, major expenditures and attitudes and expectations of a probability sample of United States households. Each year the sample consisted of some 3000 spending units, and the responses were coded onto some twelve punch card decks. The 1949, 1953, 1958 and 1961 samples each include about 1000 units interviewed in the preceding year; but essentially the basic decks of the sixteen SCFs comprise a set of successive cross sections of household sector units.

The Social Systems Research Institute has now acquired a full duplicate set of basic decks of the SCFs. We plan to utilize this set of successive cross sections in investigations of the stability of the functional form and parameters of operating characteristics and of the impact of market variables. In a pilot study, we have restricted ourselves to two special decks prepared by Charles Lininger, of the Survey Research Center, for each of the 1951–60

331

SCFs. These special decks, prepared for another purpose, are weak in asset and attitudinal data as compared with the full set of basic decks, but are quite strong in demographic, major expenditure, housing and automobile data.

Our first step was to fit least squares regression relationships for each of the ten SCFs 1951–60, with exceptions where the data were not available, for each of the following twenty-three dependent variables: total income, home ownership – probability and value of owned home – monthly rent, expenditures on additions and repairs to house – probability and amount – car ownership (probability), new car ownership (probability), multiple car ownership (probability), purchase of car in prior year (probability, total price and net outlay), purchase of new car in prior year (probability), purchase of household durables in prior year (probability and amount), mortgage indebtedness (probability, amount and monthly payment), non-car installment indebtedness (probability, amount and monthly payment), and debt incurred in connexion with purchase of car in prior year (probability and amount). The form of the relationship for any of the dependent variables is the same for all years.

For illustrative purposes, we present here three of the sets of estimated relationships: for probability of purchase of durables, for amount spent on durable purchases – given durable purchases – and for probability of new car purchase, given car purchase. Definitions of variables and symbols are given in Table 1, and the regression coefficients along with associated statistics are given in Tables 2–4. It should be noted that the SCF dated year t refers to asset, debt and demographic status as of early year t, and to income and expenditures during year $t-1$. Observations were not adjusted for price changes, nor were they weighted to reflect differential sampling rates. Farm units were excluded throughout. Unfortunately, a computing error on our part prevents us from presenting strictly comparable results for 1952 at this time.

Briefly surveying each of the tables we find what we take to be an encouraging degree of stability of each of the regressions over time – stability with respect to sign, order of magnitude and significance of the regression coefficients. For income and age, which enter nonlinearly, the intertemporal comparison is

Table 1 Definition of Symbols

Variables

Constant	a	$a = 1$ for all observations
Income; income squared	Y; Y^2	$Y =$ disposable income in 10^3 dollars
		$Y^2 =$ square of $Y =$ (disposable income squared) in 10^6 dollars

Age of head; age of head, squared $\quad A$; A^2

Age in years	A	A^2
18–24	1	1
25–34	2	4
35–44	3	9
45–54	4	16
55–64	5	25
64 and over	6	36

Sex of head	S	$S = 1$ if female; $S = 0$ if male
Race of head	R	$R = 1$ if nonwhite; $R = 0$ if white
Spending unit size	N	$N =$ number of individuals in unit
Marital status of head	W	$W = 1$ if unmarried; $W = 0$ if married
Home ownership	H	$H = 1$ if home owner; $H = 0$ otherwise
Mortgage debt	M	$M =$ mortgage debt in 10^3 dollars
Type of unit	U	$U = 1$ if primary spending unit
		$U = 0$ if secondary spending unit
Recency of marriage of head	W_R	$W_R = 1$ if married no more than two years; $W_R = 0$ otherwise
Education of head	E_1	$E_1 = 1$ if attended high school but no college degree; $E_1 = 0$ otherwise
	E_2	$E_2 = 1$ if college degree; $E_2 = 0$ otherwise
		($E_1 = E_2 = 0$ if did not attend high school)
Occupation of head	O	$O_1 = 1$ if professional, technical or self-employed; $O_1 = 0$ otherwise
	O_2	$O_2 = 1$ if manager, official or proprietor; $O_2 = 0$ otherwise
	O_3	$O_3 = 1$ if clerical, sales, skilled or semi-skilled; $O_3 = 0$ otherwise

Table 1 continued

Variables

	O_4	$O_4 = 1$ if unskilled, service, student or housewife; $O_4 = 0$ otherwise
		$(O_1 = O_2 = O_3 = O_4 = 0$ if unemployed or retired)
Durable purchases	D	$D =$ expenditures on household durables in 10^3 dollars
Durable purchaser	D_1	$D_1 = 1$ if $D \neq 0$; $D_1 = 0$ otherwise
New car purchaser	K_{PN}	$K_{PN} = 1$ if purchased new car(s); $K_{PN} = 0$ otherwise
Unemployment rate	u	$u =$ unemployment as per cent of civilian labor force, prior year
Price index	p	$p =$ consumer price index (1947–49 $= 100$), prior year

Statistics

R^2	Coefficient of multiple determination
n	Number of observations
s	Standard error of estimate
$\bar{y}$	Mean of dependent variable
ΔR^2	Increase in R^2 attributable to introduction of education and occupation variables
δ_{Y5}	'Income effect': partial derivative of dependent variable with respect to disposable income evaluated at \$5,000 disposable income (i.e. at $Y = 5$)
δ_{A3}	'Age effect': partial derivative of dependent variable with respect to age evaluated at the 35–44 age bracket (i.e. at $A = 3$)
*	Coefficient exceeds, in absolute value, 1·960 its conventional standard error
**	Coefficient exceeds, in absolute value, 2·576 its conventional standard error

Table 2: Probability of Durable Purchases

	Survey year					
	1951	1952	1953	1954	1955	1956
a	0·2456**		0·3116**	0·2820**	0·2019**	0·2817**
Y	0·0502**		0·0245**	0·0169**	0·0261**	0·0149
Y^2	−0·0012**		−0·0005**	−0·0003*	−0·0007**	−0·0002
A	−0·0168		−0·0812**	−0·0268	−0·0139	−0·0248
A^2	0·0033		0·0059**	−0·0021	−0·0038	−0·0010
S	0·0187		0·0257	0·0757*	0·0607	0·0504
R	0·0232	Strictly	0·0250	0·0420	0·0006	−0·0344
N	0·0116	comparable	0·0169*	0·0238**	0·0251**	0·0065
W	−0·1315**	results not	−0·0998**	−0·1276**	−0·0962	−0·1343**
H	−0·0309	available	−0·0268	0·0400	0·0113	−0·0188
M	0·0077*		0·0065	0·0019	−0·0002	0·0094**
U	0·1703**		0·1960**	0·1514**	0·1923**	0·2171**
W_R	0·0299		0·1488**	0·1477**	0·1076**	0·1853**
u	—		—	—	—	—
p	—		—	—	—	—
R^2	0·15		0·10	0·10	0·10	0·10
n	3026	2604	2869	2771	2906	2860
s	0·458		0·464	0·469	0·471	0·470
$\bar{y}$	0·4339	0·4320	0·3953	0·4251	0·4312	0·4343
δY_5	0·038	0·020	0·020	0·014	0·019	0·013
δA_3	−0·037	−0·040	−0·046	−0·039	−0·037	−0·031

	Survey year					
	1957	1958	1959	1960	Pooled	Extended
a	0·2620**	0·3366**	0·2714**	0·3196**	0·3012**	0·6558**
Y	0·0284**	0·0193**	0·0354**	0·0274**	0·0237**	0·0247**
Y^2	−0·0004**	−0·0003**	−0·0008**	−0·0006**	−0·0004**	−0·0004**
A	−0·0234	−0·0776**	−0·0649*	−0·0930**	−0·0547**	−0·0567**
A^2	−0·0030	0·0066**	0·0031	0·0065	0·0023*	0·0026*
S	0·0516	0·0863**	0·0531	0·0282	0·0510**	0·0503**
R	0·0044	0·0204	−0·0027	−0·0316	−0·0081	−0·0046
N	0·0032	0·0182**	0·0118	0·0258**	0·0168**	0·0173**
W	−0·1115**	−0·1535**	−0·1047**	−0·0602	−0·1236**	−0·1183**
H	−0·0096	0·0309	−0·0318	0·0308	0·0002	−0·0013
M	0·0039	0·0034	0·0023	0·0033	0·0038**	0·0041**
U	0·1834**	0·1090	−0·2067**	0·1309**	0·1687**	0·1746**
W_R	0·1705**	0·1489**	0·0961*	0·1187**	0·1288**	0·1298**
u	—	—	—	—	—	0·0045
p	—	—	—	—	—	−0·0033**
R^2	0·11	0·08	0·11	0·10	0·10	0·10
n	2854	2974	2932	2793	25982	25982
s	0·467	0·474	0·466	0·467	0·468	0·468
$\bar{y}$	0·4310	0·4126	0·4168	0·4117	0·4214	0·4214
δY_5	0·025	0·016	0·027	0·021	0·020	0·020
δA_3	−0·041	−0·038	−0·046	−0·054	−0·040	−0·041

Table 3 D: **Durable Purchases**

	Survey year					
	1951	1952	1953	1954	1955	1956
a	0·2054**		0·1768*	0·1589	0·2705**	0·1697*
Y	0·0261**		0·0387**	0·0647**	0·0354**	0·0359**
Y^2	0·0000		−0·0004	−0·0008**	−0·0003	−0·0004**
A	0·0009		−0·0224	0·0122	−0·0056	−0·0190
A^2	−0·0029		0·0010	−0·0026	−0·0002	−0·0010
S	−0·0514	Strictly	−0·0715	−0·0023	0·0637	0·0360
R	−0·0110	comparable	−0·0337	0·1918**	0·0291	0·0275
N	−0·0222**	results not	−0·0106	−0·0363**	−0·0128	−0·0025
W	−0·0070	available	0·0419	−0·0310	−0·1030*	0·0254
H	−0·0030		−0·0568	−0·1368	−0·0402	0·0034
M	0·0079*		0·0090	0·0292**	0·0145**	0·0038
U	0·1490**		0·1438**	0·1092	0·0128	0·1016
W_R	0·1819**		0·3054**	0·1927**	0·1890**	0·0764
u	—		—	—	—	—
p	—		—	—	—	—
R^2	0·15		0·14	0·16	0·12	0·11
n	1313	1125	1133	1178	1253	1242
s	0·333		0·411	0·536	0·386	0·364
$\bar{y}$	0·3818	0·4185	0·4017	0·4514	0·4018	0·3887
δY_5	0·026	0·043	0·035	0·058	0·032	0·032
δA_3	−0·017	−0·039	−0·017	−0·002	−0·007	−0·024

	Survey year					
	1957	1958	1959	1960	Pooled	Extended
a	0·2487**	0·0407	0·0620	0·1604	0·1944**	0·4292**
Y	0·0359**	0·0346**	0·0515**	0·0330**	0·0379**	0·0385**
Y^2	−0·0003*	−0·0003**	−0·0011**	−0·0003	−0·0004**	−0·0004**
A	−0·0105	−0·0098	0·0489	0·0152	−0·0076	−0·0080
A^2	−0·0003	0·0016	−0·0079	−0·0039	−0·0005	−0·0004
S	0·0759	−0·0297	−0·0082	0·0178	0·0008	0·0014
R	0·0308	0·0127	0·0236	0·0348	0·0293	0·0324*
N	−0·0038	−0·0145	−0·0157	−0·0188*	−0·0146**	−0·0140**
W	−0·1065	0·0385	0·0244	−0·0509	−0·0221	−0·0192
H	−0·0582	−0·0086	−0·0241	−0·0228	−0·0357**	−0·0374**
M	0·0066	0·0074*	0·0010	0·0091**	0·0083**	0·0087**
U	0·0384	0·1902	0·0724	0·0983	0·0904**	0·0946**
W_R	0·1939**	0·1787**	0·1883**	0·0230**	0·1941**	0·1938**
u	—	—	—	—	—	−0·0114*
p	—	—	—	—	—	−0·0016**
R^2	0·12	0·09	0·08	0·13	0·11	0·11
n	1230	1227	1222	1150	10948	10948
s	0·430	0·409	0·416	0·384	0·412	0·412
$\bar{y}$	0·4317	0·3901	0·3846	0·3980	0·4030	0·4030
δY_5	0·033	0·031	0·041	0·030	0·034	0·035
δA_3	−0·012	−0·001	0·001	−0·008	−0·010	−0·011

Table 4 K_{PN}: Probability of New Car Purchases

	Survey year					
	1951	1952	1953	1954	1955	1956
a	−0·0791		−0·0106	0·0842	0·0309	−0·0864
Y	0·0768**		0·1049**	0·0557**	0·0623**	0·0654**
Y^2	−0·0016**		−0·0029**	−0·0008**	−0·0013**	−0·0010**
A	0·1568**		0·0466	0·0736	0·0621	0·0817
A^2	−0·0174*		−0·0047	−0·0111	−0·0073	−0·0087
S	0·0373		0·0016	0·0594	0·0526	−0·0463
R	−0·0874	Strictly	0·0859	0·0413	0·0087	0·1059
N	−0·0541**	comparable	−0·0485**	−0·0431**	−0·0571**	−0·0442**
W	0·0149	results not	0·0512	−0·0633	0·0354	0·0582
H	0·0748	available	0·0082	0·0451	0·0978*	0·1137**
M	−0·0125		0·0039	0·0033	−0·0079	−0·0064
W_R	−0·0385		−0·0461	−0·0636	−0·1401	−0·0001
D_1	0·0068		0·0194	−0·0456	−0·0111	0·0073
E_1	0·0976*		0·0240	0·0847	0·0636	0·1072**
E_2	0·1412**		0·1040	0·1610**	0·1215*	0·1383**
O_1	0·1126		0·0591	0·0941	0·1039	0·0381
O_2	0·0235		0·0274	0·0097	0·1147	0·1027
O_3	0·0132		−0·0703	0·0044	0·0057	0·0496
O_4	−0·0944		−0·0486	0·0022	0·0472	−0·0270
u	—		—	—	—	—
p	—		—	—	—	—
R^2	0·27		0·28	0·20	0·21	0·24
n	750	581	615	651	722	840
s	0·434		0·416	0·448	0·435	0·438
$\bar{y}$	0·4853	0·4596	0·3740	0·4240	0·3753	0·4464
ΔR^2	0·024		0·021	0·019	0·017	0·013
δ_{Y_5}	0·060	0·074	0·076	0·047	0·049	0·055
δ_{A_2}	0·052	0·039	0·018	0·007	0·018	0·030

	Survey year					
	1957	1958	1959	1960	Pooled	Extended
a	−0·0753	0·1243	0·1530	0·0158	0·0363	0·8807**
Y	0·0543**	0·0615**	0·0770**	0·0405**	0·0561**	0·0591**
Y^2	−0·0008**	−0·0010**	−0·0019*	−0·0001*	−0·0009**	−0·0010**
A	0·1248	0·0533	0·0552	0·1071	0·0828**	0·0790**
A^2	−0·0139	−0·0052	−0·0093	−0·0104	−0·0092**	−0·0087**
S	−0·0218	0·1772*	0·0597	0·1180	0·0470	0·0507
R	−0·0489	0·0676	−0·0060	−0·0427	−0·0063	0·0009
N	−0·0317**	−0·0548**	−0·0483**	−0·0245*	−0·0450**	−0·0431**
W	0·0550	−0·0801	−0·0531	0·0142	−0·0063	0·0024
H	0·0673	0·0645	0·0878*	0·1540**	0·0828**	0·0805**
M	−0·0084	0·0011	−0·0076	−0·0144**	−0·0074**	−0·0061**
W_R	−0·0220	−0·0817	−0·0159	0·1391	−0·0315	−0·0267
D_1	−0·0281	0·0016	−0·0437	−0·0462	−0·0118	−0·0147
E_1	0·1032**	0·0506	0·0270	0·0426	0·0744**	0·0754**
E_2	0·1073	0·0093	0·0933	0·1626**	0·1237**	0·1243**
O_1	0·0054	0·0412	−0·0866	−0·0945	0·0513*	0·0401
O_2	0·0845	−0·0375	−0·1611*	−0·0749	0·0296	0·0193
O_3	−0·0097	−0·0537	−0·1496*	−0·0447	−0·0084	−0·0199
O_4	−0·0231	−0·1329*	−0·1761**	−0·1589	−0·0723**	−0·0575*
u	—	—	—	—	—	−0·0035
p	—	—	—	—	—	−0·0072**

Table 4 continued

	Survey year					
	1957	1958	1959	1960	Pooled	Extended
R^2	0·19	0·21	0·18	0·16	0·20	0·21
n	732	691	647	673	6321	6321
s	0·450	0·437	0·423	0·449	0·440	0·438
$\bar{y}$	0·4249	0·3835	0·2998	0·3759	0·4017	0·4017
ΔR^2	0·011	0·014	0·021	0·027	0·016	—
δ_{Y5}	0·046	0·051	0·058	0·034	0·047	0·050
δ_{A3}	0·041	0·022	−0·001	0·045	0·028	0·027

simplified by reference to the partial derivatives δ_{Y5} and δ_{A3} given at the bottom of the tables. For the record, each of the R^2s is significantly different from zero at the 1 per cent level by the conventional F-test. To illustrate the range of regressors being explored, the education and occupation variables are included in

Table 5 Annual Regressand Means: Observed and Predicted from Pooled Regressions

Survey year	Probability of durable purchases		Durable purchases		Probability of new car purchases	
	Observed	Predicted	Observed	Predicted	Observed	Predicted
1951	0·4339	0·3937	0·3818	0·3742	0·4853	0·3875
1952	0·4320	—	0·4185	—	0·4596	—
1953	0·3953	0·4012	0·4017	0·3842	0·3740	0·3811
1954	0·4251	0·4114	0·4514	0·3910	0·4240	0·4068
1955	0·4312	0·4206	0·4018	0·3902	0·3753	0·4010
1956	0·4343	0·4206	0·3887	0·4056	0·4464	0·4169
1957	0·4310	0·4374	0·4317	0·4314	0·4249	0·4172
1958	0·4126	0·4457	0·3901	0·4208	0·3835	0·4150
1959	0·4168	0·4249	0·3846	0·4089	0·2998	0·3736
1960	0·4117	0·4377	0·3980	0·4222	0·3759	0·4065

the regression for the probability of new car purchase, where their joint contribution is generally significantly different from zero at about the 5 per cent level by the conventional F-test, but excluded in the two durables regressions, where they fail the conventional test).

The second step was to combine all nine surveys – 1951, 1953– 60 – together and to fit each regression to the pooled sample.

The results of the pooled regressions are presented in the last but one column of Tables 2–4. A formal test of the hypothesis that the entire true regression relationship was constant for all years led to its rejection. (We have yet to formally test for stability of individual coefficients.) We have also applied the pooled regression coefficients to the annual means of the regressors to obtain a series of predicted means of the regressands. These series are presented along with the series of regressand means in Table 5. Comparison of the predicted and actual series indicates how well a single relationship is able to track the time path of the mean of the dependent variable, which may be associated with the corresponding national aggregate.

Turning finally to the impact of the market variables, we have extended the regression to include two new variables, u, the unemployment rate, and p, the consumer price index, and fitted to the pooled sample. The results of these extended regressions are presented in the last columns of Tables 2–4. We have also applied the extended regression coefficients to the annual means of the regressors to obtain a series of predicted means of the regressands; these are presented, along with their observed counterparts, in Table 6.

Table 6 Annual Regressand Means: Observed and Predicted from Extended Regressions

Survey year	Probability of durable purchases		Durable purchases		Probability of new car purchases	
	Observed	Predicted	Observed	Predicted	Observed	Predicted
1951	0·4339	0·4394	0·3818	0·3878	0·4853	0·4737
1952	0·4320	—	0·4185	—	0·4596	—
1953	0·3953	0·4020	0·4017	0·4059	0·3740	0·4006
1954	0·4251	0·4085	0·4514	0·4136	0·4240	0·4212
1955	0·4312	0·4288	0·4018	0·3816	0·3753	0·4041
1956	0·4343	0·4246	0·3887	0·4113	0·4464	0·4257
1957	0·4310	0·4351	0·4317	0·4369	0·4249	0·4198
1958	0·4126	0·4312	0·3901	0·4189	0·3835	0·3913
1959	0·4168	0·4101	0·3846	0·3729	0·2998	0·3151
1960	0·4117	0·4139	0·3980	0·3996	0·3759	0·3450

18 Kelvin J. Lancaster

Goods Aren't Goods

Excerpts from Kelvin J. Lancaster, 'A new approach to consumer theory', *Journal of Political Economy*, vol. 174, 1966, pp. 132–57.

The current status of consumer theory

The theory of consumer behavior in deterministic situations as set out by, say, Debreu (1959, 1960) or Uzawa (1960) is a thing of great aesthetic beauty, a jewel set in a glass case. The product of a long process of refinement from the nineteenth century utility theorists through Slutsky and Hicks-Allen to the economists of the last twenty-five years,[1] it has been shorn of all irrelevant postulates so that it now stands as an example of how to extract the minimum of results from the minimum of assumptions.

To the process of slicing away with Occam's razor, the author made a small contribution (Lancaster, 1957). This brought forth a reply by Johnson (1958) which suggested, somewhat tongue-in-cheek, that the determinateness of the sign of the substitution effect – the only substantive result of the theory of consumer behavior – could be derived from the proposition that goods are goods.

Johnson's comment, on reflection, would seem to be almost the best summary that can be given of the current state of the theory of consumer behavior. All *intrinsic* properties of particular goods, those properties that make a diamond quite obviously something different from a loaf of bread, have been omitted from the theory, so that a consumer who consumes diamonds alone is as rational as a consumer who consumes bread alone, but one who sometimes consumes bread, sometimes diamonds (*ceteris paribus*, of course), is irrational. Thus, the only property

1. The American Economic Association *Index of Economic Journals* lists 151 entries under category 2.111 (utility, demand, theory of the household) over the period 1940–63.

which the theory can build on is the property shared by all goods, which is simply that they are goods.

Indeed, we can continue the argument further, since goods are simply what consumers would like more of; and we must be neutral with respect to differences in consumer tastes – some consumers might like more of something that other consumers do not want – that the ultimate proposition is that *goods are what are thought of as goods*.

In spite of the denial of the relevance of intrinsic properties to the pure theory, there has always been a subversive undercurrent suggesting that economists continue to take account of these properties. Elementary textbooks bristle with substitution examples about butter and margarine, rather than about shoes and ships, as though the authors believed that there was something intrinsic to butter and margarine that made them good substitutes and about automobiles and gasoline that made them somehow intrinsically complementary. Market researchers, advertisers and manufacturers also act as though they believe that knowledge of, or belief in, the intrinsic properties of goods is relevant to the way consumers will react toward them.

The clearest case of conflict between a belief that goods do have intrinsic properties relevant to consumer theory but that they are not taken into account has been the long search for a definition of 'intrinsic complementarity'. The search was successful only where Morishima (1959) turned from traditional theory to an approach somewhat similar to that of the present paper.

Perhaps the most important aspects of consumer behavior relevant to an economy as complex as that of the United States are those of consumer reactions to new commodities and to quality variations. Traditional theory has nothing to say on these. In the case of new commodities, the theory is particularly helpless. We have to expand from a commodity space of dimension n to one of dimension $n + 1$, replacing the old utility function by a completely new one, and even a complete map of the consumer's preferences among the n goods provides absolutely no information about the new preference map. A theory which can make no use of so much information is a remarkably empty one. Even the technique of supposing the existence of a utility function for all possible goods, including those not yet invented, and regarding the prices of nonexistent goods as infinite – an incredible stretching of the consumers' powers of imagination – has no predictive value.

Finally we can note the unsuitability of traditional theory for dealing with many of the manifestly important aspects of actual relationships between goods and consumers in I. F. Pearce's (1964) recent heroic but rather unsuccessful attempts to deal with complementarity, substitution, independence and neutral want associations within the conventional framework.

A new approach

Like many new approaches, the one set out in this paper draws upon several elements that have been utilized elsewhere. The chief technical novelty lies in breaking away from the traditional approach that goods are the direct objects of utility and, instead, supposing that it is the properties or characteristics of the goods from which utility is derived.

We assume that consumption is an activity in which goods, singly or in combination, are inputs and in which the output is a collection of characteristics. Utility or preference orderings are assumed to rank collections of characteristics and only to rank collections of goods indirectly through the characteristics that they possess. A meal, treated as a single good, possesses nutritional characteristics but it also possesses aesthetic characteristics, and different meals will possess these characteristics in different relative proportions. Furthermore, a dinner party, a combination of two goods, a meal and a social setting, may possess nutritional, aesthetic and perhaps intellectual characteristics different from the combination obtainable from a meal and a social gathering consumed separately.

In general – and the richness of the approach springs more from this than from anything else – even a single good will possess more than one characteristic, so that the simplest consumption activity will be characterized by joint outputs. Furthermore, the same characteristic, for example, aesthetic properties, may be included among the joint outputs of many consumption activities so that goods which are apparently un-related in certain of their characteristics may be related in others.

We shall assume that the structure we have interposed between the goods themselves and the consumer's preferences is, in principle at least, of an objective kind. That is, the characteristics possessed by a good or a combination of goods are the same for all consumers and, given units of measurement, are in the same quantities,[2] so that the personal element in consumer choice arises in the choice between collections of characteristics only, not in the allocation of characteristics to the goods. The objective nature of the goods – characteristics relationship plays a crucial role in the analysis and enables us to distinguish between objective and private reactions to such things as changes in relative prices.

The essence of the new approach can be summarized as follows, each assumption representing a break with tradition:

1. The good, *per se*, does not give utility to the consumer; it possesses characteristics, and these characteristics give rise to utility.

2. In general, a good will possess more than one characteristic, and many characteristics will be shared by more than one good.

3. Goods in combination may possess characteristics different from those pertaining to the goods separately.

A move in the direction of the first assumption has already been made by various workers including Strotz (1957, 1959) and Gorman (1959), with the 'utility tree' and other ideas associating a particular good with a particular type of utility. The theory set out here goes much further than these ideas. Multiple characteristics, structurally similar to those of the present paper but confined to a particular problem and a point utility function, are implicit in the classical 'diet problem' of Stigler (1945), and multidimensioned utilities have been used by workers in other fields, for example, Thrall *et al.* (1954). The third assumption, of activities involving complementary collections of goods, has

2. Since the units in which the characteristics are measured are arbitrary, the objectivity criterion relating goods and characteristics reduces to the requirement that the *relative* quantities of a particular characteristic between unit quantities of any pair of goods should be the same for all consumers.

been made by Morishima (1959) but in the context of single-dimensioned utility.

A variety of other approaches with similarities to that of the present paper occur scattered through the literature, for example, in Quandt (1956), or in Becker (1965), or in various discussions of investment-portfolio problems. These are typically set out as *ad hoc* approaches to particular problems. Perhaps the most important aspect of this paper is that the model is set out as a general replacement of the traditional analysis, which remains as a special case, rather than as a special solution to a special problem.

It is clear that only by moving to multiple characteristics can we incorporate many of the intrinsic qualities of individual goods. Consider the choice between a gray Chevrolet and a red Chevrolet. On ordinary theory these are either the same commodity, ignoring what may be a relevant aspect of the choice situation, or different commodities, in which case there is no *a priori* presumption that they are close substitutes. Here we regard them as goods associated with satisfaction vectors which differ in only one component, and we can proceed to look at the situation in much the same way as the consumer – or even the economist, in private life – would look at it.

Traditional theory is forever being forced to interpret quite common real-life happenings, such as the effects of advertising in terms of 'change of taste', an entirely non-operational concept since there is no way of predicting the relationship between preference before and after the change. The theory outlined here, although extremely rich in useful ways of thinking about consumer behavior, may also be thought to run the danger of adding to the economist's extensive collection of non-operational concepts. If this were true, it need not, of course, inhibit the heuristic application of the theory. Even better, however, the theory implies predictions that differ from those of traditional theory, and the predictions of the new approach seem to fit better the realities of consumer behavior.

A model of consumer behavior

To obtain a working model from the ideas outlined above, we shall make some assumptions which are, on balance, neither more nor less heroic than those made elsewhere in our present economic theorizing and which are intended to be no more and no less permanent parts of the theory.

1. We shall regard an individual good or a collection of goods as a consumption activity and associate a scalar (the level of the activity) with it. We shall assume that the relationship between the level of activity k, y_k, and the goods consumed in that activity to be both linear and objective, so that, if x_j is the jth commodity we have

$$x_j = \sum_k a_{jk} y_k, \qquad\qquad 1$$

and the vector of total goods required for a given activity vector is given by

$$x = Ay. \qquad\qquad 2$$

Since the relationships are assumed objective, the equations are assumed to hold for all individuals, the coefficients a_{jk} being determined by the intrinsic properties of the goods themselves and possibly the context of technological knowledge in the society.

2. More heroically, we shall assume that each consumption activity produces a fixed vector of characteristics[3] and that the relationship is again linear, so that, if z_i is the amount of the ith characteristic

$$z_i = \sum_k b_{ik} y_k, \qquad\qquad 3$$

or $z = By.$ $\qquad\qquad 4$

Again, we shall assume that the coefficients b_{ik} are objectively determined – in principle at least – for some arbitrary choice of the units of z_i.

3. The assumption that the consumption technology A, B is fixed is a convenience for discussing those aspects of the model, primarily static, that are the chief concern of this paper. The consequences of relaxing this particular assumption is only one of many possible extensions and expansions of the ideas presented and are discussed by the author elsewhere (Lancaster, 1966).

3. We shall assume that the individual possesses an ordinal utility function on characteristics $U(z)$ and that he will choose a situation which maximizes $U(z)$. $U(z)$ is provisionally assumed to possess the ordinary convexity properties of a standard utility function.

The chief purpose of making the assumption of linearity is to simplify the problem. A viable model could certainly be produced under the more general set of relationships

$$F_k(z, x) = 0, k = 1,\ldots, m. \qquad\qquad 5$$

The model could be analyzed in a similar way to that used by Samuelson (1953) and others in analyzing production, although the existence of much jointness among outputs in the present model presents difficulties.

In this model, the relationship between the collections of characteristics available to the consumer – the vectors z – which are the direct ingredients of his preferences and his welfare, and the collections of goods available to him – the vectors x – which represent his relationship with the rest of the economy, is not direct and one-to-one, as in the traditional model, but indirect, through the activity vector y.

Consider the relationships which link z and x. These are the equation systems: $x = Ay$, 2 and $z = By$, 4. Suppose that there are r characteristics, m activities, and n goods. Only if $r = m = n$ will there be a one-to-one relationship between z and x. In this case both the B and A matrixes are square – the number of variables equals the number of equations in both sets of equations – and we can solve for y in terms of x, $y = A^{-1}x$, giving $z = BA^{-1}x$. $U(z)$ can be written directly and unambiguously as a function $u(x)$. Otherwise the relations are between vectors in spaces of different dimensions. Consider some x^* in the case in which $m > n$: equation 2 places only n restrictions on the m-vector y, so that y can still be chosen with $m - n$ degrees of freedom. If $r < m$, then there are $m - r$ degrees of freedom in choosing y, given some z, but whether the ultimate relationship gives several choices of z for a given x, or several x for a given z, and whether all vectors z are attainable, depends on the relationships between r, m and n and the structures of the matrixes A, B. In general, we will expect that the consumer may face a choice among many paths linking goods collections with characteristics collections. The simple question asked, in principle, in the traditional analysis – does a particular consumer prefer collection x_1 or collection x_2 – no longer has a direct answer, although the question, does he prefer characteristics collection z_1 or z_2, does have such an answer.

If we take the standard choice situation facing the consumer in a free market, with a linear budget constraint, this situation, in our model, becomes:

Maximize $U(z)$

subject to $px \leqq k$

with $\qquad z = By$

$\qquad\quad x = Ay$

$x, y, z \geqq 0$.

This is a non-linear program of an intractable kind. The problem of solution need not worry us here, since we are interested only in the properties of the solution.

The simplified model

We shall simplify the model in the initial stages by supposing that there is a one-to-one correspondence between goods and activities so that we can write the consumer-choice program in the simpler form:

Maximize $U(z)$

subject to $px \leqq k$

with $\qquad z = Bx$

$\qquad z, x \geqq 0$.

This is still, of course, a non-linear program, but we now have a single step between goods and characteristics.

The model consists of four parts. There is a maximand $U(z)$ operating on characteristics, that is, U is defined on characteristics-space, C-space. The budget constraint $px \leqq k$ is defined on goods-space, G-space. The equation system $z = Bx$ represents a transformation between G-space and C-space. Finally, there are non-negativity constraints z, $x \geqq 0$ which we shall assume to

347

hold initially, although in some applications and with some sign conventions they may not always form part of the model.

In traditional consumer analysis, both the budget constraint and the utility function are defined on G-space, and we can immediately relate the two as in the ordinary textbook in-difference-curve diagram. Here we can only relate the utility function to the budget constraint after both have been defined on the same space. We have a choice: we can either transform the utility function into G-space and relate it directly to the budget constraint; or we can transform the budget constraint into C-space and relate it directly to the utility function $U(z)$.

Each of these techniques is useful in different circumstances. In the case of the first, we can immediately write

$$U(z) = U(Bx) = u(x),$$

so we have a new utility function directly in terms of goods, but the properties of the function $u(x)$ depend crucially on the structure of the matrix B and this, together with the constraints $x \geqq 0$ and $z = Bx \geqq 0$ give a situation much more complex than that of conventional utility maximization. The second technique again depends crucially on the structure of B and again will generally lead to a constraint of a more complex kind than in conventional analysis.

The central role in the model is, of course, played by the transformation equation $z = Bx$ and the structure and qualita-tive[4] properties of the matrix B. Most of the remainder of the paper will be concerned with the relationship between the properties of B, which we can call the *consumption technology*[5] of the economy, and the behavior of consumers.

Certain properties of the transformations between G- and C-space follow immediately from the fact that B is a matrix of constants, and the transformation $z = Bx$ is linear. These can be stated as follows, proof being obvious.

4. 'Qualitative' is used here in a somewhat more general sense than in the author's work on the properties of qualitatively defined systems for which see Lancaster (1962, 1965).

5. If the relationship between goods and activities is not one-to-one, the consumption technology consists of the two matrixes, B, A, as in the technology of the Von Neumann growth model.

1. A convex set in G-space will transform into a convex set in C-space, so that the budget constraint $px \leqq k, x \geqq 0$ will become a convex constraint on the zs.

2. An inverse transformation will not necessarily exist, so that an arbitrary vector z in C-space may have no vector x in G-space corresponding to it.

3. Where an inverse transformation does exist from C-space into G-space, it will transform convex sets into convex sets so that, for any set of zs which do have images in G-space, the convexity of the U function on the zs will be preserved in relation to the xs.

The properties are sufficient to imply that utility maximization subject to constraint will lead to determinate solutions for consumer behavior.

The structure of consumption technology

The consumption technology, which is as important a determinant of consumer behavior as the particular shape of the utility function, is described fully only by the A and B matrixes together, but certain types of behavior can be related to more generalized descriptions of the technology. We shall distinguish broadly between structural properties of the technology, such as the relationship between the number of rows and columns of B and/or A and whether A, B are decomposable, and qualitative properties, such as the signs of the elements of A and B.

The leading structural property of the consumption technology is the relationship between the number of characteristics, r, and the number of activities, m, that is, between the number of rows and columns of B. It will be assumed that B contains no linear dependence, so that its rank is the number of rows or columns, whichever is less. We shall assume, unless otherwise stated, a one-to-one relationship between goods and activities.

1. The number of characteristics is equal to the number of goods. In this case, there is a one-to-one relationship between activities vectors and characteristics vectors. We have $z = Bx, x = B^{-1}z$. If B is a permutation of a diagonal matrix then there is a one-to-one relationship between each component of z and each component of y, and the model becomes, by suitable choice of units,

349

exactly the same as the traditional model. If B is not a diagonal permutation, the objects of utility are composite goods rather than individual goods, and the model has some important differences from the conventional analysis. Note how specialized is the traditional case in relation to our general model.

If B is a diagonal permutation but there is not a one-to-one relationship between activities and goods so that A is not a diagonal permutation, we have a model similar to that of Morishima (1959).

2. The number of characteristics is greater than the number of goods. In this case, the relationships $Bx = z$ contain more equations than variables x_i so that we cannot, in general, find a goods vector x which gives rise to an arbitrarily specified characteristics vector z. We can take a basis of any arbitrarily chosen n characteristics and consider the reduced $n \times n$ system $\bar{B} = \bar{z}$, which gives a one-to-one relationship between n characteristics and the n goods, with the remaining $r - n$ characteristics being determined from the remaining $r - n$ equations and the goods vector x corresponding to $\bar{z}$. In this case, it is generally most useful to analyze consumer behavior by transforming the utility function into G-space, rather than the budget constraint into C-space. What does the transformed utility function look like?

The utility function transformed into G-space retains its essential convexity. An intuitive way of looking at the situation is to note that all characteristics collections which are actually available are contained in an n-dimensional slice through the r-dimensional utility function, and that all slices through a convex function are themselves convex. The transformation of this n-dimensional slice into G-space preserves this convexity.

For investigation of most aspects of consumer behavior, the case in which the number of characteristics exceeds the number of goods – a case we may often wish to associate with simple societies – can be treated along with the very special case, of which conventional analysis is a special subcase, in which the number of characteristics and goods is equal. In other words, given the consumption technology, we concern ourselves only with the particular n-dimensional slice of the r-dimensional utility function implied by that technology[6] and, since the slice of the utility function has the same general properties as any n-dimensional utility function, we can proceed as if the utility function was defined on only n characteristics.

3. In the third case, in which the number of goods exceeds the number of characteristics, a situation probably descriptive of a complex economy such as that of the United States, there are properties of the situation that are different from those of the two previous cases and from the conventional analysis.

Here, the consumption technology, $z = Bx$, has fewer equations than variables so that, for every characteristics vector there is more than one goods vector. For every point in his characteristics-space, the consumer has a choice between different goods vectors. Given a price vector, this choice is a pure efficiency choice, so that for every characteristics vector the consumer will choose the most efficient combination of goods to achieve that collection of characteristics, and the efficiency criterion will be minimum cost.

The efficiency choice for a characteristics vector z^* will be the solution of the canonical linear program:

Minimize px

subject to $Bx = z^*$

$$x \geqq 0.$$

Since this is a linear program, once we have the solution x^* for some z^*, with value k^*, we can apply a scalar multiple to fit the solution to any budget value k and characteristics vector $(k/k^*)z^*$. By varying z^*, the consumer, given a budget constraint $px = k$, can determine a characteristics frontier consisting of all z such that the value of the above program is just equal to k. There will be a determinate goods vector associated with each point of the characteristics frontier.

6. Assuming no decomposability or singularities in the consumption technology matrix B, then, if z_n is the vector of any n components of z and B_n, the corresponding square submatrix of B, the subspace of C-space to which the consumer is confined, is that defined by $z_{r-n} = B_{r-n}B_n^{-1} z_n$, where z_{r-n}, B_{r-n} are the vector and corresponding submatrix of B consisting of the components not included in z_n, B_n.

As in the previous case, it is easy to show that the set of characteristics vectors in C-space that are preferred or indifferent to z transforms into a convex set in G-space if it is a convex set in C-space; it is also easy to show that the set of zs that can be obtained from the set of xs satisfying the convex constraint $px \leqq k$ is also a convex set. The characteristics frontier is, therefore, concave to the origin, like a transformation curve. For a consumption technology with four goods and two characteristics, the frontier could have any of the three shapes shown in Figure 1. Note that, in general, if B is a positive matrix, the positive orthant in G-space transforms into a cone which lies in the interior of the positive orthant in C-space, a point illustrated in Figure 1.

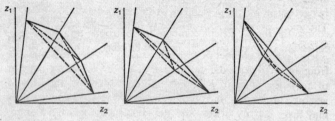

Figure 1

A consumer's complete choice subject to a budget constraint $px \leqq k$ can be considered as consisting of two parts: an efficiency choice, determining the characteristics frontier and the associated efficient goods collections; and a private choice, determining which point on the characteristics frontier is preferred by him.

The efficiency choice is an objective not a subjective choice. On the assumption that the consumption technology is objective, the characteristics frontier is also objective, and it is the same for all consumers facing the same budget constraint. Furthermore the characteristics frontier is expanded or contracted linearly and proportionally to an increase or decrease in income, so that the frontier has the same *shape* for all consumers facing the same prices, income differences simply being reflected in homogeneous expansion or contraction.

We should note that, if the consumption technology matrix

has certain special structural properties, we may obtain a mixture of the above cases. For example, a matrix with the structure

$$B \equiv \begin{bmatrix} B_1 & O \\ O & B_2 \end{bmatrix},$$

where B_1 is an $(s \times k)$ matrix and B_2 is an $(r - s) \times (n - k)$ matrix, partitions the technology into two disconnected parts, one relating s of the characteristics to k of the goods, the other separately relating $r - s$ of the characteristics to $n - k$ of the goods. We can have $s \geqq k$ and $r - s < n - k$ giving a mixed case.

Dropping the assumption of a one-to-one relationship between goods and activities does not add greatly to the difficulties of the analysis. We have, as part of the technology, $x = Ay$, so that the budget constraint $px \leqq k$ can be written immediately as $pAy \leqq k$. The goods prices transform directly into implicit activity prices $q = pA$. Interesting cases arise, of course. If the number of goods is less than the number of activities, then not all qs are attainable from the set of ps; and if the number of goods exceeds the number of activities, different p vectors will correspond to the same q vector. This implies that certain changes in relative goods prices may leave activity prices, and the consumer's choice situation, unchanged.

In most of the succeeding analysis, we will be concerned with the B matrix and the relationship between activities and characteristics, since this represents the most distinctive part of the theory.

The efficiency substitution effect and revealed preference

At this stage, it is desirable to examine the nature of the efficiency choice so that we can appreciate the role it plays in the consumer behavior implied by our model. Consider a case in which there are two characteristics, a case that can be illustrated diagrammatically, and, say, four activities.

The activities-characteristics portion of the consumption technology is defined by the two equations

$$z_1 = b_{11} y_1 + b_{12} y_2 + b_{13} y_3 + b_{14} y_4;$$
$$z_2 = b_{21} y_1 + b_{22} y_2 + b_{23} y_3 + b_{24} y_4.$$

6

Economic Factors

With activity 1 only, the characteristics will be obtained in proportion, b_{11}/b_{21} – the ray labelled 1 in Figure 2. Similarly with activities 2, 3, 4, one at a time, characteristics will be obtained in proportions b_{12}/b_{22}, b_{13}/b_{23}, b_{14}/b_{24}, respectively, corresponding to the rays 2, 3, 4 in Figure 2.

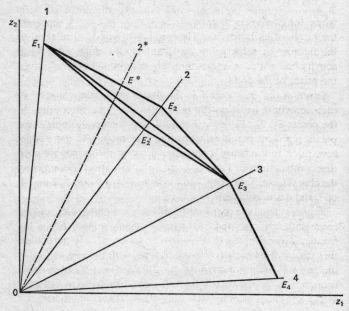

Figure 2

We are given a budget constraint in goods space of the form

$$\sum_i p_i\, x_i \leqq k.$$

If there is a one-to-one correspondence between goods and activities, the prices of the activities are given by p_i. If there is not a one-to-one relationship, but a goods-activities portion of the consumption technology

$$x_i = a_{i1}\, y_1 + a_{i2}\, y_2 + a_{i3}\, y_3 + a_{i4}\, y_4 \quad i = 1, \ldots, n, \qquad 7$$

then the budget constraint can be transformed immediately into characteristics space

$$\left(\sum_i p_i a_{i1}\right) y_1 + \left(\sum_i p_i a_{i2}\right) y_2 +$$

$$+ \left(\sum_i p_i a_{i3}\right) y_3 + \left(\sum_i p_i a_{i4}\right) y_4 \leqq k, \qquad\qquad 8$$

where the composite prices $q_j = \Sigma_i p_i a_{ij}, j = 1, ..., 4$. represent the prices of each activity. The number of goods in relation to the number of activities is irrelevant at this stage, since each activity has a unique and completely determined price q_j, given the prices of the goods.

Given q_1, q_2, q_3, q_4, and k, the maximum attainable level of each activity in isolation can be written down, corresponding to the points E_1, E_2, E_3, E_4 in Figure 2, and the lines joining these points represent combinations attainable subject to the budget constraint. In the figure it has been assumed that prices are such that combinations of 1 and 2, 2 and 3, 3 and 4 are efficient, giving the characteristics frontier, while combinations 1 and 3, 2 and 4, or 1 and 4 are inefficient.

Suppose that the consumer chooses characteristics in the combination represented by the ray z^*, giving a point E^* on the frontier. Now suppose that relative prices change: in particular, that the price of activity 2 rises so that, with income still at k, the point E_2 moves inward on ray 2. If the movement is small enough, the characteristics frontier continues to have a corner at E_2, and the consumer will continue to obtain characteristics in proportion z^* by a combination of activities 1 and 2. If income is adjusted so that the new frontier goes through E^*, the consumer will use the same activities in the same proportions as before.

If the price of activity 2 rises sufficiently, however, the point E_2 will move inward past the line joining E_1 and E_3 to E_2'. Combinations of 1 and 2 and of 2 and 3 are now inefficient combinations of activities, their place on the efficiency frontier being taken by a combination of 1 and 3. The consumer will switch from a combination of activities 1 and 2 to a combination of 1 and 3.

Thus there is an efficiency substitution effect which is essentially

355

a switching effect. If price changes are too small to cause a switch, there is no efficiency substitution effect: if they are large enough, the effect comes from a complete switch from one activity to another.

The manifestation of the efficiency substitution effect in goods space depends on the structure of the A, goods-activities, matrix. There are two polar cases:

1. If there is a one-to-one relationship between goods and activities, the efficiency substitution effect will result in a complete switch from consumption of one good to consumption of another. This might be regarded as typical of situations involving similar but differentiated products, where a sufficiently large price change in one of the products will result in widespread switching to, or away from, the product.

2. If there is not a one-to-one relationship between goods and activities and, in particular, if all goods are used in all activities, the efficiency substitution effect will simply result in less consumption of a good whose price rises, not a complete disappearance of that good from consumption. If all cakes require eggs but in different proportions, a rise in the price of eggs will cause a switch from egg-intensive cakes to others, with a decline in the consumption of eggs, but not to zero.

The existence of an efficiency substitution effect depends, of course, on the number of activities exceeding the number of characteristics, otherwise switching of activities will not, in general, occur[7], but does not require that the number of goods exceed the number of characteristics. In fact, with two goods, two characteristics and three activities, the effect may occur. With two goods, two characteristics and one hundred activities, well spread over the spectrum, an almost smooth efficiency substitution effect would occur.

Since the efficiency substitution effect implies that consumers

7. This is a somewhat imprecise statement in that, if the B matrix is partitionable into disconnected subtechnologies, for some of which the number of activities exceeds the number of characteristics and for others the reverse, an efficiency-substitution effect may exist over certain groups of activities, although the number of activities is less than the number of characteristics overall.

356

may change goods collections as a result of compensated relative price changes, simply in order to obtain the same characteristics collection in the most efficient manner, it is obvious that the existence of substitution does not of itself either require or imply convexity of the preference function on characteristics. In other words, the axiom of revealed preference may be satisfied even if the consumer always consumes characteristics in fixed proportions, and possibly even if the consumers had *concave* preferences, so that the 'revelation' may be simply of efficient choice rather than convexity.

Objective and subjective choice and demand theory

In an economy or subeconomy with a complex consumption technology – many goods relative to characteristics – we have seen that there are two types of substitution effect:

1. Changes in relative prices may result in goods bundle 1 becoming an *inefficient* method of attaining a given bundle of characteristics and being replaced by goods bundle 2 even when the characteristics bundle is unchanged.

2. Changes in relative prices, with or without causing efficiency substitutions as in type 1, may alter the slope of the characteristics frontier in a segment relevant to a consumer's characteristics choice. The change in the slope of the frontier is analogous to the change in the budget line slope in the traditional case and, with a convex preference function, will result in a substitution of one characteristics bundle for another and, hence, of one goods bundle for another. Note that, even with smoothly convex preferences, this effect may not occur, since the consumer may be on a corner of the polyhedral characteristics frontier, and thus his characteristics choice could be insensitive to a certain range of slope changes on the facets.

The first effect, the efficiency substitution effect, is universal and objective. Subject to consumer ignorance or inefficiency,[8]

8. One of the properties of this model is that it gives scope for the consumer to be more or less efficient in achieving his desired characteristics bundle, although we will usually assume he is completely efficient. This adds a realistic dimension to consumer behavior – traditional theory never permits him to be out of equilibrium – and gives a rationale for the Consumers' Union and similar institutions.

357

this substitution effect is independent of the shapes of individual consumers' preference functions and hence of the effects of income distribution.

The second effect, the private substitution effect, has the same properties, in general, as the substitution effect in traditional theory. In particular, an aggregately compensated relative price change combined with a redistribution of income may result in no substitution effect in the aggregate, or a perverse one.

These two substitution effects are independent – either may occur without the other in certain circumstances – but in general we will expect them both to take place and hence that their effects will be reinforcing, if we are concerned with a complex economy. Thus, the consumer model presented here, in the context of an advanced economy, has, in a sense, more substitution than the traditional model. Furthermore, since part of the total substitution effect arises from objective, predictable and income-distribution-free efficiency considerations, our confidence in the downward slope of demand curves is increased even when income redistribution takes place.

Since it is well known that satisfaction of the revealed preference axioms *in the aggregate*, never guaranteed by traditional theory, leads to global stability in multimarket models (see, for example, Karlin, 1959), the efficiency substitution effect increases confidence in this stability.

In a simple economy, with few goods or activities relative to characteristics, the efficiency substitution effect will be generally absent. Without this reinforcement of the private substitution effect, we would have some presumption that perverse consumer effects – 'Giffen goods', backward-bending supply curves – and lower elasticities of demand would characterize simple economies as compared with complex economies. This seems to be in accord with at least the mythology of the subject, but it is certainly empirically verifiable. On this model, consumption technology as well as income levels differentiate consumers in different societies, and we would not necessarily expect a poor urban American to behave in his consumption like a person at the same real-income level in a simple economy.

Commodity groups, substitutes, complements

In a complex economy, with a large number of activities and goods as well as characteristics, and with a two-matrix (A, B) consumption technology, it is obvious that taxonomy could be carried out almost without limit, an expression of the richness of the present approach. Although an elaborate taxonomy is not very useful, discussion of a few selected types of relationships between goods can be of use. One of the important features of this model is that we can discuss relationships between goods, as revealed in the structure of the technology. In the conventional approach, there are, of course, no relationships between goods as such, only properties of individual's preferences.

The simplest taxonomy is that based on the zero entries in the technology matrixes. It may be that both matrixes A, B are almost 'solid', in which case there is little to be gained from a taxonomic approach. If, however, the B matrix contains sufficient zeros to be decomposable as follows,

$$B \equiv \begin{bmatrix} B_1 & O \\ O & B_2 \end{bmatrix}, \qquad\qquad 9$$

so that there is some set of characteristics and some set of activities such that these characteristics are derived only from these activities and these activities give rise to no other characteristics, then we can separate that set of characteristics and activities from the remainder of the technology. If, further, the activities in question require a particular set of goods which are used in no other activities, implying a decomposition of the A matrix, then we can regard the goods as forming an *intrinsic commodity group*. Goods within the group have the property that efficiency substitution effects will occur only for relative price changes within the group and will be unaffected by changes in the prices of other goods. If the utility function on characteristics has the conventional properties, there may, of course, be *private* substitution effects for goods within the group when the prices of other goods changes. For an intrinsic commodity group, the whole of the objective analysis can be carried out without reference to goods outside the group.

Goods from different intrinsic commodity groups can be

regarded as *intrinsically unrelated*, goods from the same groups *intrinsically related*.

If, within a group, there are two activities, each in a one-to-one relationship with a different good, and if the bundles of characteristics derived from the two goods differ only in a scalar, that is, have identical proportions, we can regard the two goods in question as *intrinsic perfect substitutes*. If the associated characteristics bundles are similar, the goods are *close substitutes*. We can give formal respectability to that traditional butter–margarine example of our texts by considering them as two goods giving very similar combinations of characteristics.

On the other hand, if a certain activity requires more than one good and if these goods are used in no other activity we can consider them as *intrinsic total complements* and they will always be consumed in fixed proportions, if at all.

Many goods within a commodity group will have relationships to each other which are partly complementary and partly substitution. This will be true if two goods, for example, are used in different combinations in each of several activities, each activity giving rise to a similar combination of characteristics. The goods are complements within each activity, but the activities are substitutes. [...]

New commodities, differentiated goods and advertising

Perhaps the most difficult thing to do with traditional consumer theory is to introduce a new commodity – an event that occurs thousands of times in the US economy, even over a generation, without any real consumers being unduly disturbed. In the theory of production, where activity-analysis methods have become widely used, a new process or product can be fitted in well enough; but in consumer theory we have traditionally had to throw away our n-dimensional preference functions and replace them by totally new $(n + 1)$-dimensional functions, with no predictable consequences.

In this model, the whole process is extraordinarily simple. A new product simply means addition of one or more activities to the consumption technology. Given the technology, or the relevant portion of it, and given the intrinsic characteristic of the activity associated with the new good, we simply insert it in the appropriate place in the technology, *and we can predict the consequences.*

If a new good possesses characteristics in the same proportions as some existing good, it will simply fail to sell to anyone if its price is too high, or will completely replace the old good if its price is sufficiently low.

More usually, we can expect a new good to possess characteristics in somewhat different proportions to an existing good. If its price is too high, it may be dominated by some *combination* of existing goods and will fail to sell. If its price is sufficiently low, it will result in adding a new point to the efficiency frontier. In Figure 3, ABC represents the old efficiency frontier, on which some individuals will consume combinations of goods g_1 and g_2 in various proportions, some combinations of g_2 and g_3. If the price of the new good, g_4, is such that it represents a point, D, on the old efficiency frontier, some persons – those using combinations of g_1 and g_2 – will be indifferent between their old combinations and combinations of either g_1 and g_4 or g_2 and g_4. If the price of g_4 is a little lower, it will push the efficiency frontier out to D'. Individuals will now replace combinations of g_1 and g_2 with combinations of g_1 and g_4 or g_2 and g_4, depending on their preferences. The new good will have taken away some of the sales from both g_1 and g_2, but completely replaced neither.

If the price of g_4 were lower, giving point D'', then combinations of g_4 and g_3 would dominate g_2, and g_2 would be replaced. At an even lower price, like D''', combinations of g_4 and g_3 would dominate g_2, and the corner solution g_4 only would dominate all combinations of g_1 and g_4, since AD''' has a positive slope, so that g_4 would now replace both g_1 and g_2.

Differentiation of goods has presented almost as much of a problem to traditional theory as new commodities. In the present analysis, the difference is really one of degree only. We can regard a differentiated good typically as a new good within an existing intrinsic commodity group, and within that group analyze it as a new commodity. Sometimes there appear new commodities of a more fundamental kind whose characteristics cut across those of existing groups.

We may note that differentiation of goods, if successful, that is, if the differentiated goods are actually sold, represents a

welfare improvement since it pushes the efficiency frontier out-
ward and enables the consumer more efficiently to reach his
preferred combination of characteristics.

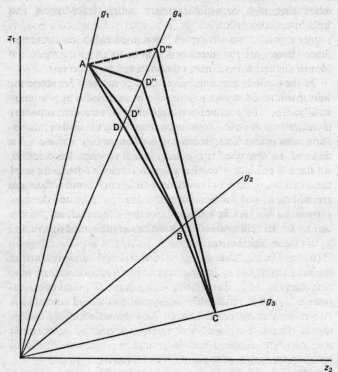

Figure 3

Many economists take a puritanical view of commodity
differentiation since their theory has induced them to believe
that it is some single characteristic of a commodity that is relevant
to consumer decisions, that is, automobiles are only for trans-
portation, so that commodity variants are regarded as wicked
tricks to trap the uninitiated into buying unwanted trimmings.
This is not, of course, a correct deduction even from the conven-

tional analysis, properly used, but is manifestly incorrect when account is taken of multiple characteristics.

A rather similar puritanism has also been apparent in the economist's approach to advertising. In the neoclassical analysis, advertising, if it does not represent simple information, and little information is called for in an analysis in which a good is simply a good, is an attempt to 'change tastes' in the consumer. Since 'tastes' are the ultimate datum in welfare judgments, the idea of changing them makes economists uncomfortable.

On the analysis presented here, there is much wider scope for informational advertising, especially as new goods appear constantly. Since the consumption technology of a modern economy is clearly very complex, consumers require a great deal of information concerning that technology. When a new version of a dishwashing detergent is produced which contains hand lotion, we have a product with characteristics different from those of the old. The consumption technology is changed, and consumers are willing to pay to be told of the change. Whether the new product pushes out the efficiency frontier, compared, say, with a combination of dishwasher and hand lotion consumed separately, is, of course, another matter.

In any case, advertising, product design and marketing specialists, who have a heavy commitment to understanding how consumers actually do behave, themselves act as though consumers regard a commodity as having multiple characteristics and as though consumers weigh the various combinations of characteristics contained in different commodities in reaching their decisions. At this preliminary stage of presenting the model set out here, this is strong evidence in its favor.

General equilibrium, welfare and other matters

Since the demand for goods depends on objective and universal efficiency effects as well as on private choices, we can draw some inferences relative to equilibrium in the economy.

A commodity, especially a commodity within an intrinsic commodity group, must have a price low enough relative to the prices of other commodities to be represented on the efficiency frontier, otherwise it will be purchased by no one and will not appear in the economy. This implies that if there are n viable commodities in a group, each in a one-to-one relation to an activity, the equilibrium prices will be such that the efficiency frontier has $n - 1$ facets in the two-characteristic case. In Figure 4, for example, where the price of commodity 3 brings it to point A on the efficiency frontier, that price could not be

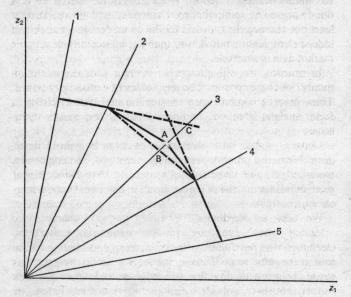

Figure 4

allowed to rise to a level bringing it inside point B, or it would disappear from the market; and if its price fell below a level corresponding to C, commodities 2 and 4 would disappear from the market. Thus the limits on prices necessary for the existence of all commodities within a group can be established, in principle, from objective data. Only the demand within that price range depends on consumer preferences. [...]

Operational and predictive characteristics of the model

In principle, the model set out here can be made operational, that is, empirical coefficients can be assigned to the technology.

In practice, the task will be more difficult than the equivalent task of determining the actual production technology of an economy.

To emphasize that the model is not simply heuristic, we can examine a simple scheme for sketching out the efficiency frontier for some commodity group. We shall assume that there is a one-to-one relationship between activities and goods, that at least one characteristic shared by the commodities is capable of independent determination, and that a great quantity of suitable market data is available.

In practice, we will attempt to operate with the minimum number of characteristics that give sufficient explanatory power. These may be combinations of fundamental characteristics, a factor-analysis situation, or fundamental characteristics themselves.

Consider some commodity group such as household detergents. We have a primary objective characteristic, cleaning power, measured in some chosen way. We wish to test whether one or more other characteristics are necessary to describe the consumer-choice situation.

We take a two-dimensional diagram with characteristic 'cleaning power' along one axis. Along the axis we mark the cleaning power per dollar outlay of all detergents observed to be sold at the same time. If this is the same for all detergents, this single characteristic describes the situation, and we do not seek further. However, we shall assume this is not so. From our observed market data, we obtain cross-price elasticities between all detergents, taken two at a time. From the model, we know that cross-price elasticities will be highest between detergents with adjacent characteristics vectors, so that the order of the characteristics vectors as we rotate from one axis to the other in the positive quadrant can be established.

The ordering of 'cleaning power per dollar' along one axis can be compared with the ordering of the characteristics vectors. If the orderings are the same, an equilibrium efficiency frontier can be built up with two characteristics as in Figure 5a. The slopes of the facets can be determined within limits by the limiting prices at which the various detergents go off the market. If the ordering in terms of cleaning power does not agree with the

365

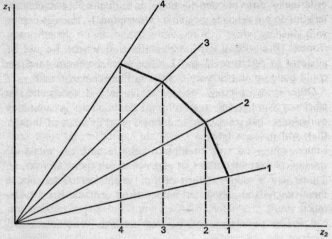

Figure 5a

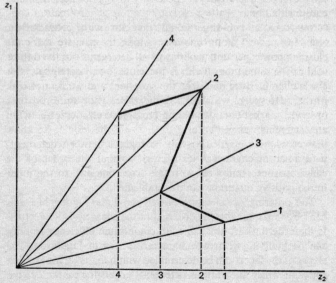

Figure 5b

ordering in terms of cross-elasticity, as in Figure 5b, two characteristics do not describe the market appropriately, since detergent with cleaning power 3 in the figure cannot be on the efficiency frontier. But with a third characteristic, detergent 3 could be adjacent to detergents 2 and 1 in an extra dimension, and we could build up an efficiency frontier in three characteristics.

Other evidence could, of course, be used to determine the efficiency frontier for a given market situation. Among this evidence is that arising from ordinary activity-analysis theory, that, with r characteristics we would expect to find some consumers who used r commodities at the same time, unless all consumers were on corners or edges of the efficiency frontier.

Last, but possibly not least, simply asking consumers about the characteristics associated with various commodities may be much more productive than attempts to extract information concerning preferences within the context of conventional theory.

In general, if consumer preferences are well dispersed, so that all facets of the efficiency frontier are represented in some consumer's choice pattern, a combination of information concerning interpersonal variances in the collections of goods chosen and of the effects of price changes on both aggregate and individual choices can, in principle, be used to ferret out the nature of the consumption technology. Some of the problems that arise are similar to those met by psychologists in measuring intelligence, personality and other multidimensional traits, so that techniques similar to those used in psychology, such as factor analysis, might prove useful.

Even without specification of the consumption technology, the present theory makes many predictions of a structural kind which may be contrasted with the predictions of conventional theory. Some of these are set out in Chart 1.

Conclusion

In this model we have extended into consumption theory activity analysis, which has proved so penetrating in its application to production theory. The crucial assumption in making this application has been the assumption that goods possess, or give rise to, multiple characteristics in fixed proportions and that it

Chart 1

This theory	*Conventional theory*
Wood will not be a close substitute for bread, since characteristics are dissimilar	No reason except 'tastes' why they should not be close substitutes
A red Buick will be a close substitute for a gray Buick	No reason why they should be any closer substitutes than wood and bread
Substitution, for example, butter and margarine, is frequently intrinsic and objective, will be observed in many societies under many market conditions	No reason why close substitutes in one context should be close substitutes in another
A good may be displaced from the market by new goods or by price changes	No presumption that goods will be completely displaced
The labor–leisure choice may have a marked occupational pattern	Labor–leisure choice determined solely by individual preferences; no pattern, other than between individuals, would be predicted
Gresham's Law. A monetary asset may cease to be on the efficiency frontier, and will disappear from the economy	No *ex ante* presumption that any good or asset will disappear from the economy
An individual is completely unaffected by price changes that leave unchanged the portion of the efficiency frontier on which his choice rests	An individual is affected by changes in all prices
Some commodity groups may be intrinsic, and universally so	No presumption that commodities forming a group, defined by a break in spectrum of cross-elasticities, in one context will form a group in another context

is these characteristics, not goods themselves, on which the consumer's preferences are exercised.

The result is a model very many times richer in heuristic explanatory and predictive power than the conventional model of consumer behavior and one that deals easily with those many common-sense characteristics of actual behavior that have found no place in traditional exposition.

References

BECKER, G. S. (1965), 'A theory of the allocation of time', *Economics Journal*, vol 75, no. 299, pp. 493–517.

DEBREU, G. (1959), *Theory of Value*, Cowles Foundation, monograph no. 17.

DEBREU, G. (1960), 'Topological methods in cardinal utility theory', in K. J. Arrow, S. Karlin and P. Suppes (eds), *Mathematical Methods in the Social Sciences, 1959*, Stanford University Press.

GORMAN, W. M. (1959), 'Separable utility and aggregation', *Econometrica*, vol. 27, pp. 469–81.

JOHNSON, H. G. (1958), 'Demand theory further revised or goods are goods', *Economica*, vol. 25, p. 149.

KARLIN, S. (1959), *Mathematical Methods and Theory in Games, Programming and Economics*, Pergamon Press.

LANCASTER, K. J. (1957), 'Revising demand theory', *Economica*, vol. 24, pp. 354–60.

LANCASTER, K. J. (1962), 'The scope of qualitative economics', *Review of Economic Studies*, vol. 29.

LANCASTER, K. J. (1965), 'The theory of qualitative linear systems', *Econometrica*, vol. 33, pp. 395–408.

LANCASTER, K. J. (1966), 'Change and innovation in the technology of consumption', *Papers and Proceedings of the Association of Economic Reviews*, May.

MORISHIMA, M. (1959), 'The problem of intrinsic complementarity and separability of goods', *Metroeconomica*, vol. 11, pp. 188–202.

PEARCE, I. F. (1964), *Contribution to Demand Analysis*, Oxford University Press.

QUANDT, R. E. (1956), 'A probabilistic theory of consumer behaviour', *Quarterly Journal of Economics*, vol. 70, pp. 507–36.

SAMUELSON, P. A. (1953), 'Prices of factors and goods in general equilibrium', *Review of Economic Studies*, vol. 21, pp. 1–20.

STIGLER, G. J. (1945), 'The cost of subsistence', *Journal of Farm Economics*, vol. 27, pp. 303–14.

STROTZ, R. (1957), 'The empirical implications of a utility tree', *Econometrica*, vol. 25, pp. 269–80.

Economic Factors

STROTZ, R. (1959), 'The utility tree: a correction and further appraisal', *Econometrica*, vol. 27, pp. 482–8.

THRALL, R. M., COOMBS, C., and DAVIS, R. L. (1954), *Decision Processes*, Wiley.

UZAWA, H. (1960), 'Preference and rational choice in the theory of consumption', in K. J. Arrow, S. Karlin and P. Suppes (eds.), *Mathematical Methods in the Social Sciences, 1959*, Stanford University Press.

Further Reading

L. Adler and I. Crespi, *Attitude Research on the Rocks*, American Marketing Association, 1968.

J. Aitchison and J. A. C. Brown, *The Log-Normal Distribution with Special Reference to its Uses in Economics*, Cambridge University, Department of Applied Economics Monographs, no. 5, Cambridge University Press, 1957.

J. Arndt (ed.), *Insights into Consumer Behaviour*, Allyn & Bacon, 1968.

S. H. Britt (ed.), *Consumer Behaviour and the Behavioural Sciences*, Wiley, 1966.

T. M. Brown, 'Habit persistence and lags in consumer behaviour', *Econometrica*, vol. 20, 1952, pp. 355–71.

M. L. Burstein, 'The demand for household refrigeration in the U.S.', in A. C. Harberger (ed.), *The Demand for Durable Goods*, University of Chicago Press, 1960.

J. S. Duesenberry, *Income, Saving and the Theory of Consumer Behaviour*, Harvard Economic Studies, no. 87, Harvard University Press, 1949.

A. S. C. Ehrenberg, *Repeat Buying: Theory and Applications*, North Holland, 1972.

M. J. Farrell, 'The demand for motor-cars in the U.S.', *Journal of the Royal Statistical Society*, *A*, vol. 117, 1954, pp. 171–201.

M. J. Farrell, 'The new theories of the consumption function', *Economic Journal*, vol. 69, 1959, pp. 678–96.

E. G. Forsyth, 'The relationship between family size and family expenditure', *Journal of the Royal Statistical Society*, *A*, vol. 123, 1960, pp. 367–97.

M. Friedman, *A Theory of the Consumption Function*, National Bureau of Economic Research General Series, no. 63, Princeton University Press, 1957.

J. R. Hicks, *A Revision of Demand Theory*, Oxford University Press, 1956.

H. S. Houthakker, 'An international comparison of household expenditure patterns, commemorating the centenary of Engel's law', *Econometrica*, vol. 25, 1957, pp. 532–51.

J. Howard and J. N. Sheth, *The Theory of Buyer Behaviour*, Wiley, 1969.

H. G. Johnson, 'Demand theory further revised, or, goods are goods', *Economica*, new series, vol. 25, 1958, p. 149.

F. T. Juster, *Anticipation and Purchases: An analysis of Consumer Behaviour*, National Bureau of Economic Research General Series, no. 79, Princeton University Press, 1964.

J. T. Klapper, *The Effects of Mass Communication*, Free Press, 1960.

Further Reading

L. R. Klein, 'Statistical estimation of economic relations from survey data', in L. R. Klein *et al.* (eds.), *Contributions of Survey Methods to Economics*, Columbia University Press, 1954.

L. R. Klein and J. B. Lansing, 'Decisions to purchase consumer durable goods', *Journal of Marketing*, vol. 20, no. 2, October 1955, pp. 109–32.

J. U. McNeill, *Dimensions of Consumer Behaviour*, Appleton-Century-Crofts, 1969.

W. N. McPhee, *Formal Theories of Mass Behaviour*, Free Press, 1963.

W. F. Massy, D. B. Montgomery and D. G. Morrison, *Stochastic Models of Buyer Behaviour*, MIT Press, 1970.

Eva Mueller, 'Ten years of consumer attitude surveys: their forecasting record', *Journal of the American Statistical Association*, vol. 58, December 1963, pp. 899–917.

L. Needleman, 'The demand for domestic appliances', *National Institute Economic Review*, no. 12, November 1960, pp. 24–44.

J. W. Newman (ed.), *On Knowing the Consumer*, Wiley, 1966.

C. S. O'Herlihy, 'Demand for cars in Great Britain', *Applied Statistics*, vol. 14, 1965, pp. 162–95.

G. H. Orcutt, *et al.*, *Microanalysis of Socioeconomic Systems: A Simulation Study*, Harper, 1961.

I. F. Pearce, 'An exact method of consumer demand analysis', *Econometrica*, vol. 29, October 1961, pp. 499–516.

S. J. Prais and H. S. Houthakker, *The Analysis of Family Budgets*, Cambridge University Press, 1955.

H. Schultz, *The Theory and Measurement of Demand*, University of Chicago Press, 1938.

J. N. Sheth, 'A review of buyer behaviour', *Management Science*, vol. 13B, August 1967, pp. 718–56.

G. J. Stigler, 'The cost of subsistence', *Journal of Farm Economics*, vol. 27, 1945, pp. 303–14.

J. R. N. Stone *et al.*, *The Measurement of Consumers' Expenditure and Behaviour in the United Kingdom*, Cambridge University Press, 1954–1966.

J. R. N. Stone and D. A. Rowe, 'Dynamic demand functions: some econometric results', *Economic Journal*, vol. 68, 1958, pp. 256–70.

J. R. N. Stone, 'Consumer wants and expenditures: a survey of British studies since 1945', in *L'Evaluation et le rôle des besoins de biens de consommation dans les divers régimes économiques*, Editions du Centre National de la Recherche Scientifique, Paris, 1963, pp. 57–87.

H. Wold and L. Jureen, *Demand Analysis: A Study in Econometrics*, Wiley, 1953.

Acknowledgements

Permission to reproduce the Readings in this volume is acknowledged to the following sources:

1 Royal Statistical Society, London and A. S. C. Ehrenberg
2 Crain Communications Inc.
3 American Marketing Association and R. E. Frank
4 *Harvard Business Review* and D. Yankelovich
5 Advertising Research Foundation
6 *Journal of the Market Research Society*
7 American Marketing Association and M. Haire
8 The Market Research Society and T. Joyce
9 The Diebold Group Inc.
10 J. Walter Thompson Company Ltd. and T. Joyce
11 Cambridge University Press
12 American Marketing Association, D. A. Brown, S. F. Buc and F. G. Pyatt
13 The Econometric Society
14 McGraw-Hill Book Company
15 American Economic Association
16 North-Holland Publishing Company
17 American Economic Association
18 The University of Chicago Press and K. J. Lancaster

Author Index

Author Index

Author Index

378

Author Index

Subject Index

Subject Index

Subject Index